Ḥakirah

The Flatbush Journal of Jewish Law and Thought

Volume 32 / Fall 2022

Ḥakirah חקירה

The Flatbush Journal of Jewish Law and Thought

Volume 32 / Fall 2022

The purpose of Ḥakirah is to promote the intellectual and spiritual growth of the Jewish community. To accomplish this Ḥakirah will:

- *Provide an opportunity for members of our community who have been studying in depth to disseminate the results of their study for careful review.*

- *Encourage others to join in this type of study.*

- *Create a forum for the discussion of issues of hashkafah and halakhah relevant to the community from a perspective of careful analysis of the primary Torah sources.*

Members of the community are encouraged to comment on the articles that they have read and subsequent issues will allow considerable space for the readers' comments and the authors' responses.

Editor
Asher Benzion Buchman

Board of Directors
Heshey Zelcer, CEO
Dov Friedberg
Ronny Hersh
Dovid Lichtenstein

Editorial Board
Sheldon Epstein
Yehoshua Grossman
David Guttmann
Eliyahu Krakowski
Shlomo Sprecher, ז"ל

Subscription requests, comments and correspondence can be directed to: HakirahFlatbush@msn.com. Visit us at www.Hakirah.org.

Cover design, production and printing: Ganz/Gross—NY
Printed in the United States of America

Ḥakirah

The Flatbush Journal of Jewish Law and Thought

Volume 32 / Fall 2022

Introduction

This volume of *Ḥakirah* emerges amidst a period of uncertainty, unease, and change, both in the world in general and in the Jewish world in particular. The articles in this issue deal with the challenges of responding to changing times and circumstances, both historically and in our own era.

Our *Jewish Thought* section deals with Israel's response to change and to modernity in general. Our opening article, "Maimonides on the Messianic Era: The Grand Finale of *Olam Ke-Minhago Noheg*," shows that Rambam's core messianic teaching is an outgrowth of his entire religious perspective "which eschews divine intervention and promotes human initiative." The second article, "For the Love of Humanity: The Religious Humanism of Rabbi Samson Raphael Hirsch," looks closely at Hirsch's universalist vision and seeks to use it as a guide for dealing with modernity. In "The Search for the Elusive Center: Norman Lamm and American Orthodoxy," the author explains that Rabbi Lamm's goal in renaming Modern Orthodoxy as Centrist Orthodoxy was to clarify the movement's ideology and enhance its attractiveness. He contends, however, that "the failure of the attempted rebranding illustrates the internal contradictions of an Orthodox Judaism open to the intellectual and social currents of the wider world" and then points out new challenges that still need to be faced.

A collection of the private correspondence of Rav Joseph B. Soloveitchik, זצ"ל, opens a window into the Rav's views on a host of issues. Of special interest are letters dealing with his relationship to the State of Israel. While the Rav never ceased his great support for the State of Israel—one letter confirms his support for Mizrachi—other letters show he also recognized secular Zionism's anti-religious trends and sought to oppose them. Ultimately, he refuses to vie for the chief rabbinate, explaining that the time dedicated to politics would not enable him to learn and teach Torah properly, and concluding, "I am a *melamed*." In yet another letter, "A Letter from Rabbi Joseph B. Soloveitchik to Aaron Zeitlin," the Rav speaks of his belief—in direct opposition to that of Israel's leaders—that the new State of Israel must be guided by the philosophy that emerges from halakhah and that, indeed, the entire world needs to be guided by it. Rambam's messianic view lies at the heart of the Rav's vision of a New World Order emerging from the sources of halakhah.

In our *Jewish Law* section, in "Tax Ethics in Rashba's Responsa to Saragossa," we see the universalist potential of halakhah, as the insights of one of our greatest *rishonim* are echoed much later by the legendary justice, Judge Learned Hand. Another article in this section, "Criminal

Proceedings Against a Jew in a Non-Jewish Court for *Get* Refusal: The Effect on the Validity of the *Get*," argues that modern government institutions can be used to aid Jewish courts in preventing the state of *igun.*

In our *History of Halakhah* section, an article titled "*Matan Torah:* What Was (and Was Not) Transmitted at Sinai" discusses which parts of the *Torah she-be-'al Peh* were revealed by Moshe and what was left for the rabbis of future generations to derive. Another article, "The Repeal of Tosefet Shevi'it: The Role of Discovered Traditions, Indirect Nullifications, and Asmakhtot in Annulling a Rabbinic Decree" gives added insight into the rabbinic process of making *takanot* and highlights different strategies taken by *amoraim* and later commentators to explain various developments in the history of halakhah.

In our *Talmud Torah* section, the author of "Solomonic Wisdom vs. the Letter of the Law: A Midrashic Reading," in a close midrashic reading, finds the reason for Shlomo's tragic error and finds in this midrash a polemic against Greek philosophy and its adaptation by Christianity. In "*Sefer ha-Tappu'ah,* The Book of the Apple: Aristotle Expresses an Interest in Jewish Concepts," we learn of a work that was of considerable importance to several cultures in the Middle Ages and during the Renaissance. In this work, "the views reputedly expressed by Aristotle are consistent with Jewish beliefs, indicating (suggesting) Aristotle's acceptance of Jewish theological concepts, articulated on his deathbed." The article titled "Shield of Abraham" gives a new perspective on the word *magen,* tracing its meaning to the garden (*gan*) of Eden. Finally, an essay on "The Sanctity of *Tefillin*" explores the nature of *kedushah* and demonstrates that the donning of *tefillin* is halachically comparable to entering the *Beit ha-Mikdash.*

One of our Hebrew articles deals with Moshe and *Parashat Mishpatim* and gives insight into the interplay between narrative and halakhah in the Torah. The other article addresses the issue of *aveilut* for one who feels no pain in the loss of his relative.

In our *History* section, "Jews Not Allowed on the Temple Mount After the British Capture of Jerusalem" asserts that "the Jewish response (or lack of response) to the changing *status quo* on the Temple Mount during the decade after the British occupation of Jerusalem made it easy for Great Britain to deal with the Arab demands for control of the Temple Mount."

As we look for a path forward in the post-Covid era—in which hostility to Torah values increases daily—we must seek guidance from the writings of Rambam, Rav Hirsch, and Rav Soloveitchik among others; the realization that our decisions have lasting consequences must be constantly on our minds.

Special thanks to all those who worked hard to make this volume of *Ḥakirah* a reality, including Nina Ackerman Indig, copy-editing; Tuvia Ganz, cover design and production; and Chaim Lam, design and maintenance of our Web page, www.Hakirah.org.

It is our continuing hope that the articles in this journal will stimulate thought, study, and discussion, and inspire other members of the public to contribute their own insights. The articles we print thus reflect a wide range of opinion and do not necessarily represent the views of our editorial board. ଔ

Instructions for Contributors

Ḥakirah, The Flatbush Journal of Jewish Law and Thought, publishes original, interesting, well-researched and well-organized manuscripts that provide new or profound insights into areas of Jewish *halakhah* and *hashkafah.*

Manuscripts should be in Microsoft Word format and sent as an email attachment to HakirahFlatbush@msn.com. Short references—for example, to a Biblical verse or to a page within the Talmud—should be embedded directly into the text of the manuscript. Insert longer references as footnotes, rather than endnotes.

The author's name should not appear on the manuscript, as it is the Journal's policy to forward the articles for evaluation without disclosing the author's identity. On a separate cover sheet, include your name, a short bio, an abstract of your article, your telephone number, fax number, and e-mail address.

After reviewing and accepting your manuscript, we are likely to request clarification of certain points. A revised electronic copy of your manuscript will then be required.

To encourage a wide variety of contributors, the Journal accepts articles employing the Hebrew transliteration style of either *Encyclopedia Judaica* or *ArtScroll.* If you have no preference, we suggest you follow the pronunciation rules used by the *Encyclopedia Judaica.* Words in languages other than English should always be italicized, unless the foreign words have become part of the English language.

For more information about writing an article for *Ḥakirah* see <www.Hakirah.org\HakirahGuideToWriting.pdf>. ☙

LETTERS TO THE EDITOR

The Limits of Orthodox Theology

Marc B. Shapiro writes:

WHEN A LEARNED READER writes a deeply scholarly essay of over forty pages analyzing a book one has written, especially a book almost twenty years old, one can only feel great satisfaction. I say this about Betzalel Sochaczewski's article on my *Limits of Orthodox Theology* that appeared in Ḥakirah 31 (Winter 2022).

Sochaczewski's article is not about looking for errors in particular citations, but is much broader in that he critiques my general approach in a few different areas. When it comes to these types of disagreements, it is not a matter of proving another wrong but of presenting an argument and then letting the readers decide which approach seems more convincing. In fact, quite apart from my book, Sochaczewski's article focuses on a number of important issues in the scholarship on Maimonides, and he offers valuable insights. I only wish to make a few comments in response to Sochaczewski.

Much of his article is focused on my claim that there are a few points in Maimonides' Thirteen Principles that Maimonides himself did not truly believe. Readers should be aware that this concept is not some

new idea invented by me, although the specific direction in which I apply this approach might be novel. There are any number of medieval scholars and commentators on Maimonides who had this same position, and it is held by many modern scholars as well. To give just one example, let me cite Moshe Halbertal, whose scholarship is widely respected. In his book, *Maimonides: Life and Thought*, pp. 146, 148, he writes:

> The suggestion that Maimonides may not have believed in one of the principles of faith that he himself established compels us to reconsider his understanding of what is meant by "principles of faith." ... Whether a belief should be classified as true or as necessary is a fundamental difficulty in Maimonides' thought. At this stage, before we examine the question in depth, we can say that several of the principles listed in the introduction to *Pereq Ḥeleq* are formulated in a manner consistent with their being necessary beliefs [but not true beliefs].

There is no need to elaborate on Halbertal's own approach, and Sochaczewski would also find a good deal to criticize in what Halbertal writes. I only mention it to show that my general approach is not revisionist, but follows in the footsteps of many scholars of the last thousand years. This is recognized by Sochazcewski, but perhaps not by all readers which is why I mention it here. Sochazcewski also does not reject out of hand the notion that Maimonides wrote things that he did not really believe. Yet he distinguishes between writings of a private nature or those written for a specific purpose, such as the *Letter on Martyrdom* (p. 16), and writings that must be regarded as "official and public teachings" (p. 14 n. 26), which would include the *Commentary on the Mishnah*, the source of the Thirteen Principles.

One problem with my approach, Sochaczewski argues, is that "it has Maimonides inventing a new, permanent category of heresy with vast practical consequences, none of which could be justified through *migdar milta*" (p. 5 n. 7). Yet this would only be the case if we assume that categories of heresy with practical consequences are to be derived from the *Commentary on the Mishnah*. Yet the matters I point to are not codified in the *Mishneh Torah* as matters of heresy. In contrast to Sochaczewski, I would argue that for Maimonides it is what appears in the *Mishneh Torah* that halakhically determines what is and what is not to be regarded as heresy, and if one sees that in the *Mishneh Torah* he does not adopt the definition found in the Introduction to *Ḥelek* (where

the Thirteen Principles appear), this is something that one needs to pay close attention to.

In dealing with the issue of creation, let me again lay out the problem. In *Guide* 2:25 Maimonides states that there is no religious objection to believing that the world was created through pre-existent matter. In the Fourth Principle, Maimonides records as dogma that one must believe in creation *ex nihilo*. (This is not in the first version of the Principle but was later added by Maimonides.)[1] We thus have a direct contradiction that needs to be explained, and the attempted solution mentioned by Sochaczewski (pp. 26–27), that so long as the theory of creation from eternal matter has not been proven normative belief is in accord with the doctrine of creation *ex nihilo*, does not solve anything. This is indeed Maimonides' opinion in the *Guide*. However, in the Fourth Principle he turns creation *ex nihilo* into a dogma, which means that it is an eternal truth, not something we affirm on a provisional basis while recognizing that further evidence could move us in a different direction. Unless you say that Maimonides changed his mind and that the addition of creation *ex nihilo* in the Fourth Principle represents his final position and is a rejection of what he says in the *Guide*, you must conclude that one of the two positions he puts forth does not represent his authentic view.

---

[1]   As I note in the book, and is mentioned also by Sochaczewski, there is another contradiction in the *Guide* itself, for in *Guide* 2:13 Maimonides describes creation from eternal matter as theologically unacceptable.

P. 16. Sochaczewski has not characterized my position correctly. I do not say that when it comes to the principle of the eternity of mitzvot that Maimonides held this belief to be "necessary," but not "true." This is the position of Yaakov Levinger, and on p. 131 of my book I specifically reject Levinger, and state that Maimonides indeed believed that the mitzvot are eternal. However, what about the view that the mitzvot might be abolished at some time in the future, a position that is found in rabbinic sources? The notion that this position is to be regarded as heresy—as indicated in the Ninth Principle—is what I suggested is a "necessary belief."

P. 17. Here Sochaczewski refers to something that appears in my *Studies in Maimonides and His Interpreters*, as well as in a more recent article. I mentioned that Haym Soloveitchik has argued that Maimonides' *Letter on Martyrdom* is a work of rhetoric that does not reflect Maimonides' true view. I then cited R. Shimon b. Zemaḥ Duran who says something very similar:

דילמא הרב ז"ל הפריז על מדותיו בזה
מלאכת שמים לחזק ידי הנאחזים
במצודה רעה להינצל מפח מוקשם
ואל תעצרם אהבת בנים ובנות

Sochaczewski replies that Soloveitchik and Duran are quite different, as Soloveitchik claims that Maimonides' words in the Letter on Martyrdom are more lenient than his true view, while Duran proposes that Maimonides presented a position that is stricter than what the halakhah requires. All this is well and good, but my point remains that both of them suggest that Maimonides expressed himself in a way that is not halakhically exact. And I would add now, that both of them suggest that Maimonides did so for important communal reasons. The fact that Soloveitchik and Duran come at this from different perspectives as to Maimonides' motivation is not relevant to my point. In fact, the connection I drew between Soloveitchik and Duran, as well as my point about the statement in the *Letter on Martyrdom* that angels have free will, is also mentioned by R. Moshe Maimon in his recent edition of the *Commentary of R. Abraham Maimonides: Bereshit*, p. 248 (which is actually referred to by Sochaczewski, p. 17 n. 34):

ויציון שכבר העיר התשב"ץ (א:סג)
שגם במילי דהלכתא נקט הרמב"ם
באגרתו זאת דברים שלא דבר לדינא
(ועוד האריך בזה פרופ' ח'
סולובייצ'יק במאמר מיוחד, ראה
קובץ מאמריו (באנגלית) ח"ב עמ'
288 ואילך), ואין פלא אפוא אם
במילי דאגדתא הרצה דברים ע"פ
מדרשים שלא כפי הפשט. במק"א
כתבתי שכך יש להבין דבריו בענין
גערת ה' בשטן על שהשטין ולימד
חובה על יהושע הכהן הגדול (מהד'
ר"י שילת עמ' לו), מה שנוגד לכאורה
דעתו בשלילת בחירה למלאכים ...
בשעת כתיבת הדברים לא חתר
הרמב"ם להעמיד את אמיתת הבנת
דברי המדרש – שאינם כפשוטם לפי
דעתו – אלא עיקר רצונו שיובן ממנו
הלקח העיקרי שהוא עד כמה חמור

עניין לימוד קטגוריה על ישראל.

Pp. 19–20. In listing various heretics, Maimonides, *Hilkhot Teshuvah*
3:7, states

וכן האומר שאינו לבדו ראשון וצור
לכל.

In *Limits*, p. 75, I translated: "He
alone is the First Cause and Rock of
the Universe." Sochaczewski questions my translation of ראשון as
"First Cause" and suggests that a
better translation is "First Existent." (In *Limits*, p. 75, I translated
מצוי ראשון in *Hilkhot Yesodei ha-Torah*
1:1 as "First Existent.") This is not
an issue that I have a vested interest
in, and it does appear that
Sochaczewski's translation is better.
I would only note, however, that
"First Cause" is how the word is
translated in the Glazer and Hyam-
son translations, and that is probably what influenced me. The problem we must confront is that
Sochaczewski, following many others, understands *Hilkhot Teshuvah*
3:7 to be stating that belief in eternal
matter is a heresy. Yet as we have
seen, this is contradicted by Maimonides' statement in the *Guide* that
such a notion is not a violation of
basic Jewish belief. I also reject
Sochaczewski's claim (p. 20 n. 44)
that *Hilkhot Yesodei ha-Torah* 1:1 is
teaching creation *ex nihilo*.

P. 25. "While the esoteric strand of

Maimonidean interpretation makes
for important study of intellectual
history, if we are indeed serious
about determining Maimonides'
true intentions, the admitted biases
of its proponents must be forefront
in our minds." The fact is that all interpreters have biases that they
bring to their interpretations (and
very few of these biases are ever
"admitted"). As R. Joseph Kafiḥ
wrote, Maimonides is like a mirror:
"Anyone who stands in front of it
sees his own reflection." [2] This
means that we must examine arguments presented, rather than try to
attribute positions to biases.

P. 33. I do not know why
Sochaczewski denies that R. Joseph
Ibn Migash assumed the non-Mo-
saic origin of the final eight verses
of the Torah. *Bava Batra* 15a states
that when the Torah is read in the
synagogue one person reads the last
eight verses. The *Gemara* offers two
different reasons for this, either that
the last eight verses were written by
Joshua or that Moses wrote them
with tears, so they are different than
the rest of the Torah. In his final
comment on this passage, summing
up, as it were, Ibn Migash cites the
view that Joshua wrote the last eight
verses. I do not know why
Sochaczewski assumes that I never
saw the complete words of Ibn
Migash when I indeed cite a recent
edition of his commentary to *Bava
Batra*. Furthermore, his crucial

[2] See his letter in *Moreh Nevukhim*,
trans. Michael Schwartz (Tel Aviv,
2002), vol. 2, p. 752. See also *Mishneh*
Torah, ed. Kafiḥ, *Sefer Hafla'ah*, p. 444.

words are also found in the *Shittah Mekubbezet, Bava Batra* 15a. Here is what Ibn Migash says:

שמונה פסוקים שבתורה יחיד קורא אותם: כלומר: הקורא פסוקים שלפניהם אינו רשאי לגמור עד סוף התורה משום שנמצא קורא מה שכתב משה עם מה שכתב יהושע, אלא מפסיק ועולה אחר וקורא פסוקים אלו בפני עצמם כדי שיהא ניכר שלא כתבן משה אלא יהושע. פירוש אחר: יחיד קורא אותם כלומר: ואינו רשאי להפסיק בהם כדי שלא יהא ניכר שיהושע הוא כתבן.

My understanding, that Ibn Migash accepted the view that Joshua wrote the last eight verses, is also stated by R. Ḥayyim Pardes, *Halakhah ki-Feshutah*, p. 97, R. Yoel Berkovitz, *Minḥat Nedavah: Menaḥot*, p. 297, as well as by Abraham Joshua Heschel, *Torah min ha-Shamayim be-Aspaklaryah shel ha-Dorot*, vol. 2, p. 387. Here is also a good place to respond to the claim made by some—but not by Sochaczewski—that "the halakhah" is in accord with the view "codified" by Maimonides, that the entire Torah was written by Moses with nothing added by Joshua. To this I would only say that R. Israel Meir ha-Kohen was unaware of such a "halakhah," as he writes as follows in *Mishnah Berurah* 428:21:

אין מפסיקין בהם: לחלקן לשני קרואים והטעם דיש בהן שינוי משאר ס"ת דיהושע כתבן ואפילו למ"ד דמשה כתבן בדמע הואיל שיש שינוי בהן שנכתבו בדמע נשתנו שלא לחלקן כשאר ס"ת.

P. 42 n. 98:

Shapiro's (p. 131), excessively subtle reading of the language in *Hil. Teshuvah* seems incomprehensible. If Maimonides leaves the door open for the possible abrogation of the Torah *in the future*, how could the assertion of that abrogation *in the past* be considered heretical? In other words: after the unspecified future point in time when the "admissible" lapsing of the Torah occurs, this repeal will be history. How, then, can any claim that the Law has already been repealed be heretical—perhaps we have indeed passed its "future" abrogation?

To begin with, I never stated that Maimonides leaves the door open for the possible future abrogation of the Torah. As mentioned already, I actually stated the exact opposite. However, I also stated that despite Maimonides' belief that there will never be an abolishment of mitzvot, because there are classic rabbinic sources that offer a different perspective, there is reason to suggest that Maimonides' positing of this idea as an authoritative dogma, as opposed to a correct notion, is a "necessary belief." I also called attention to the fact that in the *Mishneh Torah*, which is where Maimonides' halakhic rulings about dogmas are to be found, he defines a heretic as one who says that mitzvot have *already* been abolished (*Hilkhot Teshuvah* 3:8), and he does not say—as we find in the Fourth Principle—that it is heretical to believe that they will be abolished in the future.

As for Sochaczewski's question, it makes no sense to me. Leaving aside Maimonides, there are other authorities who accept the possibility that in the future there will be an abolishment of at least some mitzvot, and they still believe that it is heretical to assume that today these mitzvot are no longer binding. There is no logical problem here, and the answer to Sochaczewski's question is clear. If the Messiah has not come, or if God has not revealed himself prophetically in a public manner, then obviously there can be no abrogation of mitzvot. When these events occur, then some believe that certain mitzvot will no longer be binding. But lacking this, any claim that mitzvot have been abrogated is indeed heretical, and no one can claim that "perhaps we have indeed passed its 'future' abrogation."[3]

Betzalel Sochaczewski responds:

My thanks to Dr. Shapiro for his gracious reception of my critique of his *The Limits of Orthodox Theology* and for penning the above response. The following are my thoughts about these newest comments, in the order he presented them.

1. Shapiro emphasizes that his approach of attributing disingenuousness to Maimonides vis-à-vis parts of the Thirteen Principles is not novel, but "follows in the footsteps of many scholars of the last thousand years." Presumably, he refers to those mentioned on p. 77 of his book, regarding creation *ex nihilo*. I wonder why he feels the need to reiterate this, as I discuss all these sources on pp. 129–132 of my essay. I elaborate there on the Straussian orientation of this thinking, which prompts Shapiro (further in his comments) to observe "that all interpreters have biases that they bring to their interpretations … This means that we must examine arguments presented, rather than try to attribute positions to biases." While objective assessment of argumentation is indeed important, I

---

[3] Sochaczewski, p. 42, writes of the "extra-halakhic 'divine' repeal of the mitzvot through a prophet, such as was claimed by the Church Fathers and the Koran." This sentence is mistaken in a couple of different ways. First, the Christian claim does not refer to divine repeal through a prophet, but through God Himself, in His human incarnation. This claim is already found in the New Testament (e.g., Galatians 3:24–25). Furthermore, the notion that the mitzvot were divinely repealed is not found in the Koran and is not an Islamic position.

maintain that awareness of the general mindset of an idea's proponent is still of great value. When interpreting Maimonides' theological agenda, is it irrelevant that certain theorists subscribed to an approach that would assume him to be a closet atheist?

To these sources, Shapiro now adds Moshe Halbertal. Indeed, Halbertal's approach to Maimonides is hewn from the same Straussian bedrock, citing *Guide* 3:28 as the basis for Maimonides' endorsement of "necessary beliefs"—a reading which is disproven in my essay (pp. 117–118) and to which Shapiro declined to respond.

2. In my essay (p. 110, n. 7), I argued that there is no established precedent for Shapiro's claim that Maimonides fabricated dogma. In response to those instances in which halakhists are known to have been disingenuous, I detailed a number of crucial distinctions between them and what Shapiro attributes to Maimonides. One of these is that in some of these cases, the fabrications were of no practical import, whereas in Maimonides' case, labeling a non-heretic a heretic has vast practical import. Shapiro responded to this that only the determinations of heresy codified in the *Mishneh Torah* (*MT*) are of practical relevance and that the three items he casts aspersions on are absent there, appearing only in Maimonides' Thirteen Principles.

I would reply that this last assertion is contingent on Shapiro's personal reading of those passages in

the *MT* and does not reflect their straightforward reading:

Regarding the first, creation *ex nihilo*—on pp. 125–126 of my essay I demonstrate how *Teshuvah* 3:7 should be read in a manner which *does* codify its belief—a reading which Shapiro, later in his response, acknowledges as possibly superior. (Strangely, Shapiro there writes that he has no vested interest in this matter. Yet, it was he who advanced his own reading of this source to bolster his position. He also fails to explain why he rejects my reading—and that of the editors of the Frankel edition—of *Yesodei ha-Torah* 1:1.)

Regarding the second, the Eighth Principle—on p. 138, I completely accept Shapiro's observation that *MT* does not codify belief in the infallibility of the scriptural text. Our disagreement is whether this is Maimonides' intent in the Thirteen Principles as well.

Regarding the third, the Torah's immutability—I have already argued (p. 148, n. 48) that Shapiro's reading of *Teshuvah* 3:8 is incorrect. (See 7 below for my rejoinder to his response on this point.)

Thus, Shapiro's defense from my above criticism demands unsubstantiated readings of the two relevant passages of *MT*. More important, though, than how one reads these passages, is that one cannot simply ignore the halakhic import of the passage in the *Peirush ha-Mishnah*, as Shapiro would have us do. Maimonides concludes his detailing of the Thirteen Principles with the following (ed. Kafiḥ, v. 2, pp. 144–145; trans. from Sefaria):

וכאשר יהיו קיימים לאדם כל
היסודות הללו ואמונתו בהם אמתית,
הרי הוא נכנס בכלל ישראל, וחובה
לאהבו ולחמול עליו וכל מה שצוה ה'
אותנו זה על זה מן האהבה והאחוה,
ואפילו עשה מה שיכול להיות מן
העבירות מחמת תאותו והתגברות
יצרו הרע, הרי הוא נענש לפי גודל
מריו ויש לו חלק, והוא מפושעי
ישראל. וכאשר יפקפק אדם ביסוד
מאלו היסודות הרי זה יצא מן הכלל
וכפר בעיקר ונקרא מין ואפיקורוס
וקוצץ בנטיעות, וחובה לשנותו
ולהשמידו ועליו הוא אומר הלא
משנאיך ה' אשנא וכו'.

And when a person believes in all of these principles and his faith in them is clarified, he enters into the category of Israel; and it is [then] a commandment to love him and to have mercy upon him and to act with him according to everything which God, may He be blessed, commanded about the man towards his fellow, regarding love and brotherhood. And even if he does what is in his ability from the sins, because of desire and the overpowering of his base nature, he is punished according to his sins, but he [still] has a share in the World to Come, and is [only considered to be] from the sinners of Israel. But if one of these principles becomes compromised for a person, behold, he exits the category of Israel and denies a fundamental [dogma] and is called an apostate, a heretic and 'someone who cuts the plantings.' And it is a commandment to hate him and to destroy him, and about him it is stated (Psalms 139:21), "Do I not hate those that You hate, O Lord."

While it is true that the *Mishneh Torah* is a code and the *Peirush ha-Mishnah* is primarily a commentary, there is no question that even the latter was formulated to reflect practical halakhah, particularly when the language indicates as such. The above passage leaves no doubt that the Thirteen Principles are one such instance.

3. Regarding Maimonides' true position on creation *ex nihilo*/the Platonist model, Shapiro is fully entitled to find my proposed resolution to this difficult area of Maimonides' thought unsatisfactory. I would object, however, to his continued mischaracterization of the issues. Maimonides does not state in *Guide* 2:24 that "there is no religious objection" to the Platonic position. Rather, he says that it is not inherently contradictory to the principles of reward and punishment, miracles, or other indisputable dogma of Judaism, and that it could, *potentially*, be read into the Creation narrative. This does not mean that, as things stand at the moment, Platonism is without objection. Conversely, in 2:13, creation *ex nihilo* is not merely Maimonides' "opinion." It is "השקפת כל המאמין בתורת משה רבנו ע"ה" and "יסוד תורת משה רבינו ע"ה" בלי ספק, והיא שניה ליסוד היחוד, ואל

"יעלה בלבך זולת זה". It is incomprehensible that a mere number of pages after so strongly expressing his stance on an issue of such gravity, Maimonides would either a) change his mind on the matter, or b) put forward an inauthentic expression of his position.

If I may take the opportunity to elaborate on my suggested resolution of Maimonides' rejection of Platonism. I had proposed that while it is possible to read the Genesis 1 narrative in a manner which accommodates Platonism, so long as there are no compelling reasons to do so, the natural reading, which reflects creation *ex nihilo*, is the accepted one and deviation from it is deviation from one of the fundamental ideas of Judaism. I would add that a parallel to this approach is found in *Emunot ve-Dei'ot* (Jozefow, 1896, pp. 169–170 and Rosenblatt, pp. 423–426 [based on the version used by Ibn Tibbon in 7:5]; ed. Kafiḥ, pp. 223–224, and Rosenblatt, pp. 271–273 [based on what is presumed a later version]) regarding the nature of the scripturally promised Resurrection of the Dead. Saadiah entertained the possibility that its many scriptural references could be interpreted not as a literal resurrection of the dead, but as foretelling the national revival of the Jewish people after their long exile, providing parallel sources where the relevant expressions are indeed intended as such. He rejects this, however, by laying down a principle that Scripture is always to be read in its implied sense (כפשוטם,

Kafiḥ), unless one of four compelling reasons renders such a reading impossible and we have no choice but to reinterpret the passage. As Saadiah explains at length, if this would be incorrect and we would have license to creatively read Scripture as we wish, then all of the legal and historical narratives of the Torah could be reinterpreted in fashions which would leave us with a Judaism that bears no resemblance to the one we know. Being that none of these four factors militate against a literal reading of Resurrection, it is accepted as part of Scripture, and, as is implicit in Saadiah's extensive discussion of the topic, is elevated to being one of the hallmarks of Judaism.

More importantly for our purposes is that Maimonides (*Iggeret Teḥiat ha-Meitim*, Sheilat, *Igrot ha-Rambam*, p. 367) espouses this very train of thought regarding Resurrection:

ואנחנו כבר בארנו שבאו פסוקים, ואם הם מעטים, יורו על שוב המתים. ואם יאמר האומר: אנחנו נפרש הפסוקים ההם, כמו שפירשנו זולתם – נאמר לו ... ולזה תהיה גם כן תחית המתים אפשרית. וכל אפשר, כשתבוא בו הגדת נביא – נאמין בו, ולא נצטרך לפרשו, ולא נוציאהו מפשוטו ... ולאלו השרשים האמנו תחית המתים על פשוטה, ושמונה מפנות התורה, ואמרנו שאין ראוי לפרש שני הפסוקים הנגלים המורים עליה הוראה ברורה אשר לא תסבול פרוש.

We see here that Maimonides

was of the position that although a scriptural passage is not inambiguous, so long as there is no compelling reason to avoid it, we opt for the *peshat*, the straightforward reading, *to the point that its ideas can become fundamentals of Judaism.*

I argue that Maimonides adopted the same approach in regard to Creation. Although he acknowledges in *Guide* 2:24 that an alternative reading of Genesis 1 is *possible* and that he would utilize it were Platonism to be demonstrated (as it would activate one of Saadiah's four aforementioned rules, namely Reason), so long as that has not occurred, creation *ex nihilo* remains its default reading, to the point that Maimonides could state with confidence that this doctrine is יסוד תורת משה רבינו ע"ה בלי ספק.

4. On the matter of the eternity of the mitzvot, Shapiro has mischaracterized my characterization of his position. In the passage, he cites from p. 122, I do not claim that Shapiro has Maimonides personally denying this principle, and I explicitly write as much at the top of p. 144.

5. Regarding the use of rhetoric in the *Iggeret ha-Shemad* (p. 123), my observation of the distinction between the understandings of Duran and Soloveitchik is a brief aside (prefaced with "I assume that Shapiro was aware…"), intended to highlight that they are not identical. Indeed, as Shapiro reiterates, one may attempt to adduce evidence to his position from either source. It is

these points that I examined at great length in my essay, and to which Shapiro declines to respond. (In the quotation from Maimon, his understanding of Maimonides' loose use of midrashim for a specific goal is identical to my understanding in the given reference, not Shapiro's, leaving me to wonder why he makes mention of it in his response.)

6. Regarding ibn Migash on *Baba Batra* (p. 139), I concede that my critique as it appeared in my essay was slightly inaccurate—yet valid, nonetheless. In my essay, I pointed out that the passage of ibn Migash that Shapiro references is but a fragment of a lengthier explication of the *BB* passage. Indeed, that fragment—which Shapiro reproduced in his response—is all that appears in the *Shittah Mekubbezet*. I had mistakenly thought that this was what solely appeared in all previous editions of *Ḥiddushei ha-Ri Mi-Gash al Baba Batra* as well until the appearance of the newest edition (Politensky & DeHan, n.p., 2015, pp. 60–61) which contains much new material from manuscript. In reality, all previous editions of this work contained the following:

שמונה פסוקים שבתורה יהושע כתבן, דכתיב וימת שם משה. אפשר משה חי וכתיב וימת שם משה, אלא עד כאן כתב משה מכאן ואילך כתב יהושע, דברי רבי יהודה. אמר לו רבי שמעון בן יוחי אפשר ס"ת חסר אות אחת וכתיב לקוח את ספר התורה הזה. אלא מדאמר ליה רחמנא למשה לקוח וגו' מכלל שס"ת כולו נשלם

בימי משה ומשה כתבו כולו. אלא עד
כאן הקב"ה אומר ומשה כותב בדמע
כמו שהיה כותב ברוך מפי ירמיה,
שנאמר ויאמר אליו ברוך וגו'.
כמאן אזלא הא דא"ר יהושע בר אבין
אמר רב גידל אמר רב: שמונה
פסוקים שבתורה יחיד קורא אותן.
לימא דלא כר' שמעון, דאי ר' שמעון
אמאי קורא אותם יחיד בפירוד, והרי
משה כתבן כמו התורה כולה. אפילו
תימא ר' שמעון בן יוחי הואיל
ואישתני אישתני. כלומר הואיל
ואישתנו פסוקים אלו ונכתבו בדמע,
אשתנו נמי לקרותם בפירוד.
שמונה פסוקים שבתורה יחיד קורא
אותם, כלומר הקורא פסוקים
שלפניהם אינו רשאי לגמור עד סוף
התורה משום שנמצא קורא מה שכתב
משה עם מה שכתב יהושע. אלא
מפסיק ועולה אחר וקורא פסוקים אלו
בפני עצמם כדי שיהא ניכר שלא כתבן
משה אלא יהושע. פירוש אחר: יחיד
קורא אותם, כלומר ואינו רשאי
להפסיק בהם כדי שלא יהא ניכר
שיהושע הוא כתבן.

According to this version, ibn
Migash first explains the give and
take of the passage and concludes
with two explanations of the halakhah in question. As Shapiro clarified to me in a private correspondence, he took note of ibn Migash's
use of the opinion of R. Yehudah in
the concluding paragraph, when either opinion, that of R. Yehudah or
R. Shimon, could have been used.
This is evidence, claims Shapiro,
that ibn Migash's personal ruling
was like that of R. Yehudah that
Joshua, in fact, wrote the final eight
verses.

Besides for the weakness of this
inference, the difficulty with this

version of the text is that the concluding paragraph is out of place in
the sequence of the talmudic passage that it is explaining. Indeed, in
the newest edition of *Ri Mi-Gash*
(above) based upon the manuscripts, the final paragraph appears
between the second and third paragraphs—precisely where it ought to
be. Accordingly, the references to
Joshua writing the eight verses reflect the *hava amina* (assumption) of
the *Gemara*, as it states immediately
thereafter לימא דלא כר' שמעון. The
Gemara continues by deflecting this
assumption: the halakhah in question is compatible with R. Shimon's
position that the eight verses were
written by Moses. According to this
version, ibn Migash is merely
providing commentary to this passage without taken a position on its
subject, just as Rashi did. Thus, as I
originally wrote, the conflict that
Shapiro creates between Maimonides and Migash is without basis.

7. Regarding Shapiro's final point,
on the abrogation of the Torah, his
response to my critique (p. 148, n.
98) mixes apples with oranges. Indeed, other authorities who allow,
in theory, for the lapsing of mitzvot
through revelation would maintain
that the historical claims to such are
fallacious and irrelevant—but not
because the very notion is heretical,
rather because they did not fulfill
the standards it demands. Hence
Christianity's and Islam's position
on supersessionism is heretical, but
in the same way that any arbitrary
denial of the mitzvot is. To draw a

parallel: The possibility that rabbinic enactments could be overturned under certain circumstances is a legitimate part of the halakhic system. Yet if someone would insist that a particular *halakhah* should be disregarded on the basis of specious reasoning, it is no more than garden variety heresy.

With Maimonides, though, it is clear that he views the very suggestion of abrogation as heretical.

שלשה הן הכופרים בתורה: ... והאומר שהבורא החליף מצוה זו במצוה אחרת וכבר בטלה תורה זו אע"פ שהיא היתה מעם ה' וכו' (הל' תשובה פ"ג ה"ח).

He indicates no qualification that this is only when certain criteria have not been met. As the *Kesef Mishnah* explains, שהרי זה מכחיש כמה כתובים המורים שהתורה נצחית, the very claim that abrogation of the Torah is even *possible* is a denial of the Torah's own assertion that it is eternal. This is so under all circumstances. This is clearly Albo's (*Ikkarim* 3:13–20) understanding of Maimonides' position throughout his discussion of the topic, as well.

Indeed, this understanding is apparent from this matter's very mention as a separate subcategory of denial of the Torah. For if all Maimonides meant was as Shapiro takes him to mean, מאי קא משמע לן? Implicit in the belief in the divinity of the Torah is that its instructions are binding—do I need to single out that discarding without good reason is heresy?

8. I accept Shapiro's correction of my formulation of Christianity's and Islam's "repeal of the mitzvot through a prophet." This has no bearing, of course, on the point of that sentence: the supersession of the Torah assumed by Christianity and Islam—and rejected by Maimonides—is distinctly different than the lapse of certain mitzvot within the halakhic system.

The Exodus and Historical Truth

Nathan Aviezer writes:

I GREATLY ENJOYED the article, "The Exodus and Historical Truth" (*Ḥakirah* vol. 31) by Geula Twersky. As a physicist, I was particularly interested in her section: "Numbers in the Exodus Narrative." I would like to add strength to her thesis by commenting on a subject that her article did not discuss.

What I have in mind is the enormous population increase while the Israelites were in Egypt. The Torah states that 603,550 adult males left Egypt and this number does not include the tribe of Levi (Numbers 1:46). It is worth mentioning that when the Torah reports the number of members in a tribe, it includes only the males. One reason may be that the tribe of a child was determined by the tribe of his father, with his mother playing no role in this determination.

Although the Israelites numbered only 70 souls when they entered Egypt (Genesis, Chapter 46), when they left Egypt, they numbered over 600,000 adult males (Numbers 1:46). This number requires an explanation because it corresponds to a population growth of nearly 10,000, a population growth that is unprecedented in history.

Nevertheless, it can be shown that the data recorded in the Torah, together with some reasonable assumptions, can explain this vast population growth.

The Israelites were in Egypt for 210 years. (The oft-quoted number of 430 years refers to the period beginning with the birth of Isaac. See Rashi's commentary on Exodus 12:46.) The reported number of Israelites leaving Egypt includes only males over the age of twenty. Thus, we are speaking of a population increase during 190 years.

What is a typical population increase in history during a period of 190 years? For example, between the years 1740 and 1930, the world's population increased by a factor of 3 (from 700 million to about 2 billion). Therefore, the problem is to explain the enormous difference between this increase in the world's population (only a factor of 3) and the enormous population increase recorded in Exodus (a factor of almost 10,000) over the same period of 190 years.

It is not possible to attribute the current slow increase of the world's population to deaths caused by wars. The deadliest war in history was the Second World War, during which 60 million people died, including the six million Jews who were murdered. However, this death toll had little effect (less than 3%) on the world's population.

The reason for the very slow increase in the world's population in previous times was the lack of knowledge of medicine. Before the modern age, the majority of children died young because of disease and plagues, and this is in addition to natural miscarriages and death during childbirth. Therefore, a large fraction of pregnancies did not produce a healthy child who lived to adulthood and ultimately had children of his or her own. Hence, the population of the world increased very slowly, despite the fact that the average woman became pregnant many times during her period of fertility. The situation is summarized in the famous expression: *"Many pregnancies but small families."*

In his prize-winning book, *Guns, Germs and Steel*, Professor Jared Diamond, of the University of California at Los Angeles, describes the devastating effect that disease and plagues had on populations in the past. For example, at the time of the Exodus from Egypt, it took *a thousand years* for the world's population to double.

As stated above, the Israelites were in Egypt for 210 years. The fertility of a woman begins approximately at age 15 and continues to age 40–45. Any age between 40 and 45 years is equally reasonable to mark the end of a woman's period of fertility. We shall take the age of 45 years because this value leads to a result that is close to the population mentioned in Exodus. The length of a generation is taken to be a woman's age at the middle of her period of fertility, that is, 30 years, which lies midway between 15 years and 45 years. Therefore, *the 210 years that the Israelites were in Egypt correspond to seven generations.*

The main challenge is to determine the size of typical Israelite families in Egypt. We shall base our estimate on information given explicitly in the Torah. Jacob had twelve sons, but his family was not typical because he had four wives. Eleven sons of Jacob (not counting Levi) fathered 50 sons between them (Genesis, chapter 46). Some had many sons (Benjamin had 10 sons) whereas some had few sons (Dan had only one son). The average was 4.6 sons per family (50 divided by 11). We shall take this number of sons per family as the basis for our calculation. In addition to 4.6 sons per family, there were probably an equal number of daughters. Thus, we take the average family to consist of 9.2 children. There is nothing unusual about a family with nine children. Today, among *haredi* Jews, having nine or even more children is quite common.

In summary, the sons of Jacob (excluding Levi) sired 50 sons, and this number increased by a factor of 4.6 in every generation.

In the table below, we list the number of sons at the end of each generation (the numbers have been rounded off).

Number of Males	
Beginning	50
End of 1st Generation	240
End of 2nd	1,100
End of 3rd	5,060
End of 4th	23,300
End of 5th	107,000
End of 6th	492,000

The table does not list the sons born in the seventh generation, because at the time of the Exodus from Egypt, they were too young to be included in the census, which numbered only males *"over the age of twenty."* At the time of the Exodus, the first four generations had already died (120 years had passed). Therefore, we take into account only the fifth generation (107,000 males) and the sixth generation (492,000 males). The adult male population who left Egypt is thus calculated to be 599,000. This number is remarkably close to the figure of 603,550 adult males that appears in the Torah.

It is important to emphasize that it is not claimed that the details of the table describe exactly how many Israelites were living in each generation. Our purpose is to show that by combining the data given in the Torah with a few reasonable assumptions, one can explain the large number of Israelites who left Egypt at the time of the Exodus.

It is written twice in Exodus that the Israelites in Egypt were blessed with a large increase in population, in Exodus 1:7 (*"The Israelites were fruitful and multiplied and they became very numerous, and the land was filled with them*") and in Exodus 1:12 ("*The more that the Egyptians oppressed the Israelites, the more they increased in numbers*"). Since a family of nine children is not unusually large, how were these blessings expressed? *The meaning of the blessings is that most pregnancies resulted in children who lived to reach adulthood and to have children of their own.* This was highly unusual in the ancient world, and this was the expression of the divine blessings.

It is not necessary to assume that no Israelite children ever died young. Rather, from all the pregnancies of the average Israelite woman during her 30 years of fertility, nine pregnancies resulted in children who grew up to have children of their own. Thus, the Israelites increased in Egypt from a small tribe of seventy souls into a numerous and mighty nation.

The tribe of Levi requires a separate discussion for two reasons. First, although the increase in the number of the Levites seems impressive (from 3 males to 22,300 males), the tribe of Levi was significantly smaller than all the other tribes (Numbers, chapter 4), whose numbers ranged from 35,400 (tribe of Benjamin) to 74,600 (tribe of Judah). And this resulted in spite of the fact that the recorded population of the other tribes included only males over the age of twenty ("*males from the age of twenty*"), whereas the recorded population of the tribe of Levi included babies ("*every male from the age of one month*").

There is yet another reason for discussing separately the tribe of Levi. It is possible to carry out the same calculation for the tribe of Levi that was carried out above for the entire population of Israelites. However, it is not possible to carry out such a calculation for any other tribe because the *calculation requires the number of sons and also the number of grandsons* of Jacob. This information is given in the Torah only for the tribe of Levi. This enables one to calculate the increase of the tribe of Levi at the time of the Exodus.

Moshe and Aaron had special important tasks to fulfill during the Exodus. Therefore, the Torah found it appropriate to give detailed information about the family of Moshe and Aaron, who were members of the tribe of Levi. Regarding the other tribes, there was no reason to present such detailed information in the Torah. Therefore, it is not possible to calculate the expected increase in population of any other tribe.

We will now see that the same calculation that was carried out above for the entire population of the Israelites also explains the more modest increase of the tribe of Levi. God commanded Moshe to take a census of the tribe of Levi ("*Count the Levites … all males above the age of one month,*" Numbers 3:15).

The population of the tribe of Levi increased from the *three sons of Levi* (Gershon, Kehat, Merari) at the time of entering Egypt to 22,300 Levites at the time of the Exodus from Egypt (Numbers 3:39).

The relatively small number of Levites resulted from the smaller number of children in the Levite families. The typical size of the Levite family was 2.9 sons, whereas it was 4.6 sons for the other tribes (see previous discussion).

Levi had three sons and eight grandsons. The sons of Gershon were Livni and Shimei, the sons of Koraḥ were Amram, Izhar, Hevron and Uzziel, the sons of Merari were Mahli and Mushi (Exodus 6:17–19). This corresponds to slightly fewer than three sons per family. This datum will serve as the basis of our calculation, that is, 2.9 sons per family, and, of course, an equal number of daughters.

As stated above, the Israelites were in Egypt for 210 years. The fertility of a woman begins approximately at age 15 and continues to age 40–45. Any age between 40 and 45 years is equally reasonable to mark the end of a woman's period of fertility. We shall take the age of 40 years because this value leads to a result that is close to the population of Levites mentioned in Exodus. The length of a generation is taken to be a woman's age at the middle of her period of fertility, that is, 27 years, which lies midway between 15 years and 40 years. Therefore, *the 210 years that the Israelites were in Egypt correspond to eight generations of Levites.*

In summary, three sons of Levi entered Egypt and this number of males increased by a factor of 2.9 in every generation. In the Table below, we list the number of male Levites at the end of each generation (the numbers have been rounded off).

Number of Male Levites	
Beginning	3
End of 1st Generation	8
End of 2nd	23
End of 3rd	70
End of 4th	200
End of 5th	580
End of 6th	1,700
End of 7th	4,900
End of 8th	14,200

At the time of the Exodus, the males of the first four generations of Levites were already dead (over 100 years had passed). Therefore, we include the fifth generation (580 males), the sixth generation (1,700 males), the seventh generation (4,900 males), and the eighth generation (14,200 males). The total number of male Levites at the time of the Exodus is thus calculated to be 21,380. This number is quite close to the number 22,300 males reported in the Torah.

Our goal here is to show that it is possible to explain the numbers mentioned in the Torah, even those that seem to be exaggerated. Therefore, one should not assume that the numbers mentioned in the Torah are imaginary. The examples dealt with here are the extensive population increase of Israelites in general and the tribe of Levi in particular. Our explanation is based on the data recorded in the Torah, combined with a few quite reasonable assumptions.

Judah Landa writes:

Thank you for another great issue of *Ḥakirah*. Your encouragement of study and research into Torah and Judaism is commendable, most productive and much appreciated.

I am, however, animated to respond to Geula Twersky's article "The Exodus and Historical Truth" which appeared in volume 31 of *Ḥakirah* (pp. 151–187) as a "refutation" of the main themes of Joshua Berman's book *Ani Maamin*. The article sets grandiose goals for itself at the outset, then claims to have achieved them. Unfortunately, it falls demonstrably short of delivering on any of them. While the article makes some valid points and is well-written and well-intentioned, even impassioned in places, the numerous misstatements of fact, exaggerated descriptive appellations, wholesale ignoring of pertinent data and skewed analytical methodology, all contribute to the sense of disappointment experienced by the reader.

Twersky begins with the question of where (in what century) to look for evidence of the historicity of the exodus. After all, looking in the wrong place is bound to lead to failure. Berman is wrong to place the exodus in the 13th century BCE, claims Twersky, and this is why he and other scholars encounter "a sustained lack of evidence" for the exodus. The biblical chronology places the exodus in the 15th century BCE, asserts Twersky (p. 152), and that is where our search for evidence of it must be directed. The

biblical text (I Kings 6:1) assigns 480 years "from the exodus" to the beginning of King Solomon's construction of the Temple, an event universally attributed by scholars and historians to ca. 966 BCE. Adding 480 to 966 yields ca. 1446 BCE for the exodus, just about the middle of the 15th century BCE. This reasoning is standard fare in the Evangelical Christian community and I shall return to it later.

Twersky then goes looking for evidence in "the right place" and finds it in the form of Bryant Wood's archaeological assessment of artifacts and pottery excavated in the ruins (collapsed walls) of Jericho, which Wood dates to late in the 15th century BCE (the low 1400s). Since the exodus occurred before Jericho's destruction—a fundamental feature of the biblical chronology—this evidence, concludes Twersky, proves that Berman's Late Date Exodus in the 13th century BCE is wrong (pp. 161–2).

Wood's view is, however, a minority one, and goes against the assessment of Kathleen Kenyon, a widely respected and experienced archaeologist who actually excavated at Jericho (unlike Wood), who places Jericho's destruction in the 16th century BCE. Even more importantly than this cherry picking of disputed archaeological assessments, which Twersky goes on to repeatedly do regarding other surveyed or excavated sites in Canaan/Israel (many of which are also enmeshed in uncertainties as to which ancient city/place they represent), Twersky entirely ignores multiple sources of evidence from the hard physical sciences (as opposed to the soft, subjective, and underdeveloped field of archaeology whose conclusions at times contradict well-established history). The carbon dating and earthquake record evidence indisputably nail down Jericho's destruction to the mid-16th century BCE, in agreement with Kenyon's archaeological assessment, as I reported at length in my article in volume 14 of Ḥakirah (p. 187–235) titled "The Exodus: Convergence of Science, History and Jewish Tradition" (with follow-up material in the Letters section of volume 15). A more expansive version of that article can be accessed by all on my website www.biblical-misconceptions.com.

The "Convergence" article cited above concludes that the best date for the exodus, the one that best fits all the scientific **and** historical evidence **and** the biblical chronology, is ca. 1600 BCE, certainly not at any point in the 1400s BCE. This conclusion also best fits the destruction of Sodom 400 years before the exodus, the plain reading of the account in the Book of Judges, in which almost all the judges are presented successively, with decades between them and no overlap (contra Twersky's attempts at muddying the water on this), and Judge Jephthah's stated 300 years from Israel's taking the territories east of the Jordan River (40 years after the exodus) to his own time (Jud 11:26), a statement made in the context of his diplomatic overture to the Ammonite

king in a serious effort to avoid war.

Having promised to present the case "for the historicity of the exodus based on the evidence" and that "in fact the record lends rich support to the biblical narrative [of the exodus] as we shall see" (p. 152), and finding no such evidence in the 15th century BCE—the place to look for it as Twersky sees it—Twersky diverts our attention to a comparison of the biblical and historical depictions of the chaotic conditions in Canaan/Israel during the Late Bronze Age (1550–1200 BCE). These do generally agree with, and nicely complement, each other. But, alas, this constitutes no proof of, nor evidence for, the historicity of the exodus. Twersky is thus reduced to making the rather anemic claim that "if the evidence can be shown to work in concert with the larger biblical record, then the evidence can cautiously be understood to corroborate the biblical story." In other words, if one can be persuaded as to the historicity of one biblical narrative, one ought to be receptive of same regarding any other biblical narrative, such as the exodus. This is known as "special pleading." Needless to say, it does not work quite this way, not in the cynical world we live in these days.

What about the 480 years of I Kings 6:1? Are not ca. 1600 and 966 BCE separated by more than 480 years? The solution to this is to be found in reading the biblical text closely and carefully (as should always be done). As I elaborate in the expanded "Convergence" article (accessible on the website cited above), the text in I Kings does not refer to 480 years from "the exodus," that is, from that singular event we label "the exodus," when the Israelites crossed the threshold out of the city of Raamses. Instead, the text there refers to 480 years from [the completion of] the process of the Israelites' going forth from the land of Egypt. The Hebrew wording in I Kings is quite identical to that employed by Moses in speaking to the Israelites about an event that occurred **40 years after** the exodus. Moses describes that event as happening "when you were going forth from Egypt" (Deut 23:5). Apparently, the Israelites were on their way out of Egypt for quite some time, at least 40 years and perhaps longer, probably until they were settled securely in a land all their own and were in a position to build the Temple, which they were commanded to do. At that point they were no longer going away from their past and had arrived at the new stage of going into their future, which was to be represented by the Temple. I Kings 6:1 informs us that the Israelites were **480 years late** in commencing to perform their pivotal obligation of constructing the Temple. Otherwise, why would the Bible single out this particular event in all of Israel's history (post conquest) to date it, and only it, with respect to their emergence from Egypt?

Turning then to the matter of the size of the Israelite population, Twersky criticizes Berman's assertion (admittedly contra the plain meaning of multiple biblical texts)

that it was very small, about "enough people to fill a stadium," small enough for their departure from Egypt to have gone unnoticed by the Egyptians (thus the absence of evidence for the exodus in the Egyptian record). Berman derives support for his claim from the biblical text in which God describes the Israelites' upcoming conquest of the Promised Land (Ex 23:27–30). "I will not drive them (the indigenous inhabitants of the land) out before (in front of) you in a single year, lest the land become desolate and the wild beasts multiply against you. Little by little will I drive them out before (in front of) you, until you will have increased and [can] possess the land." To Berman this demonstrates that the Torah itself recognizes that the Israelite population was very small at the time, too small to safely possess the land on their own.

In the attempt to refute Berman's analysis, Twersky argues that "these verses refer not to the **effects** of the Israelite conquest, but rather to events that gradually **preceded** it" (p. 174). Twersky goes on to suggest that it was the (well-known) Egyptian military incursions into Canaan that unwittingly performed God's driving out of the local population **before** the Israelites entered the land. The *tzirah* of Ex 23:28 is to be translated as 'hornet' and the hornet was the ancient, long-standing symbol used by Egypt for itself. All this is then summarized by Twersky in the following tellingly head-scratching declaration: "The land's emptying out over time **prior** to the Israelite conquest prevented the formation of a void and the infiltration of wild animals" (p. 174).

This is all so utterly untenable, even risible, as to render it difficult to know where to begin. Let us start with the fact that at the time these verses were uttered (by God to Moses to be conveyed to the people) the Israelites were on the cusp of embarking directly into the Promised Land (a few months later they actually begin to do so, when the affair of the spies intervenes). There is therefore **no time** for an extended, multi-year process (per v. 29) of the gradual diminution of the indigenous population, while that of the Israelites gradually increases (per v. 30), **before** the Israelites enter the land and the conquest begins. Secondly, whether such a process happens quickly (in one year, per v. 29) or gradually (little by little, per v. 30), if it happens **before** the Israelites enter the land, the Israelites will encounter a desolate land and be greeted by wild beasts.

Thirdly, the whole point of these verses is for one population (the indigenous Canaanites) to decrease gradually and do so **concurrently** with the other population's (the Israelites) gradual increase, **while both are in the same land.** This keeps the total population stable, prevents desolation of the land and the proliferation of wild beasts. The decrease is thus hitched to the increase; they must proceed apace of each other. Since the increase in the Israelites' population proceeds gradually, so **must** the decrease in

the Canaanites' population. This is what the Torah is telling us in Ex 23:27–30 and these verses must therefore refer to the time **after** the entry of the Israelites into the land (contra Twersky).

Forty years later the Israelites are once again on the cusp of entering the Promised Land, their population is about the same as it was 40 years earlier (Num 1:46 and 26:51), and Moses reviews the same principles. "The Lord your God will dislodge these nations before you little by little; **you cannot destroy them** quickly lest the wild beasts multiply against you" (Deut 7:22). Clearly, this refers to the conquest process, with the Israelites already in the land and the pace of **their** destruction of their enemies (not by the Egyptians) is the topic being addressed.

Twersky next turns to the issue of the 22,273 firstborn males (Num 3:43) which Berman describes as a "surprisingly small number" for a population of upwards of 2 million people. (This is actually more than surprising since it is statistically a near impossibility—barring a miracle—as it necessitates a huge number of babies—about 54 by my calculations—per Israelite mother.) Twersky's solution is that the number 22,273 obtained via the census (as presented in the biblical text) represents only the firstborn males **after** the exodus (those born during the about one year between the exodus and the census), not the total number of firstborn males in the general population of Israelites. Although this is not at all stated or even hinted at in the census text, it is facilitated by associating the census of the firstborn males (Num 3:43) with the commandment to sanctify them (Ex 13:2, 11–12). That commandment, claims Twersky, applied "only to those male children born **after** the exodus" (p. 177), according to R. Yoḥanan in the Talmud (BT *Bekhorot* 4b). It follows then that the census of firstborn males was likewise limited to those born after the exodus.

Well, the association of the census with the commandment to sanctify the firstborn males is eminently reasonable, since the point of the census was to transfer the sanctification of the affected firstborn males, from them to an equal number of Levites (Num 3:45). But Twersky altogether misunderstands the pertinent Talmudic discussion. R. Yoḥanan and Resh Lakish do disagree as to whether firstborn males after the exodus were included in the commandment to be sanctified, with R. Yoḥanan saying 'yes' and Resh Lakish saying 'no.' But all agree that all Israelite firstborn males coming out of Egypt (older than one month) were included in the commandment to be sanctified. It thus follows that they all must therefore have been included in the census (based on the association described above). So the matter cannot be resolved in this manner. Neither of the Talmudic Sages would support Twersky on this.

How then is this matter to be resolved? Well, the intertwined, complex, multiple conundrums posed by the biblical numbers, for the general Israelite population and for its various subgroups, are treated thoroughly in my article titled "The Exodus: How Many?" This can be accessed by all interested parties at my website www.biblical-misconceptions.com. I highly recommend this article and the "Convergence" article cited above to both Berman and Twersky, as neither of them got it right in my view. Not even close.

Much more remains to critique in Twersky's essay, but this is a letter, not an article. Instead, I will close with a final thought regarding the big enchilada of the exodus not being reflected in the Egyptian historical record (inscriptions on tomb and temple walls and on papyri or other writing surfaces). It has been said, the best defense is a good offense. To the critics who demand to know, "How come the exodus appears nowhere in the Egyptian record?" and use this as the basis for asserting that the exodus did not happen, we may respond (with love and respect, of course), for starters, with the following question: "How come the horrific fate of two major ancient Egyptian cities, Heracleion and Canopus (not their Egyptian names), is likewise not reflected in the Egyptian record?" Those two bustling coastal cities through which the bulk of Egypt's foreign trade passed, inhabited as they were for many centuries by thousands of people—large cities with temples, statues, palaces and homes of high officials and tradesmen—sank and disappeared into the abyss of the Mediterranean Sea around the close of the 2nd century BCE, with nary a word in the Egyptian record. Were it not for the ancient Greek historians who wrote about these cities, and the modern day archaeologists who dive deep down to the bottom of the sea to uncover their mysteries, we would know nothing—dependent as we would then be on the Egyptian record—about the existence of these cities, their singularly calamitous fate and the disastrous impact their rather sudden demise had on the Egyptian economy, not to mention the many lives lost.

And while we are at it, we could also counter the critics with, "How come the century-long takeover of most of Egypt by foreigners (the oppressor Hyksos) is barely mentioned in the Egyptian record?" But for an obscure, unofficial mention found in a tomb, and artefactual discoveries later made by modern archaeologists, we would today know nothing of this monumental development in Egypt's history.

Obviously, the Egyptian historical record is grossly incomplete. This is so not only because many inscriptions have not survived the ravages of time across the millennia (they certainly have not), and not only because the Egyptian authorities preferred to avoid and hide unpleasant developments (they certainly did). This is so primarily because the absence of an event in the record, to the ancient Egyptian mind, rendered the event non-existent; the event then just did not happen. Such an event became, on some level, a non-entity. By deliberately omitting or erasing undesirable developments from the record, the ancient Egyptians also eliminated them from ever having happened. This is the basis for the ancient Egyptian practices surrounding the execration texts, their defacement of statues and their insistence on inscribing everything desirable in as permanent a format as possible.

Who knows what other important developments in the history of ancient Egypt we are utterly unaware of, due to the above described cultural proclivities? Had we not been thankfully blessed by our possession of the biblical record, God forbid, the exodus would have become another story lost to the ashbin of history. But that record **is** in our possession, and we are what we became as a result of it.

Geula Twersky responds:

I would like to express my gratitude to Professor Natan Aviezer for his kind words. It means so much coming from someone of his stature. His discussion of the topic is a welcome contribution to its elucidation. I would also like to acknowledge Dr. Landa's insightful discussion pertaining to the Egyptian practice of failing to record significant events in their historical records.

Regarding the balance of Dr. Landa's letter, I hesitate to reply for a number of reasons. First, because of the letter's gratuitous disparaging tone, which is most unbecoming. Secondly, due to the fact that so many of its critiques have already been dealt with in my article. It is pointless for me to rehash all that has been missed or ignored. Thirdly, as correctly stated in his letter, this is a letters column. Addressing each of the points properly would bring my response beyond the limited scope of this forum. Finally, and perhaps most importantly, Dr. Landa's main complaint seems to be that I do not adopt his approach. Since that issue is irrelevant to my article, this is not the appropriate place to discuss it.

Nonetheless, I would like to take the opportunity to briefly note a few important points. To begin with, Dr. Landa's letter misrepresents my article, as "a 'refutation' of the main themes of Joshua Berman's book *Ani Maamin*." This distorts the very topic of my article (and is the first of a long list of misrepresentations). As I clearly state in the opening of my article, my critique is aimed specifically at Berman's extended discussion pertaining to the Exodus.

I also wish to address the accusation of "cherry-picking." When I choose to adopt one opinion over another, despite it being a minority point of view, I consistently adduce compelling reasons for doing so. I must add that I find this complaint to be especially ironic as it is lodged against my article by someone whose approaches are not in line with even a minority of scholars.

I would like to focus briefly on one issue, as it is enormously critical to my position and to the study of archaeology in general. Dr. Landa states: "Twersky entirely ignores multiple sources of evidence from the hard physical sciences…The carbon dating and earthquake record evidence indisputably nail down Jericho's destruction to the mid-16th century BCE."

Properly addressing the questions raised by the carbon dates from Jericho requires that we delve into some of the details. The carbonized burnt grain and wood samples from Jericho's destruction layer that were initially dug up by Kathleen Kenyon in the 1950s were indeed found to support an 18th–16th cent. BCE destruction.[4] However, (re-evaluated) samples studied by the British Museum Laboratory, were calibrated to approximately 1883–1324 BCE,[5] casting a shadow on our ability to settle the debate via carbon samples alone. More recently, samples procured by an Italian excavation team in 2000, were found to calibrate Jericho's destruction to 1347 BC +/-85 and 1597 BC

---

[4] Hendrik J. Bruins and Johannes Van Der Plicht, "Tell es-Sultan (Jericho): Radiocarbon results of short-lived cereal and multiyear charcoal samples from the end of the Middle Bronze Age," *Radiocarbon* 37 (1995), 213–220.

[5] S.G.E. Bowman, J.C. Ambers, and M.N. Leese, "Re-Evaluation of British Museum Radiocarbon Dates Issued Between 1980 and 1984," *Radiocarbon* 32 (1990), 59–79, 74.

+/-91.[6] An honest evaluation of the combined carbon data points to anywhere between 1883–1262 BCE, a 600 year window! So much for the "evidence from the hard physical sciences." Indeed, the very use of the term "hard sciences" to characterize carbon 14 evaluations is nothing short of a misnomer. Additionally, the characterization of dating by means of artifacts as less empirical than by means of carbon dating is profoundly misleading. The presence of a scarab collection containing the names of an array of 18th Dynasty pharaohs, as presented in my article, is objective testimony that Jericho's destruction could not have preceded that era.

A further illustration of the limits of carbon dating is the case of the eruption of Thera and the subsequent destruction of the ancient Minoan civilization. Carbon dates for these events have yielded a 17th cent. BCE date.[7] However, the rich archaeological record from ancient Egypt and the Aegean Islands unequivocally place the Thera eruption 150 years later.[8] Manfred Bietak,

who has devoted his life's work to researching the mysterious Hyksos civilization in Ancient Egypt, cautions that relying on radiocarbon alone is far more problematic than generally acknowledged.[9]

R. Meir Simḥah of Dvinsk

Elie Bashevkin writes:

Thank you for sharing your enlightening article about the great Rav Meir Simḥah and his attitudes towards Zionism, especially as culled from his works like the *Meshekh Ḥokhmah*. At times, I believe Rav Meir Simḥah commented on important political developments—especially regarding Zionism—using veiled language. For example, *Meshekh Ḥokhmah* comments at the end of *Sefer Bereshit* (50:24) on Yosef's promise that Hashem would redeem the Jewish people and return them to Eretz Yisrael. He first quotes the *Gemara* about the "three oaths" and refers to the

---

[6] Nicolo Marchetti and Lorenzo Nigro, Excavations at Jericho, 1998: Preliminary Reports on the Second Season of Archaeological Excavations and Surveys at Tell es-Sultan, Palestine. (Quaderni di Gerico 2; Rome: Universita di Roma, 2000), 206–207, 330, 332.

[7] W.L. Friedrich, Kromer, M. Friedrich, J. Heinemeier, T. Pfeiffer, S. Talamo, "Santorini Eruption Radiocarbon Dated to 1627–1600 B.C." *Science* 312 (2006), p. 548.

[8] Manfred Bietak, "Antagonisms in

Historical and Radiocarbon Chronology," pp. 78–110 in Andrew J Shortland and C. Bronk Ramsey eds., *Radiocarbon and the Chronologies of Ancient Egypt* (Oxford: Oxbow, 2013).

[9] Manfred Bietak, "Radiocarbon and the date of the Thera Eruption," *Antiquity* 88 (2014), 277–282; cf. Paolo Cherubini *et. al.*, who concur that "caution should be applied to the dating offered by Friedrich *et al.*," idem, "Bronze Age Catastrophe and Modern Controversy: Dating the Santorini Eruption," *Antiquity* 88 (2014), pp. 267–291, 271.

disastrous results of the premature *aliyah* of the tribe of Ephraim. Then, apparently unrelated to the *pasuk* in *Bereshit*, Rav Meir Simḥah raises the issue of a *navi* who plans to bring the Jewish people up to another land and quickly labels him a *navi ha-sheker* because the Jewish people will always return to the land of Avraham, Yitzchak, and Yaakov.

Since the issue of going to another land other than Eretz Yisrael was nowhere in the *pasuk*, I can only imagine that Rav Meir Simḥah is commenting unfavorably on the Uganda Plan of the Sixth Zionist Congress of 1903 in veiled language.

Jonah Steinmetz responds:

Thank you for your feedback and input. I too mentioned this example of R. Meir Simḥah's commentary on contemporary Zionism in my article (on p. 28), though I appreciate your more detailed presentation of his point. I hope the article and our conversation encourage others to read *Meshekh Ḥokhmah* with an eye towards his implicit messages.

Women's Hair Covering

Jacob Sasson writes:

In his "Untangling the Mystery of Women's Hair Covering in Talmudic Passages" (*Ḥakirah,* Volume 31), Ari Storch surveys some of the Talmudic and Rabbinic literature dealing with the custom of women to cover their hair and, in so doing, attempts to highlight some nuance in the Talmudic discussion. For that, he is to be commended. Nonetheless, in failing to review all of the relevant Tannaitic literature, and in failing to contextualize the Talmudic discussions, the review fails to answer some of the questions it attempts to elucidate and creates just as much confusion as it seeks to clarify.

Storch's review of the Tannaitic literature begins with the Mishnah in *Ketubot.* There is, however, a parallel text in the Tosefta which, when compared to the Mishnah, helps put the development of the Mishnaic text into perspective and sets the stage for understanding the subsequent Yerushalmi and Bavli.

(Editor's Note: Sources 1, 2, 3, and 4 referenced by Jacob Sasson appear as an addendum at the end of the *Letters* Section.)

Source 1, *Tosefta Ketubot*[1] (See also the similar text in *Sotah*): Note the differences between the Mishnah and the Tosefta. For one, the Tosefta's descriptions of grounds for divorce are grouped as violative of *Dat Moshe ve-Yisrael* [sic], and not as two separate categories. Second, the "gender parity" coupled with clearly permitted actions illustrates the (im)propriety of the alleged violations, not actual *issurim*. Third, the Tosefta encourages the husband to "fix" the "sins" of the wife vis-à-vis ḥallah.

Framing the Mishnah's categorization of Dat Moshe and Yehudit (itself very odd terminology if we are speaking of prohibitions) as it is conventionally understood set the Mishnah in opposition to the Tosefta. This issue will repeat itself with the Yerushalmi and the Bavli. Viewing head covering as technically permitted but non-customary frames the sources as complementary and evolving with time.

Source 2, *Mishnah Ketubot*. [2] First, we must note the context of the discussion at hand. Prohibitions in Talmudic Law are never implied or embedded in a discussion of a different context. That makes context important. The context for this discussion is Contract Law and the husband's right vis-à-vis his wife's *ketubah*. Here, the Mishnah creates two categories of breach of contract: *Dat Moshe* and *Dat Yehudit*. It creates a cause of action, a right (though certainly no obligation!) of the husband to void the contract. It does not create an obligation to cover hair. Both Rambam and the SA codify a separate law with respect to covering hair. (More on that later.) Nothing in this *sugya* prohibits the rights of the parties to waive representations and covenants.

Let us proceed to the Talmuds.

Source 3, Yerushalmi[3] contains a clear societal factor in its analysis. יֵשׁ חָצֵר שֶׁהוּא כְּמָבוֹי וְיֵשׁ מָבוֹי שֶׁהוּא כְּחָצֵר.

(While this letter limits itself to Talmudic sources, I note that the Rif, in summarizing the *sugya* in the Bavli, includes this phrase from the Yerushalmi, presumably to highlight the societal component.)

Source 4, Bavli:[4] Here we have a further development and clarification of the Tannaitic corpus. The Bavli changes every early example of the Mishnah into a case of deception, consistent with the ḥallah example of the Tosefta. In other words, the *actus reus* is not the Mishnaic example per se but deceiving of the husband. Moreover, in its question of the *Dat Yehudit* category, the Bavli does NOT use the terminology of "*Dat Moshe*," itself a unique paradigm. Nor does it claim uncovered hair is a *d'oraita* prohibition. How could it be? The Bavli just finished evolving the *Dat Moshe* examples into cases of deception.

How best to understand these categories according to the Bavli? I propose the development of the Tannaitic material from the Tosefta/Mishnah, Yerushalmi, and finally the Bavli into two categories of breach of contract: (i) *Dat Moshe*, Breach of Contract for Fraud Acts of deception or fraud which constitute breach of contract between man and wife; and (ii) *Dat Yehudit*, Breach of Implied Covenant. In the

days in which the *ketubah* was a negotiated instrument, the parties to
the contract negotiated key business
terms and could rely on the other
party to be "normal" and acceding
to societal norms, thereby reducing
the need to negotiate every form of
behavior.

What about the Talmud's question:

פְּרוּעַ רֹאשָׁה פְּרוּעַ דְּאוֹרְיְיתָא הִיא דִּכְתִיב
וּפָרַע אֶת רֹאשׁ הָאִשָּׁה וְתָנָא דְּבֵי רַבִּי
יִשְׁמָעֵאל אַזְהָרָה לִבְנוֹת יִשְׂרָאֵל שֶׁלֹּא יָצְאוּ
בִּפְרוּעַ רֹאשׁ דְּאוֹרְיְיתָא

First, not all manuscripts contain the second reference to *d'oraita*.
Second, the terminology employed
points to an *asmakhta* and, indeed,
Rambam (*Issurei Biah* 21:17) and *SA*
(*EH* 21:2) codify this in their respective codes as *Lo*....., which in
contrast to אין or אסור is *lashon
azharah*, not prohibition. Contextu-
ally, this *azharah* or *ḥumrah* is placed
far away from the laws of *ketubot*.
This was the Jewish practice of ALL
women, single, married, and divorced but it was not law. To view
this as anything other than sociologically determined is to get lost in
confusion as to why single women
need not cover their hair or divorced women need to continue
covering their hair.

While an analysis of the treatment of women's hair covering in
Sephardic lands is beyond the pur-
view of this letter, this theme seems
to underscore the lenient positions
of the Ben Ish Ḥai, Messas, Kassin,

and the rabbis of Aleppo, Damascus, Egypt, Morocco, Turkey, and
the wider Sephardic world.

Ari Storch responds:

Jacob Sasson contends that the
Tosefta differs from the conventional understanding of the Mishnah because the Tosefta conflates
the categories of *Das Moshe* and *Das
Yehudis* into "*Das Moshe veYisrael*";
whereas, the Mishnah describes two
separate categories: (a) *Das Moshe*,
and (b) *Das Yehudis*. (It seems clear
that the synonymous words *Yisrael*
and *Yehudis* are used interchangea-
bly by these sources.) However, the
Mishnah similarly conflates these
two categories when introducing
the topic when it states, "...one who
transgresses **Das Moshe veYehu-
dis** ...." (*Kesubos* 72a). These two categories are initially conflated by
both Tosefta and Mishnah because
violation of either results in the
same loss of *kesubah*, which is the
focus of both Mishnah and Tosefta
as recorded in *Maseches Kesubos*. For
the purposes of the subject at hand,
the two categories are the same,
which is why the Tosefta does not
need to elucidate. The Mishnah's
subsequent classification of *Das
Moshe* and *Das Yehudis* is a more specific way of listing each case, but has
no bearings on the focal subject,
kesubos. Accordingly, there is no evidence to presume a difference of
opinion exists between the conventional understanding of the Mishnah and the Tosefta. The Mishnah
chose to list its cases in a way that

also demonstrates the differences between *Das Moshe* and *Das Yehudis*, which, as will be further discussed below, has bearings on prohibitions, but the Tosefta unsurprisingly chose not to separate the categories because it is inconsequential for the contractual matters of *kesubos*. The lack of any evidence of a *machlokes* between these sources demonstrates that the Tosefta and the conventional understanding of the Mishnah are not at odds.

Sasson assumes that the Talmudic texts viewed women's head covering as a *chumrah* adopted by the populace, but not actual law; meaning, there is no actual Talmudic prohibition for a woman to enter the public arena with her head uncovered. To further this point, Sasson states, "Prohibitions in Talmudic Law are never implied or embedded in a discussion of a different context." Because of this viewpoint, Sasson finds it impossible to derive prohibitions from a Talmudic discussion of *kesubos*. However, no source for this maxim is provided. Further, this maxim directly conflicts with the *Bavli*'s assertion that the Mishnah's classification of *Das Moshe* and *Das Yehudis* hinges on whether the prohibition is biblical or rabbinic (*ibid.* 72a–b). Sasson contends that is not the correct understanding of the *Bavli* as seen in some alternative texts, which omit the second reference to the word *d'oraisa*. While these alternative texts are certainly of interest, our text contains the second reference to *d'oraisa*. Further, even those alternative texts contain *d'oraisa* in its first

reference. Moreover, Rashi explicitly states that matters of *Das Moshe* are biblical prohibitions (*Rashi Kesubos* 72a *s.v. d'oraisa*), which demonstrates he felt the Talmudic text is discussing a prohibition. It seems odd that a Talmudic scholar of Rashi's erudition would be unaware that prohibitions are never implied or embedded in a discussion of a different context. It is therefore difficult to assert that one cannot derive prohibitions regarding head covering from this Talmudic passage considering the *Bavli* understands that actual prohibitions are discussed in the Mishnah.

Sasson maintains that Rambam's and Shulchan Aruch's usage of the word לא, instead of אסור or אין, demonstrates that head covering is only a *chumrah*, not law. Again, no source is provided for this tenet. In the very next chapter in their respective works, Rambam and Shulchan Aruch use the word לא when describing a prohibition regarding impermissible seclusion of the sexes. (*Issurei Biah* 22:8; *E"H* 22:5; *see also Beis Yosef E"H* 22, written by the Shulchan Aruch, describing this matter as a prohibition, possibly of biblical origin.) There are many other examples throughout both of these works that are in direct contrast with Sasson's axiom, such as in *Rambam Hilchos Shabbos* 19 and *S"A O"C* 301, and some of these examples are biblical prohibitions for which sin offerings must be brought (*e.g.*, *S"A O"C* 301:8). Further, the classical interpreters also seem unfamiliar with this axiom as they understand Rambam and Shulchan Aruch to be discussing prohibitions when they discuss women's head coverings (*e.g.*, *Terumas HaDeshen* 242; *Bach E"H* 21; *Beis Shmuel* 21:5).

I am uncertain of the relevance of Sasson's statement that societal factors play a role in the nature of women's head covering. First, this is addressed at length in my article (pp. 234–238) where I demonstrate that many authorities who maintain head covering is obligatory, not simply a *chumrah*, feel societal factors play a significant role. Second, the example Sasson provides of different requisite levels of head coverings in different locations may simply derive from the amounts of privacy afforded in each respective location, which is what Rashi suggests (*Rashi Kesubos* 72b *s.v. vederech mavoy*). No argument is supplied to suggest why *Rashi's* explanation is lacking or why Sasson's theory is superior. Rather, societal factors play a role even according to those who maintain that head covering is obligatory.

I am also uncertain of the relevance of Sasson's statement that "ALL" women covered their hair in the Talmudic era. I brought significant evidence of such in my article (pp. 228–233), and this supposition may be true even if head covering is a prohibition, not simply a *chumrah*. In fact, after my article was published, I realized there was a compelling proof that unmarried women covered their heads in Talmudic times in a passage in *Maseches Shabbos*. The Mishnah states that women may not wear *nezamim* (a type of jewelry) in public on *Shabbos*, which the *Gemara* understands is because of a concern they may remove the *nezamim* to show others and inadvertently carry (*Shabbos* 57a). The *Gemara* defines *nezamim* as nose rings (*ibid.* 59b), which Rashi understands specifically excludes earrings from this prohibition. (*Rashi Shabbos* 59b *s.v. nizmei ha'af*). *Tosafos* elucidate that earrings were worn under head coverings, so it would be too difficult for a woman to remove them in public (*Tosafos Shabbos* 59b *s.v. nizmei ha'af*). *Or Zarua* contends that wearing earrings on Shabbos is impermissible in regions where women's head coverings do not cover their ears (*Or Zarua* vol. 2, 84:2). The Mishnah's lack of distinction between married and unmarried women is thus peculiar and suggests that *Or Zarua* assumed that unmarried women covered their heads in Talmudic times. Further, the Mishnah avers that young girls who would place wood chips or string in their ears after piercing them, because they were not old enough to have earrings, are permitted to wear such chips or strings on Shabbos (*Shabbos* 65a). The *Gemara* distinguishes between non-colored strings, which may be worn because the girls will not take them out to show others, and colored strings, which may not be worn because the girls might take them out to show others (*ibid.*). *Tosafos* question why this differs from earrings, which we presume will not be removed in public because they are under a head covering (*Tosafos Shabbos* 59b *s.v. nizmei ha'af)*. *Tosafos* answer that the strings are more easily removed than earrings (*ibid.*). Considering the passage is focused on young girls, it appears that *Tosafos* presume that young girls would certainly be wearing head coverings in Talmudic times. ❧

1 *Tosefta Ketubot* 7

הדירה שלא להשאיל נפה וכברה רחים ותנור יוציא ויתן כתובה, מפני שמשיאה שם רע
בשכינותיה. וכן היא שנדרה שלא להשאיל נפה וכבר׳ רחיים ותנור תצא שלא בכתובה, מפני
שמשיאתו שם רע בשכונתו

הדירה שלא תלך לבית האבל, או לבית המשתה, יוציא ויתן כתובה, שלמחר תהא מוטלת
ואין כל בריא סופנה.

היה ר׳ מאיר או׳ מה ת״ל והחי יתן אל לבו, עביד דיעבדון לך, לוי דילוון לך, ספוד
דיספדונך, קבור דיקברונך, שנ׳ ללכת אל בית אבל וגו׳. הדירה שתהא מטעמת תבשילה לכל
אדם, או שתהא ממלא ומערה לאשפות, ושתאמר לכל אדם דברים שבינו לבינה, יוציא ויתן
כתובה, מפני שלא נהג עמה כדת משה וישראל. וכן היא שיוצא׳ וראשה פרוע, יוצא ובגדיה
פרומים, ולבה גס בעבדיה ובשפחותיה, בשכנותיה, יוצא וטווה בשוק, רוחצת ומרחצת
במרחץ עם כל אדם, תצא שלא בכתובה, מפני שלא נהגה עמו כדת משה וישראל.] ר׳ מאיר
אומ׳ אם יודע בה שמדירה ואינה מקיימת אל ישנה להדירה.] ר׳ יהודה או׳ אם היה יודע בה
שאינה קוצה לה חלה יוציא ויתקן אחריה.

אי זו היא קולנית, כל שמדברת בביתה ושכיניה שומעין את קולה. כל אילו נשים שעברו
על הדת צריכות התראה, ויוצאות שלא בכתובה. לא התרה בהן, יוציא ויתן כתובה) .כל אילו
שאמרו יוציא ויתן כתובה) אין צריך לומ׳ מאתים לבתולה ומנה לאלמנה, יתר על כן אפי׳
כתובתה מאה מנה מנה איבדה את הכל, ונוטלת בלאיות שמוצא לפניה.

2 *Mishnah Ketubot* 7

אֵלּוּ יוֹצְאוֹת שֶׁלֹּא בִכְתֻבָּה, הָעוֹבֶרֶת עַל דַּת מֹשֶׁה וִיהוּדִית. וְאֵיזוֹ דַּת מֹשֶׁה, מַאֲכִילָתוֹ שֶׁאֵינוֹ
מְעֻשָּׂר, וּמְשַׁמַּשְׁתוֹ נִדָּה, וְלֹא קוֹצָה לָהּ חַלָּה, וְנוֹדֶרֶת וְאֵינָהּ מְקַיֶּמֶת. וְאֵיזוֹהִי דַּת יְהוּדִית, יוֹצְאָה
וְרֹאשָׁהּ פָּרוּעַ, וְטוֹוָה בַשּׁוּק, וּמְדַבֶּרֶת עִם כָּל אָדָם. אַבָּא שָׁאוּל אוֹמֵר, אַף הַמְקַלֶּלֶת יוֹלְדָיו
בְּפָנָיו. רַבִּי טַרְפוֹן אוֹמֵר, אַף הַקֹּלָנִית. וְאֵיזוֹ הִיא קֹלָנִית, לִכְשֶׁהִיא מְדַבֶּרֶת בְּתוֹךְ בֵּיתָהּ וּשְׁכֵנֶיהָ
שׁוֹמְעִין קוֹלָהּ.

3 *Yerushalmi Ketubot* 7

וְאֵילוּ יוֹצְאוֹת שֶׁלֹּא בִכְתוּבָה כול׳. וְאֵי זוֹ הִיא הַקֹּלָנִית כול׳. וְכוּלְּהוֹן בְּעֵדִים. פְּלוֹנִי עִישֵּׂר.
פְּלוֹנִי רָאָה כִּיתְמָן. פְּלוֹנִי קָצָה חַלָּתָהּ. פְּלוֹנִי הִתִּיר אֶת נִדְרָהּ. בָּדְקוּן כּוּלְּהוֹן וְלָא אַשְׁכְּחוֹן.
מַאֲכִילָתוֹ שֶׁאֵינוֹ מְעוּשָּׂר וּמְשַׁמָּשָׁתוֹ נִדָּה וְלֹא קוֹצָה לָהּ חַלָּה וְנוֹדֶרֶת וְאֵינָהּ מְקוּיֶּמֶת. נִיחָה
כּוּלְּהוֹן דְּאִית לָהּ בְּהוֹן. נוֹדֶרֶת וְאֵינָהּ מְקוּיֶּמֶת מָה אִית לָהּ בְּהַדֵּיהּ. יָכִיל מֵימַר. אֵי אֶפְשִׁי אִשָּׁה
נַדְרָנִית שֶׁהִיא קוֹבֶרֶת אֶת בָּנֶיהָ. תַּנֵּי בְשֵׁם רַבִּי יוּדָן. בַּעֲווֹן נְדָרִים הַבָּנִים מֵתִים. דִּכְתִיב לַשָּׁוְא
הִכֵּיתִי אֶת בְּנֵיכֶם.

וְרֹאשָׁהּ פָּרוּעַ. לְחָצֵר אָמְרוּ. קַל וָחוֹמֶר לְמָבוֹי. רַבִּי חִיָּיה בְשֵׁם רַבִּי יוֹחָנָן. הַיּוֹצְאָה בְקַפֶּלְטִין
שֶׁלָּהּ אֵין בָּהּ מִשּׁוּם רֹאשָׁהּ פָּרוּעַ. הָדָא דְּתֵימַר לְחָצֵר. אֲבָל לְמָבוֹי יֵשׁ בָּהּ מִשּׁוּם יוֹצְאָה וְרֹאשָׁהּ
פָּרוּעַ. יֵשׁ חָצֵר שֶׁהוּא כְמָבוֹי וְיֵשׁ מָבוֹי שֶׁהוּא כְחָצֵר. חָצֵר שֶׁהָרַבִּים בּוֹקְעִין בְּתוֹכוֹ הֲרֵי הוּא
כְמָבוֹי. וּמָבוֹי שֶׁאֵין הָרַבִּים בּוֹקְעִין בְּתוֹכוֹ הֲרֵי הוּא כְחָצֵר.

4 *Bavli Ketubot* 72a–b

מַאֲכִילָתוֹ שֶׁאֵינוֹ מְעוּשָּׂר הֵיכִי דָּמֵי אִי דְּיָדַע נִפְרוֹשׁ אִי דְּלָא יָדַע מְנָא יָדַע דְּאָמְרָה לֵיה פְּלוֹנִי כֹּהֵן תִּיקֵן לִי אֶת הַכְּרִי וְאָזֵיל שַׁיֵּילֵיה וְאִשְׁתְּכַח שִׁיקָרָא

וּמְשַׁמַּשְׁתּוֹ נִדָּה הֵיכִי דָּמֵי אִי דְּיָדַע בָּהּ נִפְרוֹשׁ אִי דְּלָא יָדַע נִסְמוֹךְ עִילָוַהּ דְּאָמַר רַב חִינָּנָא בַּר כָּהֲנָא אָמַר שְׁמוּאֵל מִנַּיִן לְנִדָּה שֶׁסּוֹפֶרֶת לְעַצְמָהּ שֶׁנֶּאֱמַר וְסָפְרָה לָהּ שִׁבְעַת יָמִים לָהּ לְעַצְמָהּ לָא צְרִיכָא דְּאָמְרָה לֵיה פְּלוֹנִי חָכָם טִיהַר לִי אֶת הַדָּם וַאֲזַל שַׁיֵּילֵיה וְאִשְׁתְּכַח שִׁיקָרָא וְאִיבָּעֵית אֵימָא כִּדְרַב יְהוּדָה דְּאָמַר רַב יְהוּדָה הוּחְזְקָה נִדָּה בִּשְׁכֵינוֹתֶיהָ בַּעְלָהּ לוֹקֶה עָלֶיהָ מִשּׁוּם נִדָּה

וְלֹא קוֹצָה לָהּ חַלָּה הֵיכִי דָּמֵי אִי דְּיָדַע נִפְרוֹשׁ אִי דְּלָא יָדַע מְנָא יָדַע דְּאָמְרָה לֵיה פְּלוֹנִי גַּבָּל תִּיקֵן לִי אֶת הָעִיסָה וְאָזֵיל שַׁיֵּילֵיה וְאִשְׁתְּכַח שִׁיקָרָא

וְנוֹדֶרֶת וְאֵינָהּ מְקַיֶּימֶת דְּאָמַר מָר בַּעֲוֹן נְדָרִים בָּנִים מֵתִים שֶׁנֶּאֱמַר אַל תִּתֵּן אֶת פִּיךָ לַחֲטִיא אֶת בְּשָׂרֶךְ וְגוֹ' וְאֵיזוֹ הֵן מַעֲשֵׂה יָדָיו שֶׁל אָדָם הֱוֵי אוֹמֵר בָּנָיו וּבְנוֹתָיו רַב נַחְמָן אָמַר מֵהָכָא לַשָּׁוְא הִכֵּיתִי אֶת בְּנֵיכֶם לַשָּׁוְא עַל עִסְקֵי שָׁוְא

תַּנְיָא הָיָה רַבִּי מֵאִיר אוֹמֵר כָּל הַיּוֹדֵעַ בְּאִשְׁתּוֹ שֶׁנּוֹדֶרֶת וְאֵינָהּ מְקַיֶּימֶת יַחֲזוֹר וְיַדִּירֶנָּה יַדִּירֶנָּה בְּמַאי מְתַקֵּן לָהּ אֶלָּא יַחֲזוֹר וְיַקְנִיטֶנָּה כְּדֵי שֶׁתִּדּוֹר וְיָפֵר לָהּ אָמְרוּ לוֹ אֵין אָדָם דָּר עִם נָחָשׁ בִּכְפִיפָה

תַּנְיָא הָיָה רַבִּי יְהוּדָה אוֹמֵר כָּל הַיּוֹדֵעַ בְּאִשְׁתּוֹ שֶׁאֵינָהּ קוֹצָה לוֹ חַלָּה יַחֲזוֹר וְיַפְרִישׁ אַחֲרֶיהָ אָמְרוּ לוֹ אֵין אָדָם דָּר עִם נָחָשׁ בִּכְפִיפָה

מַאן דְּמַתְנֵי לָהּ אַהָא כָּל שֶׁכֵּן אַהָךְ אֲבָל מַאן דְּמַתְנֵי אַהָךְ אֲבָל הָא זִימְנִין דְּמִקְּרֵי וְאָכֵיל וְאֵיזוֹהִי דָּת יְהוּדִית יוֹצְאָה פְּרוּעַ רֹאשָׁהּ פְּרוּעַ הָרֹאשׁ דְּאוֹרָיְיתָא הִיא דִּכְתִיב וּפָרַע אֶת רֹאשׁ הָאִשָּׁה וְתָנָא דְּבֵי רַבִּי יִשְׁמָעֵאל אַזְהָרָה לִבְנוֹת יִשְׂרָאֵל שֶׁלֹּא יֵצְאוּ בִּפְרוּעַ רֹאשׁ דְּאוֹרָיְיתָא קַלָּתָהּ שַׁפִּיר דָּמֵי דָּת יְהוּדִית אֲפִילוּ קַלָּתָהּ נָמֵי אָסוּר

אָמַר רַבִּי אַסִי אָמַר רַבִּי יוֹחָנָן קַלָּתָהּ אֵין בָּהּ מִשּׁוּם פְּרוּעַ רֹאשׁ הֲוֵי בַּהּ רַבִּי זֵירָא הֵיכָא אִילֵּימָא בְּשׁוּק דָּת יְהוּדִית הִיא וְאֶלָּא בֶּחָצֵר אִם כֵּן לֹא הִנַּחְתָּ בַּת לְאַבְרָהָם אָבִינוּ שֶׁיּוֹשֶׁבֶת תַּחַת בַּעְלָהּ

Maimonides on the Messianic Era: The Grand Finale of Olam Ke-Minhago Noheg

By: JAMES A. DIAMOND

Moses Maimonides's vision of the messianic era expresses a universal utopian ideal toward which in a certain sense his entire philosophical, theological, and halakhic oeuvre aims at realizing. Within that vision, politics on the particular plane of Jewish national existence play a central role in achieving that ideal. Particularly significant is its relevance on a micro-level to contemporary questions related to the reestablishment of a modern Jewish state, and on a macro-level for humanity as a whole spiritually, culturally, and last, but not least, physically. Among the medievals, Judah Ha-Levi is most associated legendarily with the return to Zion,[1] while Naḥmanides, as opposed to Maimonides, famously counts settling the land of Israel as a formal mitzvah.[2] However, it is Moses Maimonides, thinking, leading, and writing in twelfth-century Egypt, geographically so

---

[1]   See, for example, Norman Stillman's assertion that "[t]he Kuzari was a glorification of rabbinic Judaism and an unabashed statement of nationalism, very much in the modern sense of the word," in *The Jews of Arab Lands: A History and Source Book* (Philadelphia, Pa.: Jewish Publication Society, 1979), p. 60.

[2]   See Naḥmanides's glosses to Maimonides's tabulation of the commandments, *Hasagot ha-Ramban* in *Sefer ha-Mitzvot*, ed. Shabse Frankel (New York: Cong. Benei Yosef, 1995), where he enumerates it as one of the positive *mitzvot* that Maimonides omitted. See the list compiled at p. 418, and also Naḥmanides's commentary to Num. 33:53 where he asserts that the verse *And you shall take possession of the land and settle in it* constitutes a positive commandment.

James A. Diamond is the Joseph and Wolf Lebovic Chair of Jewish Studies at the University of Waterloo. His principal areas of study include biblical exegesis and hermeneutics, medieval Jewish thought and philosophy, Maimonides, and rabbinics. He has published widely on various areas of Jewish thought. His most recent books are *Jewish Theology Unbound*, published by Oxford University Press, and *Reinventing Maimonides in Contemporary Jewish Thought,* co-authored with Menachem Kellner (Littman Library).

close, yet so far, from the land of Israel,[3] who remains substantively far more critical to any such discussion. His systematic project of "demythologizing" Judaism, and draining it of what he considered superstitious and pagan incursions extend to, and culminate in, his messianic vision.[4] His messianic construct is inextricably tied to the "ingathering of the oppressed Jews,"[5] a primary aspiration of modern-day Zionism. Although the messianic era in Maimonides's thought is a vast topic vigorously debated by both academic scholars and rabbis throughout the ages,[6] I wish here only to offer some further exploration of how Maimonides textually promotes an activist agenda regarding what he views as the essential accomplishments the messianic era will herald for Jews as a people.

The messianic leader is charged with the mission of restoring the monarchy, rebuilding the Temple, and reinstating a rule of Torah law, yet it is the political goal of returning Jews who have been subject to oppressive foreign regimes to the security and freedom of their own sovereign state that forms a centerpiece of Maimonides's messianic vision. Aside from the repeated emphasis on this strictly historical dimension of the messianic period,[7] Maimonides's formulation of its belief, among the thir-

---

3　Puzzlingly, this flies in the face of his categorical ruling in his Code that prohibits settling in Egypt and his description of it as the most corrupt country in the world in *Mishneh Torah* (*MT*), *Kings*, 5:8. See Isadore Twersky, "Maimonides and Eretz Yisrael: Halakhic, Philosophic, and Historical Perspectives," in *Perspectives on Maimonides: Philosophical and Historical Studies*, ed. Joel Kraemer (Oxford: Oxford University Press, 1991), pp. 257–290, note 2 at pp. 257–8.

4　Kenneth Seeskin aptly characterizes Maimonidean messianism as "deflationary" while Menachem Kellner considers it a component of Maimonides's programmatic "disenchantment" of the world. See Seeskin, *Jewish Messianic Thoughts in an Age of Despair* (New York: Cambridge University Press, 2012), pp. 179–186 and Kellner, *Maimonides' Confrontation With Mysticism* (Oxford: Littman Library, 2006), p. 294.

5　*MT, Kings*, 11:1. ‏ומקבץ נדחי ישראל.

6　For example, Jacob Dienstag compiled a vast bibliography on the subject which is already outdated by some four decades! See his *Eschatology in Maimonidean Thought: Messianism, Resurrection, and the World to Come* (New York: Ktav, 1983), pp. 242–271. In the interim, scholarship has grown extensively and I apologize to all those who have contributed importantly to the topic but I have not been able to cite here within the limited scope of this article.

7　In addition to that mentioned in note 5 see also 11:4 that lists it as one of the necessary accomplishments establishing his messianic legitimacy, ‏אם עשה והצליח, ‏ונצח כל האומות שסביביו, ובנה מקדש במקומו וקבץ נדחי ישראל – הרי זה משיח בודאי; also *Kings*, 12:3, ‏בימי המלך המשיח כשתתיישב ממלכתו ויתקבצו אליו כל ישראל; Jesus's failure to achieve this goal, and even causing further misery and dispersion for Jews, is proof positive against his messianic credentials ‏שכל הנביאים דיברו שמשיח

teen foundational principles he developed as Judaism's credo, concentrates entirely on this facet of return and political sovereignty while remaining silent about the rebuilding of the Temple and forcible imposition of Torah law. Rather, nation building is critical, for "sovereignty will be re-established in, and there will be a return to Israel… and the center of the kingdom will be in Zion." That national project toward independence and sovereignty is to be realized in a wholly natural way, for "there will be no change in reality from the way it is at present except that there will be sovereignty in Israel." As is not uncommon for Maimonides,[8] he carves out his own creative account of the messianic period. This endorsement of just one Amoraic opinion entailed rejecting the literal sense of all the extraordinary and apocalyptic upheavals anticipated by the prophets and reading such prophecies as *The wolf shall dwell with lamb* etc. (Isa. 11:6–8)… *and similar matters written regarding the messiah as parables (meshalim).*[9] Elsewhere Maimonides admits that though he does not have any rabbinic authority in support of this metaphorical reading, reason which dictates "harmonizing the Law with what is intelligible and to regard all things as following a possible natural order" unless something is explicitly characterized as a miracle, compels him to champion a non-literal interpretation.[10]

(ibid)גּוֹאֵל יִשְׂרָאֵל וּמוֹשִׁיעָם, וּמְקַבֵּץ נִדְחֵיהֶם וּמְחַזֵּק מְצַנָּתָן; וְזֶה גָּרַם לְאַבֵּד יִשְׂרָאֵל בַּחֶרֶב. Also, in *Iggeret Teiman,* "a descendant of Solomon who will gather our nation and our exiled people." Maimonides's naturalistic and historically incrementalist messianism underpins modern religious Zionism in all its various camps as Menachem Kellner states, "The messianic activism made possible by the naturalistic conception of the messianic advent is explicitly adopted by religious Zionism[,]" in "Messianic Postures in Israel Today," *Modern Judaism* 6:2 (1986), pp. 197–209, at p. 202.

8   For Maimonides's creative ways of demythologizing halakhah throughout his Code, see Marc Shapiro, "Maimonidean Halakha and Superstition" in his *Studies in Maimonides and His Interpreters* (Scranton: University of Scranton Press, 2008).

9   *MT, Kings* and *Wars,* 12:1. Although Maimonides cites the opinion in 12:2 that *there will be no change in reality from the way it is at present except that there will be sovereignty in Israel* in the name of the "sages" אָמְרוּ חֲכָמִים אֵין בֵּין הָעוֹלָם הַזֶּה לִימוֹת הַמָּשִׁיחַ אֶלָּא שִׁעְבּוּד מַלְכֻיּוֹת בִּלְבָד it is actually the opinion of one sage (Shmuel) in b.*Sanhedrin* 91b; b.*Shabbat* 63a; *Berakhot* 34b. Similarly, he cites the same opinion in *MT, Teshuvah,* 9:2 in the name of the "ancient sages" (חֲכָמִים הָרִאשׁוֹנִים). See also R. Joseph Karo's puzzlement regarding this in his *Kesef Mishneh.* Furthermore, Raavad is surely on firm rabbinic authority in his repudiation of this metaphorical reading of the prophetic messianic prognostications. For a good survey of rabbinic sources pre- and post-dating Maimonides which oppose and struggle with his position, see B.Z. Benedict, "*Atḥalta d-Geulah l-Or Mishnat ha-Rambam,*" (Heb.) *Torah She-be-al Peh* 30 (1969), pp. 81–91.

10   See Hillel Fradkin's translation in Ralph Lerner, *Maimonides' Empire of Light: Popular Enlightenment in an Age of Belief* (Chicago: University of Chicago Press, 2000),

Finally, one of the primary goals of achieving Jewish sovereignty according to Maimonides, is freedom from foreign subjugation, *"the great advantage of that time is that we will be relieved of the oppression of wicked regimes."*[11] Any discussion of the role of Jewish national sovereignty within the Maimonidean framework, or any Jewish intellectual framework for that matter, should pay heed to Isadore Twersky's warning when he cautiously approached the same topic some two decades ago: "The attitude towards Eretz Israel raises fundamental problems concerning Jews's national consciousness and historical image, and consequently demands maximum caution and meticulous analysis. It is no easy task to free oneself of the preconceived notions or deep-seated predilections, which do not necessarily stem from conclusions of disciplined study and scholarship."[12] It is a daunting task indeed, and how successful one can ever be in neatly bifurcating "deep-seated predilections" from "disciplined study and scholarship" is a vexing question, especially when approaching such a profoundly existential issue, but it is particularly incumbent upon scholars to earnestly try.[13]

While the nationalistic component of Maimonides's messianic conception is crucial to the geopolitical environment as a means toward the loftier end of nurturing a utopian climate of universal peace and harmony, the essence of its role is always vulnerable to being overcome by unbridled religious fervor and zealousness. Maimonides's profound messianic vision anticipates elements which seem to be endemic to the collective human condition that might threaten its materialization such as vicissitudes of politics, conflict, secularism, technological advance, unbridled messianic

---

pp. 154–177, at p.167, and *Iggerot ha-Rambam* (Arabic and Hebrew trans.), ed. Yitzḥak Sheilat (Ma'ale Adumim, Israel: Maaliyot Press, 1998), vol. 1, pp. 319–374, at pp. 360–361.

11 "Introduction to *Perek Ḥelek,*" in *Hakdamot ha-Rambam la-Mishnah,* ed. and Hebrew trans. Yitzḥak Sheilat (Ma'ale Adumim: Maaliyot Press, 1992), p. 144.

12 See his "Maimonides and Eretz Yisrael," supra, p. 260. Ironically, Twersky's very choice of the phrase *Eretz Yisrael,* considering its religiously loaded connotations, itself betrays certain predilections.

13 For a good overview of the various causes of bias in historical scholarship as well as an argument "that personal bias can be largely overcome by a commitment to standards of rational historical inquiry," see C. Behan McCullagh, "Bias in Historical Description, Interpretation, and Explanation," *History and Theory,* Vol. 39:1 (Feb., 2000), pp. 39–66. For an empirically based scientific analysis that demonstrates the presence of ideological bias in what is purportedly objective scholarship, see Adam S. Chilton and Eric A. Posner, "An Empirical Study of Political Bias in Legal Scholarship," *Coase-Sandor Institute for Law and Economics Working Paper no. 696,* http://ssrn.com/abstract=2478908.

passions, and theologically driven supremacist currents. It thus provides a check on theological-political impulses lapsing into petty religious and ethnic chauvinism or otherworldly metaphysical utopianism.[14]

Since it culminates in a detailed messianic agenda, the overarching thrust of Maimonides's code of law, the *Mishneh Torah*, needs to be taken into account when examining his historical/political/philosophical/theological view of the messianic era. As a whole, the *Mishneh Torah* is far more than simply a stripped-down digest of all of Jewish law culled from its biblical and rabbinic antecedents. Isadore Twersky emphasized this feature of the Code, which weaves into its texture "the thread of intellectualization and spiritualization" evident in all his writings in a project that went far beyond a simple code of law bringing about "the unity of practice and concept, external observance and inner meaning, visible action and

---

[14] A good example of this stance that is diametrically opposed to the Maimonidean naturalist vision is espoused by R. Zvi Yehudah Kook (1891–1981), son of the first Ashkenazic Chief Rabbi, R. Abraham Isaac Kook, and leading exponent of religious redemptionist Zionism, who perceives the State of Israel as divine, a notion that extends to all facets of it including its military. The following assertion could not be more opposed to Maimonides's conception: "Part of this redemption is the conquest and settlement of the land. This is dictated by divine politics and no earthly politics can supersede it." As quoted by Aviezer Ravitzky, *Messianism, Zionism, and Jewish Religious Radicalism*, trans. M. Swirsky, J. Chipman (Chicago: University of Chicago Press, 1996), at p. 131, and see generally his discussion of messianic religious Zionism in ch. 3, pp. 79–144. Of course, in line with the longue durée of engagements with Maimonides in Jewish thought, that did not deter R. Kook and others from appropriating Maimonides in support of their positions. See, for example, Dov Schwartz, "Maimonides in Religious-Zionist Philosophy: Unity vs. Duality," in *The Cultures of Maimonideanism: New Approaches to the History of Jewish Thought*, ed. James T. Robinson (Leiden: Brill, 2009), pp. 385–408 and my "A Kabbalistic Reinvention of Maimonides' Legal Code: R. Abraham Isaac Kook's Commentary on *Sefer Ha-Mada*," *Jewish Studies, an Internet Journal* 11 (2012), pp. 345–384. There is an abundance of scholarship in Hebrew on the issue. For a good overview and references to much of the Hebrew scholarship, see Ella Belfer, "*BeTzipiyat ha-Yeshuah ha-Shelemah*: The Messianic Politics of Rav Avraham Yitzchak Kook and Rav Zvi Yehudah Kook," in *Tolerance, Dissent, and Democracy: Philosophical, Historical, and Halakhic Perspectives*, ed. Moshe Sokol (Northvale: Jason Aaronson, 2002), pp. 311–361. For a recent discussion that engages much of the scholarship that preceded it on this phenomenon of chauvinist, ontologically essentialist, religious messianism, see Shai Held, "What Zvi Yehudah Kook Wrought: The Theopolitical Radicalization of Religious Zionism," in *Rethinking the Messianic Idea in Judaism*, eds. Michael Morgan, Steven Weitzman (Bloomington: Indiana University Press, 2015) pp. 229–255.

invisible experience, *gufe Torah* and their foundations."[15] The *Mishneh Torah* presents a hybrid of idealism and realism in its conception of the world, which in the end acknowledges the fruition of the national aspirations of a particular people as a medium of achieving universal ends.[16] Aside from a comprehensive and systematic presentation of halakhic statutes, it offers a grand jurisprudential/philosophical/political/social conception of Judaism and humanity in general[17] which, among other dimensions, recognizes Jews as constituents of both a global and a national village.

The *Mishneh Torah* opens with an assertion of a universal ideal, decidedly not a parochial law or a norm, of that which lies at the heart of all knowledge, "The foundation of all foundations and the pillar of all science."[18] There is neither a Jewish nor a Torah "foundation," and no Jewish "science." That foundation, or the ultimate truth in the universe, is

---

15   See his *Introduction to the Code of Maimonides* (New Haven: Yale University Press, 1980), p. 371. The question of how to classify the *Mishneh Torah* as a text in relationship to law has been recently incisively canvassed by Moshe Halbertal, but his introductory remarks are apropos my assertion that it is far more than a halakhic compendium: "Every line of the work is indeed a spectacular model of clarity, but the work overall is affected, from the outset, by a profound ambivalence that allows for strikingly varied understandings of its nature." See "What Is the *Mishneh Torah*: On Codification and Ambivalence," in *Maimonides After 800 Years: Essays on Maimonides and His Influence* (Bethesda: Harvard University Center for Jewish Studies, 2007), pp. 81–111, at p. 82.

16   For the idea of a "two-tiered system" consisting of ideal and real in the realm of halakhah, see Gerald Blidstein, "'Ideal' and 'Real' in Classical Jewish Political Theory: From the Talmud to Abarbanel," in *The Quest for Utopia: Jewish Political Ideas and Institutions Through the Ages,* ed. Zvi Gitelman (Armonk: M.E. Sharpe, 1992), pp. 41–66. Blidstein focuses on the wide discretionary powers allowed the judiciary and the monarch in ensuring an orderly society. For example, see a list of those in *MT, Sanhedrin* 24: 10–16. All those powers must be utilized only to promote the general ideals that the judiciary is meant to uphold, ibid. 24:17. A prime biblical illustration of ideal vs. real is the law of the king as stipulated in Deut. 17 and the "*mishpat ha-melekh* (practice [law] of the king)" outlined by Samuel in I Sam 8. On this topic, see Moshe Greenberg, "Biblical Attitudes toward Power: Ideal and Reality in Law and Prophets," in *Religion and Law,* eds. E.B. Firmage et al. (Winona Lake: Eisenbrauns, 1990), pp. 101–112.

17   A contrast with Joseph Karo's *Shulḥan Arukh*, the comprehensive code of Jewish law that usurped Maimonides's *MT* in terms of acceptance and authority to this day, highlights this feature. As Isadore Twersky points out, the former is marked by an "austere functionality" in its "virtually complete elimination of ideology, theology and teleology," that are endemic to the *MT*. (In "The Shulḥan 'Arukh: Enduring Code of Jewish Law," *Judaism* 16:2 [1967], pp. 141–158, at p. 153.)

18   *MT, Laws of the Foundations of the Torah* 1:1 יסוד היסודות ועמוד החכמת. Notably the Tetragrammaton is embedded in the *roshei tevot* of this formulation.

identified neither by the Tetragrammaton (*YHWH*), nor by *Elokim*, nor by any other divine epithet or cognomen that might denote a special, or worse, exclusive, relationship with one particular people, or even one that manifests its existence in the natural world or within history. It is a "*motzui rishon,*" a Prime Existent, an abstract formulation that is neither personally experienced nor worshipped in the traditional sense. Rather, it is universally accessible through reason, granted in whatever limited way, to the human, not Jewish, mind. As such it addresses the human "image of God," identified at the beginning of Maimonides's philosophical treatise *Guide of the Perplexed* as the human, not Jewish, intellect whose cultivation is an act of *imitatio dei* demanded of all human beings.[19] It is the Necessary Existence on whose existence all of existence depends, yet who exists independently of all of being.[20] In this way, its relationship to the world is defined cosmically, and not in terms of any limited geography that is part of that cosmos. It is not an object of what is traditionally considered pious devotion, but a ground of knowledge for all peoples who exercise that which constitutes their humanness.[21] Maimonides's rendition of Adam's experience vis-à-vis this knowledge in the Garden of Eden at the opening of his *Guide of the Perplexed* concerns the human, not Jewish, condition.

Maimonides's universalist posture is evident by the striking shift first from the title of this first section in the "Book of Knowledge" (*Sefer ha-Mada*), *The Laws of the Foundations of the Torah,* not to what one might anticipate as some statement relating to precisely that parochially chosen for its heading, "Foundations of the Torah," but rather to the ethnically, religiously, textually neutral *foundation of foundations.* Secondly, there is a prominent shift from the abridged listing of commandments that prefaces this first section, as every other, which identifies the object of the command "to know" as *eloha*, to the surprising object of "to know" in the very first sentence as *motsui rishon.*[22] It is not until the sixth paragraph that Maimonides normativizes this knowledge as a *mitzvah,* or a particular norm binding

---

19   See the edition of S. Pines (Chicago: University of Chicago Press, 1963) hereinafter cited as *GP*, I:1, (p. 23), where the human endeavor of intellectual apprehension "is likened unto the apprehension of the deity."

20   On this conception of Necessary Existence, see Fazlur Rahman, "Ibn Sina's Theory of the God-World Relationship," in *God and Creation: An Ecumenical Symposium*, ed. David Burrell and Bernard McGinn (Notre Dame: University of Notre Dame Press, 1987), pp. 38–52.

21   See *GP*, I:1 on the definition of "image of God (*tzelem*)."

22   לידע שיש שם מצוי ראשון vs לידע שיש שם אלוה.

only on a specific people.[23] Thus the content of this knowledge constitutes the core aim of philosophy qua philosophy, while at the same time
its juridically sanctioned formulation transforms the act of philosophizing
into a legal obligation for Jews qua Jews. All humanity qua humanity must
acknowledge the final end of that which constitutes humanness, while that
same end constitutes Jewishness only insofar as it is a norm. In other
words, for pragmatic reasons, what is an abstract truth that must attract
all human minds in its pursuit, needs to be anchored first in a narrower
concrete framework of prescribed conduct incumbent on one people, in
order to preserve and promote what should be a common human enterprise throughout history.

This dual human/Jewish enterprise that operates on both universal
and national planes, carries through to Maimonides's own reconstructed
Heilsgeschichte of biblical history. History rapidly follows a path of decline
from its origins in the truth of monotheism to a point of near irreversible
intellectual darkness until the advent of the patriarchal age. Abraham re-
discovers monotheism but not as a retrieval of some ancestral religious
cult. He reintroduces a lost philosophical truth that has been corrupted,
obscured, promoted, and exploited precisely by religious cults and their
priests. Importantly, Abraham arrives at these truths *sui generis*, *"without a
teacher, and without anyone to instruct him in anything."*[24] Abraham's philosoph-

---

23   This observation sharpens what has previously been noted that "Israel" is absent
from the initial four chapters of the code, appearing first only in chapter five
since the subject matter of the first four chapters is rationally accessible to all
human beings. See, for example, Yeshayahu Leibowitz, "Ha-Rambam: Ha-
Adam ha-Abrahami," (Heb.) *Be-Terem* 211 (1955), pp. 20–22, published in English as "Maimonides: The Abrahamic Mind," *Judaism* 6:2 (1957), pp. 148–154.
My point is that even though the account of physics and metaphysics in the first
four chapters are universal subjects of knowledge, the normative obligation to
pursue that knowledge is binding only on Jews.

24   *MT, Idolatry*, 1:3 ולא היה לו מלמד ולא מודיע דבר. As an archetype Abraham assumes
many other guises in the Maimonidean corpus, but all shaped in this mold—as
a prophet exemplifying the highest levels of prophecy short of Moses (*GP*, II:45,
pp. 401–402); as the paradigmatic "lover" of God whose love is constituted by
knowledge (*MT, Repentance*, 10:2); as a philosopher arriving independently at universal truths and teaching them universally (*GP*, II:38; *Iggeret Teiman*, 147); as an
ethical model of the golden mean (*MT, Ethical Traits*, 1:7); of supererogatory
nature (*MT, Mourning* 14:2); and the "father of all nations" and therefore of all
converts (*MT, First Fruits*, 4:3). See Masha Turner's survey of all these Maimonidean variations of Abraham, "The Patriarch Abraham in Maimonidean
Thought" (Heb.), in *The Faith of Abraham in Light of Interpretation Throughout the*

ical journey of discovery is completely divorced from familial, tribal, ethnic, or national loyalties; in other words, he had no *mesorah*. It was an unadulterated truth lost to the collective human mind, "so that the truth perished from their minds,"[25] and it was just such a truth he had autodidactically retrieved, "until he had attained the way of truth."[26] Like the statelessness of his intellectual efforts and achievements, his mission to disseminate that truth recognized no borders, neither local nor international, "*traveling, declaring, and assembling a nation from city to city and country to country.*"[27] The new Abrahamic nation was a pot that melted its kaleidoscopic populace into a unity of philosophical truths.

However, it is critical to note that in Maimonides's view of history and the devolution of monotheism into polytheism, politics is inextricably bound up with what moderns consider religion. "False prophets" (*neviei sheker*) who "fabricate" (*bada mi-libo*) and "priests" (*komrin*) who invent rites, and other charlatans (*kozvim aherim*) who speak in the name of heavenly bodies, hijack religious worship. They shore up their authority by ensuring that no one else can be privy to these "prophetic communications." Though, ostensibly, the general public's meager spiritual qualifications bar its access to them, in reality it is the chimerical nature of those "prophecies" that does so. Thus, the democratizing trend of a reason-based religion centered objectively on the fount of all truth is reversed toward its monopolization by shamans centered on their own self-declared unassailable authority to pontificate regarding "truths" to which they alone have access.

Abraham's mission then of a truth that transcends borders attracts governmental ire because its message is politically subversive. Reasoned demonstration becomes overpowering, threatening the stability of the established regime by challenging the soundness of its official pagan ideology. Only state-sanctioned violence can quell its influence, and so like Socrates, "*Once he wins over people by demonstration the king wants him dead.*"[28] Thus, the Abrahamic experiment in universalism ends up, because of political factors, constricted to its own geographical locale in Canaan in order to pursue its agenda, however practically limited in scope—"gathering them in city after city and country after country, until he came to the land

---

Ages, ed. Moshe Hallamish, Hannah Kasher, and Yoḥanan Silman (Ramat Gan: Bar Ilan University Press, 2003), 143–154.

25 שאבד האמת מדעתם.

26 שהשיג דרך האמת.

27 והיה מהלך וקורא ומקבץ העם מעיר לעיר וממלכה לממלכה.

28 כיון שגבר עליהם בראיותיו ביקש המלך להורגו.

of Canaan."[29]

Statelessness and political subjugation to foreign powers according to the *Guide*, however, cause "languor and sadness," which hamper intellectual clarity and block prophetic inspiration.[30] They cause a precipitous loss of whatever advances were made both scientifically and ethically during its period of national cohesion and integrity.[31] The implication is that, due to the exigencies of human nature, universal goals can only be achieved through particularistic means. Since Abraham's mission to propagate truths was scuttled by political intrigue, the future reinstatement of that mission requires a political corrective for its success.

Abraham's mission could not escape its political overtones since its universal message served to consolidate what paganism had fragmented by the variegated evolving cults that segregated peoples from each other rather than unifying them: "so different modes of worshipping figures became widespread throughout the world."[32] Abraham's truth reversed that political current, ultimately forging, not a religion, but a "nation that knows God,"[33] that is a polis bound by knowledge of that which is the foundation of all knowledge. But this historical interlude in the Code chronicles an ensuing phase of a seemingly inevitable collapse once again into paganism. The abstract universalism that held together Abraham's polis lapses into that which it sought to remedy. The failure of the Abrahamic experiment necessitates the new Mosaic approach of prophecy, "once Moses exercised his prophetic functions,"[34] which promoted national particularism, "God chose Israel as His heritage,"[35] exclusive religious norms, "he crowned them with precepts,"[36] singular worship, "showed them the way to worship Him,"[37] and normative barriers distinguishing between those who are accepted members of the community and those who are excluded from it, "and how to deal with idolatry and those

---

29 עד שהגיע לארץ כנען.

30 GP, II:36, p. 373.

31 GP, I:71, p. 175; II:11, p. 276.

32 ‏ופשט דבר זה בכל העולם לעבוד את הצורות בעבודות **משונות זו מזו**.

33 ‏ונעשית בעולם **אומה** שהיא יודעת את ה'.

34 ‏כיון שנתנבא משה.

35 ‏בחר ה' ישראל לנחלה.

36 ‏הכתירן במצות.

37 ‏הודיעם דרך עבודתו.

who go astray after it."[38] History then mirrors precisely the structure of the Code's initial formulation, which introduces a universal object of knowledge that is then grounded in a particularistic commandment. Likewise, intellectual history, and its political complement, evolved from an Abrahamic universalism, blind to private divine communication, exclusive norms, and national difference, to a Mosaic particularism consisting of commandments and divergent national interests. All we have just examined—philosophy, theology, history, jurisprudence—appears in what purports to be a legislative code!

The very end of the Code precisely parallels this pragmatic blend of universal idealism and religio/political particularism in its vision of the messianic era.[39] There are five overarching principles, which essentially inform that vision.

1) **The first is political.** The sole distinction between the messianic era and the historical continuum leading up to it is the relief from political oppression by the establishment of an autonomous Jewish state recognized as such by the community of nations; "there is no difference between This World and the Days of the Messiah except subservience to the kingdoms of the world alone."[40]

2) **The second is ontological.** There will be no change in the natural order of the world nor any disruption of the laws of physics: "It should not occur to you that during the days of the Messiah a single thing from the 'ways of the world' will be canceled nor will there be something novel in the Creation. Rather, the world will continue in its customary way (*Olam ke-minhago noheg*)."[41]

3) **The third is the political counterpart to this natural ontology,** conditioning the accomplishments of the messianic leader purely on political successes including the ingathering of oppressed Jews and explicitly ruling out the supernatural as a sign of his legitimacy: "It

---

38 מה יהיה משפט עבודת כוכבים וכל הטועים אחריה. See *GP*, II:39, p. 379, which parallels this account whereby Abraham did not impose norms or *mitzvot* but rather "assembled the people and called them by way of teaching and instruction to adhere to the truth he had grasped."

39 For a recent analysis of Maimonides's "messianic universalism," and especially on the symmetry between the beginning and end of the *MT*, see the final chapter of *Maimonides the Universalist: The Ethical Horizons of the Mishneh Torah,*" Menachem Kellner, David Gillis (Liverpool: Littman Library of Jewish Civilization, 2020), at pp. 278–281.

40 אין בין העולם הזה לימות המשיח אלא שיעבוד מלכיות בלבד.

41 אל יעלה על הלב שבימות המשיח יבטל דבר ממנהגו של עולם או יהיה שם חידוש במעשה בראשית אלא עולם כמנהגו נוהג.

should not occur to you that the King Messiah must bring wondrous signs or perform marvels or invent new things or revive the dead or anything like what the fools say."[42]

4) **The fourth is exegetical scepticism.** No interpretation of the meaning of biblical verses relating to the messianic period can be definitively determined until it actually materializes: "In the days of the King Messiah everyone will understand these parables and to what these matters were compared and to what was hinted."[43]

5) **The fifth is theological/halakhic.** Because of its inherent indeterminacy the exact parameters and elements of this period do not constitute a fundamental principle of belief: "But regarding all these matters and similar, no one knows how it will be until it will be. For these matters were unclear to the Prophets. Even the Sages themselves did not have a Tradition regarding these matters and only could attempt to understand the verses. Thus, there were disagreements in these

---

[42] אל יעלה על דעתך שהמלך המשיח צריך לעשות אותות ומופתים, ומחדש דברים בעולם, או מחיה מתים, וכיוצא בדברים אלו שהטפשים אומרים. *MT, Kings and Their Wars*, 11:3. However, in his *Letter to the Jews of Yemen (Iggeret Teiman),* Maimonides considers the performance of miracles an essential criterion of a messianic leader's authenticity. This is a prime example to my mind of Haym Soloveitchik's profound distinction between Maimonides's responsa and letters as works informed by rhetoric and his Code of law which is a statement of ideal law in the abstract. See the debate between David Hartman and Haym Soloveitchik, and others dealing with inconsistencies between Maimonides's responsa and his Code in H. Soloveitchik, "Maimonides's '*Iggeret ha-Shemad*': Law and Rhetoric," in L. Landman (ed.), *Rabbi Joseph H. Lookstein Memorial Volume* (New York, 1980), 281–319 and D. Hartman, "The Epistle on Martyrdom: Discussion," in *Epistles of Maimonides: Crisis and Leadership*, trans., Abraham Halkin (Philadelphia: Jewish Publication Society, 1993), pp. 46–90. See also Arye Strikovsky, "*Iggeret ha-Shemad la-Rambam: Halakhah o Retorika,*" in I. Varhaftig (ed.), *Minḥa le-Ish: Sefer Yovel for Rabbi Dolgin* (Jerusalem, 1980), pp. 242–275.
For a recent reassessment of this debate, see Yair Lorberbaum, Haim Shapira, "Maimonides's Epistle on Martyrdom in Light of Legal Philosophy," *Dine Israel* (2008), 123–169. In this case, I believe that Soloveitchik's characterization of the *Iggeret ha-Shemad* as a rhetorical work is equally apt for the letter to Yemen. Howard Kreisel expresses a similar opinion when he describes Maimonides's stance in the *Iggeret Teiman* as constructed "to meet a severe social religious challenge… [and] provides an instructive example of how the change in the focus of Maimonides's discussion of a topic in different contexts affects how he formulates his position" in his *Maimonides' Political Thought: Studies in Ethics, Law, and the Human Ideal* (Albany: SUNY Press, 1999), p. 29.

[43] ובימות המלך המשיח יודע לכל לאי זה דבר היה משל ומה ענין רמזו בהן.

matters. Nevertheless, neither the order that these events will occur nor their details are fundamental to the religion. Thus, a person must never busy himself with the Aggadot and not dwell on the Midrashim regarding these matters or similar issues. He must not make them dogma."[44]

By excluding the precise nature and order of the unfolding and realization of the messianic era as a theoretical subject of contemplation whose particular details (הֱוָיַת דְּבָרִים אֵלּוּ וְלֹא דְּקַדּוּקֵיהֶן) constitute neither a fundamental principle of belief (עיקר בדת), nor an accepted tradition (קבלה), nor are ascertainable by the normal rules of biblical interpretation (לפי הכרע הפסוקים), Maimonides brilliantly restricts the visionary focus purely on its natural, empirical, experiential, political dimensions. He thereby diverts anticipatory messianic longings toward the purely natural and political revolution that must precipitate it. For what other possible means could practically realize that vision?

Here it is important to note three opposing arguments against the view that Maimonidean messianism provides the ideological impetus for activist religious Zionism from across the spectrum of modern Jewish thought and why Maimonides resists their interpretations—an academic historian, a philosopher, and a rabbinic leader. The first is the renowned historian David Berger's insistence that "despite the reasonableness of that position they are far from Maimonides' position himself. Rambam counseled the readers of his works to wait." He further states categorically

---

44   כל אלו הדברים וכיוצא בהן לא ידע אדם איך יהיו עד שיהיו שדברים סתומין הן אצל הנביאים
גם החכמים אין להם קבלה בדברים אלו אלא לפי הכרע הפסוקים ולפיכך יש להם מחלוקת
בדברים אלו ועל כל פנים אין סדור הויית דברים אלו ולא דקדוקיהן עיקר בדת.

Ironically, Maimonides's messianic skepticism provoked the proliferation of its adversarial view. As Gerson Cohen asserts, it "gave renewed stimulus to the traditionalists to add to the corpus of Spanish eschatological literature" (in his "Messianic Postures of Ashkenazim and Sephardim," in *Studies in the Variety of Rabbinic Cultures* [Philadelphia: Jewish Publication Society, 1991], pp. 271–297, at p. 285). This is another example of how Maimonides's rationalism was in a sense responsible for the growth of what it was opposed to such as mystical literature whose "masters of Jewish esoteric lore were incubated in the shadows of the great eagle" fueled as they were by opposition to Maimonides's extreme naturalism. See Elliot Wolfson, "Beneath the Wings of the Great Eagle: Maimonides and Thirteenth-Century Kabbalah," in *Moses Maimonides (1138–1204)—His Religious, Scientific, and Philosophical Wirkungsgeschichte in Different Cultural Contexts,* ed. G. K. Hasselhoff and Otfried Fraisse (Würzburg: Ergon Verlag, 2004), 209–237, at p. 210.

that "messianic activism—even a measured kind—plays no role whatsoever in Maimonides' thought…"[45] Too much emphasis however is placed on Maimonides's phrasing that one should just "wait and believe in what we have generally exposited about it" (אלא מחכה ויאמין בכלל הדבר כמו שבארנו). Firstly, the Hebrew term "to wait" (חכה) has a wider semantic range than simply passivity or inactivity. Anticipate, or look forward to, rather than "wait" in the sense of sit back and do nothing, better captures its nuance in this context.[46] Secondly, Maimonides directs that advice in opposition to all the various forms of theoretical thinking about the messiah, including delving into *aggadot* and *midrashim* about it, since they "contribute neither to the fear nor to the love of God." Love and fear are in fact, according to Maimonides, those commandments that *are* grounded in theoretical thought and scientific understanding of the world.[47] He precisely formulates his prescription in order to avoid the theoretical that exclusively constitutes the commandments of fear and love of God, in favor of anticipating the national revival "we have generally exposited" in relation to the messianic period.

It is simply impossible for Maimonides's natural account of the messianic period to ever materialize without the human efforts required to achieve it. His account assumes activism. It is difficult to imagine what other purpose Maimonides's account would have if not to inspire some form of activism. Thus, on the subject of messianism, as with many others, Maimonides's activist model is strikingly different than its counterpart represented by Judaism's second most prominent medieval thinker (*rishon*), Moses Naḥmanides. While in Maimonides's model "the range of human responsibility is extensive," the Naḥmanidean one shifts the messianic catalyst to divine "cataclysmic intervention," the final in a series of "discontinuous ruptures in history."[48] In other words, what Maimonides

---

45   See his "Some Ironic Consequences of Maimonides's Rationalistic Messianism," (Heb.) *Maimonidean Studies* 2 (1991), pp. 1–8 at p. 7 and p. 8, note 19.

46   Marcus Jastrow translates this term which appears in the very Talmudic passage which considers both human and divine "waiting" for the messiah, as "anxiety," i.e., we are *anxious* for the messiah, in his *Dictionary of the Talmudim, Talmud Bavli and Yerushalmi, and the Midrashic Literature* (New York: The Judaica Press, 1971), p. 461. It is also important to note that the single biblical instance of this grammatical form (Isa. 30:18) (*yeḥakeh*) is interpreted by the medieval exegete David Kimhi as a transitive verb (*po'el yotze*) that takes an object, כלומר יבטיחכם שתחכו לו לחננכם שעוד יחון אתכם, יחכה פעל יוצא.

47   See *MT, Yesodei ha-Torah*, 2:2 and *Repentance*, 10:2.

48   See David Hartman in "Maimonides' Approach to Messianism and its Contemporary Implications," *Da'at* 2–3 (1979), pp. 5–33, at p. 31, 33.

has done is to inspire political activism, the heart of which is state building, rather than mere thought and belief.[49]

Maimonides ensures this kind of engagement with the notion of a messianic age when he emphasizes its exclusively natural status precisely in that section of the Code where he discusses the ultimate reward of "life in the World to Come." Enjoyment of the latter by those who qualify is perpetual and lacking nothing, while "the days of the messiah are *part of this world (olam ha-zeh) and the world acts in its customary way except for the restoration of kingship to Israel.*[50] Maimonides emphasizes the this-worldly nature of the messianic era because he is cognizant of the dangers of lapsing into quietism, when discussing future reward for present conduct that views the "World to Come" as the ultimate consequence of the good life. On its own, that wholly incorporeal world poses the danger of encouraging a life of pure contemplation, or that which most approximates "incorporeal" living in this world. He therefore accentuates the distinction between the "World to Come," that exists independently of the natural world, and the messianic period which is an integral stage in the historical evolution of the natural world. One can only trustingly wait for the former, steeped in the ethereal contemplative realm that will merit it, while the concrete physical establishment of a viable Jewish polis must galvanize the latter.[51]

---

[49]   What I present here is in stark contrast to the clear delineation Aḥad Ha-Am draws between Maimonides the rationalist who grants the intellect a place of preeminence and the Maimonides who allocates no space for nationalism, asserting categorically that "he did not recognize any value to the principle of nationhood in the thought of Judaism" (כי לא היכיר יסוד הלאומי בתורת היהדות). I agree with Lawrence Kaplan who corrects this caricature of Maimonides's thought, stating that the national motif in Maimonides's thought "forms an integral and coherent part of his political philosophy and is ultimately of a piece with Maimonides's philosophical commitment to the rule of reason" in "Shilton HaSekhel," *HaShiloah* 15, issue 85–90 (1904), reprinted in English in *Basic Writings of Aḥad Ha-Am: Nationalism and the Jewish Ethic*, ed. Hans Kohn (New York: Herzl Press, 1962), pp. 228–288. See "Maimonides on the Singularity of the Jewish People," *Da'at* 15 (1979) pp. v–xxvii, at p. xxvii, note 40.

[50]   הטובה האחרונה שאין לה הפסק וגרעון הוא חיי העולם הבא אבל ימות המשיח הוא העולם הזה ועולם כמנהגו הולך אלא שהמלכות תחזור לישראל, *MT, Repentance,* 9:2.

[51]   There is tension between the dangers of both messianic passivism and activism expressed in Maimonides's letters. In his *Iggeret Teiman,* he warns of the harm done to Jewish communities by messianic activism while in *Iggeret ha-Shemad* he deems an excessive passivity expressed as a defeatist acceptance of the status quo until the appearance of the Messiah "evil hearted, a vitiation of religion and commandments, and a great harm [or prohibition in another variant]." For a list of catastrophic messianic failures, see the former in *Iggerot ha-Rambam* (Arabic

The second is the philosopher Yeshayahu Leibowitz's opposing view, notable for two reasons. Firstly, he is one of the leading and influential Jewish thinkers of the twentieth century, and secondly, I believe his position on this subject is a sophisticated example of "preconceived notions or deep-seated predilections" coloring one's conclusions, precisely what Isadore Twersky, cited at the beginning of this article, warned against. Because of his deep disdain for what he viewed as the current sacralization, and thus "idolization," of the political state by religious Zionists, he cites this precise source as proof that Maimonides's "vision of messianic redemption is not essential for his religion and faith."[52] He went as far as to draw its inessentiality's logical extreme conclusion that would vitiate a future historical messianic reality altogether, asserting, "The Messiah is essentially he who always will come, he is the eternal future. The Messiah who comes, the Messiah of the present, is invariably the false Messiah."[53] Firstly, however, the very structure and content of the Code militate forcefully against diminishing the messiah's importance for Judaism. Addressing the messianic vision initially in the *Laws of Repentance* and then returning to it a second time at the very end of the *Mishneh Torah*, or the Code's culmination, devoting two entire chapters to it, speaks volumes to the contrary, and attests to its utmost importance and essentiality. In fact, why would he even include anything related to messianism, a subject totally devoid of halakhic consequences in a halakhic code, when it could

---

and Hebrew trans.), ed. Yitzḥak Sheilat, supra, vol. 1, pp. 161–162 and the latter, ibid., p. 58. See Aviezer Ravitzky's discussion in his "'To the Utmost Human Capacity': Maimonides and the Days of the Messiah," in *Perspectives on Maimonides*, supra, pp. 221–256, at pp. 240–241 and his insight that this wariness of both extremes expresses itself in the *MT* as well, "emphasizing the contingent factor within historical processes and negating any certain guarantees of Messianic success in advance of the fact" (p. 241). For an overview of various messianic pretenders throughout Jewish history preceding and subsequent to Maimonides's list, see Harris Lenowitz, *The Jewish Messiahs: From the Galilee to Crown Heights* (New York: Oxford University Press, 1998) and especially his examination of the excerpt from *Iggeret Teiman* which enumerates various messianic failures in his time and previously at pp. 65–67.

52   See *Ha-Rambam: Ha-Adam ha-Abrahami*, supra. See also Haim O. Rechnitzer, "Judaism and the Idea of the Law: Leo Strauss and Yeshayahu Leibowitz's Philosophical and Ideological Interpretations of Maimonides," *Hebrew Union College Annual* 79 (2008), pp. 165–191, esp. 188–191.

53   See "Lishmah and Not-Lishmah" in Eliezer Goldman, ed., *Judaism, Human Values, and the Jewish State*, trans. Goldman, et al. (Cambridge: Harvard Univ. Press, 1992), pp. 73–74, originally published in Hebrew as Yeshayahu Leibowitz, *Yahadut, Am Yehudi u-Medinat Yisrael* (Jerusalem and Tel-Aviv: Schocken, 1979).

easily have been dispensed with as it was by R. Joseph Karo's *Shulḥan Arukh*. Secondly, Leibowitz continues to argue in the very same breath that, although the two primary commandments of loving and fearing God seem to require only contemplation, it is clear to him that the world of action consisting of *mitzvot* and *halakhah* are of paramount concern to Maimonides and "only this type of worship binds man to true reality."[54] He bases this conclusion on the "fact" that it never escapes Maimonides "for an instant" that man "is not a separate intellect but rather an intellect that exists in matter and as a material existence he is destined to [a life of] conduct and action."[55] By this very same reasoning, one could forcefully argue for Maimonides's advocacy of an activist messianism. That is, it cannot solely be theorized about, but as a "material existence," human beings must bring about the messianic period by their own efforts. Contemplation alone can never succeed in realizing the messianic era envisioned at the end of the Code. That is precisely what Maimonides alludes to by excluding it from every area of pure speculation.[56]

The third is the Hasidic leader R. Yoel Teitelbaum, a Satmar Rebbe, who is another prominent example of a learned sage whose "predilections and preconceived notions" Maimonides provoked, particularly when Maimonides's explicit statements and halakhic rulings contraindicated his own positions. As a seminal rabbinic advocate of a passive supernatural messianism with respect to reestablishing sovereignty in Israel, R. Teitelbaum arguably penned the most detailed and intricate rabbinic polemic against messianic activism in its current form of Zionism.[57] For the purposes of this paper, I have no interest in evaluating the cogency of his

---

54 רק עבודת אלקים זו קושרת את האדם למציאות האמיתית.

55 ואינו שוכח אף לרגע שהאדם אינו "שכל נפרד" אלא "שכל נמצא בחומר" וכישות מטריאלית הוא נידון לפעולה ועשיה.

56 For a good analysis of Leibowitz's article see Paul Mendes-Flohr, "Maimonides in the Crucible of Zionism: Reflections on Yeshayahu Leibowitz's Negative Theology," in *Maimonides and His Heritage*, eds. Idit Dobbs-Weinstein, Lenn Goodman, James Grady (Albany: SUNY Press, 2009), pp. 181–192, where he considers this article to "construct the scaffolding of all Leibowitz's subsequent writings on Maimonides," and at the same time acknowledging that its provocative thesis, "was born of an ideological agenda, or rather a theological posture that bore a political sting." at pp. 184–185. See also in Hebrew Warren Zev Harvey's lucid explication of this groundbreaking article, "Leibowitz on the Abrahamic Person, Faith and Nihilism," in Moshe Hallamish, Hannah Kasher, Yoḥanan Silman, eds., *The Faith of Abraham: In the Light of Interpretation throughout the Ages* (Ramat-Gan: Bar-Ilan University Press, 2002), pp. 347–352.

57 "Essay on the Three Oaths," in *Va-Yoel Moshe* (Brooklyn, 1959). On this whole subject see Aviezer Ravitzky, "'Forcing the End': Zionism and the State of Israel

argument, which is indeed backed by a prodigious mastery of rabbinic sources in all their forms, and restrict my focus narrowly on R. Teitelbaum's engagement with Maimonides. Given what Maimonides actually states explicitly, including his natural historical account, one would have expected R. Teitelbaum to offer some reasoned rebuttal to Maimonides's formulations on the subject. Yet Maimonides's rabbinic stature and authority are so powerful as to elicit often desperate attempts to enlist him in support of one's theological aims and halakhic rulings, despite all evidence to the contrary. In addition, what Maimonides does not say at all, and his glaring omission in his *Mishneh Torah* of the central peg in R. Teitelbaum's argument which rests on an aggadic passage depicting God admonishing and adjuring Israel with oaths not to precipitate its own forceful return to Israel, is surely an insurmountable problem.[58] Yet he overcomes this formidable Maimonidean obstacle (not to mention the philosophical problem that a God that "adjures" militates against a Maimonidean definition of God that is immune to anthropomorphisms of any kind whatsoever)[59] by the claim that Maimonides's silence precisely points to that oath's importance so elementary and foundational to Jewish law and theology that it goes without saying. As he asserts, "The oath not to instigate the redemption independently is far more stringent than the oath taken when receiving the Torah."[60] Thus, Maimonides's omission of a crux of R. Teitelbaum's argument, patently demonstrating its insignificance and irrelevance, is turned on its head and deemed proof of how overwhelmingly foundational it is![61] The tortuous circular logic of this argument merely speaks volumes about what is, in fact, its very antithesis— Maimonides's *endorsement* of messianic activism, particularly with respect

---

as Antimessianic Undertakings," in *Jews and Messianism in the Modern Era: Metaphor and Meaning,* ed. Jonathan Frankel (New York: Oxford University Press, 1991) and particularly the literature he cites on the three oaths in fn. 53, p. 64.

58   For the oaths see b*Ketubot* 110b–111a.

59   This obstacle which space does not allow me to deal with extensively is that a literal understanding of God adjuring an oath would be impossible for Maimonides's God who cannot tolerate any anthropomorphism whatsoever. In fact, to believe this literally would be idolatrous, which is why when Maimonides specifically alludes to this midrash in his extralegal *Letter to Yemen,* he qualifies it as a metaphor. See *Epistles of Maimonides,* supra, p. 130

60   *Va-Yoel Moshe,* p. 140: שאותה השבועה לא ליקח גאולה מעצמם הוא חמורה הרבה יותר מהשבועה שהיה במתן תורה. See sections 78–81, pp. 139–147. See also Zvi Jonathan Kaplan, "Rabbi Joel Teitelbaum, Zionism, and Hungarian Ultra-Orthodoxy," *Modern Judaism,* 24:2 (2004), pp. 165–178.

61   Also at p. 139: "For the punishment and recompense related to an oath is more severe than all the other transgressions of the Torah."

to reestablishing Jewish sovereignty over Israel.

Maimonides's messianic *realpolitik* is always tempered by the universal ideal, not just on the international stage, but intra-nationally in the very way Maimonides constructs the ancient tribal makeup of the Jewish nation. Though all the tribes participated in the military campaigns and political organs of the Jewish state, the Levites were exempt from virtually everything one would associate with the political and economic life of a polis. They remain *"separated from the ways of the world—they don't wage war like the rest of Israel, they don't colonize the land, and they do not acquire anything via physical power."*[62] Their lives were wholly dedicated to the ideal of pursuing the ultimate truth in the world unencumbered by the duties that accompany any national and territorial loyalties. They are living testaments to the universal ideal that transcends land and nation by the very fact that their existential model is open to anyone, Jew and gentile alike, *"to all who enter the world,"* who opts for the ideal existence they represent.[63]

This tribal ideal links up perfectly with the last remaining legacy of the universalistic Abrahamic experiment described initially at the beginning of the Code. The Levites were the sole torchbearers of the Abrahamic teachings as the society around them devolved once again into a morass of confused theology and philosophy. Jacob, the Levites's founding father, secured his own father's legacy by designating them his missionary successors, so to speak, assigning them the task of perpetuating the universal truths of the "way of the Lord": "separated Levi and appointed him head master, and established him in a seat of learning where to instruct in the path of the Name and in the observance of the charges of Abraham. He, moreover, commanded his sons not to interrupt the succession of the sons of Levi to the presidency of the school so that the learning be not forgotten."[64]

Embedded in the realism of independent nation states which will never be overcome in "this world,"[65] is the Levitical kernel of the legacy that bridges Abraham's pioneering universalism with the messianic political leader who proves himself as the philosopher king that can instruct Jews and non-Jews in that same "way of the Lord." He will, therefore,

---

[62] *MT, Sabbatical and Jubilee Years,* 13:10, הובדלו מדרכי העולם--לא עורכין מלחמה כשאר ישראל, ולא נוחלין, ולא זוכין לעצמן בכוח גופן.

[63] Ibid., ולא שבט לוי בלבד, אלא כל איש ואיש מ<u>כל באי העולם</u>.

[64] והבדיל לוי ומינהו ראש והושיבו בישיבה ללמד דרך ה'.

[65] For Maimonides, intellectual perfection must be preceded by physical perfection, which includes politics: "the governance of the city and the well-being of the states of all its people, according to their capacity" (GP, III:27).

"teach the whole people and point out to them the Lord's path, and all nations will come to listen to him."[66] The sense is that it is not simply his intellectual acumen that will attract a universal following but his political ingenuity and success in accomplishing what no other politician prior to him has—the eradication of that age-old hatred Maimonides himself experienced and that became resurrected in the modern world in its racial iteration as anti-Semitism. The return to Zion, the particular national vehicle of Jewish aspirations and fulfillment, is the enabling historical factor for that universal return to the Levitical teaching.

At this juncture it is appropriate to focus on another important aspect of Maimonides's messianism that has not been afforded its full due to date. There are a number of differences between Maimonides's portrait of the messianic leader drawn in the *Laws of Repentance* and that in the *Laws of Kings*, but one in particular is quite striking. In the former, he will embody a near unrivalled prophetic and intellectual prowess, "possessed of wisdom greater than Solomon and an outstanding prophet nearly on par with Moses."[67] Isaiah's vision (2:2–3), echoed by Micah (4:1–2), captures this notion of the messianic leader's universal acclaim by the international consensus to ascend to "the Mount of the Lord's House" at the time when it is destined to "stand firm above all the mountains."[68] What is significant about the image of the Temple becoming the fount of philosophical wisdom is that, in Maimonides's view of biblical history, its location originally ignited jealousy, conflict, tension, and violence—precisely all those divisive forces that any messianic regime must overcome to vindicate its mission and authority. According to Maimonides's *Guide*, the Bible actually refrained from disclosing its exact location because:

1) "nations should hold fast to the place and fight for it with great violence knowing as they do that this place is the final purpose of the Law on earth";
2) "lest those who then owned the place ravaged and devastated it to the limits of their power";
3) "lest every tribe should demand that this place be *within its allotted portion* and should seek to conquer it, which would lead to conflict and sedition..."[69]

The messianic leader's transformation of what was initially a place signifying every single political malaise that fragments peoples into one

---

66   *MT, Laws of Repentance* 9:2, ‏ילמד כל העם ויורה אותם דרך ה' ויבואו כל הגוים לשומעו‎.
67   Ibid., 9:2.
68   ‏נכון יהיה הר בית ה' בראש ההרים‎.
69   *GP*, III:45, p. 576.

that unites them represents a subversion of everything peoples mistakenly conceived as the purpose of religion. Internationally, any violence exerted to conquer the Temple Mount could only have been incited by a fundamental misconception of the purpose of the Law which aims at "the welfare of the states of people in their relations with each other through the abolition of reciprocal wrongdoing," and "correct opinions."[70] Wresting possession by violence of a center that symbolizes the goals of peaceful coexistence and knowledge can only be motivated by a corrupt view of the Law, reminiscent of that prevalent during the pre-Abrahamic pagan decline. Tribal conflict expresses that very same corrupt view intra-nationally. This is precisely why the Levites maintain their isolationist existence, as a monastic ideal and antidote to this kind of attitude toward religion and the Law. Identifying the Law as an instrument of power gained by resort to violence is an exercise in self-defeat. The accomplishments of the messianic king as both the perfect teacher and politician render him the living embodiment of the two perfections at which the Law aims. The *House of the Lord* then mirrors those perfections as a symbol of political stability and philosophical truth.

However, the tangible political reality of a reconstructed Temple also belies its pristine origins during the Abrahamic monotheistic campaign.[71] During that ideal period of statelessness the Temple was also marked by its concealment, by its absence, by its placelessness, whose "place is not stated explicitly when mentioned in the Torah."[72] Its actual location could only be identified and its construction carried out once a firm political regime was in place—in this case it is the king, defined by the acute diplomatic talents that "would be qualified to give commands and quarrels would cease."[73]

The real messianic king also stands for a kind of an ideal non-king. According to Maimonides, rabbinic messianic longings arose "... not in

---

[70] *GP* III:27, p. 511. As Seeskin points out regarding Maimonides's view of the Temple and sacrificial offerings, "these activities have no inherent power to influence God or bring about atonement. They are designed to influence us by bringing about a re-evaluation of the lives we live." See his *Jewish Messianic Thoughts*, supra, p. 191.

[71] Amos Funkenstein describes Maimonides's conception of history as a "growing process of monotheization of the entire world," where the "messianic age crowns a didactic and dialectic process which began with the modest establishment of a monotheistic community by Abraham..." in *Perceptions of Jewish History* (Berkeley: University of California Press, 1993), pp. 148–149.

[72] *GP*, III:45, p.576.

[73] Ibid.

order to rule the entire world, and not so that they would subjugate the nations, and not so that the nations would exalt them... but in order that they would be free to pursue Torah and its wisdom."[74] What will nurture this intellectual freedom and curiosity is an environment in which all the social, economic, and geopolitical factors normally necessitating a king are absent, for "in that time there will be no hunger and no war and no jealousy or rivalry, goodness will be abundant and all luxuries will be as common as earth."[75] Thus, in the messianic era, the king ideally can virtually be dispensed with. I do not mean here that the world will pass into a phase of unadulterated libertarian anarchism during the messianic period, but only that the ideal king is one who presides over a kingdom in which religio/philosophical concerns predominate over all political concerns. The very political reality of a monarch and a cultic center bears witness to the ideal of their redundancy in a world where "knowledge, wisdom, and truth" are the overarching concerns.[76] Thus the meaning of Maimonides's prognostication that it is "not unimaginable that his reign will endure for thousands of years," is not that there will be an inordinate longevity to the king's rule but that there is a possibility that the messianic state might ultimately lapse once again.[77] The implication is that the global environment will reach a point of such coexistence where there is one aim for which all human beings strive, eliminating all forms of tension and conflict—that in fact the messianic *dynasty* will indeed end, but not the messianic *community* that the kingship cultivated.

---

74 *MT, Kings* 12:4, לא נתאוו החכמים והנביאים ימות המשיח לא כדי שישלטו על כל העולם ולא כדי שירדו בגוים ולא כדי שינשאו אותם העמים ולא כדי לאכול ולשתות ולשמוח אלא כדי שיהיו פנויין בתורה וחכמתה.

75 *MT, Kings* 12:5, ובאותו הזמן לא יהיה שם לא רעב ולא מלחמה ולא קנאה ותחרות שהטובה תהיה מושפעת הרבה וכל המעדנים מצויין כעפר ולא יהיה עסק כל העולם אלא לדעת את ה' בלבד.

76 *MT, Teshuvah* 9:2, הדעה והחכמה והאמת. Menachem Lorberbaum, via a different analysis, arrives at the same conclusion, that Maimonides's utopian and messianic visions work in tandem in the sense that "only through the complete success of politics can politics be overcome... The ideal polity's goal is to one day bring about its own overcoming." See his discussion in *Politics and the Limits of Law: Secularizing the Political in Medieval Jewish Thought* (Stanford: Stanford University Press, 2001), pp. 77–89, at pp. 88–89.

77 *Introduction to Perek Ḥelek*, supra, p. 139. Here I disagree with Joel Kraemer's interpretation that this implies the possibility "that even the messianic virtuous community would decompose," in his "Maimonides' Messianic Posture," p. 112. I would correct Kraemer's conclusion that "Maimonides accentuates rather the permanence of King Messiah and the indestructibility of the kingdom of Israel," to the affirmation simply of the indestructibility of the global messianic community, not of the Israelite kingship or kingdom.

Significantly, Isa. 11:9, the verse that, for Maimonides, typifies the utopian intellectual atmosphere that will pervade the entire globe, extends these Temple representations to the country of Israel as a whole. The full verse reads, "In all of my *sacred mount* nothing evil or vile shall be done, for the Land will be filled with the knowledge of God as water covers the sea." As Ibn Ezra and the modern *Jewish Publication Society* translation point out, the phrase "sacred mount" is a synecdoche for the entire land.[78] Everything that human beings perceive as evil, including natural and human manifestations of them, according to Maimonides, are really "privations" associated with the deficient nature of matter. Human evils inflicted on each other result from "tyrannical domination" rarely on an individual scale, and more commonly, on a national scale, "in the course of great wars."[79] The Temple Mount ultimately is a beacon toward its own origins of placelessness, representing intellectual focus away from falsehood signified by idolatry and toward truth signified by monotheism. Abraham manifested those truths concretely by designating the Temple Mount as the landmark by which the spatial coordinates of worship are oriented.

So does the land of Israel as a whole act in terms of politics. It is a state that ultimately veers the global community away from everything that divides states geopolitically since it projects globally the message of the unsituated Temple that "through cognition of the truth, enmity and hatred are removed and the inflicting of harm by people on one another is abolished"(GP III:12, p. 441).[80] Occurrences of evils are a result of an inverted order of priority in the human constitution where matter dominates over form since "all man's acts of disobedience and sins are consequent upon his matter and not his form" (GP, III:8, p. 431). The human form, which for Maimonides is intellect, has the potential to quell the material inclinations that cause sin by "power, dominion, and control over matter in order that it subjugate it, quell its impulses and bring it back to the most harmonious state that is possible" (ibid., p. 432). In other words, form can assert itself and subvert precisely those desires of "domination" that are at the root of human evil, harnessing them in the service of the truth rather than self-gratification. The political upheaval necessitated by the establishment of an independent Jewish state initiates a process, which practically involves violence in a world that "runs its natural course." Yet it anticipates a utopian vision toward the ultimate banishment of the will

---

[78] See, for example, Exod. 15:17; Ps. 78:54.

[79] *GP*, III:12, p. 444.

[80] See also *GP*, III:33, p. 532, where ignorance is the cause of "mutual envy, hatred, and strife, aimed at taking away what the other has," all those sources of conflict which will disappear in the messianic period.

to power first between individuals and then between states.

National sovereignty provides the free environment of *this world*, in which anti-Judaism and its various mutations under the general rubric of anti-Semitism have germinated for so long and seem to have become integral to the natural socio-political order. Political independence is conducive to the "calm" (וימצאו להן מרגוע) and the "increasing wisdom [science]" (וירבו בחכמה) that "qualifies one for the life of the *World to Come*" (כדי שיזכו לחיי העולם הבא). What is perhaps paradoxically Maimonides's favorite rabbinic maxim, "the world runs its natural course" (*olam ke-min-hago noheg*), characterizes the process and the newly initiated messianic environment. There will be no fundamental change in the laws of nature nor will the messianic leader effect the transition by any non-natural means. In other words, there is no role for divine intervention or metaphysical utopianism in this fulfillment of history.

Maimonides's natural programmatic account of history unfolding toward its ultimate fruition safeguards against a relapse into a mythic view of the world he considered fatal to achieving human perfection and, ipso facto, to the whole philosophical enterprise. Maimonides's core messianic teaching is an outgrowth of his entire religious perspective, which eschews divine intervention and promotes human initiative.[81] Although this is a vast subject, for our purposes here, I only summarize an overarching goal of Maimonides's thought. His entire philosophical project aims at distinguishing God from anything in the world so consummately as to render it impossible to actually say anything about God without violating His uniqueness and oneness. He thus constructed an impenetrable philosophical barrier between God and the world that would curtail both individuals and states from exercising the limitless power that accompanies beliefs in being uniquely endowed with divine power. As Kenneth Seeskin states, "If the line separating the divine from the human is sacrosanct, then there is no possibility of crossing it. Every human being and every institution is finite."[82] Maimonides's conception of the messianic era is the final act in his naturalistic view of the world that assigns God and the world to radically distinct realms of being that can never be traversed. It exquisitely conveys the notion that only the road of finitude, of *olam ha-zeh*, whose operative principle is the material *olam ke-minhago noheg*, can lead to the realm of infinitude, of the ethereal *olam ha-ba*.[83] ଔ

---

81   Seeskin, on this, articulates it best when he asserts that, "In the world of mythology, the line separating the divine from the human is thin. Humans become gods and gods become humans." See *Jewish Messianic Thoughts*, supra, p. 50.

82   Ibid., p. 180.

83   See *MT, Hilkhot Teshuvah*, 8:3–6.

For the Love of Humanity: The Religious Humanism of Rabbi Samson Raphael Hirsch

By: SHMUEL LESHER

I

In my teenage years, I was burning with questions. Perhaps they were not questions unique to an Orthodox young adult growing up in a modern world, but they burned nonetheless. How can I accept that the Jewish People are God's "*am segulah*" (treasured nation) when I would readily reject such a concept found in other faiths? Can I honestly be dedicated to a universal moral vision for all of humanity while being truly committed to the authentic and traditional Torah perspective?

Early on, my struggle led me to Rabbi Samson Raphael Hirsch. From the moment I started reading *The Nineteen Letters*, I was taken by R. Hirsch and his attempt to paint, with broad strokes, the overarching themes of Judaism. He was deeply rooted in Jewish tradition, and yet simultaneously engaged with the world. He confronted with confidence many of the questions I had about Judaism and its place within the world at large. But perhaps more than any particular answer that he provided, he confirmed for me that I was not wrong in my attempts to make sense of the many clashes I found between traditional Judaism and the values of universal humanism.

As I learned more about R. Hirsch, I began to realize that his thought laid much of the groundwork for other subsequent Jewish thinkers who attempted to address the confrontation between tradition and modernity, between Judaism and the world, and between the particular and the universal. This paper will attempt to paint a portrait of R. Hirsch's unique vision of religious humanism and universalism. It will also explore how R.

Shmuel Lesher is the assistant rabbi of Beth Avraham Yoseph of Toronto (BAYT). He received rabbinic ordination from RIETS where he was also a Machon Beren Kollel Elyon Fellow. He attended a number of yeshivot including Yeshivat Mir (Jerusalem) and Yeshiva Gedolah of Greater Washington. Lesher is currently pursuing a Master's Degree in Mental Health Counseling at the Ferkauf School of Psychology.

Hirsch addressed the issues of Jewish identity, chosenness, and the value of non-Jews and society at large.[*]

The Opposition: Challenges and Criticism of R. Hirsch

It is undisputed that R. Hirsch was a historic figure. His impact is still acutely felt today over 130 years after his passing. However, part of that history includes a well-established camp of opposition which had a significant amount of ambivalence for R. Hirsch and his *Torah Im Derekh Eretz* program. There have been three basic categories of opposition to R. Hirsch. Some have challenged his credentials as a Torah scholar or *gadol*.[1] Others questioned his intentions, claiming that he embraced humanism and modernity only as a temporary concession. And others even called his own authenticity into question, mistakenly arguing that R. Hirsch was "a German humanist in rabbinic garb" who was fundamentally influenced by the societal mores of his time.[2]

The rejection of R. Hirsch's *Torah Im Derekh Eretz* community model is almost ubiquitous among Eastern European Torah leaders.[3] In his day,

---

[*] I thank my dear friends Rabbis Robert Schrier and Chezkie Glatt for their friendship and encouragement. Thank you to *Mori V-Rabi* Rabbi Aaron Lopiansky who provided many important insights into this topic. Thank you to my father Michael Lesher, Rabbi Netanel Wiederblank, Rabbi Steven Miodownik, and my father-in-law, Rabbi Hanan Balk, who gave of their time and improved this article. I am indebted to professors Michah Gottlieb, David Berger, Marc B. Shapiro, and Moshe Y. Miller for their accessibility and their willingness to help. Thank you to Zvi Erenyi and the staff of the Yeshiva University Gottesman Library for their time, assistance, and dedication.

[1] Noah H. Rosenbloom, *Tradition in an Age of Reform: The Religious Philosophy of Samson Raphael Hirsch* (JPS, 1976), 60, 90. See, however, Moshe Y. Miller, *Rabbi Samson Raphael Hirsch and Nineteenth Century German Orthodoxy on Judaism's Attitude Towards Non-Jews*, Doctoral Dissertation (Yeshiva University, 2014), 182–190, who seriously challenges Rosenbloom's assertion. For a fierce rebuttal of Rosenbloom's study see Mordechai Breuer, "Review Essay: Tradition in an Age of Reform: The Religious Philosophy of Samson Raphael Hirsch by Noah H. Rosenbloom," *Tradition*, 16:4 (1977), 140–149.

[2] See R. Shimon Schwab's approbation to Joseph Elias (ed.), *The Nineteen Letters: The World of Rabbi S. R. Hirsch* (Feldheim, 1995), vii (henceforth: *TNL*). This is probably a reference to Rosenbloom's skewed depiction of R. Hirsch.

[3] See, for example, Eliyahu Eliezer Dessler, *"Al Torah im Derekh Eretz,"* Ha-Ma'ayan, 4, *Tishrei* (Jerusalem, 1963), 61–64, reprinted in *Mikhtav Me-Eliyahu*, III (Bnei Brak, 1964), 356–358; Barukh Ber Lebowitz, *Birkhat Shmuel*, I, *Kiddushin* (New York, 1972), no. 27; Elḥanan Wasserman, *Kovetz Ma'amarim*, I, 304–305; *S'ridei Aish*, II, 8, 14; Dov Katz, *Tenuat Ha-Musar*, I, 167–169, 226; *Koveitz Iggerot Ḥazon Ish*, II (Bnei Brak, 1956), 443–444. Even the iconoclastic Lubavitcher

R. Hirsch and his program were seen by many among the traditionalist camp as introducing a new and unwanted modernity into their communities.[4] His openness to secular studies put him at odds with many who rejected the pursuit of a secular education. Uncharacteristic of the rabbinate of his time, R. Hirsch chose to write in High German, the vernacular used in the contemporary non-traditional society of his time.

Unlike many other Torah authorities of his time, R. Hirsch is not particularly known for classical talmudic analysis or typical halakhic responsa. His famous writings, *The Nineteen Letters* and *Horeb,* as well as his monumental commentary on the Torah, are works filled with poetic, passionate, and sophisticated Jewish thought, but decidedly contemporary and mostly non-halakhic in their nature and content. All these factors led some to question the authoritative nature of the person, and of such works in general.[5]

A typical critique of R. Hirsch can be found in the writings of R. Shlomo Wolbe. In a passage addressing the Torah view on secular knowledge, R. Wolbe notes the *"gedolei Yisrael's"* dismissal of R. Hirsch's openness to secular culture as a *hora'at sha'ah*—a temporary ruling. He argues that *Torah Im Derekh Eretz,* as R. Hirsch conceived it, is irrelevant to the current Jewish community. Although successful for the lay community, R. Hirsch's model failed to produce a single *gaon,* Torah genius. According to R. Wolbe, Germany proved it was impossible to incorporate secular studies into a yeshiva curriculum if any measure of success was to be achieved.[6]

Although some of these grievances are not burning issues today, some of these critiques have remained, leaving the Hirschian legacy somewhat tainted. Today, some see R. Hirsch as "a masterful commentator on the Torah, a brilliant polemicist against Reform Judaism, and a great innovator in the field of Jewish education."[7] However, he is reputed to be somewhat second-rate when compared to the towering talmudists of his day.

Perhaps the most fundamental criticism of R. Hirsch and his humanism came from an unlikely source. R. Aharon Lichtenstein, an advocate

---

Rebbe, R. Menachem Mendel Schneerson, took a similarly critical view of R. Hirsch's program. See Chaim Miller, *Turning Judaism Outward* (KOL Menachem, 2014), 94–95.

4   See Jacob Katz, *"Rabbi Shamshon Raphael Hirsch, Ha-Meimin ve-ha-Masmeil,"* in Mordechai Breuer (ed.) *Torah im Derekh Eretz: Ha-Tenuah, Isheha, Ra'ayonoteha* [Hebrew] (Bar Ilan University, 1987), 13-31.

5   I recall one notable Torah scholar told me something to the effect of, "R. Hirsch was not a *gadol ba-Torah*, he was a *manhig* (communal leader). His *peirush* (Torah commentary) does not come from *Hazal.* He invented his approach."

6   Shlomo Wolbe, *Alei Shor,* I (Jerusalem, 1997), 296.

7   Ezra Schwartz, "A Gadol for the Nineties," *Ha-Mevaser* 36, Fall 1997, 13.

for religious humanism, wrote of R. Hirsch with a large degree of skepticism:

> Without in any way maligning him, it must be candidly stated that in much of his works it is precisely the sense of accommodation and concession—at times, even apologetics—that is persistent, if not pervasive... I presume...as with the Rambam...that in part we are not dealing with a graft at all but with an interpretation of the tradition; if you will, with a prism through which its thrust and content are perceived. Surely, R. Hirsch did not regard the degree of universalism which he espoused as an addendum. He undoubtedly saw it as the woof and warp of *Yahadut,* as the optimal response to an inherent question...[8]

For R. Lichtenstein, although R. Hirsch's work appears genuine, when encountering his humanism and universalism, the sense of accommodation is inescapable.

The Defense

It appears that the claim that R. Hirsch was not a proper Torah scholar is untenable. Professor Shnayer Leiman argues that the recent publications of many of R. Hirsch's halakhic responsa and *ḥiddushim* explode the myth that R. Hirsch was a second-rate talmudist.[9] R. Hirsch was clearly an expert talmudist who displayed a remarkable familiarity with the various branches of Talmudic literature throughout his writings.[10] In fact, R.

---

[8]   Aharon Lichtenstein, "Legitimization of Modernity: Classical and Contemporary," in Moshe Z. Sokol (ed.), *Engaging Modernity: Rabbinic Leaders and the Challenge of the Twentieth Century* (Aronson, 1997), 30. This critique predates R. Lichtenstein. See Gershom Scholem, *"Politik der Mystik," Juedische Rundschau* (1934), Nr. 57, 7 (German) cited in Mordechai Breuer, *The Torah im Derekh Eretz of R. S.R. Hirsch* (Feldheim, 1970), 61n117.

[9]   Shnayer Z. Leiman, "Rabbinic Responses to Modernity," *Judaic Studies,* no. 5 (Fall 2007). See also Eliyahu Meir Klugman, *Rabbi Samson Raphael Hirsch: Architect of Judaism for the Modern World* (ArtScroll Mesorah, 1996), 49–51, 288–296. Also see Leo Levi in Elliot Bondi (ed.), *Tzvi Tifarto: The World of Hirschian Teachings* (Feldheim, 2008), 187–188 and Yaakov Perlow, "Rav S.R. Hirsch: The Gaon in Talmud and Mikra," *Tzvi Tifarto* 45–59.

[10]   R. Hirsch's encyclopedic command of rabbinic literature is evident in his criticism of the fourth volume of Heinrich Graetz's *History of the Jews.* See Samson Raphael Hirsch, *Collected Writings,* V (Feldheim, 1988), 65–66,125,173,179,181 (henceforth: *CW*), and Klugman 245–250.

Hirsch communicated with the greatest Torah giants of his time.[11]

Although it is often difficult to gauge the level of scholarship or stature of any given rabbinic figure, the deference R. Hirsch was given by prominent rabbinic leaders of his generation and of later generations is instructive. Even though many criticized his *Torah Im Derekh Eretz* approach, on the whole, Torah scholars of the highest caliber and reputation had tremendous respect for R. Hirsch. R. Yitzḥak Elḥanan Spector,[12] R. Yisrael Salanter,[13] R. Ḥayyim Ozer Grodzinsky,[14] R. Avraham Binyamin Schreiber (author of the *Ketav Sofer*),[15] R. Elazer Menachem Man Shach,[16] R. Yosef Shalom Elyashiv,[17] have all expressed their tremendous respect and awe for R. Hirsch.

In regard to whether his educational program was intended as an ideal, ultimately, the greatest proof of R. Hirsch's belief in *Torah Im Derekh Eretz* as a timeless ideal can be found in R. Hirsch's own words:

> *Torah Im Derekh Eretz* is the one true principle conducive to truth and peace, to healing and recovery from all ills and religious confusion. The principle *Torah Im Derekh Eretz* can fulfill this function because it is not part of the troubled, time-bound notions; it represents the ancient traditional wisdom of our Sages that stood the test everywhere and at all times.[18]

For R. Hirsch, the application of Torah values to a particular age or culture is the historic task of the Jewish People and must be negotiated anew for every age. If properly understood and applied, R. Hirsch believed the Torah would reign supreme in every age and culture.[19] For R.

---

11 See Hirsch, "*Hitkatvut im Gedolei Doro,*" *Shemesh Marpei*, 259–269. See also Breuer, *Torah im Derekh Eretz*, 49, and Klugman 52.

12 Isidor Grunfeld, *Three Generations: The Influence of Samson Raphael Hirsch on Jewish Life and Thought* (Jewish Post, 1958), 38, and approbation to *Terumat Tzvi: The Pentateuch*, trans. Gertrude Hirschler (Judaica Press, 1986).

13 Naftali Hertz Ehrmann, *Israelit* XXIV: 22:362 (1883) cited in Klugman 369n21 and Katz, *Tenuat Ha-Musar,* I, 222–223. For an English translation see Yehoshua Leiman, *Two Giants Speak* (Jerusalem, 2002), 57–64 and Elias, *TNL,* xi-xiii.

14 *Iggerot R. Ḥayim Ozer,* I (Yeshivat Rabbeinu Yaakov Yosef, 2000), no. 296, p. 328–330.

15 See Hirschler, Preface to *Terumat Tzvi* and Grunfeld, *Three Generation*, 43-44.

16 Appropriation for Eliyahu Meir Klugman (ed.), *Shemesh Marpei* (ArtScroll Mesorah, 1992).

17 Ibid.

18 *CW,* VI, 221.

19 Isidor Grunfeld, *S.R. Hirsch: The Man and His Mission* (Soncino, 1956) xvii-xviii (henceforth: *Intro to JE*).

Hirsch, *Torah Im Derekh Eretz* is a "Torah for the Ages." In light of this, and many other such passages in R. Hirsch's writings, it appears impossible to claim that R. Hirsch's position does not represent his fundamental and ideal worldview.[20]

As R. Lichtenstein noted, when studying R. Hirsch's humanism, the most significant objection which requires a response is the question of authenticity and influence. However, here again, I believe R. Hirsch speaks for himself. R. Hirsch strongly believed in studying the Torah and Judaism from "within" (*aus sich heraus*) and arriving at our perceptions of the Torah's worldview as it emerges from the Torah itself.[21] R. Hirsch had biting criticism for both Mendelsohn, and even for Rambam, for what he saw as approaching the Torah from the "outside" and imposing their own perceptions on the Torah, instead of examining Judaism from "within."[22] This is a major theme found throughout R. Hirsch's writings. R. Hirsch constantly rejected any form of accommodation or apologetics.[23]

Furthermore, throughout his rabbinic career, R. Hirsch absolutely did not pull punches. He was often the subject of criticism when he rejected many new approaches and reforms to Judaism as inauthentic accommodations. It is almost absurd to accuse R. Hirsch of intentional accommodation or apologetics, molding the Torah into an intellectually acceptable worldview. Essentially, that would be tantamount to stating, in the most ironic way, that R. Hirsch was guilty of the very thing he so vehemently warred against his entire life. One can only conclude, as R. Lichtenstein did, that R. Hirsch must have firmly believed that his perspective of religious humanism was a genuine Torah perspective which emerged organically from the Torah. "The optimal response to an inherent question."[24]

---

[20]　For other excerpts of R. Hirsch's writings which indicate his belief in *Torah im Derekh Eretz* as ideal, see Leiman, "Rabbinic Responses to Modernity," 77–84.

[21]　See Isidor Grunfeld, *Introduction to Ḥoreb* (Soncino, 1962), xli (henceforth: *ITH*).

[22]　*TNL, Letter* 18.

[23]　See *TNL, Letter* 2; preface to Samson Raphael Hirsch, *The Pentateuch,* trans. Isaac Levy (L. Honig & Sons, 1959) often referred to as *The Commentary on the Torah* (henceforth: *COT*); *Intro to JE*, xxxvi–xxxvii; Samson Raphael Hirsch, *Judaism Eternal,* II, Isidor Grunfeld (ed.) (Soncino, 1956), 235 (henceforth *JE*). See also Samson Raphael Hirsch, forward, *Ḥoreb,* Isidor Grunfeld (ed.), (Soncino, 1962), clv-clxii.

[24]　Lichtenstein, "Legitimization of Modernity," 30.

II

R. Hirsch's Universalism and Humanism

Because humanism can mean a number of things, let us first define our terms. The term was probably first coined by theologian Friedrich Niethammer at the beginning of the 19th century[25] (just about the same time R. Hirsch was born) to refer to a system of education based on the study of classical literature. Humanism or the humanities are terms often used to describe the study of humanity and specifically the human experience. The liberal arts—literature, history, philosophy, and psychology—can all be included within humanism. However, more germane to this article, the term can also refer to a kind of ethical philosophy. Within this definition, humanism is a perspective that affirms the notion of human freedom and progress which emphasizes a concern for all human life and the universal human experience. There certainly is overlap between the two definitions. The study of humanism as a subject focuses on the human experience, which in turn enhances appreciation of the universal nature of the human condition. Although R. Hirsch embraced the study of the humanities as part of the ideal religious life, in this section we will focus on the universal and humanistic ethic in his writings.

To be sure, R. Hirsch did not invent a humanistic perspective within Judaism *ex nihilo*. He was building on a tradition certainly found in the *Rishonim*. *Rambam* (1135–1204) repeatedly emphasizes the ability of all human beings, Jew and non-Jew alike, to reach spiritual heights.[26] Humanistic themes, in particular a non-discriminatory approach to gentiles "bound by the ways of civility and religion," are also found in the writings of Meiri (1249–1306).[27] However, as will be explored below, R. Hirsch made a unique contribution to this school of thought.

---

25 Friedrich Niethammer, *The Dispute Between Philanthropinism and Humanism in the Educational Theory of our Time,* Hillebrecht (ed.), (Beltz, 1968).

26 See *Mishneh Torah, Teshuvah,* 5:2 and *Yesodei Ha-Torah* 4:8, 7:1. See also *Moreh Nevukhim* 3:28. For a fuller analysis of Rambam's perspective and how it differs from that of the Kabbalistic school, see Hanan Balk, "The Soul of a Jew and the Soul of a Non-Jew," *Ḥakirah,* 16 (New York, 2013), 61–76.

27 See his *Beit Ha-Beḥirah, Bava Kamma* 37b, *Avodah Zarah* 15b, 2a and *Yoma* 84b. For more on the approach of Meiri see Moshe Halbertal, "*R. Menaḥem ha-Meiri: Bein Torah le-Ḥokhmah,*" *Tarbiẓ* 63, 1994, 63–118, and his *Bein Torah le-Ḥokhmah: Rabbi Menaḥem ha-Meiri u-Ba'alei ha-Halakhah ha-Maimunim bi-Provence* (Jerusalem, 2000). For an English translation see "Ones Possessed of Religion": Religious Tolerance in The Teachings of Meiri," *Edah,* I, 2000, 1–24.

Torah Im Derekh Eretz: A "God-Rooted Humanism"

Torah Im Derekh Eretz is a phrase which is perhaps as elusive as it is ubiquitous. This slogan, most commonly associated with R. Hirsch, was broadly translated by Dayan Grunfeld as "God-rooted religious humanism."[28] For R. Hirsch, *Torah Im Derekh Eretz* does not just mean the study of Torah combined with an occupation. Hirschian *Torah Im Derekh Eretz* means that "Torah and *Derekh Eretz* are one." Perhaps it is in his commentary on the Torah where R. Hirsch comes closest to a definition of the philosophy most attributed to him:

> Culture starts the work of educating the generations of mankind and the Torah completes it; for the Torah is the most finished education of Man...culture in the service of morality is the first stage of Man's return to God. For us Jews, *Derekh Eretz* and Torah are one. The most perfect gentleman and the most perfect Jew, to the Jewish teaching, are identical. But in the general development of mankind culture comes earlier.
>
> But of course, where culture and civilization are used in the service of sensuality, degeneration only gets all the greater. But still, such misuse of culture does not do away with the intrinsic value and blessing of *Derekh Eretz.*[29]

R. Hirsch posits a radical, yet simple understanding of the teaching of *"Derekh Eretz Kadmah L'Torah,* the ways of culture preceded the giving of the Torah by 26 generations."[30] R. Hirsch writes that the Torah completes the educational process of cultural and social refinement (his understanding of *Derekh Eretz*).

Although "low culture" or "degenerative humanism" corrupts Torah ideals, this does not negate the intrinsic value of "good and true culture." Indeed, Jews should rejoice when mankind is informed and enlightened by this "good culture."[31] In Dayan Grunfeld's words:

> [According to R. Hirsch] As the Torah was given to develop our human gifts and faculties, it is unthinkable that it should not be in agreement with those products of human civilization and culture which bring man near to God and a life under moral law. The aim of the Torah is rather to proclaim the ideal of a religious humanism.[32]

---

28   *ITH*, xciii.
29   *COT, Bereshit* 3:24.
30   *Tanna Debei Eliyahu Rabbah* 1:1 and *Va-Yikra Rabbah* 9:3.
31   Ibid.
32   *ITH*, xciii.

Religious Humanism versus Secular Humanism

Broadly speaking, religious humanism is an integration of humanistic values and religious doctrine. Although much of R. Hirsch's thought has been categorized as religious humanism, he often contrasted the Torah's moral ethic with a purely secular humanism.[33] In his view, humanity is not fully capable of ethical morality and self-fulfillment without belief in God or religious dogma.[34] Man can only achieve the ideal humanism by heeding two existing revelations: the natural revelation in every man's soul and the divine supernatural revelation at Sinai. In the following passage, R. Hirsch expresses the ideal integration:

> Israel was chosen to symbolize the meeting between Humanism and Torah. But there are heralds of God's truth and instruments of His purposes, who show man the divine and human elements in his heart. Thus, modern Humanism is a means to combine the religious and the human ideal by striving after the true, the good, and the beautiful.[35]

In R. Hirsch's view, no room remains for a contradiction between Judaism and humanism. "Judaism is simply humanism on a higher, divine plane."[36] R. Hirsch, however, qualified this radical position by stating that although man needs to rely on his moral conscience, he may never deny his divine obligations. These obligations were revealed to the Jewish People at Sinai, and thus the divine will was recognized.[37]

R. Hirsch's approach to secular humanism is apparent in his treatment of the concept of natural morality. R. Hirsch lived at a time when the existence of an ethical morality independent of religion, essential to a secular humanistic position, was hotly debated. R. Hirsch clashed with the Reformers of his time, specifically Abraham Geiger,[38] who claimed that the character of the Torah must depend on man's individual conscience and his own moral judgment. Although R. Hirsch, too, believed in a natural morality present in the world, it must be fettered and defined by religion. As noted above, R. Hirsch stressed time and time again, "within the

---

[33] *ITH,* xc and *COT, Bereshit* 3:24. Also see R. Hirsch's criticism of Mendelssohn's philosophy in *TNL, Letter* 18.

[34] Ibid., lxxxix–xcvii.

[35] *CW,* VI, 316. See also his *Commentary* on Psalm 47.

[36] *ITH,* xci; see also *COT, Bereshit* 2:16.

[37] *Intro to JE,* xx.

[38] Abraham Geiger, *Wissenschaftilche Zeitschrift fur Judische Theologi,* IV, 11 cited in Grunfeld, *ITH,* lxxvii.

circle of Judaism the Divine Law must be the soil out of which your intellectual and spiritual life is to grow, not vice versa. You must not, from your intellectual and spiritual life, produce the basis on which to establish a Divine Law."[39] "Humanism is only a stepping stone towards a higher conception of man."[40]

An expression of this debate was the questioned acceptance of Immanuel Kant's theory of autonomy of will, i.e. moral self-legislation.[41] As a whole, the reformers used Kant's theory as the sole principle of all moral laws and all duties which accompany them. Kant posited that any law coming from outside (heteronomy), even if that outsider is God himself, must be subject to scrutiny of man's own conscience and moral self-legislation. R. Hirsch, vehemently opposed to this view, maintained that the Reformers looked at the Torah from the "outside" and applied their own preconceived notions, instead of examining Judaism from within and viewing the sources of Judaism as given phenomena.[42]

However, R. Hirsch certainly believed in the innate human desire for the moral life. R. Hirsch often wrote of a conscience which is embedded in every human breast. In fact, R. Hirsch celebrated Psalms as a book that inspires all of mankind. "For far beyond the confines of the Jewish People, even today, the Psalms still serve to lift up to God the emotions of all those who seek Him."[43] For R. Hirsch, this human conscience can be seen as "the Voice of God."[44] He explained that this innate morality is common to all human beings and is the basis for the seven Noahide Laws.[45] As noted above, R. Hirsch made one major caveat. God is the highest moral authority and, therefore, this universal morality must be seen as a commandment from God, not as a result of human logic and reasoning.[46]

According to R. Hirsch, natural morality can dictate how one should treat his fellow man. Either through Kant's categorical imperative, or

---

[39]   Hirsch, Preface to *Horeb*. For a fuller treatment of this issue see Aharon Lichtenstein, "Does Judaism Recognize an Ethic Independent of *Halakha*?", *Leaves Of Faith: The World of Jewish Living*, II (Ktav, 2004), 33–56.

[40]   *Intro to JE*, xx.

[41]   Immanuel Kant, *Critique of Practical Reason*, Book I chapter I, Theorem IV (1788).

[42]   Grunfeld, *ITH*.

[43]   *The Hirsch Tehillim* (Feldheim, 2014) xvii.

[44]   *TNL, Letter* 15.

[45]   *COT, Bereshit,* 2:16, 17.

[46]   Ibid. R. Hirsch followed the view of Rambam which we discuss in more detail below.

through Hillel's identical universal law,[47] man can logically reach a conclusion as to how to relate to his peers. Similarly, the recognition of God does not need revelation, as it can be found in nature.[48] Nevertheless, revelation is needed in order for man to know how to relate to himself and how to treat nature.[49]

In summation, R. Hirsch's position was quite contentious. While traditionalists may have dismissed humanism altogether, R. Hirsch embraced it as part of his ideal vision. On the other hand, humanists rejected the religious component which R. Hirsch saw as essential to a full understanding of humanism. Influenced by Kant's theory of autonomy, many of R. Hirsch's opponents believed everything, including divine law, must be measured by human reasoning. R. Hirsch never tired of stressing his emphatic disagreement. In R. Hirsch's view, universalism and humanism are central to Judaism. The Bible begins with man, not a Jew. Judaism welcomes every progression, enlightenment, and virtue, no matter the medium through which it comes. However, this does not mean that human reasoning gives credence to the divine law. Revelation is obligatory and valued, regardless of its conformity with human logic.

Abraham, the Religious Humanist

R. Hirsch naturally points to Abraham as the ideal for his conception of religious humanism. After both his circumcision and the *Akeidah*, acts of tremendous religious significance which may have brought about separation between him and mankind in general, Abraham remains unaltered in his behavior towards humanity.

> We see Abraham, with the pain inflicted by this sign still fresh, sitting before his tent in the heat of the sun and looking out for weary travelers, inviting idolatrous strangers into his house and showing mercy and kindness and the love of God to all his fellow-men without distinction.[50]

In contrast with how some have claimed that the Jews see themselves as the circumcised and "favored ones," R. Hirsch describes Abraham's

---

47 "That which is distasteful if done to you, do not do to your fellow man." See *Shabbat* 31a.
48 See R. Hirsch's commentary *Tehillim* 19.
49 For a fuller understanding of R. Hirsch's approach to the need for revelation see *TNL, Letters* 10, 11 and *ITH*, lxxxii-lxxxix.
50 *JE*, II, 219.

attitude towards the uncircumcised after his circumcision as "entirely unaltered." In fact, his only worry was that people would draw away from him.[51]

And again, after the *Akeidah,* Abraham and Isaac are powerfully depicted by R. Hirsch as returning to their attendants. They did not leave the rest of mankind behind on their journey towards spirituality. This, for R. Hirsch, symbolizes their returning to their duty of brotherly love for all of humanity.[52]

Appreciation for All of Mankind

'Love your neighbor as yourself' (*Va-Yikra* 19:18). R. Akiva taught that this is the great, all-embracing, comprehensive principle [of the Torah]. Ben Azai taught that *'Zeh sefer toldot ha-Adam,* This is the book of Mankind' is the great, all-embracing comprehensive principle [of the Torah].[53]

Fitting with his vision of the unity of all of mankind, R. Hirsch, interpreting Ben Azai's statement, understands *'Zeh sefer toldot ha-Adam'* as the "brotherhood of mankind" and the all-encompassing theme which encapsulates the entirety of the Torah.[54] In fact, according to R. Hirsch, "the first truth which stands at the head of the history of Man is that all men are human beings, and the image of God [in man] is never completely lost."[55]

Early in his career, R. Hirsch wrote a polemical essay in the wake of a controversy over the Jewish view of the Christian God in 1841. In this piece, R. Hirsch highlighted the Torah's humanistic approach to the stranger, the *ger,* the non-Jew. R. Hirsch responded sharply to the claim of "Jewish tribalism" by noting the Torah's emphasis on loving "the stranger."[56]

---

51 *COT, Bereshit* 18:1.

52 *COT, Bereshit* 22:19.

53 *Talmud Yerushalmi, Nedarim,* 9:4; *Midrash Rabbah Bereshit* 24; *Sifra Kedoshim* 2:4.

54 *COT, Bereshit* 5:1.

55 Ibid.

56 *CW,* IX, 109–111. Although, in this passage, R. Hirsch deviated from traditional rabbinic exegesis in his interpretations of the *ger,* Moshe Y. Miller suggests that R. Hirsch interpreted Scripture here based on his understanding of the simple meaning of the text. Traditional rabbinic exegesis allows for this form of interpretation. Miller suggests that his reliance on the simple meaning of Scripture allowed R. Hirsch to avoid some discriminatory rabbinic interpretations that did

R. Hirsch also emphasized the ability of all human beings to reach spiritual heights. In his oft-cited essay "The Jewish Woman," R. Hirsch wrote: "The view of the sages of Judaism is that every human being, regardless of class, sex or nationality, is capable of intellectual and moral perfection."[57] Similarly, R. Joseph B. Soloveitchik describes the belief that "all men are equally servants of God" and "each person has a unique mission and is equally worthy" as "Judaic humanism or democracy."[58] These statements are definitional to the humanistic outlook.

With the rise of the German Idealism movement at the turn of the 19th century, a somewhat renewed interest in the writings of Immanuel Kant began. It is therefore not surprising that R. Hirsch was very taken by Kant. In fact, he studied Kant's writings regularly with a young Heinrich Graetz.[59] This appreciation continued, and perhaps was even more fully expressed, for an admirer of Kant, the romantic poet, Friedrich von Schiller (1759–1805). R. Hirsch participated in the 100th-anniversary of Schiller's birth. At the celebration in Frankfurt, R. Hirsch delivered a famous address known as the *Schillerrede*.[60] In this speech R. Hirsch spoke of the noble expressions of compassion, justice, and human decency he saw in Schiller's writings.[61] One would be hard pressed to find a parallel to this kind of a celebratory attitude in other traditional rabbinic leaders.

In a similar vein, R. Hirsch saw many positive elements in the emergence of emancipation, a more humane society and the newfound freedom granted to Jews in his day. As early as in his *The Nineteen Letters,* he expressed his belief that the goal of *galut* and emancipation is to allow for Jewish influence on the world stage. R. Hirsch encouraged his readers to share his vision of "every son of Israel a respected, influential model of righteousness and love, spreading not Judaism—this is forbidden—but pure humanitarianism."[62]

---

not align with his humanistic perspective. See Miller, *Rabbi Samson Raphael Hirsch*, 201.

57 *CW*, VIII, 135.
58 Joseph B. Soloveitchik, *Out of the Whirlwind* (Ktav, 2003), xi and 148. I am indebted to R. Hanan Balk for this source.
59 Klugman 243 citing Graetz's personal diary.
60 *CW*, VII, 61. See also Marc B. Shapiro, "Rabbi Samson Raphael Hirsch and Friedrich von Schiller," *Torah U-Madda*, 15. (Yeshiva University, 2008–9), 172–187.
61 See Klugman 285.
62 *TNL, Letter* 16. In R. Bernard Drachman's translation (first published in 1899 and later republished by Feldheim in 1959) this line appears as "disseminating among the nations not specific Judaism, for proselytism is interdicted, but pure humanity."

R. Hirsch wrote that in his day, after experiencing centuries of persecution, the Jewish People were seeing much of this "barbarism" and "ma-
nia" disappearing. R. Hirsch contended that our ancestors would view
contemporary society as a more "humane civilization." Respect for what
is right and for the truth, for human dignity and freedom, have become
rooted in the minds of men."[63] R. Hirsch even attributed "mighty victo-
ries [for] godly truths" to this society.[64] At the same time, he was painfully
aware of the young Jews breaking from tradition and leaving in droves
because of this new-found freedom.[65]

R. Hirsch also addressed passages of the Torah which could be seen
by the modern reader as barbarous or primitive. When elucidating the
passages of the Torah commanding the annihilation of the Canaanite nations, R. Hirsch emphasized the exceptional nature of these passages.[66] In
his thorough analysis of R. Hirsch's attitude towards non-Jews, Rabbi Dr.
Moshe Y. Miller argues that because of his humanistic perspective, R.
Hirsch could not conceive of the Torah countenancing barbaric behavior
as the norm.[67] In fact, Dr. Ephraim Chamiel notes that R. Hirsch interprets the Torah's treatment of the *ger* as Judaism's complete rejection of
racism.[68] However, Chamiel notes an apparent contraction in R. Hirsch's
presentation of the *ger*.[69] Elsewhere, R. Hirsch, following rabbinic interpretations, assumes the term *ger* to refer to a convert.[70] However, in *Shemot*
22:20, R. Hirsch seems to deviate from the traditional rabbinic exegesis
and translates the term *ger* as a non-Jew. This kind of selective interpretation, which ignores the established rabbinic position, is something R.
Hirsch himself rejected in many places. How can he be guilty of this himself?

In response, Miller suggests that R. Hirsch was not re-interpreting Judaism based on an external agenda. Rather, his intention was for the
reader to read these verses according to their simple meaning and original
context. R. Hirsch believed, "rabbinic interpretation, though imbued with
halakhic weight, was never intended to negate the simple meaning of the

---

63   *CW*, I, 131–132.
64   Ibid.
65   Ibid.
66   *COT, Devarim* 7:16.
67   Miller 252. See also *COT, Shemot* 12:44 for his treatment of the non-Jewish slave.
68   *COT, Shemot* 22:20.
69   Ephraim Chamiel, *The Middle Way: The Emergence of Modern Religious Trends in Nine-
      teenth-Century Judaism*, vol. 2, trans. Jeffrey Green (Academic Studies, 2014), 319–
      323.
70   COT, *Devarim* 1:16.

verses."[71] The Torah itself commands us to treat the *ger* well because of the Jewish experience of slavery in Egypt. It is clear from the simple understanding of the verses in the Torah that its message applies to any stranger or foreigner living among Jews, regardless of race, religion, or ethnicity.[72]

Human Brotherly Love: A Study of R. Hirsch's Attitude Toward Non-Jews

In 1884, just four years before the end of his life, R. Hirsch was asked by R. Elḥanan Spector to publish a response to an anti-Semitic campaign conducted in czarist Russia against the Talmud.[73] R. Hirsch agreed and wrote his important essay "Talmud: Its Teachings on Social Virtues." Contained in this essay is one of the most radical and far-reaching examples of R. Hirsch's humanism. The particular passage of interest is short but highly significant:

> The Talmud also teaches that we have human and social obligations to all men, even to heathens and idolaters; to help their poor, to attend to their sick, to bury their dead,[74] to support their aged,[75] to respect their wise men and to recite a special blessing on seeing an outstanding and famous non-Jewish scholar.[76] That is so with heathens and idolaters; how much more so then with the non-Jews who serve the God of the Bible, the Creator of heaven and earth, who keep all the cardinal commandments (the so-called Noahide Laws)... The Talmud puts them in regard to the duties between man and man on exactly the same level as Jews. They have a claim to the benefit

---

71 Miller 200–202. Miller, however, notes that in general, R. Hirsch considered the rabbinic exegesis of biblical verses, particularly when it pertains to the halakhah, to be the only legitimate way of interpreting the text. See, for example, *COT Shemot*, 21:2.

72 Miller notes that Ibn Ezra's interpretation of *ger* in these verses as "any stranger living among Jews" may have served as precedent for R. Hirsch. See Ibn Ezra, *Shemot* 22:20.

73 See the editorial footnote, which appears in both *CW*, VII, 209 and *JE*, 155. Apparently, the essay achieved its purpose. New prohibitions on yeshivot and on printings of the Talmud did not materialize at that time.

74 *Gittin* 61a.

75 *Kiddushin* 32b.

76 *Berakhot* 58a.

of all the duties not only of justice but also of active human brotherly love.[77]

Although R. Hirsch already wrote of "the love a Jew should feel for our non-Jewish brethren," in *The Nineteen Letters*,[78] here R. Hirsch goes even further with his universalism, arguing for the equality of Jews and "believing non-Jews." To be sure, in Jewish law, respect and assistance are obligations to all human beings regardless of their religion.[79] However, traditionally, there have always been differences between Jews and non-Jews in the Jewish legal system.[80] R. Hirsch argues this only applies to non-Jews who do not accept the seven Noahide Laws. Those who do accept them are viewed on exactly the same level as Jews in Jewish law. R. Joseph Elias suggests that R. Hirsch would formally classify the enlightened contemporary non-Jewish fellow citizen he is referring to here as a "*ger toshav*," a non-Jewish resident, even without a formal acceptance of these commandments in *beit din*, a Jewish legal court.[81]

---

[77] *JE*, II, 168. To my knowledge, there have been three English translations of this essay: Grunfeld's, which I cite, *CW*, VII, 209–244, and W. Stern's, titled "The Talmud: Its Relation to Judaism and the Attitude of the Jews Towards Society," reprinted from *The Jewish Standard* (London, 1884). In the Stern translation, which appeared shortly after the original was published, the last phrase is translated as "the display of active philanthropy." In *CW*, 225, it is translated as "active charity and compassion." Perhaps both are a more loyal rendering of Rambam's citation, as I will explain below. I am indebted to Professor Michah Gottlieb for this source and the original German essay. In the original German, the passage reads, "*des Talmuds hinsichtlich der Pflichten von Mensch zu Mensch dem Juden völlig gleich und haben den An spruch nicht nur auf alle Paichten der Gerechtigkeit, sondern auch auf den Erweis thätiger Menschenliebe.*" I chose to follow the Grunfeld translation because it most closely resembles the original. Grunfeld translates "*thätiger Menschenliebe*" as active human *brotherly* love.

[78] *TNL*, *Letter* 15. Note that although R. Hirsch advocates for love for our "non-Jewish brethren," in the same *Letter* he rejects "joining his [the non-Jew's] family." He attributes the desire for assimilation into non-Jewish culture to the new advent of universalism so prevalent in his age. Interestingly, he saw his own vision of religious humanism as immune from such a critique.

[79] See for example *Avot* 1:12 and *Gittin* 61a. Noteworthy is Rambam's formulation in *Melakhim* 10:12 of the instructive of *Darkei Shalom* as an expression of "*God is good to all, and His mercies extend upon all his works*" (*Tehillim* 145:9) and, "*her ways are ways of pleasantness, and all her paths are peace*" (*Mishlei* 3:17).

[80] For example, the obligation of returning a lost object is a mandate only for co-religionists. See *Bava Metzia* 24b and *Bava Kamma* 38a.

[81] Elias, *TNL*, 219–220.

This explanation, however, is problematic. In his discussion of the subject in *Horeb*[82] R. Hirsch stresses, in accordance with the position of Rambam, that a formal acceptance of the Noahide laws in the presence of a *"beit din,"* is required to attain this status.[83] Furthermore, R. Hirsch and *Rambam* maintain that in order to achieve the status of a *ger toshav* (as well as *Ḥasidei Umot Ha-Olam,* righteous gentiles who have a portion in the World-to-Come) the Noahide laws must be accepted by the non-Jew as divinely revealed to Moshe at Sinai.[84] A gentile who merely follows the seven Noahide laws because they are logical and ethical, without a formal acceptance in *beit din* recognizing these laws as divinely ordained, would not be sufficient to grant him the status of a *ger toshav.*

It should be noted that R. Yisrael Lipshitz (1782–1860), in his *Tiferet Yisrael,* maintains that even if the contemporary non-Jew cannot attain the status of a *ger toshav,* righteous gentiles still have a portion in the World-to-Come. In an exceptional passage, R. Lipshitz extols the virtues of *ḥasidei umot ha-olam.* He asserts that even if our sages had not told us that righteous gentiles have a portion in the World-to-Come, we would know they do through logic alone. It is untenable that they not be rewarded for their contributions to the Jewish People and to society.[85]

However, R. Hirsch, accepting the position of Rambam, apparently would not subscribe to this position. Even more problematic for modern application is Rambam's position that we can only accept a *ger toshav* during the era when the Jubilee year is observed. Rambam explicitly rejects the application of the *ger toshav* status in the present era, stating that "in

---

[82] *Ḥoreb*, V, *Mitzvoth*, Ch. 77, 503.

[83] *Mishneh Torah, Melakhim* 8:10 and *Issurei Biah* 14:7. This ruling is based on the Tannaic position of *Ḥakhamim* in *Avodah Zarah* 64b. See also *Tur, Yoreh De'ah* 124 and *Shulkhan Arukh, Yoreh De'ah* 124:2 who take this position. The view of Rashi, however, is more complex. Although in *Avodah Zarah* 24b, he concurs with the above position, in many places he endorses the position of R. Meir in *Avodah Zarah* 64b that a *ger toshav* is only required to reject idol worship and need not keep all of the seven Noahide laws. See Rashi, *Va-Yikra* 25:35, Rashi, *Pesaḥim* 21b and *Yevamot* 48b.

[84] *Mishneh Torah, Melakhim* 8:11. *Kesef Mishneh* (ibid.) writes that Rambam's source for this was his own logic. However, there appear to be some sources in *Ḥazal* that support Rambam. For example, see *Mishnat Rabbi Eliezer, Parshah Shishit* (New York, 1933), 121. See also Yehuda Gershuni, *Mishpat Ha-Melukhah* (New York, 1950), 260 and Avraham Grodzinsky, *Torat Avraham* (*Yeshivat Kollel Avreikhim Torat Avraham*, 1993), 2.

[85] Yisrael Lipshitz, *Tiferet Yisrael, Boaz, Avot* 3:1.

our times, even if [a gentile] makes a commitment to observe the entire Torah with the exception of one minor point, he is not accepted."[86]

R. Elias argues that R. Hirsch may have seen the positive influence of Christianity upon the Western world and the ethical norms embraced by Western society as constituting a conscious fulfillment of God's will.[87] Although this may address why R. Hirsch did not require a formal acceptance of the Noahide laws as God-given, it remains unclear how Rambam's requirement of a *beit din* is fulfilled.[88]

Perhaps we can suggest a different approach. Professor David Berger notes R. Hirsch's position is similar to that of the non-discriminatory position of Meiri cited above.[89] Perhaps R. Hirsch is endorsing *Meiri*'s claim that non-Jews "bound by the ways of civility" are to be treated equally to Jews.

However, this approach can be challenged on multiple grounds. First of all, it is unclear how much of *Meiri's Beit Ha-Beḥirah* R. Hirsch had access to in 1884. *Meiri's* commentary to all the tractates of the Talmud was only available in 1920, after the unearthing of a single complete manuscript found in Parma and later published by R. Avraham Sofer.[90] Sec-

---

86   *Mishneh Torah, Issurei Biah* 14:7–8. See also *Arakhin* 29b. Note that there were *Rishonim* who disagreed with Rambam. See *Ra'avad, Hasagot, Avodah Zarah* 10:6 and *Shu"t Rashba*, 1, 182.

87   See Meiri, *Beit Ha-Beḥirah, Bava Kamma* 37b; *Rambam, Ma'akhalot Asurot* 11:7–8; *Kesef Mishneh*, ibid., concerning the status of the non-Jew who does not worship idols but has not formally accepted the Noahide laws.

88   For a list of authorities who do not require the gentile's formal acceptance to achieve the status of a *ger toshav*, see J. David Bleich, *Contemporary Halakhic Problems*, Vol. VII (Maggid, 2016), 176.

89   David Berger, "Jews, Gentiles, and the Modern Egalitarian Ethos: Some Tentative Thoughts" in Marc D. Stern, (ed.), *Formulating Responses in an Egalitarian Age* (Rowman & Littlefield, 2005), 100. See also Miller 271–274 who claims that R. Hirsch may have been influenced by the position of *Meiri*. Miller also suggests that R. Hirsch could have been influenced by a number of other Jewish thinkers who relegated discriminatory laws against gentiles to pagans. R. Moshe Rivkes's comments in *Be'er Ha-Golah* (*Ḥoshen Mishpat* 388:60), R. Shlomo Ben Moshe of Khelm in his *Mirkevet Ha-Mishnah, Nizkei Mamon* 8:5, and his teachers R. Ettlinger and R. Bernays took this position.

90   However, many other writings on various individual tractates were available before this time (e.g. *Megillah* Amsterdam, 1759; *Sukkah* Berlin, 1859; *Shabbat* Vienna, 1864). See Haym Soloveitchik, "Rupture and Reconstruction: The Transformation of Contemporary Orthodoxy," *Tradition* 28:4 (1994), 120–121, n. 54; J. David Bleich, *Contemporary Halakhic Problems*, IV (Ktav, 1995), 159; Gavin Michal, "The Meiri Texts: Lost or Ignored?"

ondly, if we are to assume R. Hirsch's position is based on *Meiri*, the requirement of the acceptance of Noahide laws is unnecessary. *Meiri*'s oft-repeated phrase "nations bound by the ways of religion and civility" does not explicitly invoke the requirement of accepting Noahide commandments or the *ger toshav* status. Although some[91] claim this to be the foundation of the position of Meiri, this may be difficult to maintain, as Berger notes:

> In a number of instances, Ha-Meiri extends a more advantageous legal status to the 'nations bound by the ways of religions' than the Talmud does to the individual *ger toshav*. Thus, their lives should be saved even at the cost of desecrating the Sabbath, and a Jew who kills such a person is apparently subject to the same penalty as one who kills a Jew.[92]

In fact, although R. Hirsch presents his position as "the view of the Talmud," the source indicated in his footnote is Rambam, who writes, "we treat a *ger toshav* with respect and loving-kindness (*derekh eretz* and *gemilut ḥasadim*) as we do a Jew."[93] R. Hirsch is endorsing Rambam, not *Meiri*.[94] This passage is most likely a liberal reformulation of Rambam's language. Rambam wrote, "we treat the *ger toshav* with *derekh eretz* and *gemilut ḥasadim*." R. Hirsch is translating *gemilut ḥasadim* as *thätiger Menschenliebe*, active human love.

However, this too is problematic. As mentioned above, Rambam's *beit din* requirement makes it difficult to understand how R. Hirsch is citing the opinion of Rambam. In the same vein, unlike R. Hirsch's position, Rambam does not grant the *ger toshav* completely equal standing with Jews. In Rambam's view, in contrast to the murdering of a Jew, the murdering

---

<www.kotzkblog.com/2017/01/112-meiri-texts-lost-or-ignored.html>
It should be noted that the relevant comments of Meiri cited in *Shittah Mekubetzet* (*Bava Kamma* 113a) were already known to many. In fact, the *Shittah Mekubetzet* citation of Meiri is discussed by the *Ḥatam Sofer* (*Kovetz Shu"t Ḥatam Sofer*, 90) who, believing it to be inauthentic, writes, "it is a *mitzvah* to erase it."

91 Berger 100 cites R. Avraham Yitzḥak Kook (*Iggerot Re'iyah*, I, 99) and R. Aharon Soloveitchik (*Sefer Peraḥ Matteh Aharon, Sefer Madda*, 1997, 144–145) as well as others, who argue along similar lines.

92 Ibid., 97.

93 *Mishneh Torah, Melakhim* 10:12.

94 Lest someone think that this citation was added by subsequent editors, Rambam's citation also appears in the original German version authored by R. Hirsch. See Hirsch, *Über Die Beziehung Des Talmuds zum Judenthum und zu der Sozialen Stellung Seuner Bekenner* (*Zu Frankfurt Am Maim, Verlag Von J. Kauffman*, 1884), 18.

of a *ger toshav* is not punishable in *beit din*.[95] It appears that R. Hirsch's liberal translation of the position of Rambam went well beyond the original intent of Rambam himself.

Perhaps the most formidable challenge to R. Hirsch's position is from the Talmud itself. Whether the foundation of R. Hirsch's position rests on the position of *Meiri* or Rambam, we can question the very notion of halakhic equality for *geirei toshav* altogether.

There are areas of *Halakhah* in which it is difficult to argue for a non-discriminatory position. One such area is the issue of triage. The Mishnah in *Horiot* (13b) states that in a situation of triage, "A man precedes the woman…a Kohen before a Levi, a Levi before a Yisrael." Many explain this hierarchy which decides who has priority in cases of triage is based on the different levels of *kedushah* inherent to each level. This is demonstrated by how many commandments the persons in questions have respectively in addition to other factors.[96] Accordingly, in a triage scenario, a non-Jew, who only has seven commandments, would certainly be saved after a Jew who has 613. Therefore, although the Mishnah and Talmud introduce other factors into the equation,[97] in regard to basic priority, a

---

95   *Mishneh Torah, Rotzeiaḥ Vi-Shemirat Nefesh* 2:11. *Kesef Mishneh* argues that one is liable in the heavenly courts. This, however, does not amount to equal standing. *Meshekh Ḥokhmah* (*Shemot* 21:14) claims that one is not liable for the death penalty because the sin is so egregious it is not deserving of the atonement achieved. Although tempting, this approach is radically novel and most likely cannot be attributed to Rambam. I am indebted to R. Dr. Jeremy Wieder for this source.

96   See *Taz, Yoreh De'ah* 252:6 and *Biur Ha-Gra, Yoreh De'ah*, 251:18 who quotes Talmud Yerushalmi (3:5). R. Hershel Schachter ("Piskei Corona #15: Triage in Medical Decisions, Updated," YUTorah.org, 2020)
www.yutorah.org/lectures/lecture.cfm/951531/rabbi-hershel-schachter/piskei-corona-15-triage-in-medical-decisions-updated-/
explains that *Gra* is defining the hierarchy in *Horiot* as prioritizing public need. See also R. Yaakov Emden's comments in his *Migdal Oz, Even Ha-Boḥen, Pinah* 1. R. Moshe Feinstein (*Iggerot Moshe, Ḥoshen Mishpat* II, 73:2) rules that the *Halakhah* is to treat whoever arrives first. When two people in need arrive simultaneously, the decision should be made based on medical suitability. The one who has the best chance of being treated and cured should be given the available bed. However, he does not invoke the hierarchy delineated in *Horiot*. This position of R. Moshe (as told by R. Shabtai Rappaport in a public lecture) is also cited approvingly by R. Aharon Lichtenstein in Ḥayyim Sabato, *Seeking His Presence: Conversations With Rabbi Aharon Lichtenstein* (Trans. Binyamin Shalom), (Yediot, 2016), 99. For more on this topic, see Alan Jotkowitz, "A Man Takes Precedence over a Woman When It Comes to Saving a Life," *Tradition*, 47:1 (2014), 48–68.

97   For example, one's own merit can help one move up the hierarchy. The Mishnah states that a *mamzer talmid ḥakham* (illegitimate Torah scholar) takes precedence

non-Jew is not equal to a Jew. Although normative *Halakhah* is not to give Jews precedence, this is because of a concern of animosity (*eivah*) without changing the basic hierarchy.[98] To my knowledge, neither Rambam nor *Meiri* challenge this basic hierarchy even in the case of a *ger toshav*.[99]

Perhaps one can suggest that R. Hirsch's position of complete equality may be an expression of normative *Halakhah* which is generally to treat Jews and non-Jews equally even in situations of triage, the Mishnah in *Horiot* notwithstanding. Indeed, towards the beginning of his essay on the Talmud, he writes, "I have selected texts that have become particularly embedded in the consciousness of the Jewish nation and consequently have played a decisive role in molding fundamental Jewish ideas and principles."[100] In particular, R. Hirsch cites R. Yeḥezkel Landau, R. Eleazar Fleckeles,[101] and R. Yaakov Emden as modern precedents for his position.[102]

R. Hirsch's goal was to show the Talmud's positive influence on the Jewish community and its principles. Perhaps it was more important for R. Hirsch to record what he saw as the accepted communal practice of

---

over a *Kohen Gadol* (High Priest). Another factor is public need. The *Meshuaḥ Milḥamah* (the priest anointed for war) takes precedence over the *S'gan Kohen Gadol* (deputy High Priest). Rashi explains that even though the *S'gan Kohen Gadol* has an elevated level of *Kedushah*, he comes second because of the public role of the *Meshuaḥ Milḥamah* during wartime.

[98] See *Shu"t Ḥatam Sofer, Ḥoshen Mishpat*, 5, *Hashmatot*, 194; *Shu"t Ḥatam Sofer, Yoreh De'ah*, II, 131, cited in *Pitḥei Teshuvah, Yoreh De'ah* 145:2; *Iggerot Moshe, Yoreh De'ah* no. 184. For a fuller treatment, see R. Hershel Schachter's *Be-Ikvei Ha-Tzon* (Beit Midrash of Flatbush, 1997), no. 9, 50–52.

[99] In fact, *Sifra, Behar, Parshah* 5, *Perek* 6, no. 1 is explicit that a Jew takes precedence over a *ger toshav* in a situation of triage. For other areas of discrimination between Jews and *geirei toshav*, see Shlomo Yosef Zevin (ed.), *Encyclopedia Talmudit*, VI, *Ger Toshav* (Jerusalem, 1954), 290–304.

[100] *CW*, VII, 210 and *JE*, II, 156.

[101] Besides R. Emden, who wrote of the importance of the other monotheistic faiths in his commentary on *Avot* 4:13, R. Hirsch does not cite the works he was referring to. However, he was likely referring to R. Landau's prefatory disclaimer in his preface to his *Noda Be-Yehudah* (Prague, 1776) where he posits an anti-discriminatory position towards gentiles and R. Eleazar Fleckeles's introduction to his *Teshuvah me-Ahavah* (Prague, 1808), titled *Kesut Einayim*. For more on R. Fleckeles, see my "From the Pages of Tradition: Rabbi Eleazer Fleckeles: An Early Rabbinic Humanist," *Tradition* 54:2 (2022), 133–149. For more on these and other rabbinic disclaimers about non-Jews, see Miller 36–46.

[102] *CW*, VII, 227. Both R. Landau and R. Fleckeles emphasize equality before the law for both Jews and gentiles. Neither of them, however, go as far as R. Hirsch who argues for "active human brotherly love" for gentiles.

equality for Jews and non-Jews, than to tie up the loose ends of all the relevant Talmudic passages. This may be true; however, R. Hirsch clearly emphasizes the acceptance of the Noahide laws as the rationale for granting a non-Jew equality in *Halakhah*. As we noted, this needs explanation. What happened to the *beit din* requirement for accepting a *ger toshav*?

One may ask what is the practical difference? If we are required by *Halakhah* to treat non-Jews with equality from the pragmatic standpoint (*eivah*), why is R. Hirsch's endorsement of equality—and even of brotherly love—of interest? To my mind, this is a misplaced claim. From a public policy standpoint, there may be no difference. However, from a moral perspective, there is a world of a difference between what has been deemed the "self-serving"—or even immoral—nature of the *eivah* approach and R. Hirsch's humanistic approach.[103]

R. Joseph B. Soloveitchik is said to have made this point. Professor Gerald Blidstein records that R. Soloveitchik was once asked, in reference to the traditional rationale of *darkhei shalom* or *eivah* permitting Jews to desecrate the Sabbath in order to save the life of gentiles:

> Whether, aside from the substantive content of the decision itself, he felt morally comfortable with the rationale he had given. He said no, he was in fact uncomfortable with it; and he then proceeded to propose, provisionally, an approach in which the ethical level of a culture determined its status, something very similar to what we find in Meiri (who gave a similar rationale for allowing *Ḥilul Shabbat*, clearly *de-oraita*) for saving the life of the gentile religionist of his day.[104]

---

[103] In 1965, Professor Israel Shahak wrote a letter to the *Haaretz* newspaper decrying Orthodox injustice, after he witnessed an Orthodox Jew who refused to use his telephone to call for an ambulance for a non-Jew, because it was Shabbat. See Dan Rickman, "Israel Shahak: A Voice of Controversy," *The Guardian* (London, 2009). For a fiery response claiming that Shahak fabricated the incident, see Immanuel Jakobovits, "A Modern Blood Libel: *L'Affaire Shahak*," *Tradition* 8:2 (1966), 58–65. This incident led to a legal ruling by the then Chief Rabbi Isser Yehuda Unterman (cited in Jakobovits), who ruled that the Sabbath can and must be broken to save anyone's life, based on the *eivah* principle. Shahak saw this as a cowardly response, which did not address the fundamental moral injustice. He developed this view in his *Jewish History, Jewish Religion: The Weight of Three Thousand Years* (Pluto, 1994), where he argues that rabbinic Judaism is intrinsically discriminatory against non-Jews. As a response to Shahak alone, R. Hirsch's approach is worthy of attention.

[104] Gerald Blidstein, "Halakha and Democracy," *Tradition* 32:1 (1997), 30. I am indebted to R. Dr. Jeremy Wieder for this source.

Returning to R. Hirsch and his position, it is possible that R. Hirsch's advocacy for equality for gentiles is purely an expression of the normative practice of *Halakhah*. However, his emphasis on "active human brotherly love" still remains without precedent. Although this could merely be a reformulation of the position of Rambam cited earlier, taken at face value, R. Hirsch appears to be vying for a universal love not found in Rambam, Meiri, or the Talmud. While Hillel teaches in *Avot* (1:12) "[to] love [all] mankind (*briyot*)," brotherly love, the term R. Hirsch uses, is traditionally underscored by the dictum, "Love your fellow as yourself" (*Va-Yikra* 19:18), and limited to *re'ekha* or fellow Jews.[105] Was R. Hirsch extending brotherly love to non-Jews unprecedented, perhaps even unsubstantiated, in Jewish tradition?[106] As noted above, this essay was written to counteract an anti-Semitic campaign in czarist Russia. Perhaps this is an example of R. Hirsch's accommodation or apologetics. Granted, in light of the dangers of anti-Semitism certainly justified, but for our purposes, these statements would not contribute to the picture of R. Hirsch religious humanism. The historical context notwithstanding, to my mind, one cannot merely discard this passage as unauthentic R. Hirsch. The value of all human beings and a universal emphasis are themes found throughout R. Hirsch's writings. Although this may be his most radical formulation, this passage certainly fits into the general thrust of R. Hirsch's *weltanschauung*.

Whatever approach one takes, it appears from this clause that R. Hirsch is not merely positing an endorsement of the positions of Rambam, Meiri, or the Talmud, none of which wrote of the active love granted to the *ger toshav*. We can never know what he was really thinking. However, as we noted earlier, R. Hirsch was not one to misrepresent his sources or invent an unprecedented approach because of external pressures. Furthermore, although this passage goes somewhat further than his other writings, it is not completely out of character. In fact, he wrote along very

---

105 For example, see Rambam, *Mishneh Torah, De'ot* 6:3–5; *Sefer Ha-Ḥinnukh, Mitzvah* 243; *S'mag, Mitzvot Asei,* no. 9 and *Hagaot Maimoniyot, De'ot* 6:3 exclude a wicked person from the *mitzvah* of loving your fellow man because they are not "fellows" in regard to their *mitzvah* observance. Presumably, this would also be true of gentiles.

106 Although R. Barukh Ha-Levi Epstein, in his *Tosefet Brakhah, Va-Yikra* 19:18, (*Moreshet,* 1939), 161–163, does include non-Jews even within *re'ekha*, this is certainly a minority position. I am indebted to R. Allen Schwartz for this source. R. Aharon Soloveitchik in his *Logic of the Heart, Logic of the Mind* (Genesis, 1991), 70, cites R. Ḥayyim Vital's affirmation of the obligation to love gentiles. Hs source, however, is *ahavat habriyot,* love of mankind. He (ibid. 76–78) argues that brotherly love is to be applied to all people. However, this love is not from the point of view of "logic of the heart" or blind love, but rather based on "logic of the mind." Blind or irrational love is only for Jews.

similar lines at the beginning of his career. Well before the publishing of his essay on the Talmud, R. Hirsch wrote of the "active love" a Jew must display towards Noahide law-abiding gentiles. Therefore, assuming this passage is an authentic representation of R. Hirsch's perspective, I would like to suggest the following explanation.

A careful reading of R. Hirsch will provide us with the correct understanding of his position. First let us return to the *Horeb* passage. In a piece he wrote almost 50 years before his essay on the Talmud, R. Hirsch delineated his approach to gentiles in the modern world. In the context of his treatment of the laws which govern proper boundaries between Jews and non-Jews, R. Hirsch encourages the Jewish People to celebrate humanity's abandonment, for the most part, of idolatry and acceptance of the Noahide laws:

> Israel can rejoice today in the midst of the peoples among whom it mostly lives...Rejoice that in Europe, in America, and in part of Asia and Africa non-Jewish peoples also have become illumined by the Revelation of the One God given to you and have adopted a doctrine which teaches them to perform seven duties.[107]

After noting that this acceptance must be declared before a *beit din*, R. Hirsch declares this person to be a *ger toshav*. He then pens a few sentences which are almost identical to the same passage we are discussing:

> Towards such a man you are not only to practice all the obligations of justice—as indeed also towards any idolater—but the Torah also commands you to perform toward him all the duties required by an active love (*tätiger liebe*). You must esteem him and love him as a genuine man.[108]

Again quoting Rambam who mandates "*gemilut ḥasadim* to the *ger toshav* just as we would treat a Jew," R. Hirsch clearly interprets this term as active love. This may seem strange at first, but this is in fact how R. Hirsch defines *gemilut ḥasadim*. In *Horeb*, R. Hirsch contrasts, *tzedakah* with *gemilut ḥasadim*:

---

[107] *Horeb*, V, Chapter 77, no. 503, p. 379.

[108] Ibid. In the original German, the passage appears as, *"Bflichten tatiger liebe du haft ibn ʒu achten und ʒu lieben als reinen Menfchen*—you are obligated to perform towards him all the duties of active love. You must esteem him and love him as a genuine man." See Hirsch, *Ḥorev: Verluche uber Jillroels Pflichten in der Zerltreung* (Frankfurt Am Main, 1909), 330–331.

But higher, incomparably higher, than *tzedakah*—financial and material charity—stands *gemiluth chasadim,* good works. In *tzedakah* you give away your worldly goods, your wealth; in *gemiluth chasadim* you place on God's sacred altar all the best and noblest you have...for the good of your brethren...In *gemiluth chasadim* you grow the flowers of bliss themselves, become the creator of health, the joy, the peace, the happiness of your neighbor.[109]

Later in the passage, R. Hirsch refers to *gemilut ḥasadim* only "requiring an honest mind [and] a loving heart."[110] Clearly, R. Hirsch's definition of *gemilut ḥasadim* is an active human brotherly love. So quite simply, in his essay on the Talmud, R. Hirsch is citing and translating a comment of Rambam.[111]

However, one is still left wondering, why did R. Hirsch leave out the requirement for *beit din* in his essay on the Talmud when he included it in *Ḥoreb*? Perhaps we can suggest that without a *beit din*, we cannot formally categorize most modern gentiles as *geirei toshav*. However, perhaps in R. Hirsch's view, fundamentally contemporary non-Jews still have the necessary beliefs, characteristics, and behavior of a *ger toshav*.[112] Therefore, although there may be some exceptions (e.g., situations of triage), in general, respect, equality, and love are called for when interacting with them.[113]

---

[109] Ibid., V, *Mitzvot*, 88, 575, p. 432.

[110] Ibid., no. 580, p. 435.

[111] Although one can argue that based on the strict reading of the sources one is required merely to sustain the *ger toshav*. See *Va-Yikra* 25:35 and *Avodah Zarah* 20a, 65a. See *Ramban*, ibid., citing *Torat Kohanim, Behar* 5:3, who rules there is a positive commandment to sustain and rescue a *ger toshav* from harm.

[112] See Nachum Rabinovitch, "A Halakhic View of the Non-Jew," *Tradition* 8:3 (1966), 36–39, who argues the "vast majority of non-Jews should be accorded the treatment of a *ger toshav*." Based on the position of R. Tzvi Hirsch Chajes in *Kol Sifrei Maharatz Ḥayot*, I (Jerusalem, 1958), 489–490, R. Rabinovitch maintains that Christians today have the halakhic status of *geirei toshav*. See his *Melummedei Milḥamah* (Maʻaleh Adumin, 1993), 145.

[113] R. Aharon Soloveitchik similarly argues for such a broad definition of *geirei toshav* (*Sefer Peraḥ Mateh Aharon*, 148). He argues that even for Rambam, a gentile who follows the Noahide laws with no formal acceptance, is to be treated differently than an idol worshiper. He should be supported and is allowed to live in the Land of Israel. See also *COT, Va-Yikra* 25:35, where R. Hirsch writes that the *ger toshav* is permitted to dwell in the land of Israel once he denounces idolatry and accepts the Noahide laws. Interestingly, R. Yosef Eliyahu Henkin (*Ha-Darom* 10, 5719, n8 cited in Rabinovitch 36) argues that the *beit din* requirement is only with respect to providing livelihood and the privilege of living in the land of Israel but is not required to elevate their status from idol worshippers.

If one looks carefully at the passage in *Ḥoreb*, the same point emerges. R. Hirsch encourages us to rejoice over the advent of modern society's large-scale acceptance of monotheism. Rejoicing is still called for, even without the presence of a *beit din* formally vetting the masses of non-Jews living around the world.

Earlier we questioned how R. Hirsch could advocate for brotherly love for non-Jews when this is usually a concept traditionally limited to the relationships between Jews. First, given R. Hirsch's translation of Rambam, he is simply applying what Rambam says, "we treat a *ger toshav* with respect and loving-kindness *as we do a Jew*." Additionally, the term *"Menschenliebe,"* love of humanity, is a love on a universal and human level, different from the love of *"re'ekha"*—love of your neighbor—your fellow Jew. After R. Hirsch encourages the love for the *ger toshav*, he balances this with the remainder of the crucial boundaries between Jews and gentiles. For R. Hirsch, the Jewish People symbolizes and functions in a dual role. They are the model society to be looked to from without for guidance and inspiration, a society which values universal love for all of mankind. But they are also a people with an internal society which values the love of the particular. One love is the universal *human* brotherly love, a love of the other. The other is purely *brotherly* love, a particular love of their own people. According to R. Hirsch, Jewish destiny is neither particularist nor universalist, but a complex interaction of both.[114]

Perhaps a fuller expression of this view can be found in the writings of R. Joseph B. Soloveitchik. About eighty years after R. Hirsch wrote his essay on Talmudic society, R. Soloveitchik wrote in his important essay on interfaith dialogue:

> We Jews have been burdened with a twofold task: we have to cope with the problem of a 'double confrontation.' We think of ourselves as human beings, sharing the destiny of Adam in his general encounter with nature, and as members of a covenantal community...In this difficult role, we are summoned by God, who revealed himself at both the level of universal creation and that of the private covenant, to undertake a double mission—the universal human and the exclusive covenantal confrontation.[115]

Perhaps R. Hirsch would embrace R. Soloveitchik's conception of the Jew and his twofold task resulting in two kinds of love: one of human

---

[114] Jonathan Sacks, *Tradition in an Untraditional Age* (Vallentine, Mitchell, 1990), 100.

[115] Joseph B. Soloveitchik, "Confrontation," *Tradition* 6:2, (1964), 1–29.

brotherly love for all human beings, and one of brotherly love, unique to members of the covenantal community.[116]

Israel's Chosenness: A New Interpretation

Near the beginning of *The Nineteen Letters*, R. Hirsch begins his literary career of elucidating Judaism with these few sentences:

> Let us read them [the words of the Bible] as if we had never read them before, never heard about them. Let us raise in our soul the basic questions of life: The world around me—what is it to me? What am I and what should I be in relation to it? What should I be as man and Israelite? (*Mensch Yisrael*).[117]

In typical form, R. Hirsch naturally begins with universal questions. The question of Man's place in the world and Israel's place among the nations is of primary concern. For R. Hirsch, Israel is introduced into the ranks of the nations for the good of all of mankind. Israel's role in the history of the world is to enlighten the other nations and bring about the fulfillment of God's will.[118]

Perhaps the most radical example of R. Hirsch's humanism is his interpretation of the concept of the Jewish People as the *am segulah,* chosen nation. Chosenness is a concept which seemingly is in direct contradiction to universal humanism. Addressing this, R. Hirsch claims it is an "unfortunate misinterpretation" to understand the God of Judaism as only the God of the Jewish People. He then re-interprets the concept of the *am segulah*:

> When the Torah speaks of the Jewish people as "*segullah*" (an exclusive treasure), it does not mean that God does not belong to any other people, but that this people must not belong to any other god, must not acknowledge any other being as god.[119]

---

[116] As an extension of his broad universal humanism, R. Hirsch saw many positive contributions of Christianity. See *TNL, Letter* 9; *CW,* VII, 227; Hirsch, "Haesters' Text and Reading Books for Israelite Schools," edited by Emanuel Hecht, *Jeschurun,* 4, May 1858, 394–399, recently translated into English in Marc B. Shapiro, "Rabbi Samson Raphael Hirsch on Jews in a Non-Jewish World," *Ḥakirah,* 27 (New York, 2019), 167–173. As is to be expected, R. Hirsch was also very critical of Christianity. See Elias, *TNL,* 138–140. For a full analysis of R. Hirsch's approach to Christianity, see Miller 275–290.

[117] *TNL, Letter* 2.

[118] Ibid., *Letter* 7.

[119] Ibid., *Letter* 15. This passage appears somewhat differently in Drachman's translation:

According to R. Hirsch, Israel's separateness is necessary only in order to facilitate its mission to inspire the rest of the world to God-consciousness. R. Hirsch argues that the true meaning of the Jewish nation being an *am segulah* is that God has exclusive rights to their devotion. For R. Hirsch, Israel's chosenness could not mean a rejection of the rest of humanity.

As noted above, passages like these have raised the questions of accommodation and apologia associated with R. Hirsch. Is this truly what is meant by the Torah's proclamation that the Jewish People are an *"am segulah,"* a chosen nation? Non-Jews are also subject to the prohibition of idolatry, making other beings into God.[120] How can this be the definition of *beḥirat Yisrael* when it fundamentally is no different for Jew or gentile?

The simple understanding of the chosenness concept has less to do with God's exclusive claim to Israel's devotion than it does with the choosing of Israel over other nations. Indeed, the Torah states that God chose the Jewish People because He desired them.[121] How would R. Hirsch explain classical and well-accepted sources within our tradition which clearly state that as an *"am segulah,"* Israel has an intrinsic elevated stature, a holier soul, or a greater level of God's love and favor?[122]

In R. Hirsch's defense, although there are other interpretations, perhaps one can argue, based on a passage in *Va-et'ḥanan* which links the prohibition of idolatry with Israel's chosenness, that the primary understanding of the term *"am segulah"* relates to God's claim to Israel's devotion.[123] As we noted above, Miller has argued that R. Hirsch utilized the simple meaning of the Torah to highlight the original context and meaning when he felt it necessary.[124]

The Bible terms Israel *segulah,* "a chosen treasure." This designation, however, does not imply, as some have falsely interpreted it, that Israel has a monopoly on God's love and favor. On the contrary, it proclaims that God has the sole and exclusive claim to Israel's devotion and service; that Israel may not render Divine homage to any other Being. Israel's most cherished ideal is that of the universal brotherhood of mankind.

120   *Sanhedrin* 56a.

121   *Devarim* 7: 3–6.

122   See Ramban, ibid. See also *Ohr Ha-ḥayyim* and *Kli Yakar* on *Devarim* 14:2 as well as Rashi (*Shemot* 19:5) who interpret the principle of an *am segulah* contrary to R. Hirsch's understanding.

123   *Devarim* 7: 3–6.

124   See also *Bava Kamma* 87a where R. Hirsch also found basis for his definition of the term *segulah*. He takes a similar approach in *COT* (see *Devarim* 7:6 and *Shemot*

Similarly, R. Hirsch elucidates Israel as being "God's first-born" along similar lines:

> Israel is My first but not My only child, it is only the first nation that I have won as Mine... Israel is not the first in rank, but the first in time.[125]

The Jewish People's contribution to the universal goals of mankind is a theme found in many of R. Hirsch's writings. R. Hirsch argues that Israel's most cherished ideal is that of the universal brotherhood of mankind and Israel's chosenness in no way contradicts this fundamental goal of Judaism. All nations of the world are able to contribute to the "great edifice of humanity." R. Hirsch stresses that *behirat Yisrael,* God making the Jewish People the "chosen nation," in no way is to be understood as a rejection of the rest of humanity; rather, "the choice of Israel [is] only a beginning, only the restarting of the spiritual and moral rebuilding of Mankind."[126] God chose the Jewish People as a first step in moving toward the utopian prophetic vision of the End of Days when all people will worship the one God.[127] Israel has been chosen on behalf of, and for the purpose of, the rest of humanity. In fact, in a radical interpretation of the rabbinic statement *"Ḥasidei umot ha-olam yesh lahem ḥelek la-Olam Haba,"* the pious of the nations of the world have a share in the World-to-Come,[128] R. Hirsch writes that this can be understood to mean that the righteous of all nations will have a share in attaining the goal of all of human history, the redemption at the End of Days.[129]

Along this line of thinking, R. Hirsch, embracing a more universalistic perspective, de-emphasizes the intrinsic difference between Jews and non-Jews. For example, in his commentary on the *Siddur,* he writes:

> Our entire historical significance among the nations stands and falls by the manner in which we cultivate and cherish the Torah in our midst. Should we ever cease to know the Torah, to fulfill it, we should also cease to have a place among mankind.[130]

19:5). See also *Seforno, Shemot* 19:5, who says that the Jewish People being an *am segulah* does not detract from God's love of all humanity.

125 *COT, Shemot* 4:22–23.

126 *COT, Va-Yikra* 20:26.

127 Ibid.

128 *Sanhedrin* 105a, Rashi ibid; *Sanhedrin* 110b, Rashi ibid; *Mishnat R. Eliezer, Parshah* 6; Rambam, *Mishneh Torah, Teshuvah* 3:5 and *Melakhim* 8:11.

129 *TNL, Letter* 15, footnote.

130 *The Hirsch Siddur* (Feldheim, 2013) 9. The view, that the identity of the Jewish nation is defined primarily by the Torah, is most often attributed to R. Saadiah

According to R. Hirsch, the Jewish People are only significant if they properly live up to their task. In his view, the special significance of the Jewish nation lies in their commitment to the Torah and their mission to inspire the world to the awareness of God.[131] Although the Jewish People were given a special mission by God, they are equal citizens of humanity. R. Hirsch refers to the Jewish People as "the priests among the people" (*Shemot* 19:6). However, he adds, when the Jewish People properly fulfill their task, they can become "priests to humanity."[132] For R. Hirsch, the Jewish People, by serving as a model for the rest of mankind, ultimately are facilitators of the redemption of the entirety of humanity. [133]

According to my research, the inherent elevated holiness of the Jewish soul, a concept often found in Kabbalistic sources, is not found in Hirschian thought. Unlike many of his Eastern European contemporaries, R. Hirsch saw no fundamental differences between Jews and non-Jews.[134]

A Different Approach to the *Mensch Yisrael*

However, there is a dissenting view. R. Yeḥiel Yaakov Weinberg, in his depiction of R. Hirsch's religious philosophy, claims that R. Hirsch believed Judaism to be a singular religion. In contrast with non-Jewish religions founded on the "fruit of an internal spiritual conflict within man," Judaism embraces the fullness of life. In this context, R. Weinberg contrasts Judaism with other religions:

> According to R. Hirsch, basic ethical commands were revealed by the Almighty at Sinai. There, man was given a new, higher title:

Gaon. See his *Ha-Emunot v-ha-Deot*, III, 7:1. See also R. Hirsch's sensitive interpretation of *Aleinu* (*Siddur*, 208-209), the first text which would be edited by the Reform movement. R. Hirsch emphasizes the historical significance of the Jewish people rather than metaphysical superiority.

[131] See his *COT, Shemot* 19:6.

[132] *Ḥoreb*, V, *Mitzvot*, ch. 97, no. 613, p. 465.

[133] R. J. David Bleich in his *The Philosophical Quest* (Maggid, 2013), 237, notes that R. Hirsch shared this belief with both R. Naftali Tzvi Yehudah Berlin (see his *Kidmat ha-Emek*, the introduction to his *Ha'amek Davar*, no. 4 and *Ha'amek Davar*, *Shemot* 12:51) and his teacher R. Yaakov Ettlinger. See R. Ettlinger's *Minḥat Ani*, *Parshat Bamidbar* (Bnei Brak, 2012), 285.

[134] Miller 239–240 notes the sharp distinction between R. Hirsch's position and that of the *Maharal* and *Ramḥal* who were very influential in the Eastern European traditionalist circles. The latter emphasized the intrinsic differences between Jews and non-Jews in their writings.

"Jew," his people a new moral status: "the Jewish nation"; and his soul, a new spiritual component: "the Jewish soul." This Jewish soul was blessed with a special Divine revelation which carried the spark of God deep within.[135]

Elsewhere, R. Weinberg wrote of his belief that the Jewish People have an innate gift for interacting with the divine.[136] Professor Marc B. Shapiro has noted the once widespread belief in national uniqueness (*Volkgeist*) popularized by Johann Gottfried Herder most probably influenced R. Weinberg.[137] In fact, coining a new term, R. Weinberg describes the Jews as "*das Volk der Religion*." Shapiro suggests that he probably had in mind the distinction R. Hirsch made between the Hebrew words *goy* and *am*—both words which characterize the Jewish People—and "*Volk*" (or people), which is not the proper description for the Jews.[138] Accordingly, he was adopting a view similar to R. Hirsch, that the Jewish national character is spiritual in nature and cannot be compared to any other nation in the world who are defined by their nation and land alone.[139]

Therefore, Shapiro argues that although in the piece above, R. Weinberg does not quote any passages from R. Hirsch's writings in support of his claim, it is possible that for R. Weinberg, the Jewish soul is unique just as the Jewish nation is unique. This is not a contradiction to Hirschian thought. When he speaks of the "Jewish soul," he is not speaking Kabbalisticly, of the intricately elevated Jewish soul; he is speaking romantically.

---

135   Yeḥiel Yaakov Weinberg, "*Torat Ḥayyim:* The Torah of Life as Understood by Rav S.R. Hirsch" in *Tzvi Tifarto,* 97–99. See also his *S'ridei Aish,* IV, "*Mishnato shel Rav Shamshon Raphael Hirsch,*" 364–365. In the *S'ridei Aish* passage, the belief in the elevated status of the Jewish soul is less pronounced. There, R. Weinberg emphasizes the contrast between Judaism and other religions. He explicitly rejects the view suggested below that the Jewish people have special historical significance rather than having unique spirituality. According to R. Weinberg, other religions influence their constituents "from without," whereas Judaism, for a Jewish soul, is a more natural enterprise. It is interesting to note that R. Weinberg himself expressed frustration with what he saw as anti-gentile discrimination in Jewish law. See Shapiro, *Between the Yeshiva World and Modern Orthodoxy,* 48–49, n182, 183. It is striking that in his treatment of the difference between Judaism and other religions in Hirschian thought, he makes no mention of R. Hirsch's more universalistic themes.

136   Yeḥiel Yaakov Weinberg, *Das Volk der Religion* (Geneva, 1949).

137   Shapiro, *Between the Yeshiva World and Modern Orthodoxy,* 97–98.

138   *TNL, Letter* 16 and Klugman 132n376.

139   *Between the Yeshiva World and Modern Orthodoxy,* 97–98.

R. Weinberg believed that because the Jewish People were the recipients of a special revelation, this affected and continues to affect their soul.[140]

One could also suggest this is R. Weinberg's interpretation of the Hirschian *Mensch Yisrael* concept. For R. Hirsch, the ideal religious personality, the "Man-Israelite," is committed to both his worldly role and his religious role. Perhaps this is only achieved by the Jewish humanist who is influenced by both disciplines. As noted above, the elevated spiritual nature of the Jewish soul is a belief well-founded in Jewish tradition. However, this view is not clearly spelled out in R. Hirsch's writings. On the contrary, R. Hirsch wrote that all people, regardless of sex or creed, are capable of spiritual greatness. Moreover, in his treatment of *beḥirat Yisrael* in *The Nineteen Letters*[141] and in the commentary on Torah[142] he does not invoke the principle of a singular Jewish spirituality. Rather, R. Hirsch repeatedly emphasizes the historical significance of the Jewish People and their contribution to the "great edifice of humanity."[143] If R. Weinberg is correctly portraying the Hirschian view on the elevated *Mensch Yisrael*, we are left facing an apparent contradiction.

An alternative approach to R. Hirsch's *Mensch Yisrael* concept is offered by R. Joseph Elias.[144] He argues that, for R. Hirsch, because man's abilities to intuit proper morality and God's will is limited, man is in need of an external revelation. This revelation was entrusted to the Jewish People to assure the attainment of God's goal for all of mankind. Therefore, according to R. Hirsch, the Jewish People are positioned to be an example of the highest level of morality and humanism. If one combines R. Hirsch's *Mensch Yisrael* principle with his universalistic explanation of *beḥirat Yisrael*,[145] a more holistic Hirschian perspective emerges. Although R. Hirsch does refer to the *Mensch Yisrael* as being on a "higher stage of being a man," this results from the Jew internalizing the humanism which the Torah educates.[146] R. Hirsch writes, "*Derekh eretz* (culture) and Torah are one. The most perfect gentleman and the most perfect Jew, to the Jewish teaching, are identical."[147] Torah is humanism on a higher plane, and the ideal Torah-committed Jew is the example of what it means to

---

140 Personal email correspondence (July 14–16, 2020).
141 *TNL, Letter* 15.
142 *Devarim* 7:6, *Shemot* 19:5 and *Va-Yikra* 20:26.
143 *TNL, Letter* 15.
144 Elias, *TNL,* 160–162.
145 See above.
146 See his *COT, Bereshit* 3:24. For a fuller excerpt see above.
147 Ibid.

live according to both Torah and humanistic principles. Rather than arguing that R. Hirsch's conception of the *Mensch Yisrael* cannot be reconciled with his humanistic universalism, it appears to be more compelling to argue that, for R. Hirsch, the Jewish People, informed with the Sinaitic revelation, are more significant from a historical perspective rather than being fundamentally spiritually elevated.[148]

In sum, R. Hirsch's humanism is consistent and pervades much of his work. Perhaps most significant are his positions on the equality of Jews and non-Jews, his call for human brotherly love for gentiles, and his universalistic understanding of *beḥirat Yisrael*. For those who struggle to answer claims that traditional Judaism is racist or discriminatory, R. Hirsch's humanism provides a crucial response.

Returning to Criticism of R. Hirsch

After our fuller analysis of R. Hirsch and his humanism, let us return to the criticism we outlined above. Although challenges to R. Hirsch's Torah knowledge appear to be unfounded, his status among the Yeshiva world remains somewhat on the periphery.

I believe this is because R. Hirsch still does not altogether fit the mold. It is clear from his writings that his goal was quite different from his contemporaries. From the poetic German language, the theological content and thrust of his argumentation, it is unquestionable that R. Hirsch set out to do something different.

His legacy, although debated, is certainly distinct from others of his time. Perhaps we can ask the question from a different angle: Why did he write a work like *The Nineteen Letters on Judaism?* Why, unlike most of his contemporaries, did he write a work addressed, not to his own community per se, but to the general public? Why did he generally focus on larger theological questions in his commentary on the *Ḥumash* and in *Horeb?*

---

[148] R. J. David Bleich also seems to take a position closer to R. Weinberg's in David Shatz, Chaim Waxman, and Nathan Diament (ed.), *Tikkun Olam; Social Responsibility in Jewish Thought and Law* (Aaronson, 1997), 217–218. R. Bleich sees R. Hirsch's conception of the *"Mensch Yisrael"* (for example *TNL, Letter* 10 and 12) as an expansion of R. Yehudah Ha-Levi's thesis that the Jew belongs in a category higher than other human beings and is endowed with a unique spiritual make-up (See *Kuzari*, 1:41–43 and 1:115 (3)). However, as we have argued, R. Hirsch's approach is not synonymous with that of R. Yehudah Ha-Levi's. Unlike R. Yehudah Ha-Levi, R. Hirsch saw the Jewish People as more significant from a historical perspective rather than from a spiritual one. For an example of this see *Horeb, Torot,* no. 21, p. 13, where he writes God selected the Jewish People "to be in human affairs the proclaimers of His will and His instrument for the education of humanity."

Why is his work so fresh and not dated compared to other works from his period?

Why did he take a more universal approach? Why, unlike so many others of his time, was he not content living his own religious life within his own community, alone with his own truth—not to be bothered? Why did he feel the need to address the many challenges to traditional Judaism?

The answer to all of these questions is self-evident. It is unthinkable that this man was engaged in polemics and apologetics merely to prove Judaism worthy in the eyes of his generation. Whereas R. Lichtenstein found the sense of accommodation, concession, or even apologetics inescapable, I cannot escape a quite different feeling. From R. Hirsch's writings, I sense a man emerging, a man so genuinely convinced of the humanistic and universal vision of Judaism, so singularly devoted to sharing this message with the world, his passion seeps through the text even now, over 180 years after he first put pen to paper. ❧

The Search for the Elusive Center: Norman Lamm and American Orthodoxy

By: LAWRENCE GROSSMAN

Soon after assuming the presidency of Yeshiva University in 1976, Rabbi Dr. Norman Lamm renamed Modern Orthodoxy, the religious community with which he had long identified. Calling it Centrist Orthodoxy, he hoped to clarify the movement's ideology and enhance its attractiveness. The failure of the attempted rebranding both illustrated and compounded the internal contradictions of an Orthodox Judaism open to the intellectual and social currents of the wider world.

Modernism and Its Discontents

Lamm had long expressed unhappiness with the term Modern Orthodox. In a Shavuot sermon delivered on May 23, 1969, at The Jewish Center, where he served as rabbi, Lamm said, "I flinch when I articulate the words." The same year, writing in the pages of *Jewish Life*, the organ of the Union of Orthodox Jewish Congregations of America (OU), he called them "dreadfully inadequate," to be used only "with the greatest hesitation." Calling a religious body "orthodox," Lamm felt, was "almost pejorative" since it implied "a stifling and unthinking narrow-mindedness," while "modern," with its connotation of preference for the new and trendy, "is amusingly pretentious; it adds nothing to the validity or invalidity of a proposition." Three years later, he called Modern Orthodoxy "an unhappy semantic hybrid."[1]

---

[1]   Norman Lamm, "The Arrogance of Modernism," in Lamm, *Torah Beloved: Reflections on the Love of Torah and the Celebration of the Holiday of Matan Torah,* ed. Daniel Gober (New York: Ktav and OU Press, 2020), p. 33; idem., "Modern Orthodoxy's Identity Crisis," *Jewish Life,* May–June 1969, p. 5; idem, *Faith and Doubt: Studies in Traditional Jewish Thought* (Ktav: Hoboken, NJ, 1972), p. xv.

Lawrence Grossman recently retired from the American Jewish Committee where he served as director of publications and editor of the *American Jewish Year Book,* for which he wrote the article "Jewish Communal Affairs" from 1988 through 2015. He has also published in *Modern Judaism, American Jewish History, The Encyclopedia of American Jewish History, Jewish-American History and Culture, The Forward, Jewish Ideas Daily, The New Leader, First Things,* and elsewhere.

He was hardly alone in his view.

The negative connotation of the designation Orthodox had been widespread for some time. In 1946, the year Lamm entered college, the first issue of *Jewish Life* editorialized that "'Orthodox' Judaism is an ill-fitting name" because it "suggests something rigid, motionless and static," while traditional Judaism was in fact "dynamic and progressive throughout."[2] Six years later, while Lamm was serving as assistant rabbi at the Kehilath Jeshurun synagogue in Manhattan, its senior rabbi, Joseph H. Lookstein, declared at the convention of the Rabbinical Council of America (RCA) that "there is nothing Orthodox about the word Orthodox," and said it should be replaced by "traditional."[3] At an RCA convention a few years later, Lamm's brother, Rabbi Maurice Lamm, complained that "Orthodox" was a marketing disaster. Since it had, he claimed, "no mass appeal, it provokes the old prejudice before our message is even considered, and it cripples whatever image we wish to foster." Like Lookstein, he preferred "traditional" which, in his mind, connoted "long," "honored," "hallowed," and "rich." A Hillel rabbi at the convention suggested "classical Judaism" as an alternative.[4] Rabbi Leo Jung, senior rabbi at The Jewish Center in New York City, where Lamm began serving as associate rabbi in 1958, claimed credit for introducing his preferred synonym for Orthodoxy, "Torah-true" Judaism—translated from the German—to the United States.[5]

The "Modern" modifier of Orthodox, lacking any precise meaning, hardly helped matters. It was often used to justify not just such externals as clean-shaven rabbis, decorous services, and responsive readings in English, but also the institution of mixed-gender seating and other innovations in the synagogue common to Conservative and a significant number of nominally Orthodox synagogues, but not sanctioned by Orthodox authorities. As late as the mid-20th century, the difference between Modern Orthodox and Conservative Judaism was so unclear as to be invisible to many.

---

2   "Jewish Law in the Making," *Jewish Life* 1, Oct. 1946, p. 4. The editorial was signed by Trude Weiss-Rosmarin.

3   "What's in a Name," *Orthodox Jewish Life* 19, July–Aug. 1952, pp. 3–4.

4   David Wachstock, "Orthodox Connotes Long Beard, Foreign Accent," *Jewish Post and Opinion,* Feb. 12, 1960, p. 8.

5   Leo Jung, *The Path of a Pioneer: The Autobiography of Leo Jung* (London and New York: Soncino Press, 1980), p. 126.

By the 1960s, however, Conservative Judaism had established its independent identity.[6] At the same time, the word Orthodox had lost much of its negative association with the dead past and was taking on instead— even for many who did not practice it—an aura of Jewish authenticity that also offered a wholesome alternative to the perceived hedonism and moral relativism of the youth culture of the time.[7] But as Orthodoxy's stock rose in part through its rejection of contemporary values, the adjective "Modern," suggesting at least partial validation of those values, became ever more problematic.[8]

Lamm, in the same 1969 piece that expressed his distaste for the term Modern Orthodox, introduced centrism into the debate. He wrote, "The challenge to our intellectual leadership is clear: to formulate the worldview of 'modern Orthodoxy' in a manner that is Halachically legitimate, philosophically persuasive, religiously inspiring, and personally convincing." He conceded that this was "a tall order" but one "we must fill if the great centrist mass of American orthodox Jews is not to be pulled apart in all directions...." Lamm defined "great centrist mass" as those who both rejected the idea on the right that "Orthodoxy must retreat and wait for the Messiah until it speaks to mankind," and those on the left willing to compromise with the "atavistic" sexual revolution of the 1960s, "a throwback to pagan debauchery," as he described it. Lamm gave his "centrist" thrust biblical resonance by citing the Book of Deuteronomy's command that the Jewish people shall not "turn aside neither to the right nor to the left...."[9] Refining his analysis ten years later, Lamm rejected an

---

6   The process whereby Conservatism gradually shed its Modern Orthodox associations and emerged as a separate movement is traced in Michael R. Cohen, *The Birth of Conservative Judaism: Solomon Schechter's Disciples and the Creation of an American Religious Movement* (New York: Columbia University Press, 2012). In retrospect, the decision to allow driving to synagogue on the Sabbath, documented in *Proceedings of the Rabbinical Assembly of America,* vol. 14, 1950, pp. 112–88, signaled the final break.

7   Jack Wertheimer, *A People Divided: Judaism in Contemporary America* (New York: Basic Books, 1993), pp. 114–136; Chaim I. Waxman, *Social Change and Halakhic Evolution in American Orthodoxy* (London: Littman, 2017), pp. 73–103.

8   An illuminating parallel is the negative connotation the designation "liberal" took on in American politics around that time, as elements of the Democratic Party, beginning with the Coalition for a Democratic Majority set up after the 1972 election debacle, preferred to call themselves "centrist" or "moderate."

9   Lamm, "Modern Orthodoxy's Identity Crisis," pp. 6–8. The idea of nurturing a moderate Orthodoxy was already in the air at the time, as seen in Jerry Hochbaum, "Middle-of-the Road Orthodoxy: An Alternative to Left and Right Rad-

"Anything Goes" Orthodoxy at one extreme and an "Only One Way" approach at the other, settling instead on "A dialectic of discipline and diversity, a finite pluralism" in which all members accept Torah, "especially in its halakhic commitment, and yet respect each other's singularity and differences in interpretation and style." While granting that "such a communal Paradise does not exist," he did not think it "a Pollyannaish dream."[10]

Inventing Centrism

When Lamm started publicly referring to "Centrist Orthodoxy" a few years after becoming president of Yeshiva University, others sympathetic to his ideological orientation followed suit.[11] The new term caught on especially among Orthodox educators associated with Yeshiva University, for whom it was a way to ward off criticism from their Haredi counterparts who competed for students and funding in many communities with the claim that only the most intensive yeshiva education—and certainly not a modern one—could ensure Jewish continuity.[12] Indeed, Lamm's initial public explanation of what he meant by Centrist Orthodoxy came in a 1985 talk before the YU-affiliated Educators Council of America. Titled

---

icalism," *Jewish Life,* July–Aug. 1968, pp. 27–29. Lamm's use of the word "centrist" may well have been influenced by Arthur Schlesinger Jr.'s *The Vital Center: The Politics of Freedom* (Boston: Houghton Mifflin, 1949), which appeared the year he graduated from college. It argued for a rejection of both laissez-faire and a government-controlled economy, and in favor of a New Deal-style, regulated form of capitalism.

10 Norman Lamm, "Pluralism and Unity in the Orthodox Jewish Community," *Jewish Life,* Fall 1979, pp. 41–46.

11 For Lamm's early use of the term see "So Says Dr. Norman Lamm: Authoritarian Judaism Losing Its Intellectual Independence," *Jewish Post and Opinion,* Nov. 12, 1982, p. 4, and "Yeshiva U. President Urges that Two Orthodox Congregational Organizations Be Merged," *JTA,* May 5, 1983. For its use by other rabbis, see Stewart Ain, "Rabbinical Council President Decries Holier-Than-Thou Attitude of Right Wing" (Rabbi Gilbert Klaperman), *Long Island Jewish World,* Mar. 1, 1984, p. 14; and "Orthodox Rabbi Urges Reform Movement to Drop Patrilineal Descent Decision" (Rabbi Haskell Lookstein), *JTA,* Dec. 19, 1985.

12 Mordechai Schnaidman, "Integration in Centrist Orthodox Day Schools," *Journal of Jewish Education* 47, 1979, pp. 11–18, and Alvin Schiff, "The Centrist Torah Educator Faces Critical Ideological and Cultural Challenges," *Tradition* 19, Winter 1981, pp. 275–89. In an extensive symposium on "The State of Orthodoxy" published in the Spring 1982 issue of *Tradition* (pp. 1–83), Robert S. Hirt, the only contributor to use the term Centrist Orthodoxy, did so in connection with Jewish education (pp. 36–39).

"Some Comments on Centrist Orthodoxy," his remarks betrayed a certain ambivalence about the new term, suggesting that he meant nothing more than to rebrand Modern Orthodoxy for a changing market that was not particularly impressed by modernity, and not to launch a new iteration of Orthodoxy somewhere on the ideological spectrum between the Modern and Haredi camps. Lamm said:

> We seem to be suffering from a terminological identity crisis. We now call ourselves "Centrist Orthodoxy." There was a time, not too long ago, that we referred to ourselves as "Modern Orthodox." Others tell us that we should call ourselves simply "Orthodox," without any qualifiers, and leave it to the other Orthodox groups to conjure up adjectives for themselves. I agree with the last view in principle, but shall defer to the advocates of "Centrist Orthodoxy...."

Curiously, Lamm noted that he had two reasons for preferring the centrist label but gave just one, and even that was less a reason than a verbal shoulder-shrug. He said that it was "a waste of intellectual effort and precious time to argue about titles when there are so many truly significant issues that clamor for our attention." There was little if any difference between "modern" and "centrist," Lamm assured his audience: "In no way should the choice of one adjective over the other be invested with any substantive significance or assumed to be a 'signal' of ideological position."

Lamm proceeded to refute a common right-wing argument deployed against "our Centrist outlook"—that it introduced changes in Torah and Jewish law. Yes, he granted, there had been shifts of "emphasis," but not "substance," and these did not displace "a single fundamental of Judaism." Ironically, Lamm justified them by going back to the very language he was seeking to replace, explicitly invoking "the modern experience,"

> its openness, its critical stance, its historicism; the democratic experience which, most recently, has raised the serious challenge of the new role of women in family and society; the growth of science and technology, and the scientific method applied to so many fields beyond the natural sciences; almost universal higher worldly education amongst Jews...; the historically wrenching experience of the Holocaust; the miraculous rise of the State of Israel; and the reduction of observant and believing Jews to a small minority of the Jewish people—a condition unknown since the darkest periods of the Biblical era.

He then laid out a three-part platform for Centrism: "*Torah U-madda*, the 'synthesis' of Torah and worldly wisdom" as a welcome educational goal and not just a reluctant concession to economic necessity;[13] personal and communal moderation, temperance, and tolerance, in the spirit of Maimonides's "middle way," rather than self-righteousness and extremism; and "the centrality of the people of Israel," manifested in love for all Jews and for the State of Israel.[14]

While no equivalent Modern Orthodox platform had ever been framed, Lamm's three points could be read as elucidations of the description Charles Liebman had provided of Modern Orthodox Jews two decades earlier: "On the one hand, they seek to demonstrate the viability of the *halakhah* for contemporary life; on the other, they emphasize what they have in common with all other Jews rather than what separates them."[15]

The Centrist initiative evoked a variety of responses in the Orthodox world. A reporter described the February 1986 RCA Midwinter Conference as "a forum for defining and staking out a position of 'Centrist Orthodoxy'… in the face of the apparent ascendancy of Orthodox fundamentalism."[16] Taking their cue from Lamm, some Modern Orthodox insiders sought to convey the impression of a broad consensus within non-Haredi Orthodoxy by minimizing—as Lamm did—the significance of the

---

13   See Lawrence Grossman, "The Rise and Fall of Torah U'Madda," *Modern Judaism* 41, Feb. 2021, pp. 71–91.

14   Norman Lamm, "Some Comments on Centrist Orthodoxy," in Lamm, *Seventy Faces: Articles of Faith* (Hoboken, 2002), vol. 1, p. 41 (originally published in *Tradition,* 22, Fall 1986). Clearly, in coordination with Lamm, Rabbi Aharon Lichtenstein spoke at that same conference on "Centrist Orthodoxy: A Spiritual Accounting." Since Lichtenstein was based in Israel and his approach to the subject was typically subtle and complex, his presentation attracted little attention until it was published almost two decades later in Reuven Ziegler, ed., *By His Light: Character and Values in the Service of God* (Jersey City: KTAV, 2003), pp. 220–51. Ironically, the Hebrew version at etzion.org.il translates "Centrist" as *Moderni.* On Lichtenstein's approach see Alan Brill, "An Ideal Rosh Yeshiva; *By His Light: Character and Values in the Service of God* and *Leaves of Faith* by Rav Aharon Lichtenstein," *The Edah Journal* 5, Tammuz 2005; and Alan Jotkowitz, "'I am in the Middle': Rav Aharon Lichtenstein's Vision of Centrist Orthodoxy," *Ḥakirah* 22, 2017, pp. 49–66.

15   Charles S. Liebman, "Orthodoxy in American Jewish Life," *American Jewish Year Book 1965,* p. 48, reprinted in Liebman, *Aspects of the Religious Behavior of American Jews* (New York: Ktav, 1974), p. 138.

16   Larry Yudelson, "RCA Struggles to Carve Out Centrist Orthodox Stand," *Long Island Jewish World,* Feb. 14–20, 1986, cited in "Rabbinical Council of America conference 1986—the last reign of the pulpit rabbis," kavvanah.blog/2014/05/04/rabbinical-council-of-america-conference-1986-the-last-reign-of-the-pulpit-rabbis.

linguistic innovation. The immediate past president of the Rabbinical Council of America (RCA) declared "center Orthodoxy, Modern Orthodoxy, [and] Religious Zionism" synonymous, and another past president described the rabbinical organization "as a Centrist Orthodox body, some of us a little to its left, some of us to its right."[17] And in perhaps the first published mention of centrism outside the Orthodox community, historian Marc Lee Raphael similarly referred to "signs of 'centrist', 'modern,' or mainline Orthodoxy's revival...."[18]

Others, though, thought that "modern" and "centrist" were not synonymous and considered the replacement of the former by the latter of great significance, even while differing over whether it was an improvement or not.

For those attracted to the apparent principled steadfastness of the Orthodox right and finding themselves increasingly uncomfortable in a Modern Orthodox camp they considered compromised by immersion in secular values and a degraded American popular culture, the new centrist language was a welcome change. As the editor of *Young Israel Viewpoint* put it in 1984, many rabbis who once identified as Modern Orthodox

> now call themselves "centrist" and find themselves preoccupied with justifying their ideological legitimacy to the right wing. They realize that there can be little further movement within the framework of *halachah* to accommodate feminism and other movements in contemporary society. The rabbis are ultimately constrained by the theological necessity to choose the divinely inspired Torah tradition as the highest truth, which must take precedence when in conflict with the lesser truths of man's science, logic, and standards of morality.[19]

However, other rabbis—mostly older men—who saw modernity as a potential source of positive values had their doubts. Rabbi Emanuel Rackman, an eloquent advocate of Modern Orthodoxy who had been passed over for the YU presidency due, in part, to the community's growing anti-modernist tendencies, did not directly criticize his successful rival. Yet Rackman, now president of Bar-Ilan University in Israel, undoubtedly had

---

17   Louis Bernstein contribution to symposium on "The Strength of Orthodoxy and the State of K'lal Yisrael," *Jewish Action* Holiday Issue, Fall 1986, p. 12; Bernard Rosenzweig, "The Rabbinical Council of America: Retrospect and Prospect," *Tradition* 22, Summer 1986, p. 6.

18   Marc Lee Raphael, *Profiles in American Judaism: The Reform, Conservative, Orthodox, and Reconstructionist Traditions in Historical Perspective* (San Francisco: Harper and Row, 1984), p. 170.

19   Yaakov Kornreich, "Dialogue Brings Truth to Light," *Sh'ma*, Oct. 5, 1984, p. 142.

Lamm and Centrism in mind when he insisted in a 1982 newspaper column that Modern Orthodox Jews "are the standard bearers of the authentic tradition…. They do not compromise it or falsify it." Regretting the "apologetic" tone recently adopted by those in that camp, Rackman insisted that the modernists were often more meticulous in their adherence to Jewish law than their antagonists when it came to behavior toward one's fellow man.[20] Rabbi Walter Wurzburger was even more outspoken, asserting that Lamm's avoidance of the word "modern" showed the influence of worldwide cultural trends that produced the Moral Majority in the United States and Islamist fundamentalism in the Middle East, which "hold out the promise of a safe haven offering protection from the corrosive 'acids of modernity.'" He doubted that Lamm's approach could attract many Jewish seekers of alleged Orthodox authenticity since the latter were likely to distrust centrists for not going far enough in their rejection of modernity and for making "wishy-washy compromises" with universalistic liberal values. To succeed, he wrote, Lamm's program "must vindicate itself by demonstrating that its position reflects an authentic religious vision rather than a concession to expediency."[21]

The Orthodox right wing did indeed attack centrism for stopping halfway. *The Jewish Observer,* Agudath Israel's monthly, acknowledged that centrists had correctly perceived the dangers of "a rush toward modernity," but complained that this insight had not led to a reassessment of relationships with the non-Orthodox movements. Centrists, like modernists, still spoke of reaching a modus vivendi with Conservative and Reform Judaism on conversion standards, an issue high on the community agenda at the time. Such compromise, however, was out of the question, the magazine stated. Only by ending its accommodation of "deviationist groups," most specifically by withdrawing from the multidenominational Synagogue Council of America, could centrist bodies gain the approval of the right, a demand that the latter had been making of the Modern Orthodox since the 1950s.[22]

---

20 Emanuel Rackman, "Modern Orthodox Jews Keep Authentic Tradition Alive," Nov. 26, 1982, in Rackman, *A Modern Orthodox Life: Sermons and Columns of Rabbi Emanuel Rackman* (Jersey City: Ktav, 2008), pp. 168–71.

21 Walter S. Wurzburger, "Centrist Orthodoxy: Ideology or Atmosphere?" in *Year Book: Religious Zionism, 1985–86* (Jerusalem: Mesilot, 1985), p. 7.

22 "Centrists: Between the 'Right Wing' and Whom?", *The Jewish Observer,* Apr. 1984, pp. 34–35. On the beginnings of the dispute over membership in the Synagogue Council see Raphael, *Profiles in American Judaism,* pp. 152–53.

Centrism and Pluralism

In March 1986—just five months after his public rollout of Centrist Orthodoxy—Lamm explicitly addressed the fraught issue of interdenominational Jewish relations at a conference seeking answers to the question, "Will There Be One Jewish People by the Year 2000?" Sponsored by CLAL (The National Jewish Center for Learning and Leadership), an organization created by former YU professor and Orthodox proponent of Jewish religious pluralism Rabbi Irving Greenberg, it featured addresses by such well-known figures as Elie Wiesel and Charles Silberman, and presentations by the heads of the rabbinic seminaries of the Jewish movements. The two-day event, held in Princeton, New Jersey, drew a large attendance and considerable media coverage because of growing concern about incompatible standards for conversion; the Reform movement's recent "patrilineal" decision accepting the children of Jewish fathers and non-Jewish mothers as Jews; the rising number of Jewish divorces without issuance of a *get* (Jewish document of divorce); revival of the divisive "who is a Jew" controversy in Israel; and incendiary rhetoric from some sectors of Orthodoxy seemingly denying the Jewish identity of the non-Orthodox, all of which could lead to schisms within the Jewish people.[23]

Lamm had championed Jewish unity long before he made it a pillar of Centrist Orthodoxy, speaking out consistently for continued RCA and OU membership in the Synagogue Council of America.[24] In 1981, when he became the first denominational leader to address the General Assembly of the Council of Jewish Federations, Lamm was reported to have "electrified the audience" by showing how love for Torah must go hand-in-hand with an inclusive love for all Jews.[25] But fully aware that his role at the CLAL conference would be carefully scrutinized by right-wing critics, Lamm agreed to speak only if he did not have to be in the room for the rest of the program, and so would not appear together with the leaders of the Conservative, Reform, and Reconstructionist seminaries.

---

23 For contemporary reports of the gathering see "Reform, Conservative and Orthodox: Are They One?" *Jewish Post and Opinion,* Apr. 2, 1986, pp. 15–16, and "Calling for a Truce in the War of Incivility," *Baltimore Jewish Times,* Apr. 18, pp. 40–41.

24 Irving Spiegel, "Orthodox Jews Back Unity Role; Delegates Reject Proposal to Quit Synagogue Council," *New York Times,* Nov. 22, 1966, p. 38; "Orthodox Rabbi Urges Creation of a United Orthodox Council," *JTA,* Dec. 3, 1974.

25 "Rabbi Norman Lamm Tells G.A.: Dare Not Exclude Anyone from House of Israel," *Jewish Post and Opinion,* Nov. 20, 1981, p. 7. The text of his talk, "A Story of Two Loves: Creating Jewish Leadership and Jewish Community," is in Lamm, *Seventy Faces,* I, pp. 123–34.

In his conference address titled "Unity and Integrity," Lamm stressed that for him religious pluralism did not extend to "anything goes," and that the Orthodox, who considered Torah of divine authority, could not be expected to legitimize positions clearly outside halakhic boundaries. Even so, he continued, no Jew, no matter how nonobservant, could be excluded from the Jewish fold. Lamm proceeded to address the religious status of non-Orthodox Jews and their rabbis in a way sure to disturb Orthodox leaders to his religious right. Since the non-Orthodox movements were "vital, powerful, and dynamic," he said, their leadership had functional validity; to the extent that they were sincerely religious, they had spiritual dignity; and yet their denial of the transcendent authority of Jewish law denied them "Jewish legitimacy." Criticizing some in his own Orthodox camp for incivility toward the non-Orthodox, he urged the latter to avoid responding in kind. To deal with the interdenominational rifts that threatened to split the Jewish people, Lamm urged creation of a national *bet din* (Jewish court) to handle conversions and divorces, its judges to be appointed on the basis of their rabbinic scholarship and halakhic observance irrespective of denominational affiliation—although he acknowledged that most of the qualified candidates were likely to come from the Orthodox community.[26]

One person in the audience later reported that when Lamm, during his presentation, identified as a "centrist," a young man sitting nearby whispered to a friend, "Boy, is he going to catch hell when he gets back to Yeshiva University!"[27] In fact, Lamm's centrist embrace of interdenominational cooperation generated opposition from many points on the Orthodox institutional spectrum—though his name was usually kept out of the discussion. OU President Sidney Kwestel, who placed the entire blame for Jewish disunity on non-Orthodox rejection of Torah, insisted that all halakhic personal-status issues remain under Orthodox control, and called for strengthening ties with right-wing Orthodoxy and disengaging from the heterodox groups.[28] In April 1987, when Rabbi Milton Polin, president of the RCA, joined with his Conservative and Reform counterparts in signing onto a pre-Passover "Statement of Jewish Unity,"

---

26   A version of Lamm's talk under the title "Seventy Faces," almost identical with the "Unity and Integrity" text distributed at the conference, was published in *Moment,* June 1986, and subsequently in Lamm, *Seventy Faces,* I, pp. 135–49. Lamm's proposed *bet din* was never implemented.

27   Alfred Fleishman, "Orthodoxy Coming to Terms," *Jewish Post and Opinion,* May 12, 1993, p. 9.

28   *Jewish Action,* Winter 1986–87, p. 65–68.

criticism came not only from *The Jewish Observer* but also from RCA members, and he yielded to pressure to withdraw from participation in a planned Jewish interdenominational program in Boston.[29] At the RCA annual convention that year, Rabbi Aharon Soloveitchik, younger brother of the now incapacitated Rabbi Joseph B. Soloveitchik and his successor as senior *rosh yeshiva* at YU, castigated the Jewish Unity statement and all other forms of cooperative endeavor with non-Orthodox rabbinic bodies, implicitly condemning Lamm, president of his own institution. "What kind of common dialogue can there be," Soloveitchik asked, "between Jews *shlemim be-emunah* [of perfect faith] and Conservative and Reform rabbis?" And he denied that the position of his brother—universally acknowledged as the RCA's authority—was any more liberal than his own.[30]

Lamm responded to his critics with a strongly worded address, "Centrist Orthodoxy: Agenda and Vision, Successes and Failures," delivered at the Fifth Avenue Synagogue on March 22, 1988, which was reported in *The New York Times*. Prefacing his remarks by stressing that he spoke as president of YU's rabbinical seminary—and hence as Soloveitchik's employer—Lamm expressed far greater criticism of those to his religious right than of those to his left. He accused "the ultra-Orthodox" of "triumphalism," the belief that "We are winning, therefore we are right." Lamm asserted that Centrist Jews differed in no way from the rightists in their adherence to Halakhah as "the authoritative norm for daily conduct." He restated the three ways in which Centrism differed from Haredi Orthodoxy: openness to secular culture as embodied in Yeshiva's Torah U-Madda (Torah and general knowledge) curriculum; the priority of Jewish peoplehood and Zionism; and a tolerant and moderate approach to differences of opinion. It was in regard to that last feature—moderation—that Lamm asserted his own camp "needs an injection of courage right now":

> Moderation should never be confused with indecisiveness. On the contrary, a lack of self-confidence in one's most basic commitments

29   "One People, One Torah, One Voice: An Editorial Statement," *The Jewish Observer,* May 1987, pp. 19–22; Rabbi Fabian Schonfeld, "The RCA and the 'Torah Community'," letter to the editor ibid., pp. 33–34; Rabbi Milton Polin, "From the President's Desk," *Rabbinical Council Record,* Sept. 1987, pp. 3–4; Judith Antonelli, "Orthodox Leader Pulls Out of Unity Meeting," *Boston Jewish Advocate,* May 14, 1987, pp. 1, 18.

30   Larry Yudelson, "After the Rav: RCA Rabbis Listening for Master's Voice," *Long Island Jewish World,* May 29–June 4, 1987, p. 20.

is often expressed in extremism. Only one who is sure of what he stands for can afford to be moderate. A strong heart can risk being an open heart.

While chastising Reform Judaism for abandoning Halakhah and Conservatism for "tampering" with it, Lamm repeated his earlier designation of both as "valid groupings" that "possess spiritual dignity," and urged that they be treated with respect even when disagreeing with their views.[31]

Praising Lamm for "forcefully delineating a new, affirmative path for centrist Orthodoxy," the YU student newspaper welcomed this "return to moderation."[32] Expressions of satisfaction came from outside the Orthodox world as well. Rabbi Wolfe Kelman, executive vice president of the (Conservative) Rabbinical Assembly, told a reporter that "the centrist Orthodox have not been our problem." Rabbi Alexander Schindler, president of the (Reform) Union of American Hebrew Congregations, wrote Lamm: "This is the kind of voice that I and many others have been longing to hear. You express the kind of Orthodoxy that I was taught to revere."[33]

Fire from Right and Left

Right-wing Orthodoxy—the chief target of Lamm's critique—could hardly ignore such a full-barreled assault in the pages of the nation's newspaper of record. Agudath Israel chose to respond through Professor Aaron Twerski, whose rabbinic beard and Hasidic garb had not hampered his career as a respected professor at leading law schools, providing living proof that an Orthodox Jew did not have to demonstrate centrist leanings to succeed in America. Indeed, Twerski began an "open letter" to Lamm by asserting that while he and others like him "do not embrace Western culture," they were not "country bumpkins" ignorant of it. He asked how Lamm could possibly call the non-Orthodox movements "valid groupings" while at the same time denying them religious legitimacy, and wondered, tongue-in-cheek, whether the "spiritual dignity" Lamm ascribed to them had any Jewish significance or was meant to equate a non-Orthodox rabbi to "a Jesuit priest, or to a Tibetan monk's search for nirvana...." He concluded with a challenge to Lamm:

---

31   Ari L. Goldman, "Jewish Moderate Urges Believers to Take a Stand," *New York Times,* March 24, 1988, p. 16.

32   "Welcome Return to Moderation," *Commentator,* May 17, 1988, p. 2.

33   Goldman, "Jewish Moderate," p. 16; Andrew Silow Carroll, "Call For Orthodox Moderation Earns Praise from Reform Leader," *JTA,* March 27, 1988.

Your lecture… was most disturbing. In the guise of a call for moderation, you in effect misled the broader public in regard to the Torah view on basic issues, and you maligned the 'Ultra-Orthodox' camp in the process…. Torah Jewry has the right to ask that as president of the Rabbi Isaac Elchanan Theological Seminary and spokesman for 'Centrist Orthodoxy,' you make the positions you espouse unequivocal and clear. The public has a right to know that behind the silk language of diplomacy lies acceptance of the harsh reality that *halacha* confers no rabbinic status whatsoever on Conservative and Reform rabbis…. Dr. Lamm, are you there with us?[34]

Lamm responded in a subsequent issue of the magazine by claiming that Twerski had gotten the wrong impression from the *Times* report. His acceptance of non-Orthodox groups as "valid," Lamm explained, meant nothing more than "de facto recognition" in the same sense that the Torah sometimes referred to pagan priests as "priests"—although he now wished he had "chosen a less equivocal and ambiguous word than 'valid.'" And as for "spiritual dignity," all he meant was that many non-Orthodox Jews were "religiously sincere."[35] Twerski, though, had the final word. If, he asked, the *Times* had misreported Lamm's speech to give the impression that he endorsed the legitimacy of the non-Orthodox streams, why had he not immediately demand a retraction? Twerski proceeded to pin Lamm to Irving Greenberg and his explicitly pluralist CLAL, at whose major conference Lamm had appeared to legitimize the non-Orthodox by proposing establishment of a *bet din* made up of rabbis from all Jewish denominations. Twerski bitingly chastised Lamm: "the Conservative and Reform leadership has been writing the music of 'pluralism'; Greenberg has furnished the orchestration; and, sadly, you wrote the lyrics."[36] Explaining to an interviewer that he had "anticipated a strong reaction when I criticized certain policies of the right wing," Lamm let the matter drop.[37]

---

[34] Aaron Twerski, "Open Letter to Dr. Norman Lamm," *The Jewish Observer,* April 1988, pp. 6–9. Nowhere in their correspondence does Twerski refer to Lamm as "Rabbi." An even sharper right-wing rebuke of Lamm, conveyed by Rabbi Mordechai Gifter in an address on Apr. 5, 1988, and circulated by audio recording, is excerpted under the title "Gifter Slaughters Lamm for Passover," in Zev Eleff, *Modern Orthodox Judaism: A Documentary History* (Philadelphia: Jewish Publication Society, 2016), pp. 355–58.

[35] Norman Lamm, "An Open Reply to Professor Aaron Twerski," *The Jewish Observer,* June 1988, pp. 13–16.

[36] Aaron Twerski, "A Rejoinder," ibid., pp. 17–26.

[37] "The Commentator Interview: President Norman Lamm," *Commentator,* Nov. 22, 1988, p. 6.

He turned his attention instead to a critique emanating from the other ideological extreme of Orthodoxy, conveyed to him privately rather than publicly. Greenberg, his host at the CLAL conference, complained to Lamm that his adoption of the "centrist" term seemed "a way of trying to distance himself from the left wing of modern Orthodoxy, i.e., people like me." And he asked:

> What does the term "centrist" mean? If you mean that the center is located in the middle of the Jewish people, with fifty percent to its right and fifty to its left, then that is where Orthodoxy would be. If you mean by "centrist" that modern Orthodoxy should station itself halfway between Yitz Greenberg and the Satmar Rebbe, then you turn Orthodoxy into some lunatic fringe—because more than ninety percent of the Jewish people is to my left.

Greenberg felt that Modern Orthodoxy should constitute the bridge between the Orthodox and the rest of the Jewish community, not, as he feared Lamm's centrist designation signified, a group of slightly secularized fellow travelers of the Haredim.[38]

At the 1989 RCA convention Lamm sought to clear up what he considered a misinterpretation of Centrism by denying both of Greenberg's proposed 50-yard-line hypotheticals. Without mentioning Greenberg by name, Lamm said he had never envisioned "that we locate ourselves midpoint between Orthodoxy and assimilationism and claim that territory as our religious home," since that was to abandon Torah Judaism. Neither was it his intention to stand at the center "between Satmar and the few intellectuals who presumably constitute the Orthodox Left," which would require "walking about the religious terrain with a yard-stick, calipers, and a pocket calculator." Rather than seeking such a mathematically determined center, Lamm explained that by centrism he intended "moderationism," a word he coined to invoke the "middle way" that Maimonides advocated for individual behavior. On the communal level, Lamm said, this entailed mutual respect, tolerance for dissent, consideration of all reasonable opinions—sometimes choosing one direction and sometimes another—and above all, avoidance of extreme solutions that all too often led to fanaticism. Urging his fellow Centrists to drop their overly "apologetic and defensive" posture, Lamm noted: "Our problem is a pedagogical one: how do we educate our people to be reflective and yet passionate,

---

[38]   Irving Greenberg, *Living in the Image of God: Jewish Teachings to Perfect the World, Conversations with Rabbi Irving Greenberg, as Conducted by Shalom Freedman* (Northvale, NJ: Jason Aronson, 1998), pp. 111–12.

civil and yet committed, enlightened and yet spirited."[39] To buttress his case for cooperation with the non-Orthodox, Lamm separately published a detailed halakhic analysis making the case that "the overwhelming majority of non-observant and non-religious Jews in our times" were not heretics in the eyes of Jewish law and were thus "fully within the Jewish people."[40]

Immoderation Rampant

Lamm's promulgation of moderationism neither mitigated the ongoing attacks from his rightist critics nor prevented an escalation of infighting within the Centrist/Modern Orthodox world. Even as Agudath Israel continued to accuse Lamm of legitimating heresy by promoting a joint *bet din* for conversions,[41] rabbis on the YU faculty spread the identical charge against their president and his centrist philosophy, eleven of them signing a letter denouncing Lamm's position that was leaked to the press. Rabbi Aharon Soloveitchik went so far as to compare such a *bet din* to the sin of the Golden Calf.[42]

The OU leadership too sided with Twerski rather than Lamm. President Kwestel echoed Agudath Israel by blaming the intensification of polarization within Orthodoxy on "so-called Orthodox groups euphemistically known as 'Centrist'" that taught "the flawed and erroneous premise that for the sake of Klal Yisrael [unity of the Jewish people], the Torah community must somehow recognize the non-Torah movements as legitimate expressions of Judaism." He argued that the OU should leave the Synagogue Council and, instead, help create a united Orthodox front.[43]

---

39   "Lamm's Moderationism Talk Convention Program Highlight," *Rabbinical Council Record,* Oct. 1989, pp. 1, 4. A revised version of Lamm's address under the title "Centrist Orthodoxy and Moderationism: Definitions and Desiderata," is in Lamm, *Seventy Faces,* I, pp. 54–64.

40   Norman Lamm, "Loving and Hating Jews as Halakhic Categories," *Tradition* 24, Winter 1989, pp. 98–122.

41   "Sherer tells Yeshiva U. 'don't connect with HUC'," *Jewish Post and Opinion,* Dec. 13, 1989, p. 41.

42   Jonathan Mark, "Yeshiva U's Lamm: A Rabbi Under Siege," *New York Jewish Week,* p. 24; Josh Fruchter and Tommy Werzberger, "The Making of Jonathan Mark's 'Siege,'" *Commentator,* Oct. 5, 1989, p. 6; Josh Fruchter and Daniel Oshinsky, "Rabbis' Letter Leaked," ibid., Nov. 9, 1989, pp. 1, 8.

43   Sidney Kwestel, "Appropriate and Inappropriate Legitimation," *Jewish Action,* Fall 1988, p. 9; Kwestel, "Truth, Peace and Ahavas Yisroel," ibid., Spring 1989, pp. 63–66; Kwestel, "President's Message," ibid., Fall 1989, p. 12.

The OU moved to purge its membership to facilitate such a rapprochement with the right. The organization, which as late as the 1960s had included many synagogues that lacked a *meḥitzah* (physical separation) between men's and women's sections and had sought for years to coax them to install such dividers, informed those congregations in 1985 that it would expel synagogues that refused to conform. Explaining the move, Rabbi Pinchas Stolper, the executive vice president, declared that *meḥitzah* "has become a weathervane of whether the congregation takes its Orthodoxy seriously or not."[44] In response, several rabbis serving in such pulpits and others sympathetic to them founded a new rabbinic group, the Fellowship of Traditional Orthodox Rabbis (FTOR), which held its first conference in August 1988. The fifty rabbis in attendance, about half of them also members of the RCA, called themselves centrists to denote their dissent from what they considered Orthodoxy's "turn to the right." Norman Lamm, who had coined the centrist label for that very purpose, declined comment. Both the OU and the RCA urged the new group to disband.[45] In 1990, the RCA notified its members who also belonged to FTOR that they risked expulsion, but reversed course under the threat of lawsuits. Another example of the turn to the right that year was the decision of the RCA *Va'ad Ha-Kavod,* a tribunal consisting of its former presidents, to investigate charges against Irving Greenberg for publicly suggesting that Christianity had much to teach Judaism and that Jesus was a "failed" rather than a "false" messiah, and for allegedly participating in non-Orthodox services as part of CLAL's interdenominational activities. Adverse publicity eventually convinced the RCA to drop the matter.[46]

In his keynote address to the 1993 RCA convention, Rabbi Lamm

---

44 Elena Neuman, "Thriving Orthodox Movement Split Between Strict and More Permissive," *JTA*, July 16, 1990.

45 Andrew Sillow Carroll, "New Centrist Group: A Splinter or a Branch?" *JTA*, Sept. 9, 1988.

46 Jonathan Mark, "Modern Orthodox Rabbis Claim Assault from RCA Right Wing," *New York Jewish Week,* July 13, 1990, pp. 4, 29, and letters to the editor ibid., July 27, 1990, pp. 22–23; Irving Greenberg, *For the Sake of Heaven and Earth: The New Encounter between Judaism and Christianity* (Philadelphia: Jewish Publication Society, 2004), pp. 33–35; Zev Eleff and Seth Farber, "Antimodernism and Orthodox Judaism's Heretical Imperative," *Religion and American Culture: A Journal of Interpretation* 30, Spring 2020, pp. 254–57; Irving "Yitz" Greenberg, "Modern Orthodoxy and the Road Not Taken: A Retrospective View," in Adam S. Ferziger, Miri Freud-Kandel, and Steven Bayme, eds., *Yitz Greenberg and Modern Orthodoxy: The Road Not Taken* (Boston: Academic Studies Press, 2019), pp. 34–35.

fiercely denounced the burgeoning extremism, declaring, "Much of Orthodoxy today is in the grips of a straightjacket on personal autonomy and independent thought imposed on even the most learned and distinguished who yield all to easily to blatant terrorism." He told the rabbis: "Anyone who submits to this kind of a threat ought to get out of the rabbinate and seal his mouth forever from uttering any opinion on anything other than the weather. The rabbinate must never become the sanctuary for moral cowards."[47]

The next year, prospects for more harmonious relations among the Orthodox factions improved when the Synagogue Council of America disbanded due to lack of funds and diminished interest on the part of its constituents. Relieved now of the constant need to justify its membership to Orthodox separatists, the OU believed that the closure "rid the Torah community of a gratuitous problem." A leading OU rabbi celebrated the occasion by pronouncing the traditional *Sheheheyanu* blessing thanking God who "granted us life and sustenance and enabled us to reach this time." Agudath Israel, too, expressed hope for better intra-Orthodox relations.[48]

The disappearance of the Synagogue Council, however, hardly muted the battle within Orthodoxy. At YU, Norman Lamm 's decision in 1995 to allow student-activity fees to be used for gay clubs at three of the university's graduate schools so as not to risk the withdrawal of government funding—even while he maintained that homosexual acts were contrary to Jewish law—drew not only the ire of the *Jewish Observer* but also a letter of protest signed by twenty-four members of his own rabbinic faculty.[49] The next year, the Young Israel network of Orthodox synagogues, originally Modern Orthodox but now strongly influenced by the separatists, rebuffed a proposed merger with the much larger OU on the grounds that the latter still included four member congregations without *mehitzot* and was insufficiently answerable to rabbinic authority. Young Israel proceeded to adopt Star-K, a private company, as its kosher certification

---

[47] "President of Yeshiva University Calls for Renewed Rabbinic Leadership," YU press release, June 16, 1993.

[48] Saul Bernstein, *The Orthodox Union Story: A Centenary Portrayal* (Northvale, NJ: Jason Aronson, 1997), p. 359; *American Jewish Year Book 1996* (New York: AJC, 1996), p. 163; Rabbi Shmuel Bloom, "Synagogue Council of America (1926–1994): A Post-Mortem," *Jewish Observer,* Feb. 1995, pp. 28–31.

[49] "A Letter That Should NOT Have Had to Have Been Published," ibid., Summer 1995, pp. 30–32; Binyamin Jolkovsky, "Sages of Yeshiva Issue a Dissent on Lamm's Law," *Forward,* July 17, 1995, pp. 1, 4.

agency, in direct competition with the OU, which, it claimed, had lower kashrut standards.[50]

Even in the absence of the Synagogue Council, Modern/Centrist fear of seeming to countenance non-Orthodox forms of Judaism continued to affect its policies. In 1997, the OU refused to participate in "Shabbat Across America," a broad-based project to encourage Jews to observe the Sabbath, because it might appear to condone non-Orthodox forms of Sabbath observance, even though many individual Orthodox synagogues took part. In 1998, the OU declined to be part of Jewish Web/Net Week that linked over 600 Jewish websites, because participation might seem to associate the organization with non-Orthodox sites. The RCA president that year turned down an invitation to a joint study session with non-Orthodox rabbis at the Council of Jewish Federations General Assembly. And the basketball league of New York yeshiva high schools refused to admit the (Conservative) Solomon Schechter schools, one principal explaining that he wanted his students to associate only with those "who share our philosophy of Judaism." Meanwhile, Lamm's association with ongoing efforts to devise an interdenominational mechanism for facilitating conversions to Judaism in Israel earned him the sobriquet "hater of God" from a leading Agudath Israel sage.[51] Eventually, even Lamm succumbed to the rhetoric of delegitimization, predicting, in 2009, "with a heavy heart," that "we will soon say Kaddish on the Reform and Conservative movements."[52]

A Proliferation of Centrisms

Lamm's promotion of Orthodox centrism as updated Maimonidean moderationism not only failed to moderate the religious climate, but it also opened the door to others who—against his clearly stated wishes—reified Centrism into a separate form of Orthodoxy different, ideologically and behaviorally, from both the right-wing Haredi and the Modern varieties, though opinions differed widely over its exact nature.

---

50 Debra Nussbaum Cohen, "Young Israel Resists Effort by OU Head to Merge Agencies," *JTA*, May 28, 1996; Stewart Ain, "Unholy Alliance?" *New York Jewish Week*, Jan. 26, 1996, p. 7.
51 Debra Nussbaum Cohen, "Streams Join Forces to Promote Shabbat Experiences for Everyone," *JTA* Mar. 28, 1997; *American Jewish Year Book 1999*, p. 180; Mendy Ganchrow, MD, *Journey Through the Minefields: From Vietnam to Washington, An Orthodox Surgeon's Odyssey* (Silver Spring, MD: Eshel Books, 2004), pp. 198–201.
52 Matthew Wagner, "Non-Orthodox Judaism Disappearing," *Jerusalem Post*, May 10, 2009, jpost.com/Jewish-World/Jewish-News/Non-Orthodox-Judaism-disappearing.

Journalists reporting on the impressive growth of Orthodox communities found the term useful because it helped them lay out a taxonomy of Orthodoxy's divergent forms. For example, an extensive 1989 account of Orthodoxy in Baltimore—said to have the largest percentage of Orthodox Jews of any American city—divided the community into four segments. The right wing, dominated by the "yeshiva world," according to the authors, "tend to separate themselves from the rest of society... are generally passive when it comes to the secular State of Israel... and are wary of modernity." The centrists, in contrast, are portrayed as "open to secular culture, unabashedly Zionist, and tolerant of varying opinions." Orthodoxy's left wing is associated with the few "observant feminists" in town, and Modern Orthodox is described as a "nebulous term" that may be synonymous with centrism in some cities but in Baltimore meant the nonobservant, nominally Orthodox.[53]

Social scientists professionally attuned to changing trends and novel terms to describe them, quickly picked up the nomenclature as well. First out of the gate were sociologists Samuel C. Heilman and Steven M. Cohen, whose 1989 book *Cosmopolitans and Parochials* sought to define the distinctions between what they considered three forms of Modern Orthodoxy—nominal (relatively nonobservant), centrist, and traditional (highly observant)—on the basis of answers to a questionnaire completed by some 1,000 self-identified Modern Orthodox Jews in the New York area. Respondents were asked about their Jewish ritual practices (ranging from Sabbath observance to not eating on the little-known fast of the Tenth of Tevet); belief in such tenets of Judaism as the existence of God, revelation, and the coming of the Messiah; friendship patterns with Orthodox and other Jews; giving to Jewish causes; the Jewish education of their children; leisure pursuits; political and social opinions; and attitudes toward premarital sex. The book described the centrists, those with scores in the middle range, as "sitting at the epicenter of the crossroads of the traditional and contemporary worlds," a situation they manage "by compartmentalizing their lives." Heilman and Cohen called them "an aggregate of the ambivalent"—hardly what Rabbi Lamm could ever have imagined when he conceived Centrism.[54] The book drew criticism for employing

53   Arthur J. Magida and Gary Rosenblatt, "Orthodox Judaism: A Surge to the Right," *Baltimore Jewish Times,* June 9, 1989, pp. 52–53.

54   Samuel C. Heilman and Steven M. Cohen, *Cosmopolitans and Parochials: Modern Orthodox Jews in America* (Chicago: University of Chicago Press, 1989), quotations on pp. 209–10.

an allegedly skewed and unrepresentative sample and for positing a "centrist" category lacking "conceptual coherence."[55] The search for a sociologically meaningful category of centrist Orthodox Jews continued.

It was not until 2017 that a more sophisticated portrait of centrism emerged from the Nishma organization under the direction of research and marketing professional Mark Trencher. Nishma worked with a sample of almost 4,000 Jews across the country who called themselves Modern Orthodox. Instead of categorizing them on the basis of responses to a questionnaire, it asked them to self-identify as either Open Orthodox (12 percent), Liberal Modern Orthodox (22 percent), Modern Orthodox (41 percent), Centrist Orthodox (14 percent), or "Right-wing Centrist Orthodox (tending toward Yeshivish)" (11 percent). Respondents were also asked about their theological views, observance patterns, the importance of Orthodox practice in their lives, their opinions on the role of women in Judaism and whether gays should be accepted as synagogue members. Responses correlated almost exactly with the self-identifications, the proportion of those supplying the most traditional answers rising steadily from the more left-wing categories to the center and on to the right. Perhaps the most significant finding was that 39 percent of the entire sample said they had become more observant over the past decade and 23 percent less observant, evidence both of growing polarization in the Orthodox community and its overall move to the right.[56]

The Jewish day-school world also found the distinction between Centrist and Modern Orthodoxy a valuable explanatory tool. In the late 1990s, the Avi Chai Foundation sponsored *A Census of Jewish Day Schools in the United States 2000*. It would go on to fund and publish three more such reports, at five-year intervals, by 2014. Alongside Ḥasidic, Ḥabad, yeshivaworld, non-Orthodox, and nondenominational community schools, the *Census* categorized Centrist and Modern Orthodox schools as two separate types, the major difference between them being the coeducational schooling provided by the Modern, in contrast to the separate-gender setup of the Centrist. Also, the Modern schools, unlike the Centrist, "generally" used Hebrew for Jewish studies, emphasized the significance of the State of Israel, took "a modernist approach to contemporary issues, such

---

[55] David Berger, "Modern Orthodoxy in the United States: A Review Essay," *Modern Judaism* 11, Dec. 1991, pp. 261–72.

[56] *The Nishma Research Profile of American Modern Orthodox Jews Summary Report,* Sept. 28, 2017, http://nishmaresearch.com. Samuel Heilman came to a similar conclusion when he revisited his centrists in a work whose title indicates what he thought happened to them and their children: *Sliding to the Right: The Contest for the Future of American Jewish Orthodoxy* (Berkeley: University of California Press, 2006).

as feminism," and included "marginally Orthodox and non-Orthodox students."[57] A decade later, the third *Census* added the "intensity" of Jewish studies as another distinguishing mark of Centrist schools, and—with probably unintentional irony—girls studying Talmud as an identifying feature of Modern Orthodox institutions.[58] Both that *Census* and the final edition in 2014 reported the reassignment of a number of schools from the Modernist to the Centrist categories, a shift the author ascribed to changes in the schools—most notably separation of the sexes at earlier ages—made necessary by the desire of Modern Orthodox parents to give their children a Centrist education.[59]

By then the Centrist label had also taken on another function—a pejorative way to designate trends in the Orthodox community that one found unserious, even counterfeit. Depending on one's ideological preferences, Centrism could be "just a form of Charedi Judaism that speaks English passably and wears Western clothes," or else "Torah and popular culture" for wealthy Jews who were fixated on "the NCAA playoffs and Netflix movies" and whose children spent their leisure time at "birthday parties, play dates, and continuous recreation."[60]

Second Thoughts

"The semiotics of being Orthodox have never been more complex," a 1994 JTA report began, noting that while "centrist" had been gradually replacing "modern" over the previous ten years, "not everyone is happy about it or even sure what it means." Jews, apparently, like many other Americans, were "growing increasingly suspicious of anything smacking of modernity," and "no matter how liberal an interpreter of Jewish law

---

57   Marvin Schick, *A Census of Jewish Day Schools in the United States* (Avi Chai, Jan. 2000), p. 8.

58   Marvin Schick, *A Census of Jewish Day Schools in the United States 2008–09* (Avi Chai, Oct. 2009), p. 9.

59   Ibid, p. 12; Marvin Schick, *A Census of Jewish Day Schools in the United States 2013–14* (Avi Chai, Oct. 2014), p. 8.

60   Rabbi Michael Chernick, "Condemning Unfairly: A Reply to Avrohom Gordimer," *Jewish Link,* Sept. 24, 2015, https://jewishlink.news/features/9700-condemning-unfairly-a-reply-to-avrohom-gordimer; Alan Brill, "The Emerging Popular Culture and the Centrist Community," in Yehuda Sarna, ed., *Developing a Jewish Perspective on Culture* (Jersey City: KTAV, 2013), pp. 39, 37.

someone may be, they describe themselves as centrist" to avoid identifi-
cation with the left.[61] Four years later journalist Samuel G. Freedman drew
an analogy to the rise of political conservatism in the United States, writing:

> The very term "Modern Orthodox" has become so pejorative—it is
> to observant Jews what "liberal" is to Democrats—that even its
> practitioners prefer to call themselves "centrist" or "traditional."[62]

Rabbi Rafael Grossman, rabbi of the Baron Hirsch Synagogue in
Memphis and a past president of the RCA, opined that while "the majority
of Jews identifying as Orthodox are centrist… none can clearly assert
what centrist Orthodoxy is about."[63] Richard Joel, who succeeded Lamm
as YU's president, evinced similar puzzlement, responding to a question
about centrism by recalling that someone once told him that "a centrist is
someone who agrees with me."[64]

By then, however, it made little difference: Rabbi Lamm, who found
the words Modern Orthodox so objectionable thirty years earlier, had already disowned his replacement for it and reverted to the original brand.
Telling a reporter in 1994 that he regretted the confusion, Lamm declared,
"I wear the name 'Modern Orthodox' as a badge of honor." Eight years
later Lamm published two volumes of his essays, including those through
which he had introduced and elucidated Centrist Orthodoxy. He explained in the introduction that he had, indeed, avoided the term Modern
Orthodox "for a while" because it seemed "as if we were boasting of our
modernity when, indeed, we were hardly uncritical of it even though we
stand for engaging it openly and forthrightly." He had introduced Centrist
Orthodoxy in its place "intending not a mathematical mean between two
extremes, but… Maimonides' principle of moderation." Since his intentions continued to be misunderstood,

> I have therefore reverted to the term Modern Orthodoxy. I assure
> the reader that there was and is no difference in my mind between
> the two, and I apologize to the sociologists and other pundits for
> having wasted their time and intellectual effort as they labored to
> define the differences between the two.[65] ෬

---

61 Debra Nussbaum Cohen, "The Changing Orthodox World—What's in a Name:
    A Lot," *JTA*, Dec. 30, 1994.
62 Samuel G. Freedman, "Yeshivish at Yale," *New York Times Sunday Magazine,* May
    24, 1998, p. 34.
63 Debra Nussbaum Cohen, "Modern Orthodox Jews Engage in Public Search for
    New Identity," *JTA*, Feb. 3, 1999.
64 Mindy Schiller, "The Middle Man: A Conversation with Richard Joel," *World
    Jewish Digest,* Aug. 2008, p. 51.
65 Cohen, "The Changing Orthodox World"; Lamm, *Seventy Faces,* I, p. 1.

A Letter from Rabbi Joseph B. Soloveitchik to Aaron Zeitlin[*]

Edited By: ELIYAHU KRAKOWSKI, HESHEY ZELCER and MARK ZELCER

Rav Soloveitchik wrote this letter to Aaron Zeitlin on September 14, 1955, just a few days before Rosh Hashanah, and seven months before he would deliver his famous lecture that became *Kol Dodi Dofek*, outlining the Jewish people's obligation to the State of Israel. Zeitlin[1] was a professor of Hebrew literature at Jewish Theological Seminary, a poet and playwright, who authored various books and articles in both Yiddish and Hebrew.[2]

Rav Soloveitchik, in his letter, mentions that he "read and greatly enjoyed" a *kuntres* (pamphlet) that Zeitlin wrote, but does not mention its title. Nonetheless, it appears that Rav Soloveitchik is responding to Zeitlin's 1955 Hebrew pamphlet, *המדינה והרוח: מסה פוליטוסופית בי"ג פרקים*, *The State and the Spirit: An Essay on Political Philosophy in Thirteen Chapters* (NY: *Ha-Doar*, 1955). The underlying theme of the book is how to structure an ideal state. The first seven chapters summarize and discuss how philosophers throughout the ages—from Plato and Aristotle to Cervantes, Shakespeare (in *Hamlet*), Hegel, Marx, Ernst Cassirer, and others—had envisioned an ideal state. Chapters 9 through 13 are Zeitlin's view on how to structure an ideal Jewish State. Chapter 8 transitions from states in general to a Jewish State in particular.

Zeitlin sees the history of Jewish nationhood as bracketed by two visions. At the beginning of Jewish history, we have the vision presented by Moshe Rabbeinu. At the other end of Jewish history—in our current era in which we have regained sovereignty in the Land of Israel—we need to implement the messianic vision of the prophets. Instead of phil-

---

[*] The editors thank: Tzemach Glenn for providing Ḥakirah with a copy of Rav Soloveitchik's letter; Tina Weiss of the Mendel Gottesman Library of Yeshiva University for her invaluable research assistance; and Deborah Schranz of the Library of the Jewish Theological Seminary.

Eliyahu Krakowski is associate editor of OU Press. Heshey Zelcer is on the editorial board of Ḥakirah. Mark Zelcer teaches philosophy at Queensborough Community College, CUNY. Heshey and Mark Zelcer coauthored *The Philosophy of Joseph B. Soloveitchik* (Routledge, 2021).

osophical ideas forming the foundation of a Jewish State, we must instead use the divine ideals of the Torah. The goal of a Jewish State is to form a holy nation, composed of holy people, exemplifying the universal ideals envisioned by the prophets. Judaism will then be in a position to realize the prophetic ideals and become a light unto the nations.

In the letter, Rav Soloveitchik tells Zeitlin that he agrees with many of his assumptions and conclusions. Nonetheless, without directly contradicting or criticizing him, Rav Soloveitchik points out that one of Zeitlin's central ideas—that the State of Israel should seek to mirror the messianic universalistic vision of the prophets—is used by some to denigrate the Judaism of the last two millennia. Rav Soloveitchik is especially critical of Ben-Gurion who "is in love" with Spinoza,[3] and for whom "the Oral Torah is totally non-existent. The biblical period ended; the period of chaos began and it continued until the emergence of modern Hebrew literature."

While Rav Soloveitchik believed that the then-new Jewish State was a great and important event for the Jewish people, he did not view it necessarily as a messianic event.[4] Zeitlin, however, saw the formation of the State of Israel in messianic terms. Rav Soloveitchik in his letter does not mention that he disagrees with Zeitlin on this issue.

A few points of contact between the letter and Rav Soloveitchik's other works are worth noting. First, Rav Soloveitchik's letter was written around the same time he gave a course on "The Relationship between Halakhah, Aggadah and Kabbalah."[5] This triad is noted in the letter. Second, the letter notes that Halakhah should be the source for Jewish philosophy. This is an idea Rav Soloveitchik formulated in *The Halakhic Mind* and pursued for the rest of his writing career. Finally, Rav Soloveitchik mentions that he had suggested to Rabbi Samuel Belkin, then president of Yeshiva University (who also received a copy of Zeitlin's pamphlet),[6] "that it is incumbent upon us to establish a center for research into our worldview and to formulate our stance with regard to the problems that echo through the void of our cultural world, confused about itself and seeking its repair."[7]

(Editor's note: The handwritten text of our letter, as opposed to the signature, does not appear to be that of Rav Soloveitchik. Apparently, Rav Soloveitchik had dictated this letter and someone else transcribed it into written form. Rav Soloveitchik subsequently reviewed it, made corrections and signed it.)

Front page of Aaron Zeitlin's pamphlet   *First page of Rav Soloveitchik's letter*

Following is the transcription of Rav Soloveitchik's three-page Hebrew
letter, and facing each page is an English translation. An image of each
page follows.

1

יוסף דוב הלוי סולוביצ'יק

Joseph Soloveitchik

34 Hutchings Street

Roxbury 21, Mass.

Wednesday, 27th day of Elul, 5715 [9/14/1955]

To the sublime author, enlightened man of exemplary character, Mr. Aaron Zeitlin, may he[8] live and be well, greetings and blessings!

Forgive me, my honorable master, for aligning myself with those who "mourn the appointed time," and for being among those who procrastinate when answering letters. Exertion does much to a person, and I desperately needed to rest and relax from my routine work—which exhausts body and soul—such that I was unable during the summer months to accomplish even that which is of utmost importance. Your honor's good heart makes me confident he will understand and judge me favorably.

I read your pamphlet and greatly enjoyed it. I was delighted both by its lively, bubbling content, overflowing with clear ideas, sensitivity and refined emotions (when dealing with Jewish thought, it is also necessary to have an affective [or emotional] approach, warm and heartfelt. Cool and complacent logic, as objective as it may be, does not suffice), and also by its beautiful form that radiates light and splendor. I already stressed in my first letter, without any trace of flattery, God forbid, that many of our assumptions and conclusions converge onto the same path.

Thank you for your brilliant efforts to clarify and formulate the essence of Jewish political philosophy. Now that the Jewish State is being conceived—born and formed—we need this type of research, as it [the Jewish State] has not yet found its essence and uniqueness. I have discussed many times with my friend Rabbi [Samuel] Belkin, president of Yeshivat Rabbi Yitzhak Elhanan, that it is incumbent upon us to establish a center for research into our worldview and to formulate our stance with regard to the problems that echo through the void of our cultural world, confused about itself and seeking its repair. It appears to me that we need to start, not with theological-metaphysical investigations, as our sages did in the Middle Ages, but rather with a practical philosophy, with religious values that affect the existence of the real human being, and which flow into the cauldron of his clamorous day-to-day life. Our contemporaries, who strive for a safe harbor, expect redemption and salvation not through abstract thinking and a grasp of the ontic essence via metaphysical speculation [*ma'aseh bereishit u-ma'aseh merkavah*], but rather by combining our cultural consciousness with firm values and an absolute axiological vision. Truthfully, our Halakhah was never addicted to the speculative which is detached from reality, and which deals with the transcendental world. It [Halakhah] was always interested in the most real-life question: What is the duty of man within his physical surroundings,

א

יוסף דוב הלוי סולוביצ'יק
Joseph Soloveitchik
34 Hutchings Street
Roxbury 21, Mass.

יום ד',כ"ז אלול, תשט"ו

כבוד הסופר הנעלה, איש האשכלות ובחיר המדות, מר אהרן צייטלין, שיחיה,
שלום וברכה!

יסלח לי אדוני הנכבד על אשר השתיקתי ל"נוגי מועד"[9] והייתי מן המפגרים בעניני
כתיבת אגרות שלום. הרבה היגיעה עושה, ואני כה הוצרכתי לנופש ולמנוחה מעבודתי
השיגרתית המפרכת את הגוף וגם את הנפש עד שלא נזדקקתי בירחי הקיץ אפילו לדברים
היותר חשובים. מובטחני בטוב לבו של מע"כ, כי ילמד עלי סניגוריה ויזכני.

קראתי את קונטרסו ונהניתי מאד ממנו. התבשמתי בין מן התוכן החי והמפעפע, גדוש
רעיונות בהירים, רגשות והרגשות עדינים (כשדנים על מחשבת היהדות זקוקים גם לגישה
אפקטיבית, חמה ולבבית. אין ההגיון השאנן והצונן על כל האוביקטיביות שבו מספיק.), בין
מן הצורה הנאה השופעת אור וזוהר. כבר הדגשתי במכתבי הראשון, ללא כל שמץ של
חנופה, ח"ו, כי אנו נפגשים בשביל אחד בנוגע להרבה הנחות ומסקנות.

יישר כחו על נסיונו הנהדר ללבן ולנסח את יסודות הפילוסופיה הפוליטית של היהדות.
אנו צריכים למחקר כזה עכשיו בשעת הרת מדיניות ישראלית–לידתה והתהוותה–שלא
מצאה עדיין את עצמותה ואת יחודה. הרבה פעמים שוחחתי את ידידי, הרב בלקין, נשיא
ישיבת רי"א, כי עלינו ליסד מרכז לחקירה בהשקפת עולמנו ולניסוח עמדתנו ביחס לכל
הבעיות המנסרות בחללו של העולם התרבותי התוהה על עצמו ומבקש את תיקונו. מדומני,
שעלינו להתחיל לא בחקירות תיאולוגיות-מיטפיסיות, כמו שנהגו חכמינו בימי הביניים, כי
אם בניסוח פילוסופיה שימושית ומערכת ערכים דתיים המשתבצים לתוך קיום ישות-אדם
ממשי והזורמים לתוך קלחת חייו הגועשים, היום-יומיים. בן דורנו החותר לקראת חוף
מבטחים מצפה לפדיון ולגאולה לא דרך המופשט ההגיוני והתעלות ההכרה הטהורה בתפיסת
המוחלט האונטי, בבחינת מעשה בראשית ומעשה מרכבה, כי עם על ידי התערוב התודעה
התרבותית בערכים יציבים ובחזון המוחלט האקסיולוגי. לאמתו של דבר, ההלכה שלנו
מעולם לא התמכרה למופלא הספקולטיבי, המנותק מן הממשיות והרוחץ בעולם
טרנסצנדנטלי, ותמיד התעניינה בשאלה האקטואלית ביותר: מה היא חובתו של האדם בתוך
הסביבה המוחשית,

<u>2</u>

within the world containing a plethora of colors, sounds, smells, impressions and reactions; and how can he realize his true self? It is now appropriate to abandon for a short while the inquiry into "what is ahead" and "what is behind" and concentrate on our actual religious experience, which takes place in real-time, and which constitutes a central, durable fact in the ever-changing stream of man's being. This experience requires us to clarify our stance, our fate and our destiny, our obligations and our abilities. We do not need help from the schools of existential philosophy of Kierkegaard or the circles of Heidegger, Jaspers, and contemporary French thinkers; we may compare and evaluate but we need not imitate.

The time is right for such research and formulation. American philosophy of religion and theology is beginning to break free from the stagnation of pragmatism[10] and from the grasp of superficial liberalism,[11] and it now desires its own self-image. The erroneous system that was so prevalent among religious leaders here—that the purpose of faith is to sweeten the bitterness of existence and provide comfort and peace of mind for the hardships of the day for those who are lost and dejected, and that it is but a useful device which was only created to serve man and his practical needs[12]—is slowly subsiding. In its place arises the correct understanding: that the bond between man and his Creator has a different mission, and that there are new dimensions, and spectacular and shining horizons, beyond a [mere] sweet night's sleep. They roll their eyes at the man of faith. It is true that these ideas are ancient, and many have already trodden in this path. Our State, however, is full of pioneering spirit, fast paced, and bold and daring economically and technologically. It has not managed until now to follow this line of thinking, and dismissed it as a European creation rooted in the bankruptcy of the poor, passive man of the old country. [They say] that the dynamism and assertiveness of such an aggressive type cannot coexist with her [the Jewish religion]. Now the situation is changing, and the buds are seen in the Land. Judaism with its Halakhah—the great religious imperative—can be a sublime and pure lifestyle in such a spiritual atmosphere.

Such research should be based, as I have emphasized above, not on apologetics and imitation, on categories and templates of thought from foreign sources; nor on adornments and eye-shadow for the sake of seeking favor, honeycombs of homiletical sentimentalism which lack any flavor. Only a sharp and smooth analysis of our religious consciousness against the backdrop of an affective [or emotional] connection, strengthening our awareness, will produce for us the true results. The main point is not to lose sight of the Halakhah which embodies the essence of Judaism.[13]

When I read occasionally (not often) writings of Ben-Gurion on the essence of Judaism,[14] when he begins to quote Tanakh and to plant nails and spurs with assurances of "everyone knows," I am frightened both by the haughtiness that oozes from every word, and by the Karaism hovering over his "sensational" statements. For him, the Oral Torah is totally non-existent. The biblical period ended; the period of chaos began and it continued until the emergence of modern Hebrew literature. (I forgot Spinoza, with whom Ben-Gurion is in love!)[15]

ב

רבת צבעים וקולות, ריחות, רשמים ותגובות, ואיך הוא יכול להגשים את עצמותו הממשית?
עתה יאה להזניח לשעה קטנה את החקירה ב"מה לפנים" וב"מה לאחור"[16] ולהתרכז
בחוויתנו הדתית הריאלית, המתרחשת בזמן, והמהווה עובדה צנטרלית יציבה בהוויתו
השוטפת של האדם. חוויה זו דורשת מאתנו בירור עמדתנו, גורלנו ויעודנו, חובתנו ויכלתנו.
אין אנו זקוקים לעזר מצד הפילוסופיה האכסיסטנציאלית מבית מדרשו של קירקגור או
מחוגי היידגר, יספרס וההוגים הצרפתיים העכשויים, אנו יכולים להשוות ולדמות, אבל אין
אנו צריכים לחקות.

השעה מסוגלת למחקר ולניסוח מעין זה. הפילוסופיה של הדת והתיאולוגיה
האמריקאיות מתחילות להשתחרר מקפאונם הפרגמטי ומחרצובות הליברליזם השטחי
ומבקשת דמות דיוקן עצמאית לאט לאט שוקעת השיטה המוטעת שהייתה רווחת כל כך בין
מנהיגים דתיים כאן, כי האמונה באה לשם המתקת מרירות הקיום ומתן נוחיות ומנוחת הנפש
לקשי יום, לאובדים ולנדחים, ואינה אלא מכשיר שימושי שכולו לא נוצר אלא לשרת את
האדם וצרכיו הממשיים. במקומה בוקעת ועולה ההבנה הנכונה שמשימה אחרת מיועדת
לזיקת האדם ליוצרו ושדימנסיות חדשות ואופקים מרהיבים ומזהירים מלבד שינת ליל
מתוקה, קורצים עין לאיש הדת. אמנם עתיקים המה דברים אלה, וכבר הלכו במקצוע זה
הנמושות. ברם, מדינתנו ספוגת חלוציות, בעלת קצב מהיר וחרג כלכלי-טכנולוגי נועז, לא
הסתגלה עד הנה להלך מחשבה כזה והביטה עליו בביטול כעל תוצרת אירופאית המושרשת
בפשיטת הרגל של האדם העדל והסביל של היבשת הישנה, שאין הדינמיות והתקיפות של
הטיפוס האגרסיבי הכא יכולות לדור עמדה בכפיפה אחת. עכשיו נשתנתה המצב, והנצנים
נראו בארץ. היהדות עם ההלכה שלה, בת האימפרטיב הדתי הכביר, יכולה להיות אורחות
חיים נעלים וטהורים באווירה רוחנית כזו.

מחקר כזה צריך להתבסס, כפי שהטעמתי למעלה, לא על אפולוגיטיקה וחיקוי דברים,
קטגוריות ודפוסי מחשבה מתחומים זרים, לא על פירכוס וכחילת עין לשם העלאת חן ולא
על נופת צופים של סנטימנטליות דרושית חסרת-טעם רק ניתוח חד וחלק של התודעה
הדתית שלנו על רקע זיקה אפקטיבית, רפודת[17] הכרה, ימציא לנו את התוצאות האמתיות.
עיקר העיקרים הוא מבלי להסיח דעת מן ההלכה התופסת טיבורית של היהדות.

כשאני קורא לפרקים (רחוקים) את מאמרי בן גוריון על אודות מהותה של היהדות,
כשהוא מתחיל לצטט את התנ"ך ולטעת מסמרים ודורבנות בבטיחות של "כל יודע", אני
נבהל בין פני מפני הגאווה המבצבצת מכל מלה ומלה, ובין מפני הקראות המרחפת על פני
הצהרותיו ה"סנסציונליות." אין בכלל תורה שבע"פ קיימת בעדו. תקופת התנ"ך מסתיימת,
תקופת תהו ובהו מתחילה ונמשכת עד הופעת הספרות העברית החדשה. (שכחתי את
שפינוזה, שבן גוריון התאהב בו!)

<u>3</u>
יוסף דוב הלוי סולוביצ'יק
Joseph Soloveitchik
34 Hutchings Street
Roxbury 21, Mass.

Ben-Gurion, to our great sorrow, is not the only one with this false and inane perspective. Many writers and thinkers see the unfolding of our history in this fashion. There was [a period of] being, of nothingness, and again of being. Of course, the nothingness exceeds the [period of] existence. Surely, from a numerical perspective, the prophetic era was short, and the era of the Oral Torah was long! The term "Talmud" leaves a bad taste in their bones, like that which the Christian theologians tasted throughout the generations. It is therefore no surprise that Ben-Gurion said what he said about our political views, and prostrated himself before the scholars of Athens and their works in which he "specializes."

It is impossible to speak about our Written Torah as a stand-alone unit. We have our Tanakh, which is woven through with the Oral Law, or perhaps the reverse; we have an Oral Law which encircles the prophets, whose words were also meant to be written. We do not have the right, however, to distinguish between the Written [Torah] and our heritage; between the letter and the thought of the heart. I am therefore uncomfortable with the terms "prophetic Judaism," the "prophetic conception," the "prophetic ethic," etc. They have double-meanings. Sometimes the reader gets the impression that [these terms] are only meant to stress the distance between those things which are connected, and to declare the bifurcation of Judaism, which is the basis of Christian understanding of our history. How disturbed I become when I stumble across expressions like these by Jewish scholars, who speak about the view of the Talmud as opposed to the outlook of the prophets! This is precisely the theological basis of the Church. We believe in all the power our historical consciousness; prophecy too folds into the infinite stream of the transmission and the tradition which flows forever. The Written Torah and the Oral Torah are a firm and interwoven unity. It is impossible to separate them, just as we cannot separate the flame from the candle.

I therefore cherish and love his honor and his opinions, for he is one of the few Jewish authors who insists on the unity, the continuity and the identity of the Divine spirit in its trans-historical revelation, whether in the Holy Writings or in the thought of the Oral Torah—Halakhah, Aggadah, the esoteric teachings, etc.

I wish him a good writ and sentence, for a year of life and peace, a year of creation and innovation.

Yours, with great appreciation,
Yosef Dov ha-Levi Soloveitchik

ג
יוסף דוב הלוי סולוביצ'יק
Joseph Soloveitchik
34 Hutchings Street
Roxbury 21, Mass.

בן גוריון, לדאבוננו הגדול, איננו יחיד במינו ביחס לתפיסה מסולפת ושגעונית כזו. הרבה
סופרים והוגי דעות רואים את ההשתלשלות ההיסטורית שלנו בדמות כזו – יש, אין ויש.
כמובן, האפסות מרובה על הקיימת, לכה"פ מבחינה מספרית, כמה קצרה היא תקופת
הנביאים, וכמה ארוכה היא תקופת תורה שבע"פ! המונח "תלמוד" נותן טעם לפגם
בעצמותיהם כמו אותו הטעם שטעמו בו התיאולוגים הנוצריים מדור דור. לפיכך אין כל
תימה בדבר, שבן גוריון אמר מה שאמר ע"ד תפיסתנו הפוליטית וכרע ברך לפני חכמי
אתונא ש"התמחה" בהם ובתורתם.

אי אפשר לדבר על תורה שבכתב כחטיבה בפני עצמה. יש לנו תנ"ך שלתוכו משתבצת
תורה שבע"פ, או להיפך, יש לנו תורה שבע"פ המקיפה את הנביאים שדבריהם נתנו גם
להכתב. ברם, אין לנו רשות להבדיל בין הכתב והמסורה, בין האות והגות הלב.

לכן אין דעתי נוחה מן המונחים "היהדות הנבואית" "התפיסה הנבואית", ה"מוסר
הנבואי" וכיוצא בהם. דו-משמעות ישנו בהם. לפעמים הקורא מתרשם כאילו לא באו אלא
להדגיש את הרווח בין הדבקים ולהכריז על השניות שביהדות שנעשית לבסיס התפיסה
הנוצרית של ההיסטוריה שלנו. כמה ירגז בטני כשאני נתקל בביטויים כאלה אצל חכמי
ישראל המדברים על התפיסה התלמודית בניגוד להשקפה הנבואית. הלא על גישה כזו
מבוססת התיאולוגיה של הכנסיה. אנו מאמינים בכל עצמת תודעתנו ההיסטורית, כי גם
הנבואה מתקפלת לתוך הזרם הנצחי של קבלה ומסורה השוטף מעולם עד עולם. תורה
שבכתב ותורה שבע"פ מהוות אחדות גמורה ומשוכללת, ואי אפשר להפרישן כמו שאין
לנתק את השלהבת מן הנר.

לכן אני מוקיר ומחבב את מע"כ ואת דעותיו, כי הלא הוא מן יחידי סגולה, בין סופרי
ישראל, שעמדו על אחידות זו ועל המשכיות הרוח האלקי וזהותו בהתגלותו העל-היסטורית
בין בכתבי הקודש ובין במחשבת תורה שבע"פ – הלכה, האגדה, תורת המסתורין וכו'.
אני מאחל לו כתיבה וחתימה טובה לשנת חיים ושלום, שנת יצירה וחדוש.

שלו בהוקרה רבה,
יוסף דוב הלוי סולוביי'צ'יק
ଓଃ

HIGHLANDS 5-4687

K

יוסף דוב הלוי סולוביצ'יק

JOSEPH SOLOVEITCHIK

34 HUTCHINGS STREET

ROXBURY 21, MASS.

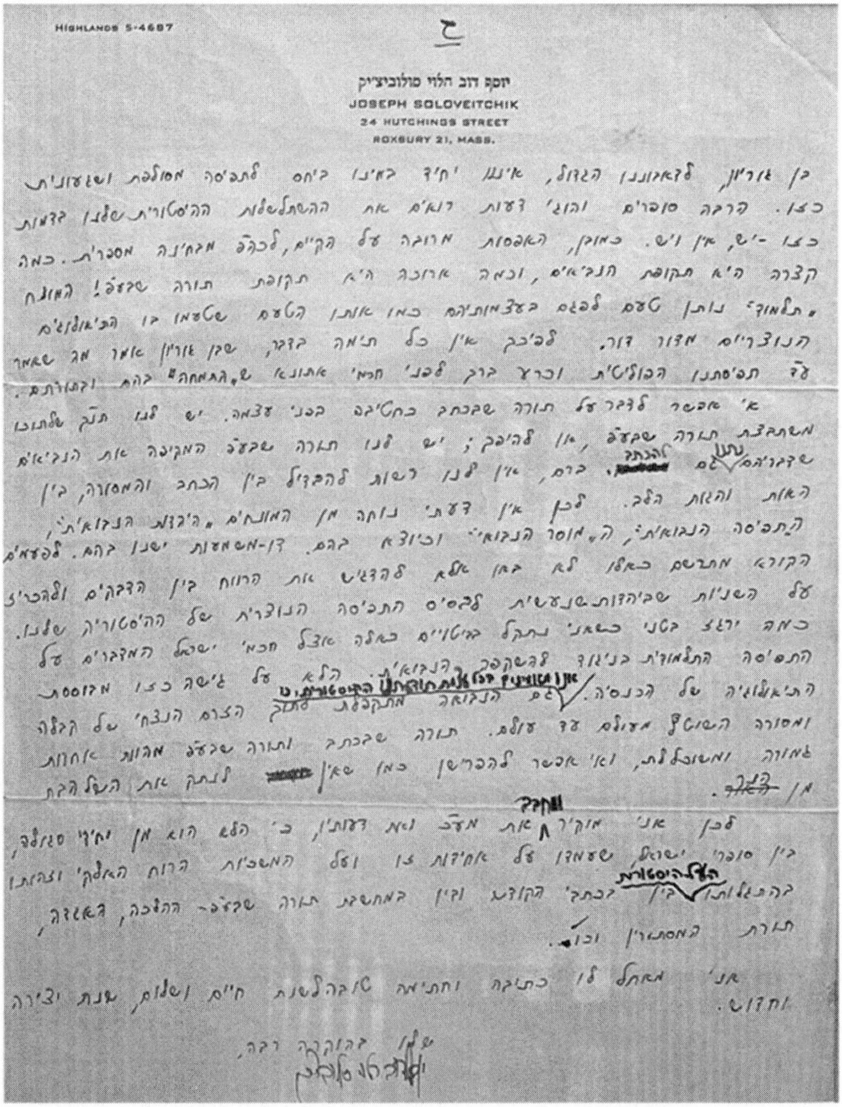

HIGHLANDS 5-4687

ב״ה

יוסף דוב הלוי סולוביצ׳יק
JOSEPH SOLOVEITCHIK
24 HUTCHINGS STREET
ROXBURY 21, MASS.

בן גוריון, לדאבוננו הגדול, אינו יחיד באינו ביחס לתפיסה מסולפת ושגעונית
כזו. הרבה סופרים והוגי דעות רואים את ההשתלשלות ההיסטורית שלנו בדמות
כזו - יש, אין ויש. כמובן, האפסות מרובה על הקיום, לכה״פ מבחינה מספרית. כמה
קצרה היא תקופת הנביאים, וכמה ארוכה היא תקופת תורה שבע״פ! המונח
"תלמודי" נותן טעם לפגם בעצמותיהם כמו אותו הטעם שטעמו בו הביאולוגים
הנוצריים מדור דור. על כל פנים אין כל תמיה בדבר, שבן גוריון אומר מה שאמר
על תפיסתנו הפוליטית וכרוך בדרך לבני חוגי אתונאי ש"המאחה" בהם ובתורתם.

אי אפשר לדבר על תורה שבכתב בחטיבה בפני עצמה. יש לנו תנ״ך שלתוכו
משתרבבת תורה שבע״פ, ואין להיפך; יש לנו תורה שבע״פ המקיפה את הנביאים
שדבריהם נתנו גם להכתב, ברם, אין לנו רשות להבדיל בין הכתב והמסורה, בין
האות והגות הלב. לכן אין דעתי נוחה מן המונחים "היהדות הנבואית",
"התפיסה הנבואית", "המוסר הנבואי" וכיוצא בהם. דו-משמעות ישנן בהם. לפעמים
הקורא מתרשם כאילו לא באו אלא להדגיש את הרווח בין הדבקים ולהבריג
על השניות שביהדות שנעשית לבסיס התפיסה הנוצרית של ההיסטוריה שלנו.
כמה ירגז בטני כשאני נתקל בביטויים כאלה אצל חכמי ישראל המדברים על
התפיסה התלמודית בניגוד להשקפה "הנבואית" הלא על גישה כזו מיוסדת
התיאולוגיה של הכנסיה. גם הנבואה מתקבלת מתוך הזרם הנצחי של קבלה
ומסורה השוטף מעולם עד עולם. תורה שבכתב ותורה שבע״פ מהוות אחדות
גמורה ומשוכללת, ואי אפשר להפרישן כמו שאין לנתק את השלשלת
מן הקבלה.

לכן אני מוקיר מאד את מר ... ואת דעותיו, כי הוא הוא מן יחידי סגולה
בין סופרי ישראל, שעמדו על אחדות זו ועל המשכיות הרוח האלקי וצהרתו
בהתגלותו ההיסטורית בין כתבי הקודש ובין המחשבת תורה שבע״פ - ההלכה, האגדה,
תורת הסתרים וכו׳.

אני מאחל לו כתיבה וחתימה טובה לשנת חיים ושלום, שנת יצירה
וחדוש.

שלו בהוקרה רבה,
יוסף דוב הלוי סולוביצ׳יק

Notes

[1]   Aaron Zeitlin (1898–1973) was the oldest son of Hillel Zeitlin. In 1942, when
the Nazis were rounding up the Jews in his town, Hillel Zeitlin, then 71 years
old, left his home to face his death wrapped in his *tallit* and *tefillin*, clutching a
copy of the *Zohar.* See the introduction to (תל *בפרדס החסידות והקבלה,*
ר"ה תש"ג. עטוף בטליתו ומוכתר בתפיליו, כשהספר הזוהר, בו הגה כל ימיו, בידו – כך יצא
אביב: יבנה, תשל"ג), עמ' ז: "הלל בר' אהרן אליעזר צייטלין קידש את השם בפולין בערב
.הילל צייטלין לקראת המרצחים הנאצים. עובדה זו אושרה על ידי עדי ראייה משארית הפליטה"
[2]   Among his many works, Zeitlin published two pamphlets and one book dealing with Zionism and the State of Israel:
In 1943, Zeitlin published a 31-page Yiddish pamphlet, אין קאמף פאר א אידישער
מלוכה, *The Struggle for a Jewish Nation* (NY: Jewish National Workers Union,
1943), a polemic against anti-Zionism and anti-Zionist Jews. Available at:
https://ia802604.us.archive.org/32/items/nybc211998/nybc211998.pdf.
In 1955, Zeitlin published a 40-page Hebrew pamphlet, מסה *המדינה והרוח.*
*פוליטוסופית בי"ג פרקים, The State and the Spirit: An Essay on Political Philosophy in
Thirteen Chapters.* This was a slightly expanded version of the same article that
had been serialized in the journal *HaDoar.* Rav Soloveitchik's letter is commenting on this pamphlet.
In 1965, Zeitlin published a 227-page Hebrew book, מדינה וחזון מדינה, *The State
and the Vision of the State* (Tel Aviv: Yavneh, 1965). This book discusses how
various philosophers envisioned the ideal state. In the last few chapters Zeitlin
lays out his own vision for the newly established Jewish State. This work can
be viewed as an expansion and fine-tuning of his previous 1955 essay.
A copy of this book sent to Rav Soloveitchik is inscribed by the author:
לכבוד הרב הגאון יצ"ו, מעמיק במחשבת היהדות, הרב דר. יוסף דוב סולווייטשיק, מנחת
.ידידות, אהרן צייטלין, חשון תשכ"ו
[3]   Ironically, Aaron Zeitlin's father had published a book on Spinoza, ברוך
שפינוזה, (Warsaw: Tusija, 1900). See Hillel Zeitlin, ibid. וכן פירסם באותה תקופה"
.ספר על שפינוזה (הוצ' "תושיה" תר"ס)"
[4]   See Gerald J. Blidstein, "A Religious-Zionist Thinker?" in *Society and Self: On the
Writings of Rabbi Joseph B. Soloveitchik* (OU Press, 2012), pp. 19-35. For more details on Rav Soloveitchik and Zionism see Heshey Zelcer and Mark Zelcer, *The
Philosophy of Joseph B. Soloveitchik* (Routledge, 2021), pp. 12–14, 173–197.
[5]   These lectures, edited and annotated, will appear in future volumes of *Ḥakirah.*
[6]   A copy of the book at Yeshiva University library is inscribed by Aaron Zeitlin:
.לכבוד הרב דר. ש. בעלקין, יצ"ו, בברכה ויקר – המחבר
[7]   The short-lived Israel Rogosin Center may have been an outgrowth of this
idea. See, "Yeshiva University Opens Two New Colleges; Starts Its 81st Year,"
JTA, 9/7/1966, "…Yeshiva launched at its graduate center today the Israel
Rogosin Center for Ethics and Human Values, a pioneering program that will
focus on teaching and research into the history, philosophy and practical application of Jewish ethics." We thank Jacob Sasson for this source.

8   Rav Soloveitchik refers to Aaron Zeitlin in the third person, a literary flourish used to show respect.

9   נּוּגֵי מִמּוֹעֵד אָסַפְתִּי מִמֵּךְ הָיוּ מַשְׂאֵת עָלֶיהָ חֶרְפָּה (צפניה ג:יח).

10   In philosophy, pragmatism is an approach popularized by William James that measures the truth of theories or beliefs in terms of the success of their practical application.

11   For Rav Soloveitchik's definition and discussion of "religious liberalism" (including the ideology of Reform Judaism), see *The Halakhic Mind*, pp. 88–91: "The basic error of religious liberalism is to be discerned less in its ideology than in its methodical approach. Liberalism has travelled in the wrong direction—from subjectivity to objectivity—and in so doing has misconstrued both. Religious liberalism is based upon a very 'simple' methodological principle. Subjective religiosity, the moderns say, is subordinated to the omnipotent authority of time and change" (pp. 88–89). In other words, religious liberalism is the idea that religion is subordinate to, and ought to be comprised of, the values in which we believe at that moment in time and place. Later in *The Halakhic Mind*, Rav Soloveitchik, in response to Rambam's approach to *Ta'amei Ha-Mitzvot*, i.e., giving commandment an ethical purpose, phrases this critique as "making religion the handmaid of ethics" (p. 93).

12   See *Halakhic Man,* pp. 139–143, n. 4.

13   In *The Halakhic Mind*, Rav Soloveitchik developed the idea that Halakhah should be used to create a Jewish Philosophy. For detailed analysis, see Zelcer and Zelcer, *The Philosophy of Joseph B. Soloveitchik*, ch. 4. Halakhah as a source for Jewish philosophy is further developed in Rav Soloveitchik's lectures, "The Relationship between Halakhah, Aggadah and Kabbalah," mentioned above.

14   See, for example, Anita Shapiro, "Ben-Gurion and the Bible: The Forging of an Historical Narrative?" *Middle Eastern Studies* (Vol. 33, No. 4, October 1997, pp. 645–674): "Thus his heroes were those of Scripture of the era of the First Temple" (p. 658); "Moreover, 'the human and social values we espoused—including Jewish redemption and universal human salvation—were articulated most forcefully by the prophets'" (p. 660); "The younger generation discovers in the Bible what it cannot find elsewhere in Jewish letters: there is no other Hebrew book written in the period after the Bible and all the way down to fifty or sixty years ago that is so close and intimate to the young as the Bible" (p. 662).

15   For Ben-Gurion's feelings about Spinoza, see, for example, "Ben-Gurion Demands Abolition of 300-Year Ban on Spinoza," *JTA*, December 28, 1953. Available at https://www.jta.org/archive/ben-gurion-demands-abolition-of-300-year-ban-on-spinoza. See also, Jacob Adler, "The Zionists and Spinoza," *Israel Studies Review*, Volume 24, issue 1.

16   אין דורשין בעריות בשלשה ולא במעשה בראשית בשנים ולא במרכבה ביחיד אלא אם כן היה חכם ומבין מדעתו. כל המסתכל בארבעה דברים ראוי לו כאילו לא בא לעולם מה למעלה מה למטה מה לפנים ומה לאחור. וכל שלא חס על כבוד קונו ראוי לו שלא בא לעולם (משנה חגיגה ב:א).

17   סַמְּכוּנִי בָּאֲשִׁישׁוֹת רַפְּדוּנִי בַּתַּפּוּחִים כִּי־חוֹלַת אַהֲבָה אָנִי (שיר השירים ב:ה): ועיין שם ג:י, ועיין איוב יז:יג.

Letters from the Rav

Edited By: MARC B. SHAPIRO

The private correspondence of R. Joseph B. Soloveitchik opens a window into the Rav's views on a host of issues. In addition to the important volume of letters published by R. Nathaniel Helfgot,[1] other letters have been published by Helfgot,[2] Dov Schwartz,[3] and Amihai Radzyner,[4] and there are also scattered letters that appeared in different places. (Unfortunately, we do not have a complete bibliography of all of the Rav's published correspondence.) Over the years, I have also collected a number of letters from the Rav, in both Hebrew and English. Some of them I found in archives and others were given to me. For a few of the letters, I no longer remember how I came to them. From these letters, I have selected some that I think *Ḥakirah* readers, and the Jewish world at large, will find of interest. A few of the letters contain typos, spelling mistakes, and rabbinic texts that are not quoted exactly, and I have corrected these. On occasion, I have also added punctuation and put the date at the top of the letters even when in the original it appeared at the bottom. In typed versions of the Rav's letters, the signature appears in different ways. This is because the person transcribing the letter could not make out exactly how the Rav signed his name. Sometimes the transcriber added הרב before the name, which the Rav never used in his correspondence. I have corrected these letters so that the Rav's signature appears the way he wrote it: יוסף דוב הלוי סולוביצ'יק. I thank the Rav's son, Professor Haym Soloveitchik, for granting me permission to publish these letters. I also thank R. Helfgot and R. Aharon Rakeffet for helping me decipher some of the Rav's difficult handwriting. As indicated in the

---

1   *Community, Covenant and Commitment: Selected Letters and Communications* (Jersey City, 2005).

2   "From the Rav's Pen: Selected Letters of Rabbi Joseph B. Soloveitchik," in Rafael Medoff, ed., *Rav Chesed: Essays in Honor of Rabbi Dr. Haskel Lookstein* (Jersey City, 2009), pp. 315–330.

3   *Haguto ha-Filosofit shel ha-Rav Soloveitchik* (Ramat Gan, 2008), pp. 360–368; "Igarto shel ha-Rav Y. D. Soloveitchik be-Nose ha-Ortodoksyah ha-Modernit," in Dov Schwartz, ed., *Tziyonut Datit* 1 (Ramat Gan, 2017), pp. 199–203.

4   "Shtei Iggerot Nosafot me-ha-Rav Soloveitchik le-Yitzhak Goldschlag," in Dov Schwartz, ed., *Tziyonut Datit* 4 (Ramat Ran, 2020), pp. 219–234.

Marc B. Shapiro holds the Weinberg Chair in Judaic Studies at the University of Scranton.

notes, a number of the letters are found in the Central Zionist Archives, which graciously allowed me to include them in this article.

Letters 1-3

Letters 1–3 were sent to Rabbi Mordechai Kirshblum (1910—1993).[5] Kirshblum was a Religious Zionist leader in the United States, and in 1952 became president of the Mizrachi Organization of America. In 1956 he was appointed to the Jewish Agency Executive, and in 1968 he moved to Israel where he continued his Religious Zionist activism.[6] Letter 1 is significant in that it shows some of the Rav's inner tension when it came to Zionism. While the Rav never ceased his great support for the State of Israel, he also recognized secular Zionism's anti-religious trends. Letter 2 shows how on occasion the Rav could be very annoyed with the Chief Rabbinate when in his opinion it did not have the courage to make decisions.[7]

Letter 1

בין המצרים יהפכם ד' לששון ולשמחה!

ד' מנחם אב, תשט"ז

July 12, 1956

Dear Rabbi Kirshblum,

Thank you for your letters. I appreciate greatly your efforts on behalf of Tovah[8] and her friends. I was very much disturbed and indignant when I received a phone call from Tovah advising me that the El-Al people were trying to persuade her and other passengers to board the plane in London on Friday. I resented the deliberate attempt on the part of El-Al officials to mislead a group of sincere boys and girls and to place them in a precarious position in which they would have been compelled to violate the Sabbath. The El-Al officials knew very well that it was impossible for a plane which was supposed to take off from the London airfield on Friday noontime to land in Lydda, Israel, before sunset. Nevertheless, they kept on asserting that such a miracle of קפיצת הדרך was possible and quite probable and they have repeatedly assured the passengers that their arrival in Israel before the Sabbath was almost a certainty. Such false predictions reflect a cynical and brutal disregard for religious values which is so characteristic of the officialdom in Israel.[9]

---

[5] Letters 1-2 are found in the Central Zionist Archives, Z7/2701. Letter 3 is found in the Central Zionist Archives, Z7/368.

[6] For Kirschblum's biography, see *Entzyklopedia shel ha-Tziyonut ha-Datit* (Jerusalem, 2000), vol. 6, cols. 776-780.

[7] See *Community, Covenant and Commitment*, pp. 179ff., where the Rav offers other criticisms of the Chief Rabbinate.

[8] The Rav's daughter.

You know my emotional and intellectual involvement in the sacred cause of שיבת ציון and my relationship to the State of Israel as a miraculous grant of infinite Divine grace to a martyred, abused and persecuted people. You are also aware of the fact that whenever zealots and bigots tried to create imaginary religious issues and I felt that the motivating force of such actions was sheer hatred of the State of Israel, I stood up and voiced my protest in no uncertain terms. That is why I feel that when I encounter irresponsible conduct and willful interference in matters which affect the religious conscience, on the part of certain officials of the State of Israel, doubts of a very unpleasant nature begin to assail my head and willy-nilly I question myself whether I am always right in refusing to give credence to the slanderous rumors circulated by the extremists with regard to the intentions of officials of the State. Can not the [Jewish] Agency understand once [and] for all that to thousands of young boys and girls, born and reared in the U.S., religion means a great deal more than mere ceremony, and that they are ready to forego many activities for the sake of complying with the Law. They have observed the Sabbath while they were in school—sometimes at great sacrifice—and they are not going to forsake this sacred principle because of a trip to Israel. Not even Ben Gurion with his illiterate philosophy of Judaism will succeed in changing their mode of living.

As to the Hapoel Hamizrachi convention, permit me to express my doubts about the sincerity and candor of the administration with respect to the מיזוג issue.[10] If the leadership had been honestly interested in the implementation of the resolution, it would not have engaged in parliamentary fireworks and filibuster and would have instead accepted in humility the will of the party in Israel. Mildly speaking, I was very disappointed in such political maneuvers.

I take the liberty of expressing to you my heartfelt wishes for unlimited success in your new post as head of the Department of Religious Culture of the J.A. [Jewish Agency]. May you bring the message of our perennial Torah to our brothers who find themselves in the abyss of ignorance.

With kind regards, I remain

Sincerely yours,

Joseph Soloveitchik

---

9   For another incident where El Al did not follow Halakhah, and the Rav's response, see R. Berel Wein, *Teach Them Diligently* (New Milford, CT, 2014), pp. 96–97.

10   He refers to the 1956 merger of Mizrachi and Ha-Poel ha-Mizrachi in Israel.

Letter 2

חזון, ה' מנ"א, תשט"ו, בין המצרים – יהפכם ד' לששון ולשמחה ערב שבת

July 13, 1956

Dear Rabbi Kirshblum,

I wrote you a letter last night but I forgot to mention that I have been very annoyed by the telegrams from the Chief Rabbinate. I resent the delaying tactics and maneuvers practiced by the members of a great and venerable institution. It took my brother exactly several hours to arrive at definite conclusions and offer <u>voluntarily</u> advice and guidance to young people who were perplexed and confused. Why should the Rabbinate whose duty it is to render clear cut decisions on all matters pertaining to Halachah debate the issue for weeks and months and attempt to evade responsibility? In the future I am not going to cooperate with the Chief Rabbinate since it is beset by fears and ludicrous cowardice, and engages, from time to time, in hypocrisy. I told you in our phone conversation that I also can wrap myself in the mantle of a "saint" and קנאי and let myself be proclaimed a צדיק. . . .

Excuse my emotional excitement. I have become, lately, a bit tired of playing the childish game of hide and seek with a certain segment in our community (a game at which the רבנות הראשית has displayed considerable skill) and I shall not cooperate with anybody who engages in similar methods. That is why I am also determined not to maintain any liaison or have any dealings with the leaders of Hapoel Hamizrachi in America since I am indignant about their shameful political maneuvers with respect to the merger issue at the last convention. There is no place for double talk and צביעות in our midst.

I hope that you will succeed in reorganizing the Department of Religious Culture. It should be put on a solid educational basis. The courses you intend to offer should be integrated into the program of an existing graduate school and conducted in the same manner as it is done, for instance, at Harvard with regard to its Russian or Middle Eastern Institute. I believe that the Yeshiva will be glad to cooperate with you. Please do not continue the old policy of reducing the Israeli Institute to some public lecture forum. You may arrange from time to time public lecture-meetings. Yet this should not exhaust the scope of activities of the Institute. I would also recommend that the Institute publish in English a periodical dealing with religious, philosophical and popular halachic topics which have a bearing upon our statehood problematics. This would enhance the prestige of our movement and help us to disseminate knowledge among the cultured laity. I told you that I am willing to cooperate with you, provided the work will be organized along these lines.

I wish you success in your new endeavor.

Sincerely yours,

J. Soloveitchik

Letter 3

י"ג טבת, תשי"ח

January 5, 1958

Dear Rabbi Kirshblum,

There is no doubt in my mind that the ZOA [Zionist Organization of America] should be set up as an autonomous movement without being subject to the decisions of the World Zionist Organization. Any stigma of this sort attached to the Zionist movement in this country could automatically spell the doom of all Zionist projects.

With kindest regards, I remain

Sincerely yours,

Joseph Soloveitchik

Letter 4

The following letter shows the Rav's support of the Chinuch Atzmai school system in Israel.[11] Although Chinuch Atzmai was controlled by Agudat Israel and the Rav identified with the Mizrachi party, he was always happy to lend his assistance.

Adar II 8th 5722

March 14th, 1962

Dear Colleague:

I have heartily endorsed the sacred work done by the חינוך עצמאי–Torah schools in the Holy Land, since their establishment some eight years ago.

Today this movement has spread the influence of Torah to 90 communities in Israel by providing religious education to nearly 40,000 children in 200 schools.

In order to assist in providing adequate facilities for the existing schools and to establish the religious schools in those communities where none exist, the American Friends of Chinuch Atzmai–Torah Schools for Israel are holding a dinner at the Hotel Pierre, 5th Avenue and 61st Street, New York, on Tuesday, April 3rd, 1962.

I appeal to my friends in the Rabbinate to do their utmost to make this undertaking a financial success. Your attendance at the dinner together with your congregants will be of great help.

Sincerely yours,

Joseph B. Soloveitchik[12]

---

[11] The letter is found in the Central Zionist Archives, Z7/15.
[12] For another appeal for Chinuch Atzmai, see the Rav's letter in www.jewishpress.com/sections/features/features-on-jewish-world/a-letter-by-rav-soloveitchik/2020/08/27/
A recording of the Rav's famous talk at the 1956 Chinuch Atzmai dinner has been placed on Youtube. See www.youtube.com/watch?v=drIHuygZ2C4

Letter 5

This letter was sent to Rabbi Irving Greenberg (b. 1933) and relates to Greenberg's involvement with a certain group, although it is not clear if the issue was interfaith dialogue or Greenberg's involvement with non-Orthodox streams of Judaism.[13] *Strangely enough, Greenberg himself does not recall the exact circumstances of the letter, but he assumes that the Rav was referring to interfaith dialogue, against which he had recently published his famous essay "Confrontation."*[14] *From the letter we see that despite his own opinion, the Rav did not insist that Greenberg follow it. This is in line with other times where the Rav made clear that if people found his opinion convincing then they should adopt it, but he did not expect compliance merely out of respect for his stature, à la Da'as Torah.*

יום ג' י"ג תשרי, תשכ"ו[15]

Dear Rabbi Greenberg,

I acknowledge receipt of your letter. Thank you for your good wishes. Please accept my greetings and felicitations on the occasion of the New Year. May you and your dear ones enjoy health, joy and happiness throughout the year.

גמר חתימה טובה לשנת חיים ושלו' וכל טוב!

There is absolutely no need of apologies or explanations. You are certainly entitled to your opinion as much as I am to mine. I have never demanded conformity or compliance even from my children. I believe in freedom of opinion and freedom of action. When you consulted me about your participation all I said was in the form of a hesitant advice, which I addressed not to you but to myself. In fact, I spoke in the first person, namely, if I were invited I would not accept. I did not instruct nor did I try to convince you. Since you have made up your mind in accordance with your own view all I can say to you is עלה והצלח go and may God be with you!

Please accept my fond wishes and greetings. מועדים לשמחה!

Sincerely,

Joseph Soloveitchik

---

[13] The letter is found in the Irving Greenberg Papers, 58:17, Harvard University Library. I thank Rabbi Greenberg for granting me permission to publish the letter.

[14] See Joshua Feigelson, "Relationship, Power, and Holy Secularity: Rabbi Yitz Greenberg and American Jewish Life, 1966—1983" (unpublished doctoral dissertation, Northwestern University, 2015), p. 108 n. 2. Feigelson discovered this letter and published most of it, ibid., p. 107.

[15] This has to be an error as 13 Tishrei, 5726 was Shabbat, not Tuesday.

Letter 6

One point concerning which the Rav was very eloquent and forceful was the necessity of having a meḥitzah *in shul. In Baruch Litvin's 1959 book,* The Sanctity of the Synagogue, *pp. 109—114, there is a letter from the Rav to an RCA convention dealing with this matter. (This letter has been reprinted in* Community, Covenant and Commitment, *pp. 139–142.) Moshe Schwartz found a copy of the original letter in the papers of his grandfather, R. Gedaliah Dov Schwartz, and I thank him for sending it to me. From the original letter we see that some paragraphs, in which the Rav offers an important personal statement about the halakhic process, were deleted when the letter was published in* The Sanctity of the Synagogue. *This was apparently done because these paragraphs are not specifically related to the* meḥitzah *issue.*

As chairman of the Vaad Halachah I intended to inform the conference about our activities during the past year. Since I am prevented from doing so I have asked my friend Rabbi Joseph Weiss to take my place.

Permit me to say the following. One of the fundamentals of my faith is that the Halachah is an all-inclusive discipline and system of thought capable of meeting any challenge of modern times and of confronting the most perplexing problems which a technically progressive and scientifically minded society may periodically pose. This optimistic formula, however, cannot always be successfully applied because of the limited knowledge and the imperfect intellectual capability of the human being. I for one, am not always able to behold the Halachic truth and to see the light under all circumstances. Many a time I grope in the dark, pondering, examining and re-examining an intricate Halachic problem— and find myself unable to arrive at a clear decision. Even the Talmud has not solved all problems and has not answered all questions. The *Teiku* is a very prominent and characteristic feature of *Torah She'B'al Peh.* We members of the Halachah Commission are not partners in a contracting firm whose task it is to provide every member of the Rabbinical Council of America with a clear-cut answer to his problems. Quite often the solution eludes us. We are beset by grave doubts. We face many alternatives not knowing which to choose since each is supported by sound logical reasoning. We cannot be guided in our decisions by emotional factors or pragmatic arbitrariness and hence we are impelled to employ in such situations the principle of *"B'divrai Torah Haloch Achar Hamachmir"* which seems to inconvenience some of our members.

Religious Jews have of late developed an intolerant attitude towards what they call the shyness and reluctance on the part of scholars to commit themselves on Halachic issues, not knowing that there is no omniscience in this world and that doubt is an integral part of the Halachic experience as it is of every scientific performance. A rabbi who thinks that he can solve all problems is implicitly admitting his own ignorance. I implore the convention to abstain from leveling charges of evasion at the Halachah Commission. Let us not repeat the complaints which are so common in religious circles in Israel about a lack of boldness on the part of the rabbinate. They come, for the most part, from people who are not conversant with Halachic scholarship. If there is in our ranks someone wise enough to undertake to answer all Halachic questions by return mail, I would not hesitate to relinquish my position as chairman to him.

The P.S. found in the Rav's letter is also of interest.

P.S. I would suggest that the convention adopt a resolution condemning the Humphrey Bill pertaining to humane method of slaughter. The convention should also send a letter of thanks to the State Department for the special attention of Assistant Secretary Herbert Hoover, Jr., for its stand against the proposed calendar reform.

Letter 7

This letter is to Zorach Warhaftig (1906–2002), Mizrachi leader and Knesset member.[16] From the letter we see that there was a plan to bring musmakhim of Yeshiva University's Rabbi Isaac Elchanan Theological Seminary to study in Israel. Noteworthy in the letter is the Rav's high regard for the young American Orthodox Jews who retained their commitment to the Torah while also achieving the same intellectual and professional heights as the non-Orthodox. He also notes that most of them are not committed to the ideals of Mizrachi, a situation he very much wished to change.

יום שלישי, ט"ז מנחם אב, תשט"ז
לכבוד ד"ר ז' וואַרהַפטיג, שיחי'
שלום וברכה!

קבלתי את אגרתו הנכבדה. אתחיל בקל הקל תחילה. אי אפשר לי לתייר את הארץ בחדשי החורף. עסוק הנני במלאכתי, מלאכת שמים, ואין לאל ידי להפסיקה אף לדבר מצוה חשובה ותכלית נשגבה כעליה לארץ ישראל. שכיר יום אנכי. אשתדל, ברצות ה', לגשם מאוויי ולעלות ציונה בקיץ הבא, בעונת הפגרא. אני תפלה וגם תחינה, כי אעברה ואראה את הארץ הטובה.

ביחס לתכניתו של מע"כ על אודות מוסמכי ישיבת רי"א, הנני לחזור על דברי שאמרתי לידידנו, הרב קירשבלום, כי אי אפשר לסדר את כל העניין מבלי שאחד מקרבניטי תנועתנו יבא ניו-יורקה לשם זה ביחוד וידין [!] על ההצעה בכובד ראש עם נשיא המוסד, ד"ר בלקין. הדבר נכבד ורציני מאד – ועלול הוא להשפיע חיובית על התפתחות תנועתנו וקליטתה בשורות הנוער התורני כאן – וכדאי הוא לכתת עליו את הרגלים ולשוט למדינת הים. מוכרחים אנו לחזור לתוך לבות הדור הצעיר הדתי שזה עכשיו התחיל להגיח מן הצללים ולצאת מן רשות היחיד לרשות הרבים ולהטביע את חותמו על החיים הציבוריים כאן (אם לא עכשיו – אימתי?). ישנם הרבה גורמים פסיכולוגיים וגם פוליטיים – שלא בנקל יעלה בידינו לסלקם – המפריעים את חובבי רעיונו של מע"כ מלהוציאו לאורה. האשמה תלויה בנו על אשר הזנחנו את עבודתנו החינוכית והתעמולתית בבתי היוצר לעתיד היהדות הנאמנה בארצות הברית וחצבנו בארות נשברים של ויכוחים פוליטיים שאינם מעלים ולא מורידים. ברם, יהיה איך שיהיה, הצעד הראשון צריך להעשות בכיוון שהתווה מע"כ. המוסמכים אשר יבלו בארץ שנה או שנתים יוכשרו להחלץ כנושאי הרעיון והאיד"יאל של תחיה דתית בארץ הקודש. עדיין לא נצלנו לטובת תנועתנו את הפלא הגדול אשר לא יאומן כי יסופר – דור אמריקאי, בן תרבות והליכות עולם, שאינו נופל בערכו האינטלקטואלי והמקצועי מחבריו הבלתי דתיים (ולפרקים גם עולה עליהם), מושרש בקרקע מסורת אבות, מצויד בידיעות תורתיות רבות, בר הכי של המשך ובעל אחריות ומעש. לדאבוננו אין בני הדור הגבור הזה הוגים חיבה למשאת נפש של המזרחי והפועל המזרחי. ישנם, כמובן, יוצאים מן הכלל, אבל רובם ככולו אינם משתייך לתנועתנו. מעוות זה עדיין הוא בגדר אפשרות

---

16   The letter is found in the Israel State Archives, 12277/10-גל (000ijek).

של תיקון אם לא נחמיץ את השעה. לכן אל תחוסו על עתכם ובאו הנה. מצדי אעשה
הכל כדי להביא את הדבר לידי גמר טוב.

בנוגע לשאלה הראשונה, מי כמוני יודע את צערם של כל אלה העומדים במערכה
למען הצלת הדור מרשת הטמיעה וההתנכרות, ומי כמוני מרגיש את הודה והדרה של
הגבורה הנפשית המתבטאת לא בבריחה מן החזית והסתייגות מן החיים אלא בהתיצבות
אמיצה בתוך תוכם ובמאבק על-אנושי על טיהורם וקידושם. בשעה שבקשתי את ידידי
הרבנים למסור את דברי למנהיגי תנועתנו הדגשתי כי אין אני דן על עצם התכנית ורק
מפאת נימוקים פוליטיים-תכסיסיים באתי בבקשתי לדחות את הענין לפי שעה ולהסירו
מסדר היום. יסוד בית האולפנא יגרום למאבק חדש מעין זה[17] אשר קפץ עלינו בימים
שעברו בעטיו של החוק שרות לאומי. כחבר נאמן למזרחי אני ממאן בפולמוס חדש אשר
יגזול זמן ומרץ מחברינו. מדומני, שישנן עכשיו משימות יותר חשובות מלהתוכח עם
אנשי ריב ומדנים כאן ולהגן על תנועתנו בפני אלה שאינם רוצים להאזין להגיון ישר
ולהתחשב עם עובדות. תפקידנו עתה הוא להעמיק את האידיאולוגיה ולהרחיב את
התנועה ולקנות לבבות ולעשות נפשות למשאת נפשנו ולא לשאת ולתת עם מנדינו
ומתנגדינו.

אני חותם בחיבה ובכבוד רב,

יוסף דוב הלוי סולוביצ'יק

ד"ש חמה לאביו הנכבד, הרב הגאון, שליט"א[18]

---

17   Although the sentence reads well, it is possible that one or two words are missing here, as the paper is cut.

18   R. Yerucham Warhaftig.

Letter 8

This letter is to Leon Gellman (1887–1973), a leader of Mizrachi first in the United States and later in Israel.[19] One of the issues the Rav dealt with was the plan by the Zim shipping line, owned by the Israeli government, to install two kitchens—one kosher and one not—on its cruise liner, the SS Shalom. *This created a good deal of controversy, and after great pressure was exerted on the government, in both Israel and the Diaspora, plans for a non-kosher kitchen were abandoned. The letter also mentions the need to stop the missionary threat in Israel.[20]*

יום ה, ט' שבט, תשכ"ד

ידידי החביב, חו"ב סוע"ה . . .[21] והוגה דעות, מוהרא"ל גלמן שיחי'
שלום וברכה,

קבלתי את אגרתו. עשיתי מה שעשיתי ודברתי מה שדברתי בועדת המזרחי (הדברים
סולפו ולקו בחסר וביתר, בשגגה וגם בזדון ע"י הכתבים) משום שהרגשתי כי גורל
תנועתנו היקרה לי מאד נתון בכף מאזנים ויזרע לחסד או לשבט לפי פעולותנו ביחס
לשאלת המיסיון ואנית "שלום". החדשות שהגיעו מא"י הסעירו את הלבבות וביחוד
עשו רושם אמיץ על הנוער הדתי בכלל (אינני מטפל בצעירי וויליאמסבורג או לייקווד).
הרבה התחילו לשאול שאלות ולהקשות קושיות ולתהות על דרכה של תנועתנו. מובן,
שהקיטרוג מן הימין גדול מאד. הנוער נבוך. אלה שרוצים להבנות מחורבנה של תנועתנו
עסוקים בשקידה ובחריצות רבה בהשמצתה. עמדה תקיפה נחוצה היתה כאוויר לנשימה.
עכשיו הכל מודים, כי היחידים העומדים בפרץ המה מנהיגי תנועתנו. הקנאים, גרוריהם
ומשרתיהם מתפללים כי הממשלה תנקט עמדה נוקשה בענין האניה ולא תטה אוזן קשבת
לדברינו. יש להם עוזרים בארץ ישראל הממטירים במכתבים, כי אין שאלת האניה
חשובה כלל. עיקר העיקרים הוא מלחמה בקונסרבטיבים. רצונם להפריד בין הדבקים
ולבלבל את המוחות. לכן אני מבקש את ידידי היקר למסור לחברנו הגדול, מוהר"מ
שפירא,[22] שלא להתפשר ביחס לשני המטבחים. רק מטבח אחד כשר הוא הפתרון
היחידי. עיני הציבור הדתי נשואות לנו ויש בתוצאות המאבק משום סמליות גורלית
לעתידה של תנועתנו.

בנוגע למסיון אני מבין את הבעיה בכל חומרתה ותסבכתה הכרוכה בחקיקת חק.
אינני משפטן, ולא ברורה לי התשובה. ברם דבר מה צריך להעשות גם מפאת נימוקים
הלכיים וגם בשל לחץ דעת הקהל. צריכים לבלם את "מסע הצלב" בארצנו הקדושה.
הרבה דרכים לממשלה, במישרין או בעקיפין, לחסם את הדרך בפני המיסיונרים, שונאי
דתנו עמנו ומדינתנו. יאמין לי ידידי, כי קשה מאד לשתף פעולה עם ה"צדיקים", בבחינת

---

[19] For Gellman's biography, see *Entzyklopedia shel ha-Tziyonut ha-Datit*, vol. 6, cols. 268–272.

[20] The letter is found in the Central Zionist Archives, A374/161.

[21] The paper is torn and one word is unreadable.

[22] Haim-Moshe Shapira

"עבודה קשה במקדש".[23] יש ביניהם הנגועים בצרות עין ובתסביכים שונים, שרק פסיכואנליטיקון יכול להבינם. הדבר עולה בטרחה מרובה ומיגעת. יש להשגיח מן החלונות ולהציץ מן החרכים, שלא יעשו דבר מרגיז ויפגעו בכבודה של ארץ ישראל, ח"ו. איסורים, חרמות ו"קנאות" המה מן הדברים הפשוטים [ו]אני לא הורגלתי בזה. לפתע פתאם הוטלה עלי המשימה של שומר חנם ה"חייב" (מתנה ש"ח להיות כשאול![24]) לא ביחס לכסף וכלים (כמו שלמדנו בפרשת משפטים) כי אם לאנשים. הפוליטיקה של הממשלה דוחפת הרבה מידידי וחובבי המדינה לזרועותיהם של קנאים. על מה נלחמת הממשלה? על מטבח של בשר חזיר!! נא לסדר את ענין האניה בהקדם האפשרי כדי שאוכל להשתחרר קצת מהשגחתי על הולי מח ולב. אינני רוצה לטפל בדברי סילוף של העתונות. נפשי סולדת בהרבה שקרים שנפוצו ע"י כתבים שלא שמעו את דברי ומעולם לא ראוני. מימי לא אמרתי כי דת חדשה נולדה בא"י ברם השתיקה יפה לגוף וגם לנפש.

אני מאחל למע"כ אריכות ימים ושנים, מרץ יצירה וכחות רעננים עד כי יבא שילה.

בכבוד רב

יוסף דוב הלוי סולוביצ'יק

---

23 See *Yoma* 47b.

24 See *Bava Metzia* 94a.

Letters 9, 11–14 were sent to Yitzhak Goldshlag (1921–1992), a Mizrachi leader who often corresponded with the Rav.[25] Letter 9 focuses on the "Brother Daniel" controversy, in which Oswald Rufeisen, a Jew who had converted to Catholicism and become a Carmelite friar, wished to be accepted as a citizen in Israel under the Law of Return. His case went to the Israel Supreme Court which ruled against him. The Court stated that according to halakhah Rufeisen was to be regarded as Jewish, but since the Law of Return was not established on halakhic parameters, the government was within its rights to refuse citizenship to one who converted to another religion. The Rav, while happy with the Court's ruling, was very disappointed at what he regarded as a basic error, namely, that halakhically a Jew retains his status as a Jew even if he apostatizes. The Rav's position is explained in Letter 10. In addition, R. Aharon Lichtenstein's analysis of the matter in his famous article "Brother Daniel and the Jewish Fraternity"[26] reflects the Rav's position. At the end of his detailed discussion, R. Lichtenstein concludes:

> *As long as there is an identification with Knesset Yisrael, and not merely with a political state, the gravest of sinners remains a Jew. As a member of a spiritual community (even though he may not acknowledge and appreciate its true nature), he retains its quintessential character, at once a spiritual quality and a legal status—kedushat Yisrael, the personal sanctity of the Jew. With the loss of identification, however, there is a loss of identity. Personal status as a Jew—be it for marriage or any other purpose—is lost. The distinctive mark of Jewry, what being a Jew essentially means, is effaced. Kedushat Yisrael is destroyed… . Kedushat Yisrael may be a native endowment, but it is not an irrevocable patrimony. It is received, but it must also be taken; and it can be thrown away.[27]*

---

25 See the Rav's letters to him in the sources mentioned above, notes 2–4; *Community, Covenant and Commitment*, no. 41. Goldschlag also wrote an article on the Rav. See "Ha-Gaon Rabbi Yosef Dov ha-Levi Soloveitchik Shlita," in Yitzhak Rafael, ed., *Shragai* 2 (Jerusalem, 1985), pp. 151–163. For Goldschlag's biography, see *Entzyklopedia shel ha-Tziyonut ha-Datit*, vol. 6, cols. 244–246.

26 The article originally appeared in *Judaism* 12 (1963), pp. 260–280, and has been reprinted in Lichtenstein, *Leaves of Faith* (Jersey City, 2004), vol. 2, ch. 3.

27 *Leaves of Faith*, vol. 2, p. 78.

Letter 9

יום הששי עש"ק, א' טבת, תשכ"ג
ידידי הנכבד מוהר"י גולדשלג, שיחי',
שלום וברכה!

תשואות חן חן לו על אשר שלח לי באחרונה תגובת העתונות לפסה"ד על אודות המשומד.
אדוני אינו יודע כמה חשובה היתה שאלה זו בעד הרבה מיהודי אמריקה התלושים מממסורת
ומשרשיה ואין להם אחיזה בקרקע היהדות הנאמנה. ישנם הרבה יהודים בארבע כנפות
ארצות הברית שאינם מצטרפים אל הכנסיה הנוצרית משום שראים בפעולה זו בגידה באומה
הישראלית. אם, ח"ו, ביה"ד הגבוה היה מוציא המשומד לטובת פסק כי זכאי הוא להכנס
לא"י על סמך חוק השבות, הסכר האחרון היה מתפרק, ומי יודע מה היו עושים אחינו בני
ישראל, שאין להם זיקה כלל ליהדות מלבד רגש של לוויליות (נאמנות). שמח אני לראות כי
גם העתונות החילונית ברכה את פסק הדין, אולם דברי השופטים כי ההלכה מכירה בו כיהודי
גמור, ולו פסקו על פיה, כי אז היה יוצא זכאי, בלבלה את מוחות יהודי ארצה"ב. אני מקבל
שאלות למאות (בלי גוזמא) האם נכון הדבר. גם רבני א"י יודעים ללקט מקורות, וכמו שעשה
השופט זילברג, הידועים לבר בי רב דחד יומא ושתינוקות של בית רבן יודעים אותם, להראות
כי קדושתו לא "נפגמה" ח"ו אף כחוט השערה. לישראליזם הלכתי זה בלי להתעמק אף כל
שהוא במושגים ולהתעלם ממקורות אחרים ומהלכות שלמות המעידים בעליל כי מומרות
מפקיע בהרבה מובנים קדושת ישראל, סופו עלול לסכן את מצב ישראל בגולה. רבנים אלה
כנראה אינם מבינים ואינם מרגישים את גודל האחריות שהם נוטלים על עצמם באמרם כי
המומר הזה ישראל גמור הוא. לפני שלשה שבועות נאמתי במכון הטכנולוגי של
מאסאטשוסעטס לפני סטודנטים ופרופיסורים ע"ד יסודות היהדות. לאחר ההרצאה סבוני
כדבורים הרבה מתבוללים גם אינם יהודים, ושאלה אחת בפיהם: האם אמת ונכון הדבר כי
ההלכה מכירה במשומד כיהודי. אין התחזקות זו פרי סקרנות לבד. מהווה שאלה זו ענין
אקטואלי להרבה יהודים אמריקאים שנתרחקו מן המקור, אבל אינם רוצים להתכחש לעמם.
המה מבקשים תשובה ברורה. מעונינים המה בנקודת מבט ההלכתי יותר מבפסק הדין של
ביה"ד הגבוה לצדק. פיסיקאי אחד, פרופ' במכון זה!, אמר לי כי אם ההלכה תכיר במשומד
כישראל גמור, אז אפשר לפתור הרבה שאלות סוציאליות העומדות על הפרק. האם יודעים
הרבנים בא"י את המצב כמו שהוא בבחינת "מעשה ידי טובעין בים", והם מתעסקים בלומדות
של סרק ואומרים שירה ל"בקיאותם" אשר איש ואשה תינוק ותינוקת יודעים. מוכן אני
להסכים כי היהדות המסורתית זכתה בדין משום שביה"ד היה חילוני. במשטר "הלכתי",
במדינה היה המשומד יצא [יוצא] זוכה. החילוניות "הגינה" על הדת . . .[28] טרגי קומדיה!
אינני מתפלא כלל שמצב הרבנות ירד פלאי פלאים בארץ הקודש. יסלח לי אדוני שאני
משתמש בביטויים חריפים. אולם אין אדם נתפס על שעת צערו. אני יודע את המצב בארצות
הברית היטב.

בברכה רבה ובתודה

יוסף דוב הלוי סולוביצ'יק

---

[28] Ellipsis in the original.

Letter 10

The following is taken from a December 27, 1962 letter written by Yisrael Friedman to Shabbetai Don-Yaḥya (also known as דניאל .ש), the editor of Ha-Tzofeh.[29] The letter offers the Rav's explanation as to why an apostate is no longer regarded as Jewish.[30]

בשיחה שהתקיימה בימים אלה בין הרב ד"ר בן-מאיר סגן יו"ר הכנסת, הנמצא כעת בארצות הברית, והגאון ר' יוסף דב סולוביציק, הביע הגאון שליט"א את תמיהתו על שבכלל קיימת בעיה שכזאת, והצביע על גמרא ורמב"ם מפורשים הפוסקים בדרך חותכת הלכה בנידון. והרי:

במסכת יבמות דף טז ע"ב במימרא של ר' יהודה בר רב אסי שחוששים לקידושין של עובד כוכבים, שמא מעשרת השבטים הוא, נאמר בדף יז ע"א כי אמריתה קמיה דשמואל, א"ל לא חזו משם עד שעשאום עובדי כוכבים גמורים, שנאמר (הושע ה,ז) "בה' בגדו כי בנים זרים ילדו". ומקשים המפרשים איך יכלו חכמים לעקור דבר מן התורה כלפי היתר לאשת איש, כידוע שבכל מקום (כלפי כותים לדוגמא) שנאמר שעשאום לעובדי כוכבים גמורים הכוונה היא לחומרא, ולא לקולא, והרי כאן יוצא שגם לקולא דינו כעובד כוכבים גמור. והסביר הגאון בשם אביו ז"ל שהנקודה הקובעת כאן היא מה שנאמר בפסוק "בה' בגדו כי בנים זרים ילדו", כי יתכן שיהודי יכול להיות מומר לכל התורה כולה ואפילו לעבודת כוכבים, אבל איננו עד כדי כך מנתק השתייכותו לעם ישראל, עד שיהא בטוח כי בנים זרים ילדו. אולם מומר שעובר לגמרי לדת אחרת, הרי יוצר ניתוק שכזה כלפי עצמו וצאצאיו.

והביא הגאון ראיה נוספת לכך מפירוש המשניות לרמב"ם במסכת נדה פרק ז משנה לפני האחרונה, ד"ה: כל הכתמים הנמצאים בכל מקום טהורים, ואומר הרמב"ם כלפי כותים בסוף המימרא: "וזה מאז, אמנם היום הנה הכותי עצמו אם מת לא יטמא באהל לפי שהם עובדי כוכבים ואין מטמאין באהל." והרי כידוע שבקשר לכותים בזמן הגמרא קבעו אותם כעובדי כוכבים גמורים לחומרא ולא לקולא. והרמב"ם פוסק שכיוון שבימים אלו כבר הסתבר שכותים אינם חלק מעם ישראל, הרי גם לקולא הם כעובדי כוכבים גמורים ואינם מטמאים באהל כדין ישראל, אלא דינם כדין מי שאינו יהודי. ברור הדבר אם כך כי מומר גמור, להבדיל מכופר או עובר עבירות—מומר שעוזב את עם ישראל על-ידי קבלה על עצמו דת אחרת—הרי הוא מבחינת [!] "בה' בגדו כי בנים זרים ילדו", ואז דינו כדין עובד כוכבים גמור אפילו לקולא ולא רק לחומרא.

---

29 For Don-Yaḥya's biography, see *Entzyklopedia shel ha-Tziyonut ha-Datit*, vol. 6, cols. 317–320.

30 The letter is found in the Israel State Archives, 14923/5-גל (000j33d).

Letter 11

The following two letters also deal with the plan to have two kitchens on the Israeli ship Shalom, one kosher and one not. From these letters we see that the Rav viewed this issue as a most significant matter, with great symbolic significance. In his opinion, the Orthodox had to exert all of their influence to ensure that the ship not install a non-kosher kitchen. He also expresses a strongly negative view of Prime Minister Levi Eshkol's handling of this matter. The first letter concludes with comments about the missionary threat in Israel.[31]

ידידי הנכבד מר יצחק גולדשלג שיחי',
שלום וברכה!

תשואות חן חן לו על אגרותיו וכל החומר שהוא מספק לי מדי פעם בפעם. הדברים יגעים. הידיעות סותרות ומכחישות הדדית, וראש הממשלה אומר ואינו עושה ומשתלב בעירבוביא של הבטחות. שיחתו עם העתונאי מר פלינקר ע"ד אנית שלום שהופיעה ב"טאג" עשתה רושם נורא כאן. רק במאמצים גדולים הצלחתי לעכב את הרבנים מפרסום האיסור. אוי לו לדור כי מנהיגיו מדבר ומפטפט דברי שטות, הבל והבאי. מקווה אני כי ביחסיו עם המציאות הוא משתמש בשכלו (אם דבר זה קיים בו) ולא בלשונו. חבל, חבל, כי ע"י הערות מטומטמות מרחיקים את הנוער הדתי ואת היהדות החרדית בכלל. כבר כתבתי לידידי החביב כי אני עומד על המשמר ומשתדל להשגיח על חברי שלא יעשו דבר תקלה. אמנם לכל תכלה וגבול וגם לסבלנות. אם אנית שלום תצויד בשני מטבחים יפורסם האיסור וגם <u>יבוצע</u>, ואל ישאו <u>הרבה</u> מן האורחים הבאים לא"י את חברינו,[32] כי אין דבר זה אלא איום. אין אנו מאיימים ואין אנו נותנים אולטימטום לשום איש. ענין שני מטבחים הפך סמל [!], וגורל תנועתנו תלוי בתוצאות המאבק. לא נחשה ולא נשב בחיבוק ידים. אני מקווה שלא נצטרך להשתמש בתחבולות כאלו, אבל אם אחרים יכריחו אותנו לא ננוס מן המערכה. עוד הפעם אל תטו אוזן קשבת לדברי פיתוי של אנשים שאין להם שום השפעה על היהדות החרדית כאן. עתידה של תנועתנו תלוי בתוצאות ההתנגשות ע"ד האניה. פשרה כל שהיא עלולה להחריב את התנועה ולהרחיק ממנה את הכחות היותר יפים. דברתי עם ידידי החביב, הרב קירשבלום, על אדות זה והסברתי לו את המצב כמו שהוא, והוא בדעה אחת עמדי.

נא להאמין לי, כי רק חיבה יתרה לתנועתנו מדברת מתוך גרוני. אמנם ישנן בעיות אחרות, שמצד מהותן חשובות יותר מבעית "אנית שלום", אבל אניה זו הפכה "ערקתא דמסאנא" [!] ונעשית עיקר גדול בדת.

עכשיו בדבר מסיון. בודאי ידוע למע"כ, ידידי, כי היהדות החרדים באנגליה לכל זרמיה מימין ועד שמאל שלחה אגרת לראש הממשלה שבו היא מבקשת אותו הדבר שיהדות הנאמנה כאן בקשה: לבלום את תיאבון המיסיונרים ולהציל נפשות משמד. חזית

---

31 Letter 11 is found in the Central Zionist Archives, A374/161. Letter 12 is found in the Central Zionist Archives, Z7/584.

32 See 2 Kings 18:29. The meaning is: Let not the many visitors arriving in Israel deceive our colleagues into thinking that this is only a threat.

מאוחדת של היהדות החרדית כאן הולכת ומתגבשת ותעשה כח עצום, בפרט, כי חזית זו מורכבת מב"כ הנוער התורני בעל תרבות והשפעה. אפילו הנוער הקונסרבטיבי הולך ומצרף לחזית זו. אני פקדתי עליהם שלא לפרסם שום דבר ושלא להפגין ושלא להשתמש "בפובליסיטי". לכן אין הרבה יודעים על תנועה זו המתעסקת לא רק בענין המיסיון בא"י כי אם בכלל ביחסים ההדדיים שבין עמנו והכנסיה הקתולית בקשר עם המועצה האקומנית וה"הצהרה" שלא הוצהרה שהיא חטיבה אבנגלית כולה.[33] החלטנו להוציא את כל הענין מידיהם של הארגונים הסקולריים שיכולים להביא את עם ישראל לתהום של התנצרות, ר"ל.

הנני כותב כל זה לידידי כדי שחברינו ידעו שהענין לא ירד מן הפרק. אינני משפטן, אבל דבר מה צריך להעשות. אם נוכל להשיג דבר ממשי נהפך התנועה [!] היותר חזקה בארצות הברית.

בברכה

יוסף דוב הלוי סולוביצ'יק

[לפי תאריך הדואר המכתב יצא בה' אדר תשכ"ד. נתקבל י' אדר תשכ"ד.[34]]

---

[33] He is referring to a draft of the Vatican document *Nostra Aetate* which he regards as a missionary text. I thank Prof. David Berger for helping clarify this point.

[34] The bracketed sentences appear in the typed version of the letter.

Letter 12

August 26, 1963

יום שני, ו' אלול, תשכ"ג

Dear Rabbi Kirshblum

In this morning's mail I found a copy of a letter, concerning the Kashruth problem on the ship Shalom, addressed to you by Mr. Shragai.

    I wholeheartedly approve of his suggestions and I take the liberty of urging you to implement them as soon as possible. The introduction of a double menu on an Israeli boat under governmental auspices will have a corrosive effect upon many American institutions. If my assistance is needed, please call upon me.

With personal regards,

כתיבה וחתימה טובה לשנת חיים ושלו' וכל טוב!

Sincerely yours,

Joseph Soloveitchik

Letter 13

In this letter the Rav again speaks about issues of religion and state in the State of Israel.[35]

עש"ק, כ"ח ניסן, תשכ"ד
כבוד ידידי מוהר"י גולדשלג, שיחי',

שלום וברכה!

קבלתי את מכתבו. גופא דעובדא הכי הווי. כשהסכמתי לשיחה התניתי שתופס [!]
השיחה קודם שיפורסם ימסר לי להגהה. הוא קיים את התנאי ושלח לי את התופס. אני
עברתי עליו, הוספתי עליו וגרעתי ממנו הרבה והמצאתיו לו. הנוסחה שפורסמה ב"על
המשמר"[36] היא הראשונה שהעתונאי כתב בעצמו ושלח לי. בעתונות האנגלו-יהודית
פרסמו את התופס המוגהה. מדוע נזדמן ל"על המשמר" הנוסחה המשובשת, הבלתי
מתוקנת – לא אבין.

כשמע"כ יקרא בתשומת לב את התופס השני, יראה את השינויים והחילופים, כבדי
משקל.

החלטתי להביע דעות אלו לא באה בקלות ראש. נמלכתי בעצמי וגם בתלמידי וחברי
מהסתדרות הרבנים והישיבה. עייפים אנו מכל מעשה התעתועים של החילוניים לרבות
גם חברי הממשלה המתערבים בעניני הוראה ורבנות ומאיימים תמיד בביטול
ה"קידושין". כאן בארצות הברית השיחה עשתה רושם טוב ואמיץ לטובת תנועתנו. אל
יחשבו החילוניים וגם המתקנים כי הננו כעניים העומדים בפתח הממתינים לפירורים
מעל שולחן "גבוה" של המפא"י, שבחסדם מעניקים לנו "קונצסיות" דתיות. אם אין
אתם רוצים בנישואין אלה אנו נכונים לקבל גט פטורין או לבטל את הנישואין. יחדלו
נא לאיים! המצב כאן עקב הטלגרמה של שבעת האירגונים דרש עמדה חזקה בלתי
תלויה כזו. יאמר נא מפא"י כי היא רוצה במדינה חילונית!

בכלל ענין ה"נאמנות הכפולה" ביחס למדינה סקולרית שכנע את הרבה מן
המתבוללים כאן אשר חתמו על המברק לאשכול כי אסור "להשתעשע" בעניני דת
ומדינה. הלא פחדנים המה!

מובטחני כי במשך הזמן קבלתם תופסים אחרים של השיחה בצורתה המתוקנת.
כאן נדפסה בהרבה עתונים אנגלו-יהודיים במילואה. ה"טאג מארגן זשורנאל" תרגם
אותה ולא הבין את האנגלית וגם לא ידע איך לכתוב אידית ויצאה מקולקלת "בלי ידים
ורגלים". אם אדוני רוצה בתופס השיחה אמציאנה אליו.

בנוגע לריפורמים, אלה הנלחמים בהם מגדילים אותם ומפרסמים את פולחנם.
כנראה שהרבה מאתנו החרדים עדיין חיים בעיירות קטנות בליטא או בפולניה ונאבקים
בתכסיסים העלולים לחזק את האויב.

בדבר ביקורי בא"י בקיץ זה, כתבתי כי אם רעיתי שתחי' תרגיש עצמה טוב נשתדל
לבקר בארץ חמדת אבותי ברצות ד'.

---

35   The letter is found in the Religious Zionist Archives, Mossad ha-Rav Kook.
36   *Al ha-Mishmar*, March 31, 1964, p. 2.

בברכה רבה,

יוסף דוב הלוי סולוביצ'יק

Letter 14

Here we have an example of the Rav's concern for members of the Boston community. Alan Solomont (born 1949), the subject of the letter, went on to have a distinguished career, and is a well-known philanthropist and Democratic Party activist. I thank Mr. Solomont who provided the information that enabled me to date the letter.

[קיץ תשל"א]

כבוד ידידי הנעלה, מוהר"י גולדשלג, שיחי',

שלו' וברכה!

דבר לי אל כבוד ידידי. בן למשפחה עשירה וחשובה בבוסטון נמצא בארץ ישראל כאורח הקיבוץ "כפר בלום". בחור זה שגודל בבית נטול אמונה ואהבת ישראל תועה עכשיו בדרכי החיים ומבקש אידיאה, אידיאל, ז.א. משמעות לקיומו. (בינתיים גם המשפחה לבשה צורה אחרת והפכה לדתית עקב קשריה עם ישיבת רמב"ם שיסדתי.) הוא מבקש את מזלו ויעודו בארץ אבות. לכן אני מעונין מאד, כי צעיר זה יבלה זמן מה גם בקיבוץ דתי. דברתי עם אביו והלה שמח מאד לקראת הזדמנות כזו כי עכשיו הוא רוצה להחזיר את בנו בתשובה. בניו הצעירים שהספיקו להספח על תלמידי ישיבת רמב"ם מפגינים את יהדותם והתמסרותם לתורה ולמצוה בראש גלי. ברם הבן הבכור שלא גרם מזלו לבקר את בית ספרנו מחפש לו נתיב בחיים מתוך מבוכה וסנורים. האם יש לאל ידו לבקש את אחד מן הקיבוצים הדתיים להזמין צעיר זה לחודש ימים או פחות או יותר. מי יודע, אולי ביקור בקיבוץ דתי ישפיע עליו לשנות את דרכו, וישוב וינחם על מעשיו. כתבת הצעיר הוא: אלן סולומנט, כפר בלום, גליל העליון.

אני מודה לאדוני מאד מאד.

ידידו מוקירו

יוסף דב הלוי סולוביצ'יק

Letter 15

In this letter from the Rav to the Mizrachi leader Yisrael Gan-Zvi,[37] the Rav reaffirms his commitment to Mizrachi. This is one of a number of letters that the Rav sent to Mizrachi figures who were worried that the Rav's public criticism of various political positions adopted by Mizrachi signaled that his enthusiasm for the movement as a whole had cooled.[38] In all of these letters the Rav strongly affirms his support for Mizrachi and its vital role in fostering religious life in the State of Israel.[39]

יום ב', כ"ט אדר, תש"כ

למר י. גן-צבי

שלום וברכה

קבלתי את אגרתו מיום י"ז לחודש זה. אודה ולא אבוש, כי תוכן האגרת גרם לי עגמה וגם עלבון. אין בי הרבה מדות טובות, ברם ב"מעלה" אחת ברכני א'. נפשי בוחלת בדברי רכילות ולעז, ומימי לא השתייכתי לכת מקבלי לשון הרע. העובדה עצמה, כי חברי המרכז העולמי מלאו את ידי אדוני לכתוב אלי אגרת הכחשה, עשתה עלי רושם מוזר. צורך הכחשה מבוסס על הנחה חשד, כי עלול אני להטות אוזן קשבת לדברים טפלים ובטלים כאלה, ובהנחת חשד זו יש משום פגיעה בכבודי ובכבוד כל אדם נורמלי, בן דעת ובעל נימוס. אמנם בינה יתרה לא נתנה לי מן השמים, אבל, בכל זאת, אינני נמנה על חבורת הפתאים המאמינים בכל דבר, בסיפורי בדים ובמעשיות שאין להן שחר. אטו בשופטני עסקינן?

היחסים ביני ובין התנועה בעינם יעמדו גם להבא. המה יהיו לא רק מתוקנים אלא גם לבביים, רפודי חיבה וידידות הדדית. השתייכותי לתנועתנו מבטאת זיקה פנימית אשר מים רבים לא יוכלו לבטלה. סיסמתנו[40]— המתבטאת במטבע קצרה רבת תוכן וענין: עמידת גבורים בתוך מערכות העולם המודרני על כל נפתוליו במקום בריחה, שהיא תחילת נפילה, ומאבק בני אמונה ומסורת על טיהורם וקידושם של החיים במקום פרישה בת היאוש—משמשת לנו לעינים גם כאן, בארצות הברית, בעבודתנו החינוכית, אשר הרבה ברכה ראינו בה בעונה האחרונה. כל זמן שמפלגתנו תדגול בסיסמה זו אשאר נאמן לדגלה.

אמנם, מפעם לפעם אין אני מסכים לקו הפוליטי שתנועתנו נוקטת בו. ברם אין בחילוקי דעות עראיים שבין אחים לדעה משום פירוד הלבבות הדופקים בריתמוס אחד. לו הייתי תושב ארץ הקודש הייתי מחווה את דעתי בעליל, אולם כבן חוץ לארץ אין אני

---

[37] For Gan-Zvi's biography, see *Entzyklopedia shel ha-Tziyonut ha-Datit*, vol. 6, cols. 277–278. His article, "Against 'Separation' in Israel," appeared in *Tradition 2* (Spring 1960), pp. 218–236.

[38] See *Community, Covenant and Commitment*, pp. 195–206, Helfgot, "From the Rav's Pen," pp. 325ff.

[39] The letter is found in the Central Zionist Archives, Z7/855.

[40] He is apparently referring to the Mizrachi slogan, "The Land of Israel for the People of Israel according to the Torah of Israel."

רשאי לקפוץ בראש ולבקר אפילו לפעמים בלתי תכופות. לכן אתי תלין הבקורת, ואין אני מגלה אותה לשום איש. אחד אני יודע: לולי תנועתנו משוללת היתה היהדות החרדית חלק ונחלה בבנין הארץ ותקומת המדינה, פעולות גורליות, טעונות הוד היסטורי. דייני בהכרה זו כדי שארגיש עצמי מקושר לתנועה שהצילה את כבוד היהדות הנאמנה בתקופה מכריעה כזו.

אגב גררא רצוני להוסיף דבר אחד. נתקלתי בידיעה ב"הצופה", כי בעתון פלוני אלמוני הופיעה שמועה כאילו הבעתי את דעתי בשיחתי עם ראש הממשלה שיש להפריד בין הדת והמדינה. לא היו דברים מעולם. לא נגענו בשיחתנו בנושא זה. אמנם בשקלא וטריא עם העיתונאים רצה אחד להטיל פירוש כזה בהשקפתי על הרבנות ותפקידיה, ואמרתי לו בפירוש כדברים האלה: אין אני בעד הפרדת הדת מן המדינה כי אם בעד הפרדת הרבנות ממשרד הדתות.

בברכת שמחת הרגל ובכבוד רב,

יוסף דוב הלוי סולובי'ציק

דרישת שלום מיוחדת לידידי הנאמן, מר משה שפירא. אברך אותו ואת כל משפחתו בברכת מועדים לששון ולשמחה. עוד הפעם אני מודה לו על ידידותו אלי.

Letter 16

In this letter we see the Rav's fond feelings for two long-time Mizrachi leaders, Shlomo Zalman Shragai (1899–1995)[41] and Yitzhak Rafael (1914–1999).[42]

יום הששי ערב ש"ק ט' מרחשון, תשל"ח
כבוד ידידי היקר, הרב הג' והנעלה, מוהר"ם קירשבלום, שיחי',
שלו' וברכה!

נא למסור לשני ידידי, מוהרש"ז שרגאי ומוה"ר יצחק רפאל, את איחולי הכי לבביים
לרגל המסיבה הנערכה לכבודם.

לא איש דברים אנכי. קשה עלי לבטא במלים מסוימות את חשרת רגשותי ורחשי לבי.
עולמי האימוציונלי גנוז וטמון מעין מעין רואים. לכן אל אאריך בדברי שבח על שני חתני החגיגה.
אולם ליהווי ידוע לכולכם כי יותר ממה שאני אומר לפניכם כתוב עלי לבי.

האחד הוא איש מחשבה והרגשה, בעל נפש עדינה ובישנית, מאציל הוא הוד וחזון
על הקרובים אליו.

השני הוא איש מרץ ופעולה, בעל שכל ישר ומוח חריף מאציל הוא על כל הנספחים
אליו עוז פנימי וגבורה המתבטאים במעשה.

שניהם כאחד טובים ושניהם כאחד תרמו תרומה גדולה לתנועתנו. אלמלא המה אין
אני יודע אם היינו מגיעים עד כה!

האחד בצלותא ובבעותא, פשוט מיט זאגען תהלים. השני בחרבו ובקשתו. האחד
בלבביות ובחזון. השני בתכנית ברורה, משמעת דיקנית ויד יוצרת – שניהם הקדישו את
חייהם לשיבת ציון הדתית. שניהם חשבו, פעלו, נלחמו ועמדו בראש התנועה שנים
רבות.

כולנו חייבים להכיר טובה להם. מה אמר ר"ע לתלמידיו כשדחפו את רחל שבאה
לקבל פני בעלה המפורסם אחרי רבות של פירוד ועוני? "הניחו לה, שלי ושלכם – שלה
הוא".[43] כך אנו אומרים לחתני המסיבה: שלנו – שלכם הוא!

הקב"ה יתן להם חיים ארוכים, חיים שיש בהם מן האושר הפנימי ומן ההצלחה
המעשית.

בכבוד רב

יוסף דוב הלוי סולוביצ'יק

---

41   For Shragai's biography, see *Entzyklopedia shel ha-Tziyonut ha-Datit*, vol. 6, cols. 930–942.

42   For Rafael's biography, see *Entzyklopedia shel ha-Tziyonut ha-Datit*, vol. 6, cols. 858–877.

43   *Nedarim* 50a.

Letter 17

In this letter to Shlomo Zalman Shragai, the Rav defends the religious legitimacy of something Shragai wrote, apparently dealing with the "Who Is a Jew" issue. Unfortunately, I do not know the particulars of why some found Shragai's words problematic.

מוצאי ש"ק, י"ד שבט, תשכ"ה

ידידי החביב והנכבד מוה"ר ש"ז שרגאי, שיחי',
שלו' וברכה!

יסלח לי אדוני את עוון שתיקתי. טרדתי מעבירה אותי על דעתי ועל דעת חברי. אמנם אין בה מחוסר רגש כיבוד וידידות לאדוני. אני מחבב כל אגרת ואגרת שהנני מקבל ממנו וקורא בעיון רב וגם בעונג רב את דבריו הנחמדים המופיעים מעונה לעונה ובהזדמנויות שונות והחוצבים להבות אש של אהבה עזה וגדולה לא', לעמו ולארצו.

קראתי את דבריו שהמציא לי ולא מצאתי בהם אף שמץ של סטיה מדרך האמונה והמסורה. לכן "לך איעצך" שאל יתענין בדבריו בקורת שרק איבה וקנאה מבצבצות מהם ותוססות בהם, ולבטלם בתכלית הביטול ובהיסח דעתו הגדולה והרגישה. כולנו יודעים, כי מע"כ הוא העומד בפרץ והמגין בדמי לבו ובמסירת נפשו על עיקרי ההלכה ביחס לטהרת עם ישראל וספר וספר יוחסין שלו. אלה הרואים "מומים" בשיטתו ובהתנהגותו לא נקפו אפילו באצבע קטנה למען עיקרון זה. יודעים המה איך לבקר ולפסול אבל לא איך לתקן ולטהר. עוד הפעם, אין המה מעליבים את מע"כ כי אם את עצמם. אני מודה לו על ספר "פתיל תכלת" ששיגר לי. תשואות חן חן לו!

אני דורש בשלומו הטוב ובשלום רעיתו הכבודה ואני חותם בכל טוב,

יוסף דוב הלוי סולוביצ'יק

Letter 18

This letter, whose recipient is unknown, relates to the Rav's well-known harsh public criticism of Rabbi Emanuel Rackman's (1910–2008) claim that in contemporary times the ḥazakah of tav le-meitav tan du mi-le-meitav armelu (that a woman prefers almost any husband to being single) is no longer applicable.[44]

יום ב', יב תמוז, תשל"ח
כבוד ידידי הנעלה, הרה"ג, איש האשכולות, שיחי',
שלום וברכה!

תודה לבבית על אגרתו. מעולם <u>לא</u> אמרתי דברים כאלה. מעולם <u>לא עלו</u> ברעיוני
מחשבות כאלו. <u>להד"מ!</u> לא דבר ולא חצי דבר! לפני שנתים הופיעו בעתון *The Jewish*[45]
Examiner מאמרים ע"ד האשה בהלכה. המאמרים הם פרי עטו של ידידנו. באספת
הסתדרות הרבנים הרצה דברים דומים לאלה שפרסם בעתון. כשנודע לי הדבר אח"כ
מחיתי נגד המאמרים וההרצאה. קשה היה עלי הדבר מאד, מאד, כי הלא הוא מידידי
הנאמנים זה רבות בשנים. ברם למרות צערי שגרמה לי מחאתי לא יכלתי לעבר
בשתיקה, מחיתי בנוכחתם של יותר ממאה איש!

עוד הפעם אני מודה לו על שהעיר את תשומת לבי.

בברכה ובחיבה,

יוסף דוב הלוי סולוביצ'יק

---

[44]   The text of the Rav's address at the Rabbinical Council of America's 1975 convention, where he criticizes Rackman's approach, can be seen at www.arikahn.blogspot.com/2013/03/rabbi-soloveitchik-talmud-torah-and.html. Regarding the Rav and Rackman, see Lawrence Kaplan, "From Cooperation to Conflict: Rabbi Professor Emanuel Rackman, Rav Joseph B. Soloveitchik, and the Evolution of American Modern Orthodoxy," *Modern Judaism* 30 (Feb. 2010), pp. 46–68.

[45]   The title of the newspaper was actually *The Jewish Week and the American Examiner*.

Letter 19

On February 24, 1969, Rabbi Ẓemaḥ Zembrowski (1911–1996)[46] wrote to the Rav informing him that he told the leadership of Mizrachi-Ha-Poel ha-Mizrachi about the Rav's suggestion that a world council of Torah sages be formed, and they agreed to do so. Before beginning this process, they wanted to know which rabbis the Rav would recommend for this international body. In response to this, the Rav states that Zembrowski had misunderstood him, as he did not intend a council of Torah sages as is found in Agudat Yisrael, but rather that the religious Zionist leadership should consult with Torah scholars regarding the important issues that arise. In this letter we again see the Rav's concern for young people from the Boston community who were on their own in Israel.

יום ב', כז אדר, תשכ"ט
ידידי הנכבד, הרב צ. זמברובסקי, שיחי',
שלו' וברכה!

קבלתי את אגרתו. לא נתכוונתי למועצת רבנים רשמית. אין אנו משתעשעים במועצות גדולי, חכמי או גאוני תורה. זוהי זכות מיוחדת של אגו"י. אין אני רוצה בזה. מה שרציתי הוא דבר שונה לגמרי. אם תלמידי חכמים, הוגי תורה ולנים באהלה של תורה משתייכים לתנועתנו, אז מחובתה של התנועה לעמוד עמם בקשר ובמשא ומתן ביחס לשאלות חמורות (פוליטיות, חברתיות, וכו') העולות על הפרק. אם דעתם של ת"ח שבתנועה מבוטלת לגמרי, אז אין שום ערך בהשתייכותנו אליה. אנו עומדים בתנועה ומגינים עליה בכל לב ונפש. עדיין לא הרגשתי בשום מחווה שיש בה משום הכרה סתמית, או הכרת טובה מצד התנועה אלינו. אם אין צורך בת"ח, למה לנו להלחם בעדה? אין צורך בהחלטות, ובוויכוחים, כי אין רשמיות לדברי אלה. אם ראשי התנועה מבינים את אשר בלבי יכולים המה לתקן את הדבר. אם אינם רוצים להבין אז אין ממש במינוי מועצות רבנים. [!]

דרך אגב, אני מבקשו לנהוג מנהג הכנסת אורחים בשלש תלמידות של האוניברסיטה העברית, ולראות כי יבלו את ימי החג (עיקר העיקרים את ליל הסדר) בחוג משפחות דתיות. הבחורות הן מבוסטון, בנות בתים מהודרים שאצילות חופפת עליהם.
אני רושם את שמותיהן של התלמידות ומקום מקוריהן.
1) תמר סיון – שיכון הסטודנטים, רחוב גבטמלה [גואטמלה] 35/3 קרית היובל
2) חיה גבורין – "   "   "   "   "
3) רחל לייטמן – מטודלה 34
מובטחני, כי תמלאו את בקשתי.

אני מאחל לו ברכת מועדים לששון ולשמחה, בכבוד רב,

יוסף דוב הלוי סולוביצ'יק

---

[46] For Zembrowski's biography, see *Entzyklopedia shel ha-Tziyonut ha-Datit*, vol. 6, cols. 428–431.

Letter 20

After the passing of Chief Rabbi Isaac Herzog (1888–1959), many hoped that the Rav would be one of the candidates when the next chief rabbi was voted in. In the following letter, the Rav writes to R. Reuven Katz (1880–1963), chief rabbi of Petaḥ Tikvah, explaining why he does not wish to be considered for the position of chief rabbi. While most of this letter (with minor changes) appeared in Ha-Doar, March 11, 1960,[47] this is the first time the complete letter has appeared in print.

יום ג', י"ח שבט, תש"כ

כבוד הרב הגאון הגדול, עטרת ישראל ותפארתו, מרביץ תורה ויושב בישיבה, מוה"ר ראובן כ"ץ, שליט"א
שלום וברכה מרובה!

קבלתי את מכתבו הראשון יומים קודם שנהייתי נחליתי[48] ונפלתי למשכב. ימים קודרים, מלאי דאגה סבל ובדידות אלמת עברו עלי. עולמי נטרף לפתע פתאום. אולם זכות אבותי עמדה לי בשעת זעם, והקב"ה ברחמיו המרובים פדה בשלום נפשי ולא נתנני למות. יהי שמו מבורך.

לפיכך לא נזדקקתי לאגרתו של מעכ"ג. גם עכשיו, כשאני הולך ומחלים, עוד לא התנערתי מן החולשה הגופנית וההבהלה הנפשית שקפצו עלי בשעות קשות ומרות של חולי ויסורים. עדיין אין לי העצמה לנסח הרהורי במטבעות לשון מתוקנות ולהכריע בדברים העומדים ברומו של עולם. אולם אשתדל עתה להשיב תשובה ברורה ומחוורת כשמלה על מכתביו הנכבדים.

אני מגלה לו את כל לבי ללא שום נסיון של חיפוי פוליטי על כוונותי. לכתחילה, כשבני מעכ"ג, הרבנים הגדולים ואנשי האשכלות, מסרו לי בשמו, כי הוא רוצה לעמוד לימיני ולתת את אימונו לי [!], הצעיר בבית הלוי, הכרעתי לציית להצעתו ולשאת במשא הרבנות הגדולה.

קוויתי, כי יעלה בידי להפריד את הצד הטכני-הפוליטי מן העבודה הרוחנית הגדולה, הרבצת תורה ודעת א', וכי אוכל להקדיש את זמני ומרצי לעיון, ללימוד ולמחשבה, כמו שעלה ביד מעכ"ג באופן נפלא כל כך.

אולם המאורעות האחרונים בקשר עם הרבנות הראשית, ההתנגשויות האישיות וגם המפלגתיות ונסיון השתלטות על הרבנות על ידי בני אדם שאין להם שום זיקה לדת, הפיצו אור חדש על המצב, ומספוקני אם אוכל לעסוק בתורה מתוך מנוחת הנפש. ישנה אומדנא דמוכח, כי אשתלב בכל נפתולי הפוליטיקה, דבר שאינו לרוחי ולרצוני.

לכן הנני מוכרח להודות, כי במצב הנוכחי אין אני ראוי לכהונה זו. מלמד הנני, ואין לי בעולמי אלא ד' אמות של הלכה. אינני רוצה לצאת מהן אף אם יתנו לי מלכות שלמה.
אין די מלים בפי להודות לו על חיבתו אלי. לעולם לא אשכח את ידידותו.

---

47   A translation of what appears in *Ha-Doar* is found in *Community, Covenant and Commitment*, p. 177.
48   See Daniel 8:27.

בהערצה ובאהבה,

יוסף דוב הלוי סולוביצ'יק

Letter 21

Dr. Marvin Fox (1922–1996) taught for many years at Ohio State University in Columbus, Ohio. When the synagogue he attended in Columbus, Agudas Achim, built a new building and instituted mixed seating (while still calling itself Orthodox), Fox was placed in a quandary and wrote to the Rav. The Rav's reply is in line with his consistently strong stand against mixed seating, which he viewed as a desecration of the synagogue.[49]

יום הששי, ג' תמוז, תשט"ו

June 23, 1955

Dr. Marvin J. Fox
Department of Philosophy
Ohio State University
Columbus, Ohio

Dear Dr. Fox,

Please excuse the delay in answering your letter. I have been unwell these past few weeks and I have abstained from any kind of work.

My attitude towards a synagogue with a mixed seating arrangement has been explained to rabbis and laymen many times and it unequivocally censures any deviation from the architectural pattern of sex segregation which is as old as the synagogue itself. Women and men must be segregated in the synagogue by a partition; otherwise the synagogue not only forfeits its Halachic status but becomes a secularized and vulgarized house of worship unworthy of its name. Whoever quotes me to the contrary is deliberately lying.

Relative to your problem, I must say that since I am not familiar with circumstances prevailing in Columbus I am unable to guide you. All I can say is that I would advise you to pray at home (even on Rosh Hashanah and Yom Kippur) rather than to participate in a service which contradicts the basic elements of עבודה שבלב. Of course, if you are able to organize a strictly orthodox synagogue you should certainly engage in this most worthy undertaking. The issue of the synagogue today has assumed central significance, and therefore we must ascribe to the synagogue

---

[49]   For other letters of the Rav dealing with prayer in a synagogue with mixed seating, see *Community, Covenant and Commitment*, pp. 125–142. The Rav's letter to Fox is found in the Marvin Fox Papers, Box 29, Brandeis University, and appears here courtesy of the Robert D. Farber University Archives and Special Collections Department, Brandeis University. I hope to soon publish Fox's letter to the Rav which is also of great interest.

tradition almost dogmatic significance and to the struggle for its survival—the character of a מלחמת מצוה. Orthodoxy has until now been too lenient toward the problem of mixed pews. Orthodox rabbinical seminaries have tacitly endorsed this semi-reform trend and they send their graduates into conservative temples. A conspiracy of silence has been organized by many orthodox leaders who have neither faith nor courage to fight for a sacred cause. It is high time that a few pioneers whose hearts are aching at the pitiable sight of self-betrayal and self-deception bring the issue into the open and take a courageous stand on matters dear and sacred to us. Their voices will certainly echo throughout the Jewish community and many will follow their lead.

With kindest personal regards, I remain

Sincerely yours,

Joseph Soloveitchik

CR

The Repeal of Tosefet Shevi'it:
The Role of Discovered Traditions,
Indirect Nullifications, and Asmakhtot in
Annulling a Rabbinic Decree[1]

By: SHLOMO BRODY

The Talmud records how Rabbi Yehudah Ha-Nasi and his son Rabban Gamliel[2] made significant changes to nullify work restrictions in the periods immediately preceding and following the *shemittah* year (*shevi'it*). The motivations for these changes are not hard to understand. Even according to the base requirements of the Torah law, the idea of leaving one's land fallow for the year was very difficult, especially once compounded by a weak economic situation and heavy Roman demands for tax payments.

---

1   This essay draws from chapters of my doctorate, Shlomo M. Brody, *Repealing Rabbinic Laws: Talmudic and Medieval Perspectives on the Authority to Nullify Halakhic Norms* (Bar Ilan University Law School, 2018). Many thanks to my advisor, Rabbi Prof. Yitzhak Brand, for his many suggestions, as well as my father, Prof. Baruch Brody, Baruch Alter ben HaRav Eliezer Zev *a"h*. My last extended conversation with my father before his death related to material covered in Section III of this study, and it is dedicated in his memory.

2   I follow Ra"sh Sirilio to y*Shevi'it* 1:1 (*d.h. lamah ne'emar*) and Rabbi Gedalia Nadel, *Be-Torato Shel R. Gedalia* (Maale Adumim, 5764), p. 63, in identifying Rabban Gamliel as the son of Rebbi, known in academic literature as Rabban Gamliel III. For sources and argumentation, see R. Shaul Lieberman, *Tosefta Ki-Feshutah: Shevi'it*, 482–483. Hereafter, references to *Tosefta Ki-Feshutah* are designated as TKF.

Shlomo Brody is the co-dean of the Tikvah Online Academy and a columnist for the *Jerusalem Post*. For a decade he served as a rebbi at Yeshivat Hakotel and as a junior research fellow at the Israel Democracy Institute. A *summa cum laude* graduate of Harvard College, he received rabbinic ordination from the Israeli Chief Rabbinate, an M.A. in Jewish philosophy at Hebrew University, and his Ph.D. from Bar-Ilan University Law School, where he continues to serve as a post-doctoral fellow. His work has appeared in *Mosaic, First Things, The Federalist, Tablet, Tzohar, The Forward, Ḥakirah*, and other popular publications, and has been cited in Israeli Supreme Court decisions. His book, *A Guide to the Complex: Contemporary Halakhic Debates* (Maggid), won a National Jewish Book Award.

The additional days or months to this prohibition, known as *tosefet shevi'it*, only added to the burden while increasing the probability that people would violate these laws to maintain economic sustenance.[3]

Nonetheless, these legal nullifications seemingly violate the rule established in the mishnah in *Eduyyot* (1:5). *Ein bet din yakhol le-vatel divrei bet din ḥavero ad she-yihiyeh gadol mimenu be-ḥokhmah u-be-minyan*, loosely translated as "A judicial court cannot nullify the edicts of a fellow court unless it is greater than the latter in wisdom and numbers" (hereafter known as the *ein bet din* rule). In the case of Rabban Gamliel, the Talmud asks how he was able to make this change to the pre-Sabbatical year period in light of the mishnah's rule. The Talmud gives multiple answers that have important implications for understanding the *ein bet din* rule and ways of circumventing it. In the first section, we document these answers and try to understand the different strategies that they represent. In the second section, we examine the texts regarding Rebbi's successful attempt to nullify the limitations in the post-Sabbatical-year period and ask why the Talmud did not question his authority to make this significant change in light of the *ein bet din* rule. We will suggest that Rebbi's actions entailed an indirect nullification through a series of legal proclamations without directly repealing a rule, and therefore was not seen to conflict with the *ein bet din* rule. We will further argue that our findings in the first two sections indicate that the *ein bet din* rule was understood to mandate direct repeals of earlier laws but not indirect nullifications. In the third section, we will use this insight to focus on one of the strategies taken by the Talmud to justify Rabban Gamliel's innovation and explore the rule of Biblical hermeneutics in justifying rabbinic innovation.

---

3   The impact of economic pressures was already noted in *Tiferet Yisrael: Yakhin* to m*Shevi'it* 1:3 and are documented most systematically in Shmuel Safrai, *Bi-Yemei Ha-Bayit U-Bi-Yemei Ha-Mishnah,* Vol. 2 (Jerusalem, 5754), pp. 421–466. See also Daniel Sperber, *Roman Palestine: 200–400 The Land: Crisis and Change,* pp. 92–93.

Section I
How Did Rabban Gamliel III Nullify the
Pre-Sabbatical-Year Prohibition?

1. The Repeal

In the beginning of *Tosefta Shevi'it*, we are told about the following rescind-
ment.

רבן גמליאל ובית דינו התקינו שיהא מותרין בעבודת הארץ עד ראש שנה
Rabban Gamliel and his court ordained that the working of the land
be permitted until the New Year [of the Seventh Year].[4]

Apparently, before this declaration, there was some form of prohibition of working the land even before the Sabbatical year began. What exactly was the existent rule beforehand and how did Rabban Gamliel nullify
it? This is a matter of dispute discussed in both the Jerusalem and Baby-
lonian Talmuds.[5] A few mishnayot in the beginning of tractate *Shevi'it* discuss the extent of the period before the Sabbatical year (colloquially
known as *shnei perakim* of *tosefet shevi'it*) in which the different types of agricultural activity are prohibited.[6] The two Talmuds present various theories, with some differences, about the origins of this prohibition and
which elements of the law were nullified by Rabban Gamliel.[7] Yet both

---

4   t*Shevi'it* 1:1 (Lieberman edition).
5   *Mo'ed Katan* 3b, y*Shevi'it* 1:1, 33a (= Felix, *Masekhet Shevi'it*, Vol. 1, p. 22). See also
     y*Shevi'it* 1:7, 33b (=Felix, *Masekhet Shevi'it*, Vol. 1, pp. 66–68). The default version
     of y*Shevi'it* is *Talmud Yerushalmi im Masekhet Shevi'it*, ed. R. Yehuda Felix, 2 vol-
     umes (Jerusalem 5740).
6   See m*Shevi'it* 1:1, 1:4, 2:1, for example. Regarding theories of when this enact-
     ment was originally created, see Felix, *Masekhet Shevi'it*, Vol. 1, pp. 84–85, who
     himself believes it was enacted around the time of Shammai, based on his com-
     ment in t*Shevi'it* 3:10. See also Safrai, *Mishnat Eretz Yisrael: Shevi'it*, p. 6. (Hereaf-
     ter, books from the *Mishnat Eretz Yisrael* series will be abbreviated as MEY).
     Most commentators assume that the law was enacted out of concern that farm-
     ers were tilling the land in preparation to illicitly work the land in *shevi'it* itself (as
     opposed to preparing it for the year following *shevi'it*). Felix suggests that this
     was a generic *shvut* to warn people of the prohibition during the *shevi'it* year itself.
     Regarding the agricultural basis for why preparing the land at the end of the
     sixth year might be beneficial, see Y. Felix, *Ha-Ḥakla'ut Be-Eretz Yisrael Be-
     Tekufat Ha-Mishnah Ve-Talmud* (Jerusalem, 1963), pp. 34–42.
7   Most significantly, it is clear within the Tosefta and Yerushalmi that Rabban
     Gamliel's pronouncement permitted working the land until Rosh Hashanah.
     Within Bavli, however, some explanations maintain that an earlier prohibition
     (originating before the decree of Hillel and Shammai) would remain in place for

include admissions (at least by some Sages) that at least part of the pre-Sabbatical-year period had initially included some form of rabbinic decree which was entirely rejected by Rabban Gamliel.[8] In both Talmuds, this bothered different *amoraim* since the nullification of the law by later figures seemingly violates the *ein bet din* principle. Indeed, Bavli records that one of the Sages was initially confounded by this problem.

ואמר רבי שמעון בן פזי אמר רבי יהושע בן לוי משום בר קפרא: רבן גמליאל
ובית דינו נמנו על שני פרקים הללו ובטלום.[9]
אמר ליה רבי זירא לרבי אבהו, ואמרי לה ריש לקיש לרבי יוחנן: רבן גמליאל
ובית דינו היכי מצו מבטלי תקנתא דבית שמאי ובית הלל? והא תנן: אין בית דין
יכול לבטל דברי בית דין חבירו אלא אם כן גדול ממנו בחכמה ובמנין! **אשתומם
כשעה חדה...**

And Rabbi Shimon ben Pazi said that Rabbi Yehoshua ben Levi said in the name of bar Kappara: Rabban Gamliel and his court voted about the prohibitions of these two periods (i.e., from Passover or *Shavuot* until Rosh Hashanah) and nullified them.

Rabbi Zeira said to Rabbi Abbahu, and some say that it was Reish Lakish who said to Rabbi Yoḥanan: How could Rabban Gamliel and his court nullify an ordinance instituted by Beit Shammai and Beit Hillel? Did we not learn, "A court cannot nullify the ruling of another court unless it surpasses it in wisdom and in number?" **Rabbi Abbahu was dumbfounded for a moment...[10]**

---

a limited period (e.g., 30 days) before Rosh Hashanah. See bMo'ed Katan 3b and Felix, *Masekhet Shevi'it*, Vol. 1, p. 23.

8   A different problem raised by this prospect is why did the mishnah continue to state the law of *tosefet shevi'it* even after it had been nullified. This question is addressed in the Yerushalmi (1:1, 33a). For other examples, see Yaakov N. Epstein, *Mevo'ot Le-Sifrut Ha-Tanna'im* (Tel Aviv, 1957), pp. 227–229 and David Beit-Halaḥmi, *Ha-Ukimta Ba-Talmud* (Tel Aviv, 1987), pp. 81–84.

9   It should be noted that several Bavli manuscripts (including Munich 95) all use the term התירו (or similar variation) as opposed to בטלום. This language is also used in the Yerushalmi, and the Tosefta also used the verb of ה.ת.ר. There is no reason to assume that the term *heter* means something different than *batel*. The relationship between the word התירו and בטלו is discussed further in appendix #4 of my doctorate.

10   bMo'ed Katan 3b. Translation adapted from the William Davidson Talmud on Sefaria.

2. Talmudic Explanations for Rabban Gamliel's Authority

In both Bavli and Yerushalmi, justifications for Rabban Gamliel's authority are ultimately given. Each answer represents its own type of resolution and will be presented thematically.

a) Stipulation: The Law Was Limited to Specific Conditions

One strategy interprets the original law as being limited in scope to specific conditions, namely the standing of the Temple.[11]

אמר רב אשי: רבן גמליאל ובית דינו סברי לה כרבי ישמעאל דאמר הלכתא גמירי
לה, וכי גמירי הלכתא - בזמן שבית המקדש קיים, דומיא דניסוך המים, אבל בזמן
שאין בית המקדש קיים - לא.

Rav Ashi said: Rabban Gamliel and his court held in accordance with the opinion of Rabbi Yishmael, who said that they learned this prohibition as a *halakhah* (i.e., transmitted to Moses from Sinai). But they learned this *halakhah* only with regard to the time period when the Temple is standing, similar to the law of water libation (in the Temple). But when the Temple is not standing, [this law] does not apply.[12]

According to Rav Ashi, Rabban Gamliel believed, in accordance with the position of R. Yishmael,[13] that *tosefet shevi'it* before the Sabbatical year was derived as a *halakhah le-Moshe mi-Sinai* along with two other unrelated laws that were relevant to the Temple. Once the Temple was destroyed, *tosefet shevi'it* was automatically nullified, just as the other two laws were nullified. As such, Rabban Gamliel was in fact not nullifying anything, but rather merely pronouncing (or clarifying) that the ancient law of *tosefet*

---

11 This is the last answer offered in the Bavli's presentation but is presented here first because it is the simplest approach to resolving the question and was also deemed normative by many later halakhic figures. See Rambam, MT *Shemittah ve-Yovel* 3:1 and the comments of Radbaz. This answer is not found in the Yerushalmi.

12 b*Mo'ed Katan* 4a. The position of R. Yishmael that attributes *tosefet shevi'it* as a *halakhah le-Moshe mi-Sinai* might run into a conflict with a different tradition in his name regarding *tosefet Shabbat* in b*Rosh Hashanah* 9a. See the commentaries there for attempted resolutions.

13 Menachem Katz, "Halakhah Le-Moshe Mi-Sinai' ke-even boḥen ideologit," *Uquimta* 6 (5780), pp. 1–21, argues that there is broader difference between the schools of R. Yishmael that will attribute unsourced norms to "*halakhah le-Moshe mi-Sinai*" whereas the school of R. Akiva will support them with an *asmakhta*.

shevi'it, which has the status of a *halakhah le-Moshe mi-Sinai*,[14] was always intended to apply only when the Temple stood.[15] Accordingly, the original legislation stipulated that the prohibition was only binding under certain circumstances.

This interpretation, which is connected to a parallel passage in b.*Sukkah* 44a,[16] solves the problem of the authority of Rabban Gamliel's court's action by interpreting the law in light of its supposed legislative history. In general, legislative history is a well-known tool for judges to try to understand the purpose and meaning of a statute.[17] Yet this depiction of the law's historical evolution goes against the thrust of the tradition that *tosefet shevi'it* was enacted in the time of Beit Hillel and Beit Shammai (as Bavli calls it, "תקנתא דבית שמאי ובית הלל"), and that Rabban Gamliel and his court convened a quorum to nullify it. Or to put it another way, it offers a conflicting narrative to the assumed legislative history of this law and, to a certain extent, brings the authenticity of both into question.

Moreover, while many laws were deemed by the Sages as applying in the Temple era alone, it is not clear why the rule of *tosefet shevi'it* should be particularly tied to the standing of the Temple. The fact that it was allegedly announced at the same time as two other laws that are more naturally tied to the Temple service does not mean that the third law is also contingent on the Temple.[18] Rav Ashi's interpretive recreation of the law's

---

14   In discussion of this passage in *Mo'ed Katan*, as well as other circumstances in which *halakhah le-Moshe mi-Sinai* or the forgotten/reestablished strategy are invoked, R. Gedalia Nadel asserts that these are cases in which we are dealing with old, recognized laws whose origins we do not know. While they could go back to the days of Sinai, they might not go back that far, and in any case, are treated as rabbinic laws. See Nadel, *Be-Torato shel R' Gedalia*, pp. 66–68. For earlier sources who assert that "*halakhah le-Moshe mi-Sinai*" refers to ancient traditions, see the commentary of R. Ovadiah Bartenura to m*Yadayim* 4:3 and *Tosafot Yom Tov* to m*Yevamot* 8:3.

15   See Meiri (*Bet Ha-Beḥirah, Mo'ed Katan* 3b d.h. *halakhah*) and *Shittah al Mo'ed Katan Le-Talmido R. Yeḥiel Me-Paris* 4a d.h. *dumya*. Accordingly, the law of *tosefet shevi'it* would be revived in a future Temple era.

16   See Moshe Benovitz, *Lulav Ve-Aravah Ve-Ha-Halil*, pp. 132–135.

17   Aharon Barak, *Purposive Interpretation in Law*, pp. 344–350.

18   This explanation works better in accordance with the position of *Tosafot* 4a d.h. *ela amar Rav Ashi*, who claims that all three of the laws were given together. As noted in *Hagahot ha-Baḥ*, however, Rashi (*Sukkah* 34a d.h. *asarah*) asserts that these three laws were taught in the *bet midrash* at the same time. If this is the case, the logic of why the default dormancy of one law would impact the status of another unrelated law is not clear. For questions on the attribution of a *halakhah le-Moshe mi-Sinai*, see Benovitz, *Lulav Ve-Aravah*, p. 114 fn. 5 and pp. 124–126.

history and its built-in stipulation is therefore somewhat surprising; indeed, it is not found in Yerushalmi. It is possible that in addition to his take on the disputed origin of these laws, Rav Ashi was also uncomfortable with the alternative answers given to the *ein bet din* problem, and therefore proposed his own solution which neutralized the innovation made by Rabban Gamliel.[19]

b) Stipulation: Revisionist Bias. A second solution, offered by R. Abbahu after being dumbfounded by the question, also follows the model of historical re-creation that posits that the original enactors included a stipulation. Yet unlike the model of Rav Ashi, which narrowly interpreted the intended scope of the original law, R. Abbahu made a broader claim that the legislators empowered a later court with the prerogative to nullify the decree should this be deemed necessary.

אשתתומם כשעה חדה. אמר ליה: אימור כך התנו ביניהן: כל הרוצה לבטל - יבוא
ויבטל.

He [R. Abbahu] was dumbfounded for a moment. He said to them: Assert [that when they established their decree,] they stipulated among themselves: Anyone who wishes to nullify this decree may come and nullify it.[20]

As such, the initial decree included a provision that in effect neutralized the *ein bet din* principle by allowing for a later *bet din*, even of lesser stature, to nullify the law. In practice, the condition introduces what legal scholar Guido Calabresi has called a "revisionist bias" to the law.[21] That is to say, it creates a built-in condition that makes this particular law inherently more liable to being nullified. This overrides the *ein bet din* principle, which creates a strong "retention bias" that would preserve the

---

[19] See R. Gedalia Nadel, *Be-Torato shel R' Gedalia*, p. 73, who speculates that Rav Ashi believed this was an ancient decree (not a *de-oraitta* law) which was understood as a stringency that could only be kept under good political and economic conditions. The original enactors therefore stipulated that should things turn for the worse (as exemplified by the destruction of the Temple), the stringent practice would not apply. This interpretation would make his opinion more similar to that proposed by R. Abbahu, below.

[20] In y*Shevi'it* 1:1, 33a, this concept is formulated as שאם בקשו לחרוש יחרישו. Note that whereas *Korban ha-Edah d.h. le-kakh nitnah* gives the authority to the court, *Pnei Moshe d.h. be-sha'ah* seems to give the authority to the people to decide. As Benovitz, *Lulav Ve-Aravah*, p. 134, notes, this was a problematic formulation which was clarified in the Bavli to assert that the authority rests with the court.

[21] Calabresi, *Common Law*, pp. 123–124.

law.[22] It is not difficult to speculate why such a provisional clause might be built into this law. As the Tosafists already note, given the hardships already posed by observing the Sabbatical year, there might have been some concern that the law would cause undue damage to the land or strain for its owners.[23]

Yet this stipulated legislative history in Bavli begs the question of how R. Abbahu[24] knew that this *takanah* had such a clause built into it. As we saw, when originally challenged by the problem of *ein bet din*, the Sage was silent for a moment, as indicated by the word אשתומם. This term is used elsewhere in the Talmud in circumstances when a Sage was initially stumped on the origin of a law.[25] Following his recovery, he asserted, "Assert (אימור) that they have stipulated amongst themselves that whoever might want to nullify that measure can come and nullify it." The hesitation, followed by the postulation of this condition, might give the impres-

---

[22] See Meiri 3b *d.h. ein bet din*, who assumes this as a regular rule. אין בית דין יכול לבטל דברי בית דין חברו אא"כ גדול ממנו בחכמה ובמנין או שהתנו הראשונים על כל...

[23] *Tosafot* 3b *d.h. kol ha-rotzeh*.

[24] Or R. Yoanan, according to a different tradition in Bavli and the passage in Yerushalmi.

[25] The term, which is derived from Daniel 4:16, is used in b*Shabbat* 47a, b*Ḥullin* 21a, and b*Sukkah* 44b. Significantly, in each case, the Sage responds to the challenge with a significant revisal of his previous statement. Particularly interesting is the use of אשתומם in the related *sugya* in b*Sukkah* 44b, in which R. Abbahu, when dealing with conflicting traditions about whether the practice of *aravah* was a *halakhah le-Moshe mi-Sinai* or a *takanat nevi'im*, asserts that the law was given, forgotten, and then re-established by decree. In the parallel in y*Sukkah* 4:1 (54b), which discusses *tosefet shevi'it* and the ten saplings, the passage states, "R. Yosi the son of R. Bun said in the name of R. Levi: This decree was a halakhah they had in their hands [by tradition], but they forgot it. The second ones arose and conceived of the same things as the earlier [Sages]. This serves to teach you that any matter for which a [members of a] court sacrifice themselves will ultimately become established by them as it was told to Moshe on Sinai." For a similar use of this expression with regard to various laws, see b*Yoma* 80a, b*Shabbat* 104a, b*Megillah* 2b–3a, y*Pe'ah* 1:1 (15c), and y*Shabbat* 1:4 (3d)). For more on this forgotten/reestablished strategy, including our case, see C. Hayes, "Halakhah Le-Moshe Mi-Sinai in Rabbinic Sources: A Methodological Case Study," in *The Synoptic Problem in Rabbinic Literature*, ed. Shaye J.D. Cohen (Providence, 2000), pp. 102–108. This statement would seem to indicate the necessity of finding new interpretations or traditions to deal with the challenges presented in the *sugya*, as argued by R. Ḥayyim ibn Attar, below.

sion that an invented tradition or fiction was created to solve this problem.[26] The importance of understanding this strategy is compounded by the fact that a similar stipulation is asserted in other Talmudic passages where rabbinic authority was challenged.[27]

Such a response might have broad implications. As R. Shlomo Algazi wondered in the 17th century, why does the Talmud not simply give this answer to other circumstances in which later Sages have nullified a previous law?[28] To answer this question, some interpreters like R. David Sinzheim assert that it must be that the given Sage had a bona fide tradition about this given clause. Otherwise, one cannot assume such a "revisionist" clause was built into the decree.[29] Others, like R. Yitzhak Goyta (19th century), assert that in order to assume that such a clause was made, we must have good reason to believe that the propagators of the law believed that the law might cause severe financial loss (as the Tosafists claimed in this case), as opposed to other decrees.[30] In other words, some decrees

---

26 It may also lead to ridicule of the system. See, for example, Solomon Zucrow (1870–1932), a teacher at Hebrew Teacher's College in Boston, who writes, in his *Adjustment of Law to Life* (Boston, 1928), p. 39, that this one of the "far-fetched explanations to which the later rabbis of the Talmud resorted in their attempt to explain away the apparent violation" of the *ein bet din* principle. In the postscript to the book, he writes that the *ein bet din* rule is "counter to the facts of Jewish history" and is "quite illogical."

27 This idea is also used in the end of y*Shabbat* 1:4, 3d to explain the nullification of the decrees against gentile oil and the law regarding five *hatat* offerings that are left to die. The notion of a law that is created with such a clause may also be found in m*Ma'aser Sheni* 5:2 with regard to *kerem reva'i*. A similar idea might be found in the concept of *masero ha-katuv la-hakhamim*. See the comments of R. David Frankel, *Shirei Korban, Sukkah* 4:1 *d.h. she-kakh*, regarding the prohibition of *melakhah* during *hol ha-mo'ed* and further discussion in chapter nine of my doctorate.

28 *Halikhot Eli* #168, *d.h. bitul*, p. 64.

29 R. David Sinzheim (d. 1812, France), *Yad David*, Vol. 2, *Mo'ed Katan* 3b *d.h. kakh*. He is cited favorably in R. Menachem Munisch Heilpern, *Menahem Meishiv Nefesh*, Vol, 3, pp. 109–110. For R. Sizhheim's position on the *ein bet din* rule regarding the prohibition of shaving on *Hol Ha-Mo'ed*, see the article of Moshe Samet within Meir Benayahu, *Tiglahat Be-Holo shel Mo'ed*, p. 64, as well as the various primary sources recorded in his name in Benayahu's collection.

30 *Sedeh Yitzhak*, Helek Rishon, *Mo'ed Katan* 3b *d.h. Tosafot*, based on *Tosafot* 3b *d.h. kol ha-rotzeh*. He goes on to claim that such a concern would not have been inherently present in the case of gentile oil, which is why this solution was not presented in that case.

present complications which the original enactors undoubtedly anticipated and therefore we can assume that such a stipulation was made.[31]
Despite their differences, both of these interpretations of R. Abbahu's
solution assert that the original enactors had reason to introduce a revisionist bias to this particular law.

Yet other figures assert that later Sages made a post-facto claim when
there was no other explanation for the authority used to change the law.
As R. Ḥayyim ben Attar (known by the name of his popular Biblical commentary, *Or Ha-Ḥayyim*) posits,[32]

ומינה (=מהסוגיא במועד קטן, ש.ב.) דכל דאשכחן דאתא בי"ד וביטל גזירת בי"ד
חבירו שלפניו ולא אשכחן פירוק', אמרי דהכי התנו ביניהם. ולהכי אשתומם ר"י
כשעה חדא ואהדר לשנויי ולא אשכח שיניא, אז אמור הכי התנו וכו'.

In other words, R. Abbahu conceived this tradition in the absence of
other explanations. For this reason, he hesitated in his answer, seemingly
to look for other explanations, and then proceeded to assert this stipulation.[33]

R. Ben-Attar's interpretation goes significantly further than the first
two explanations to assert that not only did R. Abbahu give a post-facto
justification for a legal repeal that would otherwise be unauthorized because of the *ein bet din* principle, but that he knew fully well there was no
tradition of such a stipulation being made in the original decree.[34] One

---

31 Such an idea may also be found in Meiri's comments to *Megillah* 2a and *Avodah
   Zarah* 35b.

32 *Rishon Le-Tzion*, *Beitzah* 5a *d.h. gemara*. Rabbi Binyamin Zeev Wolf Boskowitz (d.
   1818), in his *Shoshan Edut* commentary to *Masekhet Eduyyot* 1:5 (10b in the book's
   pagination), formulated matters slightly more moderately. He interprets the Talmud to assert that whenever a nullification took place, later Sages assume that
   there must have been an oral tradition that the initial decree was made with the
   proviso that a later (and lesser) *bet din* could nullify that decree. Both statements
   are cited approvingly by R. Moshe Tzvi Neriah, "Davar She-be-minyan Tzarikh
   Minyan Aher," in *Mazkeret* (Rabbi Herzog Festschrift), ed. Shlomo Zevin and
   Zerah Warhaftig (Jerusalem, 5722), pp. 327–328.

33 R. Ben-Attar significantly goes on to claim that when the Sages themselves explicitly stated the rationale of the decree, it does not require a greater *bet din* to
   nullify it because the original legislators are implicitly stating that should the
   law's rationale no longer be germane, any *bet din* could nullify it. These broader
   questions are discussed in chapters 10–12 of my doctorate.

34 All three of these interpretations understand R. Abbahu to be offering a post-
   facto justification for R. Gamliel's action. Yet a fourth, more liberal strand
   emerged to assert that R. Abbahu's statement was a broader programmatic assertion that *all* rabbinic decrees could be nullified (*ab initio*) if the social circumstances change or the original decree creates unanticipated hardships. R. Abbahu

might explain his reasoning as a hermeneutic method based on legislative history: sometimes subsequent legislation sheds light on the purpose and scope of the earlier legislation.[35] Since Rabban Gamliel's court nullified the law, we assume that the original legislators anticipated the potential pitfalls of the law and took measures to prevent it from doing harm. It *must be* that the original law had a built-in stipulation since otherwise he could not explain the subsequent legislative history. For R. Abbahu, this provided a satisfactory answer to justify Rabban Gamliel's authority in repealing this decree.

In fact, this strategy is already found in a Genizah fragment possibly composed by Sherira Gaon but elsewhere attributed to Rav Hai Gaon.[36] The *gaon* was asked how R. Yehudah ben Beteirah could nullify Ezra's decree regarding *tevillat ba'al keri*.[37] In response, he asserts that a condition must have been made, citing as precedent the stipulation made with *tosefet shevi'it*. Once again, the assumption is that later legislative history tells us something about the earlier stages of the enactment. The *gaon* then further

---

teaches that the original legislators would have never wanted to make their decree in such a circumstance and tacitly understood that their decree could be nullified if later Sages deemed it necessary. This interpretation of R. Abbahu was made by Weiss, *Dor Dor Ve-Dorshav*, Vol. 2, p. 58 and Yitzhak Shmuel Reggio in his *"Ma'amar Ha-Tiglaḥat,"* reprinted in Meir Benayahu, *Tiglaḥat*, pp. 295–296. A similar type of claim was made by R. Moshe Ashkenazi of Odessa, known as the author of *Sefer Leḥem Avirim*. In a major *agunah* case discussed within rabbinic circles in Turkey, he asserted that the entire rabbinic decree of *"mayim she'ein lahem sof"* was no longer relevant in an era of mass communication. Citing the statement of R. Abbahu, he asserted that every rabbinic decree had within it a condition that allowed for its nullification should it cause greater hardship. This position drew scorn from other rabbinic figures of the time, who asserted that one could only assert that such a condition was placed on a decree when *Ḥazal* themselves made that declaration (as in *Mo'ed Katan*). Ashkenazi's position, along with the responses, are found in R. Ḥayyim Palagi, *Shu"t Ḥayyim Ve-Shalom*, Vol. 2, EH *Siman* 1 and R. Shalom Gagin, *Shu"t Yismaḥ Lev*, EH *Siman* 5. For a thorough discussion, see Raphael Etzion, *Hilkhot Ḥakhamim She-Batal Ta'aman Be-Peskiat Ha-Dorot Ha-Aḥaronim,* unpublished PhD thesis (Bar Ilan University Law School, 2008), pp. 232–234 and p. 254. Indeed, it seems difficult to assert that there is any textual indication that the statement of R. Abbahu should be taken in a manner that was meant to be a broader *de jure* statement regarding the powers maintained for *all* decrees of Ḥazal.

35 Barak, *Purposive Interpretation in Law*, pp. 348–349.

36 Shraga Abramson, *Inyanot Ba-Sifrut Ha-Geonim* (Jerusalem, 1974), p. 98.

37 For different strategies regarding the nullification of *tevillat ba'al keri*, see chapter eight of my doctorate.

adds a broader, more systematic statement, which we will cite from the version as later recorded in R. Zehariah Agmati's *Sefer Ha-Ner*.

יש דברים **שעיקר תקנתן על תנאי** שאימתי שירצו בית דין יבטלוה, לפי' בזמן שאנו רואין תקנה שתיקנוה בית דין הגדול בחכמה ובמנין, ובא מי שוא קטן ממנו ובטלה, וקיבלו את דברי השני ועשו בו מעשים, **אנו אומ' שאלמלא שלא היה לו כוח לבטל, לא היה מבטל ואף לא היו מקבלין ממנו.**[38]

The argument of the *gaon* is clear: when we see that a lesser court nullified the decree and the masses accepted such a decision, we assume that a stipulation was made by the original legislators, since the later court would have never acted (or been accepted) had they not had such powers. In the more complete responsum re-created by Abramson, the *gaon* further cites the case of *tosefet shevi'it* as proof for this point, while contending that this matter was already discussed and resolved in a *kallah* gathering.[39] This basic explanation was later cited by *Tosafot* and others.[40] The formulation of the *gaon*, however, is particularly significant since he articulates a programmatic statement. If we find lesser courts nullifying earlier decrees and their actions are accepted by the masses, it must be that the original legislators gave them such powers.

Thus three different interpretations emerged within later rabbinic literature to explain the answer of R. Abbahu: 1) he possessed a specific tradition about this clause; 2) he did not possess a specific tradition, but there was a particularly good reason to think that such a clause would have been made in this case; or 3) such a clause is stipulated in all circumstances to post-facto explain how Sages had the power to nullify a decree when the *ein bet din* principle would seemingly preclude such a possibility. However plausible one might deem these interpretations of R. Abbahu's statement, all three highlight the struggle R. Abbahu had in explaining the actions of Rabban Gamliel.

c) Connection to Verses: Perhaps because of these difficulties, a third strategy was presented in both Talmuds to justify Rabban Gamliel's repeal. This explanation asserts that the original law was based on Biblical exegesis, which Rabban Gamliel rejected. Since the original decree was

---

38   *Sefer Ha-Ner: Berakhot* 22a *d.h. ke-Rebbi Yehudah*, pp. 40–41.
39   Abramson, *Inyanot*, p. 98, line 8.
40   See *Tosafot, Bava Kamma*, 82b *d.h.* and Rosh, *Bava Kamma* 7:19, who cite this interpretation amongst three possibilities. See also Rashba, *Bava Kamma* 82b *d.h. ve-tiken, Ḥidushei Ha-Ra'ah, Berakhot* 22a *d.h. ke-de-Rav Ḥisda*, and Ritva, *Mo'ed Katan* 3b *d.h. ein bet din.*

built on Biblical interpretation, it could be subject to a reinterpretation by later courts. In the words of Yerushalmi,

רבי אחא בשם רבי יונתן בשעה שאסרו למקרא סמכו ובשעה שהתירו למקרא סמכו.

R. Aḥa said in the name of R. Yoḥanan, "When they issued the prohibition, they relied on support from Scripture. When they released the prohibition, they relied on support from Scripture."[41]

Bavli presents a similar explanation.

ורבי יוחנן אמר: רבן גמליאל ובית דינן **מ[ן]דאורייתא בטיל להו**. מאי טעמא? גמר שבת משבת בראשית, מה להלן היא אסורה, לפניה ולאחריה - מותרין, אף כאן, היא אסורה, לפניה ולאחריה - מותרין.[42]

And Rabbi Yoḥanan said that Rabban Gamliel and his court nullified based on a source written in the Torah. What is the reason? He derives [from the word] Shabbat [stated with regard to the Sabbatical Year in the verse: "But in the seventh year shall be a sabbath of solemn rest for the land" (Leviticus 25:4)] and the word Shabbat [which commemorates] the Shabbat of Creation. Just as there [on Shabbat itself] it is prohibited to perform labor, but before and after Shabbat it is permitted, so too here [in the case of the Sabbatical Year] itself it is prohibited [to perform labor during the Sabbatical Year] but before and after it is permitted.

Both Yerushalmi and Bavli suggest that Rabban Gamliel had the power to change the law because the original decree was based on Biblical verses. The later interpretation, by its nature, could undermine the original rabbinic statement and thus lead to a law's nullification. In Yerushalmi's formulation—"at the time when *they* prohibited... *they* permitted"—it is clear that both the original proclamation and its nullification were rabbinic pronouncements. The verses are being used as an *asmakhta* ("they relied on support from Scripture"). As Rashi notes, this also seems to be the meaning of Bavli as well.[43] The premise of this strategy is that the reliance of the original law on Biblical text makes it easier to nullify it. This strategy requires a more extended explanation to which we will return in Section III of our study.

Summary of Section I

---

41 y*Shevi'it* 1:1, 33a. See Felix, *Masekhet Shevi'it*, Vol. 1, pp. 24–25.

42 *Mo'ed Katan* 4a.

43 See Rashi *Mo'ed Katan* 4a *d.h. me-deoraitta*. See also the discussion in *Tosafot* 4a *d.h. ela*, Ritva 4a *d.h. R. Yoḥanan*, and *Shittah al Mo'ed Katan Le-Talmido R. Yeḥiel Me-Paris* 4a *d.h. deoraitta*.

The *amoraim* perceived Rabban Gamliel's action as a formidable legal declaration that violated the *ein bet din* principle. This seems to be the case because he sought to entirely repeal the decree that had been issued by Beit Hillel and Beit Shammai. Yet the Sages ultimately justified his court's innovation, albeit through different types of strategies to circumvent the *ein bet din* principle. Two major models emerged to resolve this problem. According to one model, a tradition was revealed which asserted that the original law had a stipulation built into it which undermined the authoritative status of the law. In one version, this went so far as to declare that Rabban Gamliel's court issued no nullification, as the original ancient law (*halakhah le-Moshe mi-Sinai*) originally asserted that it would not apply in an era without the Temple. According to another version of this strategy, Rabban Gamliel's court did issue a formal nullification which was nonetheless justified since the original legislators built in a revisionist stipulation which would allow for the law's easy nullification. According to the second model, Rabban Gamliel's court outright rejected the earlier law. Nonetheless, this was permissible, since the original law and its nullification were connected to Biblical verses.

Section II
How Did Rebbi Nullify the Post-7th-Year Prohibitions?

Rabban Gamliel III's pronouncement regarding *shnei perakim* before the Sabbatical year continued a trend initiated by his father R. Yehudah Ha-Nasi (known as Rebbi). Interestingly, while the innovations of Rebbi received much opposition, the *ein bet din* rule was not marshalled in Talmudic texts to challenge his authority. To understand why that might be the case, we must first appreciate the nature of his innovations and especially his nullification of the prohibitions extended to the post-*shevi'it* period.[44]

Rebbi made a series of declarations that were clearly intended to reduce the financial pressures created by agricultural laws. For starters, he

---

44   This post-Sabbatical-year period is sometimes also colloquially known as "*tosefet shevi'it.*" While the two decrees relating to before and after the *shevi'it* year are sometimes lumped together (as in m.*Shevi'it* 1:4 and *Mekhilta De-Rashbi* to *Shemot* 34:21), this might stem from post-facto *derashot* which were used to explain pre-existing decrees, as discussed below. See Safrai, *MEY: Shevi'it*, 40–41 and Felix, *Masekhet Shevi'it*, Vol. 1, p. 50; and Yisrael Ta-Shma, *Minhag Ashkenaz Ha-Kadmon*, p. 111. In any case, it should be clear that we are dealing with separate decrees, which is why they would need separate nullifications, even as both had the same overarching goal of preventing the illegal working of the land during *shevi'it* itself.

made several controversial pronouncements that excluded significant population territories from the (costly) agricultural laws in an era of economic hardship.[45] These declarations engendered significant controversy, with some Sages refusing to participate in the quorum. Similarly, he allowed imports of produce from outside the land of Israel, thereby increasing supply and markets at the same time.[46] The most significant ruling was his pronouncement that the Sabbatical years were only in force from rabbinic law (*me-derabanan*) in the current era in which the laws of *yovel* were not applied.[47] This declaration, which also had direct implications for *shemitat kesafim* and *prozbul*, was premised on an interpretive statement that *shemittah* and *yovel* were directly tied to each other. This reasoning is sensible but is certainly not the only way to think about these laws; moreover, it was not the assumption of all *tannaim* in previous eras.[48] By the Sages' own admission, the reduced status of the *shemittah* year created a legal basis for additional dispensations,[49] while further creating a cultural atmosphere that tolerated even greater popular deviancy, especially given the economic hardships.[50] In fact, there is even a tradition that Rebbi tried to

---

45 y*Demai* 2:1, discussed below. The significance of borders for legal purposes has regularly been a matter of deep halakhic significance with contentious debates. See m*Yadayim* 4:3, t*Oholot* 18:13–18 and the discussion in David Levine, "Rabbi Yehudah Ha-Nasi U-Tehumei Arim Be-Eretz Yisrael," *Katedrah* 138 (December 2010), pp. 7–42. pp. 41–42. For broader discussions on the significance of legal borders in different realms, see Eyal Ben-Eliyahu, *Ben Gevulot* (Jerusalem, 2016).

46 y*Shevi'it* 6:4 and sources discussed below.

47 y*Shevi'it* 10:3, 39c. See the parallel versions in b*Gittin* 36a and b*Mo'ed Katan* 2b. The version in b*Gittin* significantly adds that the Sages explicitly decreed to continue to observe *shevi'it*, a claim not explicated in the parallel versions. See Felix, *Masekhet Shevi'it*, Vol. 2, pp. 311–312.

48 See, for example, *Sifra Behar* 2. See also the comments of Rashi *Gittin* 36a *d.h. ba-shevi'it* and *Tosafot* 36a *d.h. bazman* and the sources cited in *Otzar Mefarshei Ha-Talmud: Gittin II*, pp. 603–609. See also Safrai, *Be-yemei Ha-Bayit*, Vol. 2, pp. 456–457 and Yitzhak Gilat, "*Ha-Im Yovel Meshamet Kesafim?*" in *Yad Gilat*, pp. 116–126.

49 y*Demai* 2:1, 22d, the statement of R. Yohanan. See also y*Shevi'it* 9:9, 39a which depicts someone as being punctilious regarding the (Biblical laws) of *hallah* but lax on *shevi'it*, since it is a mere law of "Rabban Gamliel and his colleagues." See Felix, *Masekhet Shevi'it*, Vol. 2, p. 286.

50 y*Ta'anit* 3:1, 66b–c, in which Rebbi reflects sympathy for a schoolteacher who is suspect of violating *shemittah* restrictions, since he is dependent on this work for his livelihood. The tolerance for such behavior also impacts the status of *shevi'it* violators as witnesses in court. In m*Sanhedrin* 3:3, their status is suspect. In b*Sanhedrin* 26a, however, R. Yannai declares them legitimate witnesses since they acted under pressure to pay government taxes. The rest of the passage,

nullify all of the *shemittah* restrictions, but ultimately recanted because of the protests of the saintly R. Pinḥas b. Yair.[51]

In this regard, it is particularly significant to note Rebbi's dispensation to allow the consumption of vegetables that were picked immediately after the end of the *shevi'it* year. The story of his declaration is recorded without fanfare in the Tosefta.

רבי ובית דינו התירו ליקח ירק במוצאי שביעית מיד.[52]

Yet within the mishnah, his position is cited as a dissenting opinion. The first position asserts that a prohibition exists in the initial period of the eighth year until one can reasonably assume that vegetables currently picked had been planted following the Sabbatical year.

מאימתי מותר אדם ליקח ירק במוצאי שביעית משיעשה כיוצא בו עשה הבכיר הותר האפיל.רבי התיר ליקח ירק במוצאי שביעית מיד.

When in the year following the Sabbatical year is one permitted to buy a [given type] of vegetable? Once [the new crop of] that same vegetable has become ripe. Once the [portion of the crop which] ripens early [in the year] has become ripe, the [portion of the crop which] ripens later [in the year] is also permitted (i.e., may be purchased).[53] Rebbi permitted the purchase of vegetables immediately

---

however, makes clear that not everyone, including Resh Lakish in the next generation, was pleased with this attitude. This is also clear in y*Shevi'it* 4:2, 35b. See Safrai, *MEY: Shevi'it*, pp. 117–120 and Felix, *Masekhet Shevi'it*, Vol. 1, pp. 227–236.

51 See y*Ta'anit* 3:1, 66c (and parallel in yDemai 1:3, 22a). See also b*Ḥullin* 7b. See Moshe Benovitz, "*Be-Sha'at Ḥerum Shanu*," pp. 21–22. For analysis of Rebbi's relationship with R. Pinḥas, see Ofrah Meir, *Rebbi Yehudah Ha-Nasi* (Tel Aviv, 1999), pp. 145–154. Note that R. Pinḥas ben Yair did not oppose all of Rebbi's actions, such as those relating to the status of Ashkelon. Felix, *Masekhet Shevi'it*, Vol. 2, pp. 442–443 discusses the possibility that this was not an attempt to permanently nullify the law, but rather a) a temporary measure because of drought, or b) an attempt to permit *sefihin* (aftergrowth). This approach is rejected by Benovitz, "*Be-Sha'at Ḥerum Shanu*," p. 21 fn. 45. Either way, there is a clear general lenient trend in his approach, as well documented in Safrai, *Be-yamei Ha-Bayit*, Vol. 2, pp. 453–457.

52 t*Shevi'it* 4:17 (Lieberman edition).

53 It should be noted that even within the *tanna kamma*, there is an attempt here to create a formal rule that allows for certain leniencies since any crops that are already ripe at this stage (but would normally would only be ripe later) might have been presumed to have grown during *shevi'it*. See also t*Shevi'it* 4:14 and the discussion in Safrai, *MEY: Shevi'it* p. 207 and Felix, *Masekhet Shevi'it*, p. 438.

in the year following the Sabbatical.[54]

From several places in the Talmud, we know that this declaration of Rebbi received reproach from his colleagues, along with the other dispensations which he declared. For example,

ר' התיר בית שאן ר' התיר קוסרין ר' התיר בית גוברין ר' התיר כפר צמח **ר' התיר ליקח ירק במוצאי שביעי' והיו הכל מליזין עליו.** אמ' להן בואו ונדיין כתיב וכתת נחש הנחוש' וכי לא עמד צדיק ממשה ועד חזקיהו להעבירו אלא אותה עטרה הניח לו הקדוש ברוך הוא להתעטר בה ואנן העטרה הזאת הניח הקדוש ברוך הוא לנו להתעטר בה. רבי יהושע בן לוי הוה מפקד לטלייא לא תיזבון לי ירק אלא מן גינתא דסיסרא.

Rebbi permitted [i.e., exempted] Beit She'an. Rebbi permitted Caesarea. Rebbi permitted Beit Guvrin. Rebbi permitted Kfar Tzemah. **Rebbi permitted [people] to purchase vegetables immediately following the Shevi'it year, and everyone spoke derogatorily about him** (*malizin alav*).[55] Rebbi said to them: Come and let us judge [the merits of my action]: It is written, 'And he [King Ḥizkiyahu] crumbled the copper' (II Kings 18:4). Was there no righteous person who arose from Moshe until Ḥizkiyahu to remove [the copper serpent from the world]? Rather, that crown God decided for Ḥizkiyahu to

---

54   m*Shevi'it* 6:4. As Safrai notes (*MEY: Shevi'it*, p. 208), the citation of a position of Rebbi within the mishnah likely indicated the editorial role of one of his students. On the broader phenomenon, see Epstein, *Mavo Le-Nusaḥ Ha-Mishnah*, pp. 946–950.

55   Emphasis added. R. Yisachar Tamar, *Alei Tamar: Yerushalmi Seder Zeraim,* Vol 1, p. 412, correctly argues, based on parallels to b*Ḥullin* 6b, that the Sages spoke derogatorily about all of Rebbi's declarations, not just the last one related to the period after *shevi'it*. R. Tamar believes that the criticism stemmed from Rebbi's hubris of disagreeing with his predecessors. Rabbis Yehudah Levi and Aryeh Carmel, *Talmud Yerushalmi im perush Kav Ve-Naki*, p. 39, argued that the term used in the Talmud (*malizin*) is connected to the problem of being *motzi laz* (casting aspersions) on previous generations. They contend that Rebbi's actions would surely incite the masses against those Sages whom they will now perceive as having been overly stringent on them. In contrast, Rebbi would be asserting in his response that it is justified for later figures to sometimes disagree with their predecessors. This is precisely the conclusion made by R. Menaḥem Meiri (*Seder Ha-Kabbalah,* p. 103) from this passage. וכמ"ש דרך כלל מקום הניחו לנו כו' (חולין ז.) כלומר שאין השלימות נמצא בנבראים, ואפי' במובחרים שבהם, עד שלא יהיו אחרונים רשאין לחלוק עמהם בקצת דברים. Indeed, the premise of the larger *ein bet din* principle is that there are times when later scholars may be greater than their predecessors. See the commentaries of *Tosafot Yom Tov* and *Ahavah Be-Ta'anugim* to m*Eduyyot* 1:5 and the discussion in appendix #2 of my doctorate.

be crowned with. R. Yehoshua ben Levi would command the boys, 'Do not buy vegetables for me [in Beit She'an] except from the garden of Sisera.'[56]

This is, in fact, one of several stories which indicate that the Sages did not accept his lenient rulings regarding *shemittah*, as seen below.[57] The dramatic story shows how Rebbi did not back down from his dispensation in spite of the scorn he received from his colleagues for his lenient ruling and their refusal to accept his position.

Why Did Rebbi's Actions Not Raise the Problem of the *Ein Bet Din* Rule?

What remains important for our purposes is that in the various discussions about Rebbi's *shevi'it* dispensations, he is never challenged as violating the *ein bet din* principle. This is particularly interesting because he was challenged on these grounds regarding his repeal of a prohibition of gentile oil (*Avodah Zarah* 36a), just as we have seen that his son's related nullification of the period of *tosefet shevi'it* before the Sabbatical year was also challenged.[58] One explanation might be that invoking the *ein bet din* principle was not necessary because of the rapid opposition to the merits of Rebbi's decree, let alone his authority to act.[59] One might additionally add that given the idiosyncrasies of the editing of the Talmuds, one cannot derive anything from such an omission.[60]

---

[56] y*Demai* 2:1, 22c. See Levine, "Rabbi Yehuda Ha-Nasi," p. 37. Levine also analyzes the larger story, as well as differences with the parallel in b*Ḥullin* 6b–7a. For additional analysis, see Ben-Eliyahu, *Ben Gevulot,* pp. 250–253; Felix, *Masekhet Shevi'it,* Vol. 2, pp. 424–431; and Oppenheimer, *Rebbi Yehudah Ha-Nasi,* pp. 67–73. Previously in the passage in the Yerushalmi, we also learn that R. Zeira opposed Rebbi's declaration. For other examples of R. Zeira's opposition to Rebbi's legal declarations (including his attempt to serve as the *makhria* who resolves disputes), see y*Yevamot* 4:11, 6a.

[57] For examples, see the forthcoming passages. Many of these sources showing opposition to Rebbi are discussed in Alon, *The Jews in Their Land,* pp. 722–725, and Albert Baumgarten, "Rabbi Judah I and His Opponents," *Journal for the Study of Judaism in the Persian, Hellenistic and Roman Period* 12:2 (1981), pp. 135–172.

[58] On this repeal, see chapters 6–7 of my doctorate.

[59] Alternatively, one might state that this was perceived as a personal declaration, and not that of his *bet din*. Yet in t*Shevi'it* 4:17, these actions are attributed to Rebbi and his court.

[60] As I show in my chapters 7–8 of my doctorate, there is evidence within the Talmud that two other decrees were nullified (gentile bread and *tevillat ba'al keri*), even as the *ein bet din* principle was not invoked. In those cases, however, there are disputes within the text whether such a nullification took place.

Even with those caveats, it pays to explore whether there is a more fundamental explanation for why the *ein bet din* principle might not have been invoked. Rebbi's pronouncement to permit post-*shevi'it* vegetables was the result of a series of his declarations, as seen in the presentation in both Tosefta[61] and Yerushalmi.[62] The latter tells the following history regarding Rebbi's declaration:

בראשונה היה הירק אסור בספרי ארץ ישראל התקינו שיהא הירק מותר בספרי ארץ ישראל. אף על פי כן היה אסור להביא ירק מחוץ לארץ לארץ התקינו שיהא מותר להביא ירק מחוץ לארץ לארץ. **אף על פי כן היה אסור ליקח ירק במוצאי שביעית מיד**, רבי התיר ליקח ירק במוצאי שביעית מיד בר מן קפלוטא. מה עבדון ליה ציפוראיי אלבשוניה סקא וקיטמא ואייתוניה קומי רבי אמרין ליה מה חטא דין מן כל ירקא ושרא לי לון.

At first (בראשונה),[63] vegetables were forbidden [for import] to the border settlements of the land of Israel. [The rabbis] instituted (התקינו) that [foreign-grown] vegetables should be permitted to the border settlements of Israel. Nevertheless, it was prohibited to bring vegetables from outside the land into [the central areas] of the land. They instituted that it should be permissible to bring vegetables from outside the land into [all parts of] the land. **Nevertheless, it was prohibited to buy vegetables immediately following shevi'it. Rebbi permitted buying vegetables immediately following shevi'it,** with the exception of the leek. What did the residents of Tzippori do?[64] They took it [a leek] and dressed it in sackcloth and ashes and brought it before Rebbi. They said to him, 'In what has this leek sinned more than all other vegetables?' Rebbi permitted the leek to them.[65]

Based on this depiction, Rebbi's permissive stance regarding post-*Shevi'it* produce stemmed from the previous declaration (also made by

---

61   t*Shevi'it* 4:16–19.

62   Safrai, *Be-yamei Ha-Bayit*, Vol. 2, pp. 451–455 and Haim Licht, *Masoret ve-Ḥidush*, pp. 95–110. Both Safrai and Licht follow in the footsteps of the brief remarks of Lieberman, TKF, Vol. 2., p. 542.

63   The use of this term, which will also arise in section three, is discussed at length in appendices #6 and #7 of my doctorate. For now, note that it clearly connotes significant halakhic change, even as the *ein bet din* principle is not invoked.

64   Regarding the actions of the residents of Sephoris, see Stuart Miller, *Sages and Commoners*, pp. 42–44.

65   y*Shevi'it* 6:4, 37a (Felix, *Masekhet Shevi'it*, Vol. 2, pp. 91–92). See also the parallel in t*Shevi'it* 4:16. The passage continues with stories of rabbinic opposition to his actions.

him, as made clear further in the passage)[66] that one may import vegetables outside of Israel, first into border towns and later throughout the country. Initially, this prohibition had been made to prevent landowners within Israel from selling *shevi'it* produce under the guise of being imported produce.[67] Yet this decree was no longer deemed implementable, either because many border city residents owned land outside of the territory of Israel, or because their communities were naturally awash with such produce anyway.[68] Alternatively, or additionally, the decree may have become unfeasible given the need for increased supply of food[69] and broader economic struggles in later eras.[70] Once this prohibition was removed, and further applied to the rest of Israel, there was no reason to prohibit consumption of vegetables right after *shevi'it* since one could readily assume that the produce purchased in the market was imported.[71] As such, it no longer made sense to impose a law that prohibited the purchase of vegetables immediately after *shevi'it*. This declaration, of course,

---

[66] See as well y*Pe'ah* 1:5 (18d) and y*Shekalim* 1:2 (46a), amongst other places which attribute these decrees to Rebbi. t*Shevi'it* 4:16 attributes them to "*raboteinu.*"

[67] See Pnei Moshe *d.h. ba-rishonah* and Mahar"a Fulda *d.h. af al pi*. This interpretation is also adopted by contemporary scholars. See Felix, *Masekhet Shevi'it*, Vol. 2, p. 437 and Lieberman, *TKF*, Vol. 2, p. 541 Yet some commentators (*Ra"sh Sirilio d.h. assur* and *Ḥazon Ish, Shevi'it* 20:3) elected to interpret the Yerushalmi in light of the Bavli, which claims that the alleged initial prohibition decree was based on whether we are concerned with the implantation of impure dirt from outside of Israeli into Israeli soil. Bavli gives no direct indication of any form of historical development. This was simply a matter of disagreement, which had ramifications regarding the intercalation of the calendar. See b*Nedarim* 53b and b*Sanhedrin* 12a.

[68] Mahar"a Fulda *d.h. she-yehe mutar*. See Lieberman, TKF, Vol. 2, p. 542, for various explanations.

[69] This explanation is offered by Rabbi Chaim Kanievsky in his edition of the Talmud Yerushalmi, *Pe'ah* 5:1, p. 76.

[70] See Rash Sirilio *d.h. assur* and Felix, *Masekhet Shevi'it*, Vol. 2, p. 437. Unfeasible laws can become nullified under the important principle found in y*Shabbat* 1:4 (and elsewhere), as discussed in chapters 6–8 of my doctorate.

[71] See Mahara Fulda *d.h. be-motzei shevi'it*. A similar explanation is found in the commentary of Rabbenu Asher to m*Shevi'it* 6:4. According to a parallel version (y*Pe'ah* 7:3), a tale of nearly-miraculous speedy vegetable growth led to his declaration. According to this version of the legal development, Rebbi permitted the immediate consumption of the food because produce in Eretz Yisrael could be plausibly blessed to grow incredibly quickly. Yet as Ḥazon Ish (*Shevi'it* 20:3) notes, it is hard to think that Rebbi based his lenient ruling on an extraordinary miraculous occurrence. On the use of miracle stories in these narratives, see Albert Baumgarten, "Rabbi Judah I and His Opponents," pp. 166–167.

removed the strongest social sanction against those who had, in fact, violated the *shevi'it* restrictions[72] since, in effect, it allowed consumers to purchase vegetables from the marketplace without concern. It might be that it was precisely for this reason that Rebbi's colleagues believed he had gone too far. Yet as Rebbi made clear,[73] he had no interest in issuing moral judgments (and certainly social sanctions) against those who felt compelled to violate these laws which, after all, was no longer a Biblical command—at least according to Rebbi, who had made that declaration.[74]

Accordingly, Rebbi Yehudah Ha-Nasi's dispensation regarding post-*Shevi'it* produce never entailed the outright and direct repeal of a decree made by earlier figures.[75] Instead, a series of incremental legal developments made in light of the economic and agricultural situation—including those made by proclamation (*hora'ah*) by him—allowed for the evolution of a law in a manner which made the initial prohibition no longer relevant. Once one could reasonably assume that produce found in Israel after *shevi'it* came from abroad, a legal rationale emerged to lighten the burden on the people. Rebbi found a way to change the law without directly repealing any given decree,[76] even as the result was the same.

A similar explanation can be made regarding the changes he initiated over which cities were within the borders of Eretz Yisrael. As we saw, many Sages held different opinions, both before and after his declaration,

---

[72] Either those who had actively grown their crops during the *shemittah* year, as Safrai claims (*Be-yamei Ha-Bayit,* Vol. 2, p. 454) or those who did not accept the restrictions regarding *sefiḥin* (aftergrowths), as claimed by Felix (*Masekhet Shevi'it,* Vol. 2., p. 91 and pp. 437–439).

[73] y*Ta'anit* 3:1, 66b–c. See the discussion in Safrai (*Be-yamei Ha-Bayit,* Vol. 2, p. 455.)

[74] See Rash Sirilio to y*Shevi'it* 6:4 *d.h. rebbi hitir,* who argues that the ultimate basis for these leniencies was Rebbi's belief that *shevi'it* was no longer a Biblical law. That being the case, he was lenient to prevent major economic hardship, even to allow produce which could not regularly grow in such a short period of time.

[75] The Bavli neutralizes this question by connecting this question to a general dispute regarding concerns over impure soil and never mentioning any historical development. Accordingly, we have a disagreement over a technical halakhic issue which Rebbi resolved in a different manner and which has subsequent consequences on the issue of post-*shevi'it* restrictions. Within the Yerushalmi, however, it is clear that there initially was such a prohibition of importing foreign produce which was released by Rebbi. This is seen in the multiple places in which the Yerushalmi will discuss legal implications before and after Rebbi's declaration. See, for example, the statement in y*Shevi'it* 6:4, 37a. The passage goes on to give other implications of Rebbi's decision. For other examples, see Lieberman, TKF, p. 541 fn. 76.

[76] In this case, the term *hitir* means to permit an act, not to nullify a law.

arguing that there were clear traditions which affirmed various cities within the halakhic territory of the land of Israel. Rebbi's innovations may have stemmed from alternative traditions, a strong sense of legal prerogative and independence, or, most likely, something in-between.[77] Yet ultimately, he and his colleagues were making a legal declaration (*hora'ah*) regarding the application of a norm which had not originated in legislation.[78] The basic law that produce in the land of Israel was liable to tithings and other laws was known; the interpretation of those borders, however, was subject to dispute and different rulings. Rebbi and his court gave a different interpretation which changed the law. They were not repealing the

---

[77]   What was the basis for Rebbi's declaration? According to Meiri (*Ḥullin* 6b *d.h.* *Bet Shean*), Rebbi based his declaration entirely on an earlier tradition regarding which territories were sanctified in the time of Ezra. As such, he was not making a novel declaration, and therefore could assert that the previous practice was a mistaken *hora'ah*. For a similar interpretation, see the commentary of *Pnei Moshe* to y*Demai* 2:1 *d.h. ve-hitir et kulah* and R. Yisrael Schepansky, *Ha-Takanot Ba-Yis-rael*, Vol. 1, pp. 390–391. Bavli (*Ḥullin* 6b) indicates such an interpretation, based on the claim of Rebbi's opponents that he was relying on an inaccurate tradition in the name of R. Meir. Noah Aminah, "*Eizoh Hee Eretz Yisrael La-Da'at Rebbi Yehudah Ha-Nasi?*", *Or Ha-Mizraḥ* 32 (5744), pp. 44–47, more moderately sees this declaration as a *sha'at deḥak* ruling based on a combination of earlier opinions. Schepansky notes that many contemporary scholars are more skeptical of this interpretation and saw Rebbi's action as decree that overturned earlier decisions. Yet a closer look shows a more nuanced approach in their writings as well. See, for example, Alon, *The Jews in Their Land*, p. 731, who writes, "In another of his enactments, Judah I dispensed Caesarea, Beth Guvrin, and Beth Shean from the payment of tithes. The motivation for this was undoubtedly the decrease in the number of Jewish farmers in those areas and the desire to enable those who remained to cling to their holdings." Yet Alon then adds, "The measure also had sound theoretical underpinnings and had been discussed earlier." Safrai, "*Mitzvat Shevi'it*," ties these declarations to Rebbi's broad halakhic approach which greatly weakened the status of the Sabbatical year, as Ra"sh Sirilio previously asserted. Felix, *Masekhet Shevi'it*, Vol. 2, pp. 424–431, ties Rebbi's declarations to a broader strand of thought in medieval commentaries who understood that the determination of borders for agricultural laws would take into consideration the economic needs of the power. See, for example, Rashi. *Ḥullin* 7a *d.h. harbeh kerakhim* and Rambam MT *Terumot* 1:5. Accordingly, Rebbi's declarations were consistent with a broader trend of keeping in mind the economic consequences regarding the determination of legal borders for agricultural laws.

[78]   In this respect, see the formulation Rambam gave in his Commentary to m*Ohalot* 18:9 for the ruling given to the area of Kini, which he deems was a matter of dispute that became resolved in the time of Rebbi.

decree of a previous court, and therefore did not violate the *ein bet din* rule. The *ein bet din* rule, it would appear, only applies for direct repeals.[79]

Summary of Section II

The comparison between the treatments of the two different periods of *tosefet shevi'it* highlights how far the Sages in the post-Temple period went to alleviate the economic pressures imposed by agricultural laws. It also shows us the difference between two different methods of nullifying a law in practice. In the case of Rebbi, the nullification of *tosefet shevi'it*, while controversial, occurred through a series of declarations that weakened the law to its ultimate nullification. In the case of Rabban Gamliel III, however, there was no such indirect development. As many mishnayot in the beginning of *Shevi'it* make clear, a decree was widely known against tilling the land before the Sabbatical year began. Rabban Gamliel III nullified that prohibition outright, seemingly in contradiction to the *ein bet din* principle.[80] Two important models emerged to resolve this tension. The first argued that there were built-in stipulations that the law applied only under certain circumstances or that it more broadly included a "revisionist bias" to undermine the *gadol mimenu* requirement. As such, the *ein bet din* principle did not apply to this law. The second approach argued that the legal

---

79   As I argue in my doctorate, the Talmuds also perceived the nullifications (or attempted nullifications) of *prozbul,* gentile oil, and the days on which one can read *Megillat Esther* as direct repeals, which is why the *ein bet din* rule was invoked to challenge the authority of those nullifications. On many other occasions, however, laws were changed in more indirect manners and therefore did not violate this rule.

80   This is not to say that Rabban Gamliel operated in a legal vacuum. Clearly, he was aware of the precedents of his father's broad legal activity regarding *shemittah*. Moreover, the continued discussion within rabbinic literature of what activities might be permitted on the land (even during the *shemittah* year itself, let alone beforehand) clearly reflect shifts in what dispensations might be allowed to make the land usable in the period immediately following *shevi'it*. Unfortunately, the chronology of those developments is somewhat complex. For relevant sources, see m*Shevi'it* 4:2, t*Shevi'it* 3:10, y*Shevi'it* 4:2 (35a–b), m*Sanhedrin* 3:3, b*Sanhedrin* 26a, and y*Sanhedrin* 3:5 (21b). These sources include traditions regarding the dispensation of R. Yanai (challenged by other authorities) to permit plowing the land in *shevi'it* because of taxes *("annona militaris")* imposed by the rulers. For plausible chronologies of these developments, see Felix*, Masekhet Shevi'it,* Vol. 1, pp. 85–86, 226–229, and Vol. 2, pp. 339–353, and Safrai, *MEY: Shevi'it*, pp. 115–121. That being said, none of these developments seem to have affected the period before *shevi'it* until Rabban Gamliel made his declaration. As such, Rabban Gamliel's actions were an outright challenge to the decree that had been made in previous generations.

decree was built on a Biblical verse which could be interpreted differently. As we will now argue, the logic behind this strategy is that the utilization of alternative *derashot* to support a law's nullification prevent it from being deemed a direct repeal and therefore not a violation of the *ein bet din* rule.

Section III
How Does the Connection of *Tosefet Shevi'it* to Biblical Verses Make It Easier to Nullify?

The Yerushalmi, as we saw, clearly indicates R. Yoḥanan treated these *derashot* regarding *tosefet shevi'it* as *asmakhtot*. Yet when reading some Talmudic presentations of the original notion of *tosefet shevi'it*, one might have thought these were understood to be full-fledged *deoraitta* laws based on Biblical *derashot*. This is certainly the impression that one may get from the mishnah in *Shevi'it*, based on its citation of Exodus 34:21.

> ...שנאמר (שמות לד) בחריש ובקציר תשבות אין צריך לומר חריש וקציר של
> שביעית אלא חריש של ערב שביעית שהוא נכנס בשביעית וקציר של שביעית
> שהוא יוצא למוצאי שביעית
>
> … As it says (Exodus 34:12), "From the plowing and the reaping you shall rest"; [this verse] is not needed to discuss the plowing and reaping of the Sabbatical year, rather the plowing of the pre-Sabbatical year that enters the Sabbatical year, and the reaping of the post-Sabbatical year that leaves the Sabbatical year. [81]

As such, according to those who adopt the approach of R. Yoḥanan, it required them to clarify these *derashot* to have been mere *asmakhtot* and that the original law stemmed from a rabbinic pronouncement.[82]

For our purposes, the key question is how does the decree's connection to Biblical verses ("*la-mikra samkhu*") help obviate the *ein bet din* problem? One might have actually thought the opposite—the fact that the original law was "supported" by a Biblical verse should make it harder to nullify. Unfortunately, the Talmuds postulate this approach without further explicating how this addresses the problem of overcoming the *ein bet*

---

[81] m.*Shevi'it* 1:4. The *derashah* is referring back to the basic idea of *tosefet shevi'it*, as found in m.*Shevi'it* 1:1. Indeed, the Yerushalmi begins its discussion of the first mishnah with this *derashah*. See *Melekhet Shlomo* to *Shevi'it* 1:4, the comments of Vilna Gaon to y.*Shevi'it* 1.3, along with Felix, *Masekhet Shevi'it*, Vol. 1, pp. 48–50 and Safrai, *MEY: Shevi'it*, p. 40. The midrash is cited in the name of R. Akiva in b.*Mo'ed Katan* 3b–4a, b.*Rosh Hashanah* 9a, and b.*Makot* 8b. The mishnah (and Bavli) go on to give an alternate reading of the verses in the name of R. Yishmael.

[82] On this general issue, see, most recently, Rabbi Shmuel Ariel, *Nata Betokheinu: Perakim Be-Yesodot Torah She-be-al Peh* (Otniel, 5778), Vol. 2, pp. 225–236.

din principle. Moreover, the strategy is also utilized in other prominent cases to justify legal repeals, including the alleged nullifications of laws relating to gentile oil[83] and *tevillat ba'al keri*.[84] On this basis, Rambam asserts that the *ein bet din* rule (and more specifically, the requirement of a greater court) does not apply to laws based on the rules of hermeneutics but does apply to rabbinic decrees, further highlighting the significance of this strategy.[85] Thus, the question becomes how the utilization of Biblical verses lowers the barriers to halakhic change.

Do *Asmakhtot* Create Legal Stability?

As is well known, rabbinic scholars have long disagreed over the relationship between traditional practice, law, and midrash. They have particularly questioned which came first: the law or the *derashah*? Did the *derashah* generate the law, or does it support the declared law or contemporary practice?[86] Without entering the fray over the larger debate, it seems clear that there are times when the Torah is being used to buttress a pre-existing practice or a new rabbinic decree. That is to say, the law came first, and the verse followed it. This can be classically seen in the passages in which we find the following statement.

---

83 See *Avodah Zarah* 36a-b and the comments of Rabad, *Perush Ha-Rabad Le-Avodah Zarah*, ed. A. Sofer (Jerusalem, 5738), 36a *d.h. bishlama*, pp. 73–74.

84 See *Berakhot* 22a and the comments of Meiri, *Bet Ha-Behirah, Berakhot* 22a *d.h. tevillah.*

85 *Mishneh Torah, Mamrim* 2:1–2. See also Rabbi Abraham di-Biton, *Leḥem Mishneh, Mamrim* 2:2; Rabbi Abraham Hayim Schor, *Torat Ḥayyim, Avodah Zarah* 36a *d.h. kesavar*; Rabbi Yosef Shaul Natanson, *Shu"t Shoel U-Meshiv Kamma* 2:100; Maharatz Chajes, *Kol Kitvei,* Vol. 1, pp. 384–385. See also the position of Rav Hai Gaon, as cited in Rabbi Meir Abulafia, *Yad Ramah, Sanhedrin* 33a *d.h. ve-ibaye,* and the comments of Meiri at the end of his commentary to *Beitzah* 5a.

86 Many positions on these questions, from earlier centuries, are explored in Jay Harris, *How Do We Know This?* (New York, 1995). In recent years, the trend within academic scholarship favors the opinion that legal declarations came first and then were given support through Biblical exegesis. See Ephraim Urbach, *Me-Olamam shel Ḥakhahim,* pp. 50–66 and his *Ha-Halakhah,* pp. 79–88. See also Epstein, *Mevo'ot Le-Sifrut Ha-Tana'im,* p. 511, who asserted, "While Scriptural prooftexts are provided for halakhah, one does not derive or innovate legal traditions on the basis of Scripture." Vered Noam, "*Ben Sifrut Qurman La-Midrash Ha-Halakhah,*" p. 94 fn. 99, affirms that this is the current trend in scholarship. For a primary opposing position who sees the exegesis as preceding the law, see David Weiss Halivni, *Midrash, Mishnah, and Gemara,* pp. 18-37, who also provides earlier literature on the topic.

מדרבנן, וקרא אסמכתא בעלמא הוא.[87]

Here the Talmud asserts that a law is of rabbinic origin and that the text was only an *asmakhta* invoked to provide "support."[88]

One of the Talmudic passages which is frequently cited[89] to support the notion that *derashot* came to support existing laws is a mishnah in *Sotah* in which R. Yehoshua praises R. Akiva for buttressing a law developed by an earlier Sage, R. Yoḥanan ben Zakkai, with a midrashic teaching.

בו ביום דרש רבי עקיבא (ויקרא י"א) וכל כלי חרש אשר יפול מהם אל תוכו כל אשר בתוכו יטמא אינו אומר טמא אלא יטמא לטמא אחרים לימד על ככר שני שמטמא את השלישי. אמר ר' יהושע מי יגלה עפר מעיניך רבן יוחנן בן זכאי שהיית אומר עתיד דור אחר לטהר ככר שלישי שאין לו מקרא מן התורה שהוא טמא, והלא עקיבא תלמידך מביא לו מקרא מן התורה שהוא טמא שנאמר כל אשר בתוכו יטמא.

On that day Rabbi Akiva expounded, "Any earthenware vessel into which any of them fall, whatever is within it shall become impure" (Leviticus 11:33). It does not say "impure" but "becomes impure" —thus it makes others impure. This teaches that a loaf of second-degree impurity can make impure a loaf to the third-degree. Rabbi Yehoshua said, "Who will remove the dirt from your eyes, Rabban Yoḥanan ben Zakkai? You used to say that in the future another generation will purify a third-degree loaf, because there is no verse

---

[87] See, for example, b.*Sukkah* 28b, b*Yevamot* 24a, b*Ḥullin* 17b, and b*Niddah* 25a. See also b*Sukkah* 6a and b*Eruvin* 4a, where it is used to buttress an old legal tradition (*hilkhata*).

[88] On the many different meanings offered to the term "*asmakhta*," see R. Ḥanan Gafni, *Peshutah shel Mishnah* (Jerusalem, 2011), pp. 245–251, R. Yehoshua Inbal, *Torah She-be-al Peh: Samkhutah U-Derakheihah* (Jerusalem, 5775), pp. 304–309, and *Encyclopedia Talmudit*, Vol. 2, pp. 105–108 (*d.h. asmakhta*). It should be noted that even Halivni recognizes that the term "*asmakhta*" connotes in later Talmudic literature a rabbinic law. As he writes, in some cases, "The text is, as it were, merely ornamental, a rabbinic decoration with no Biblical force." See Halivni, *Peshat and Derash*, p. 157. In contrast, we will argue that the use of the prooftext in our cases was clearly not meant to just be "ornamental."

[89] See, for example, anokh Albeck, *Mavo La-Mishnah*, pp. 47–48; Shmuel Safrai, *The Literature of the Sages*, Part 1, p. 159; Gafni, *Peshutah Shel Mishnah*, pp. 244–245, as well as the literature discussed in Yishai Rosen-Zvi, "'*Mi Yigaleh Afar Me-Eina-kha*': Mishnat Sotah Perek 5 U-Midrasho shel R' Akiva," *Tarbiẓ* 75:1–2 (5766), pp. 101–102.

from the Torah that makes it impure. Now behold, Akiva your student brings a verse from the Torah that it is impure! As it says, 'All
that is in it becomes impure.'"[90]

R. Yehoshua congratulates R. Akiva for solidifying a law which lacked
bona fide textual proofs.[91] According to Bavli (*Sotah* 30a), R. Yoḥanan
ben Zakkai derived this law from a *kal va-ḥomer* which he believed was
compelling but nonetheless had flaws, thereby making it subject to rever-
sal. As such, R. Akiva gave the claim greater strength. The prooftext of
the Torah, R. Yehoshua hoped, will solidify the law and prevent it from
being rejected or overturned in later generations, as R. Yoḥanan ben Zakkai feared.[92] The mishnah plainly acknowledges the creativity used by R.
Akiva in fortifying the halakhah though the support of Biblical exegesis.

In recent years, academic scholars like Menaḥem Kahana have pains-
takingly documented how R. Akiva's strategy was to confer authority to
these new rabbinic teachings. This can be seen in the many *midrashim* in
which a Biblical text is cited only to give support to a complete mishnah
or other halakhic teaching, as introduced by the term *mikan amru* (מכאן
אמרו).[93] This process, which has been aptly called "re-scripturizing," uses

---

90 m*Sotah* 5:2.

91 Rosen-Zvi, "*Mi Yigaleh Afar*," pp. 98–101.

92 As Jay Harris notes, the historical motivation for this fear is not easy to determine and it may not have been uniform among all Sages. However, as he goes
on to write, specifically commenting on this mishnah, "What is important is that
at some point in the tannaitic period, a concern was expressed that law passed
on without explicit scriptural authority might fail to stand the test of time. The
position attributed to Yoḥanan ben Zakkai here gives voice to that anxiety precisely. One cannot know how widespread such anxiety may have been in the
rabbinic world of the second century, or that the teaching attributed to Akiva
was motivated by it; nor, finally, can one conclude that *midrash halakhah* originated in response to such anxiety. The only thing one can know is that in the
tannaitic period, some large or small segment of the rabbinic estate developed a
deep-seated concern that unjustified law would not seem compelling to later
generations. A suggestion can be made that midrashic activity, no matter its origins, serves inter alia to address such anxiety. (It is striking that such anxiety
finds expression in the Mishnah, which, with important exceptions, is the vehicle of unjustified law par excellence.)" See Harris, "Midrash Halachah," in *The
Cambridge History of Judaism, Vol. 4: The Late Roman-Rabbinic Period*, ed. Steven
Katz (Cambridge, 2006), pp. 340–341.

93 Menaem Kahana, "*Hadrashot Ba-Mishnah Ve-Ha-halakhot Ba-Midrash*," *Tarbiz*
84:1–2 (5776), pp. 17–76. An earlier English summary of the major claims can
be found in Yakir Paz, "Re-Scripturizing Traditions: Designating Dependence
in Rabbinic Halakhic Midrashim and Homeric Scholarship," in *Homer and the*

exegesis to connect a self-standing legal tradition to a Biblical word, verse, or passage. By showing a close connection between the rabbinic law to the Bible, R. Akiva and his school gave authority to the rabbinic teaching which has been attached to the text. Significantly, R. Akiva's midrashic teachings are not just innovating new laws, strengthening independent rabbinic teachings, or arbitrating standing disagreements.[94] Rather, they are innovations which fundamentally *change* halakhic practice and nullify the previous norm.[95] Accordingly, R. Akiva utilized *derashot* as a mechanism to justify halakhic changes, which he was introducing.

A good example of this phenomenon in which an *asmakhta* supports a legal change found in a mishnah relates to the case of how the *bikkurim* ritual was performed. In *Sifre Devarim*, a work of *midrash halakhah* generally attributed to the school of R. Akiva, a change in the ritual is recorded alongside support from a Biblical verse, using similar linguistic expressions (*samkhu al ha-mikra*) to those in the case of *tosefet shevi'it*. The *derashah* is wrapped around a citation of the mishnah in tractate *Bikkurim* (3:7) which describes how the Sages changed the protocol of reciting the appropriate verses because illiterate people were too embarrassed to bring their sacrifice.

עניית ואמרת, נאמר כאן עניה ונאמר להלן עניה מה עניה האמורה להלן בלשון
הקדש אף עניה האמורה כאן בלשון הקדש. **מיכן אמרו בראשונה** כל מי שהוא

Bible in the Eyes of Ancient Interpreters, ed. Maren R. Niehoff (Leiden, 2012), pp. 269–298.

94   On the use of the expression *ad she-ba R. Akiva* ("until R. Akiva came and asserted") which appears in several of these texts, see Epstein, *Mevo'ot La-Sifrut Ha-Tana'im*, pp. 74–80.

95   On R. Akiva as a *darshan* and innovator, see the literature cited in Menaḥem Kahana, *Sifre Zute Devarim*, p. 373 fn. 31. One classic collection of his innovations, including those that go against *mishnah rishonah*, is Epstein, *Mevo'ot Le-Sifrut Ha-Tana'im*, pp. 71–84. A representative sentiment is expressed by Shmuel Safrai (*Literature of the Sages*, Part I, p. 200): "R' Akiva is one of the greatest innovators in the history of halakhah." He goes on to add (p. 204–205, emphasis added), "But R. Akiva's contribution consisted not only of reformations, expansions, and clarifications of existing mishnayot, but also of conscious innovations in explicit opposition to the accepted Halakhah. The Sages prior to R. Akiva, as was all his contemporaries, did not alter or rework the mishnayot which they had received from their teachers. They added to them and used them for creating new halakhot, for example, by comparing a new problem with an appropriate accepted halakhah... To be sure, R. Akiva himself also derived many new halakhot in this way. **What was new was that R. Akiva altered accepted traditions and thus made them what was subsequently called the 'First Mishnah.'**"

יודע לקרות קורא ושאינו יודע לקרות מקרים אותו נמנעו מלהביא **התקינו** שיהו
מקרים את היודע ואת מי שאינו יודע. **סמכו על המקרא** וענית אין עניה אלא מפי
אחרים.

(*Devarim* 26:5) 'And you shall answer': 'answer' is written here, and
elsewhere (ibid. 27:14): Just as there, in the holy tongue; here, too, in
the holy tongue. 'And you shall answer and you shall say': **From here
they said: In the beginning**, whoever could recite the formula (by
himself) did so, whoever could not, recited after another—where-
upon they stopped bringing *bikkurim* (to avoid embarrassment). **It
was, therefore, ordained** to have one who knew how (to recite it)
do so; and for those who did not know how to recite it, **they relied
on the verse** 'and you shall answer'—'answering' is in response to
another. [96]

This is clearly a case in which the *derashah* justifies or solidifies the
legal change that was instigated for social reasons (in this case, embarrassment from illiteracy causing people to not bring the sacrifice). [97] The text
testifies to the fact that that this was a rabbinic innovation (*hitkinu*) which
departs from the earlier practice (*ba-rishonah*), [98] and that the *asmakhta* (*samkhu al ha-mikra*) is being marshalled (*mikan amru*) to support the change
already known from the mishnah.

In this case, we are dealing with a new exegesis regarding a law to
which there was no recorded earlier, alternative interpretation or *derashah*.
For our purposes, we will call this a "reinforcing *asmakhta*" in that it but-
tresses a legal declaration without challenging an earlier *derashah*. [99]

---

[96] *Sifre, Devarim* #301.

[97] Safrai, *MEY: Bikkurim*, pp. 257–258.

[98] For more examples of legal changes indicated by this word, as well as an explanation why these developments did not violate the *ein bet din* rule, see appendices
6–7 of my doctorate.

[99] Other examples of a "reinforcing *asmakhta*:" 1) See mNedarim 9:6 and yNedarim
1:1, 36c. (Note that that the *derashah* does not appear in bNedarim 27a.) For discussion of parallel ideas and sources, see Lieberman, *TKF*, Vol. 6, pp. 468–470
(to tNedarim 5:1) and Kahana, *Sifre Bamidbar*, Vol. 4, p. 1260 fn. 57. 2) mYoma
2:1–2 states that the job assignments in the Temple were initially decided on a
first-come, first-serve basis, but that after a violent incident, the Sages enacted a
lottery system. The violence of this incident is greatly elaborated upon in parallel
sources, such as tKippurim 1:12. Less noted, however, is that in *Sifre Bamidbar*
#116, the lottery system is established on the basis of a *derashah* with no refer-
ence to such an incident. Many classic commentators have noted that this is just
an *asmakhta*, yet as Kahana notes, the later *derashah* is being employed to justify
a change in practice (in this case, a "reinforcing *asmakhta*"). See Kahana, *Sifre
Bamidbar*, Vol. 4, p. 879. 3) The type of land from which one collects damages.

"Revisionist *Asmakhtot*": Challenging Earlier Interpretation to Make Legal Changes

In different cases, however, an *asmakhta* is used when there were alternative Scriptural interpretations supporting the competing and earlier legal practices. For our purposes, we will call this a "revisionist *asmakhta*" since it challenges and revises the earlier meaning derived from Scripture. An example of this is the disagreement given in the mishnah regarding the minimum amount a *nazir* must consume to violate the prohibition. The original law (*mishnah rishonah*) was that a *revi'it* must be consumed, yet the law changed to follow the opinion of R. Akiva that a *kezayit* was necessary. In the parallel Yerushalmi, it becomes clear both opinions were based on competing *asmakhtot*, with R. Akiva using his own *derashah* to buttress his opinion. Thus, the *asmakhta* in this case comes to undermine the "*mishnah rishonah*" that was based on an alternative *derashah*.[100]

Another case in which alternative exegesis supports multiple legal changes relates to the complex development of the law that came to prohibit a woman betrothed (*arusah*) to a *kohen* from eating his *terumot* before they are married (*nesu'in*). The mishnah[101] asserts that the *mishnah rishonah* (i.e., original law) was that a betrothed woman was only entitled to eat from *terumot* if the 12-month deadline had passed and she had still not been formally married. A later *bet din* changed the rule to assert that she could not eat from the *terumot* under all circumstances until she was married under the wedding canopy.[102] From other sources, however, we learn that there was an even earlier position which asserted that the *arusah* could eat from *terumot* already from the beginning of the betrothal period, based

---

See t*Ketubot* 12:2. As Lieberman notes (*TKF*, Vol. 7, p. 370), the parallel Yerushalmi (y*Gittin* 5:1, 46c) makes clear that this is a departure from the Biblical law, with (once again) R. Akiva basing the change on a Biblical verse. The matter, however, is more complicated within Bavli (*Gittin* 48b), which initially asks how this can be attributed to a rabbinic law and asserts that this is a case in which the norm derived from the logic of the Torah.

100 See m*Nazir* 6:1, y*Nazir* 6:1, 55a and the discussion in Kahana, *Sifre Bamidbar*, Vol. 2, p. 219 to *Sifre Bamidar* #24.

101 m*Ketubot* 5:2–3. See also the parallel in t*Ketubot* 5:1 (Lieberman edition). On the text, see Yeraḥmiel Brody, *Mishnah ve-Tosefta Ketubot*, pp. 146–149. See also Epstein, *Mavo Le-Nusaḥ Ha-Mishnah*, pp. 972–973, Lieberman, TKF, Vol. 6, pp. 256–259; Adiel Schremer, *Zakhar u-Nekevah*, pp. 326–333 and 341–345 (which includes important discussion regarding parallels to Roman law); Safrai, *MEY: Ketubot* (to m*Ketubot* 5:2–3); and Kahana, *Sifre Bamidbar*, pp. 898–901 (to Sifre #117), who provides textual variations to texts as well as parallel sources.

102 This position also appears in m*Yevamot* 9:4 and y*Yevamot* 9:6, 10b.

on *Vayikra* 22:11 (regarding an analogous case of legal responsibilities with slaves[103]) or *Bamidbar* 18:13 (allowing "all of your household" to consume *terumot*).[104]

The Yerushalmi explains the different positions by providing a depiction of a three-stage historical development with significant implications for the role of *derashot* in supporting rabbinic pronouncements.

מתניתי' לא כמשנה הראשונה ולא כמשנה האחרונה אלא כמשנה האמצעית. דתני
בראשונה היו אומרים ארוסה בת ישראל אוכלת בתרומה **דהוון דרשין** וכהן כי
יקנה נפש קניין כספו דלא כן מה בין קונה אשה ובין קונה שפחה. **חזרו לומר**
לאחר שנים עשר חדש לכשיתחייב במזונותיה. **בית דין של אחרון** אמרו לעולם
אין האשה אוכלת בתרומה עד שתיכנס לחופה.[105]

Accordingly, the original law (*mishnah rishonah*) was that a betrothed woman could eat *terumot*. This ruling, as the text stresses, was based on a *derashah*, in this case from the verse in *Vayikra*. Later, in the interim stage, the Sages asserted (חזרו לומר) that only a betrothed woman whose wedding day had passed was entitled to eat from the *terumot*.[106] Ultimately, in the final ruling, the later court ruled that no betrothed woman could consume *terumot* until she made it under the wedding canopy. Accordingly, we had two rabbinic decrees: the first which significantly amended the Biblical law, and the second which nullified the first rabbinic decree.

How did this prohibitive position win the debate? The Yerushalmi continues to explain that R. Yehudah ben Beteira felt that the original permissive law was correct based on the Biblical verses. Moreover, he had a *kal va-ḥomer* argument to show why that should be the case, based on an

---

103   b*Ketubot* 57b.

104   *Sifre Bamidbar (Koraḥ)* #117. There is good indication in various Talmudic passages that this was the practice in certain times or places. See Safrai, *MEY: Ketubot,* pp. 318–320. The midrash, moreover, explicitly rejects an interpretation which would only allow a fully married woman to consume this food. Yet it is precisely this stringent exegesis which is adopted in *Sifre Zuta Bamidbar* 18:13 and asserts, based on the same word in the verse, that a woman cannot eat from the *terumot* until she is married. Moreover, in the latter text, the prohibitive position is presented as an outright *derashah*, with no comments on any historical development and no assertion (as found in Bavli) that the strict ruling was a decree to prevent mishaps. Yerushalmi, cited below, also relies upon this strict interpretation of *Bamidbar* 18:13 but does present the historical development.

105   y*Ketubot* 5:4, 29d, emphasis added.

106   The position recorded as *mishnah rishonah* in m*Ketubot* 5:2 is here labeled the *mishnah ha-emtza'it*, "the intermediate teaching."

analogous discussion regarding the laws of slaves.[107] Nonetheless, he re-morsefully concludes,

ומה אעשה והן אמרו לעולם אין האשה אוכלת בתרומה עד שתיכנס לחופה
וסמכו להם מקרא כמה שנאמר כל טהור בביתך יאכלנו.[108]

What can I do? For they have declared, "A woman may not partake of *terumah* until she has actually entered the wedding canopy." And they relied on the verse, as it says…

"What can I do?," he bemoans, seemingly reflecting his frustration that his position has been defeated as the later court marshalled Biblical verses (וסמכו להם מקרא) for their position. From this presentation, the final ruling of the latter *bet din* is clearly a mere *asmakhta,* as noted by medieval commentators.[109]

What did this *asmakhta* accomplish? The original law was also clearly supported by a Biblical verse, either from *Vayikra* or *Bamidbar*. Yet the law was changed by the Sages, possibly out of concern from the misuse of the *terumot* to those not entitled to it. This was a clear rabbinic development. It seems there were two stages in this process, including an interim decree when the Sages were generally stringent yet allowed the woman to partake in the food, albeit only after the planned wedding date had passed. This interim stage had no support verse, highlighting the fact that the later developments were clearly of rabbinic origin. In the final stage, the later *bet din* was supported by a *derashah*, being a departure from both the original Biblical law as well as an interim rabbinic ruling. For

---

[107] In the continuation of the story, the strength of the logic of this *kal va-ḥomer* is questioned. In any case, the stress of the narrative is that even if the *kal va-ḥomer* had been strong, it still would not have overridden the rabbinic decision.

[108] This critical line, which clearly indicates that they saw this interpretation as an *asmakhta*, does not appear in the parallel presentations of the dialogue in tKetubot 5:1, Sifre #171, and bKiddushin 10b. See Kahana, *Sifre Bamidbar*, pp. 900–901.

[109] This position is already asserted by Rabbenu Tam (*Sefer Ha-Yashar: Ḥiddushim, Siman* 7 (p. 17 in Schlesinger edition) and Rabbenu Asher (*Tosafot Ha-Rosh, Kiddushin* 10b *d.h. arusah*), where he makes the interesting claim that many *derashot* in the Sifre are *asmakhtot*. (He makes a similar claim in Rosh, *Bava Kamma* 7:3. See also Ramban, *Derashah Le-Rosh Hashanah* in *Kitvei Ramban*, Vol. 1, ed. Chavel, p. 218, in which he makes the same claim about the Sifra and the Sifre.) See Lieberman, TKF, Vol. 6, p. 258, as well as p. 83 and p. 233. Kahana, *Sifre Bamidbar*, p. 901 fn. 16, notes that the *amoraim* regularly understood a *derashah* to be an *asmakhta*, even as the presentation within tannaitic literature makes no indication of it. As one example, he cites *Sifre Bamidbar* #116 which claims that *netilat yadayim* is of Biblical origins, even as many other sources indicate otherwise.

whatever reason,[110] these Sages were adamant to prohibit these women from eating *terumah*, and they used a "revisionist *asmakhta*" to undermine the earlier law that also had Biblical support.[111]

These cases in which *derashot* are used to support legal changes (as indicated by *barishonah* or *mishnah rishonah*) highlight the fact that "re-scripturizing" does not necessarily preserve a legal ruling, as R. Yehoshua hoped. This method may have initially developed as a way of grounding the authority of a legal tradition or innovation, as in the case of "reinforcing *asmakhtot*." While the *asmakhta* might grant the law its initial authority or help win an opening dispute, it can also make the norm fleeting. Just

---

110 Schremer, *Zakhar U-Nekevah,* pp. 326–329, attributes the motivation for this change to shifting visions of the nature of marriage and whether the union begins at *erusin* (contractual agreement) or *nesuin* (personal relationship). Accordingly, *terumah* is an ancillary consequence to a larger shift. Safrai, *MEY: Ketubot,* Vol. 1, p. 320, however, reads certain texts to indicate that the shift relates to the perceived severity of *terumah*, and not necessarily larger questions regarding the status of *erusin*.

111 Other cases of a "revisionist *asmakhta*": 1) The question of when non-tithed produce (*tevel*) is subject to the laws of *bi'ur*. See m*Ma'aser Sheni* 5:8. The original stringent ruling had attached to it a well-attested procedure in which scholars provided practical guidance to landowners how to fulfill this law. The Tosefta and Yerushalmi provide extensive documentation of this process, indicating that this was a rooted historical practice. Yet R. Akiva successfully introduced a significant lenient change to exempt much produce. According to a parallel version (*Midrash Tena'im* [ed. Hoffman], pp. 175–176 to *Devarim* 26:13), the Sages in the generations which preceded R. Akiva had rejected this lenient ruling when it was introduced by R. Neḥunia ben Ha-Kana. In that parallel, the two different practices are in fact attributed to a *derashah* of a Biblical verse. Ultimately, as the mishnah asserts, R. Akiva's ruling won the day, in part with the support of the *derashah* of his teacher which was used to overturn the existing practice, which itself had Scriptural support. On this ruling of R. Akiva and the practice beforehand, see the detailed study of Safrai, *MEY: Ma'aser Sheni*, pp. 403–413.

2) In another case, R. Akiva expanded the number of relatives who are ineligible to testify to include several relatives of one's mother. See m*Sanhedrin* 3:4. As Menaḥem Kahana (*Sifre Zute Devarim,* pp. 369–374) has documented, this ruling of R. Akiva was built on *derashot* found in several halakhic midrashim. See, for example, *Sifre Devarim* (*Ki Tetze*) #260, b*Sanhedrin* 27b, *Sifre Zute Devarim* 24:16.

3) t*Pesaḥim* 1:7, emphasis added. While not explicit in this source, it seems that previous eras believe that "*tashbitu*" in the Torah meant that *ḥametz* must be eradicated entirely from the world, whereas R. Akiva believed that it simply had to be out of a Jew's possession. See Rashi *Pesaḥim* 21a *d.h. ve-lav*, Meiri *Pesaḥim* 21a *d.h. u-mokhrah*, R. David Pardo, *Ḥasdei David* to Tosefta *Pesaḥim* 1:6 (p. 242–243). As R. Pardo makes clear, R. Akiva's position goes beyond that established by Beit Hillel. See also Shamma Friedman, *Tosefta Atikta*, p. 138.

as one can easily establish one law through exegesis, so too can one change the law through alternative exegesis, as we saw in the cases of "revisionist *asmakhtot.*"

A Taste of His Own Method: A Revisionist *Asmakhta* to Justify Nullifying *Tosefet Shevi'it*

This, in fact, seems to have happened to the law of *tosefet shevi'it*, and most tellingly, with a *derashah* of R. Akiva as the victim. The *derashot* to support *tosefet shevi'it*, especially as derived from the verse in Exodus 34:21, is deeply tied to the school of R. Akiva, as we saw previously in the mishnah in *Shevi'it* 1:4.[112] In another *midrash halakhah* tied to this school, R. Akiva's students disagree on some of the details, but share the basic assumption of this law.

ר' יהודה אומר בחריש ובקציר תשבת חריש שקצירו אסור זה חריש שלערב שביעית וקציר שחרישו אסור זה קציר שלמוצאי שביעית. ור' שמעון אומר שבות מן החריש בשעת קציר ושבות מן הקציר בשעת חריש.[113]

Yet there is good reason to believe this practice pre-dated R. Akiva's era, as much earlier sages from Beit Hillel and Beit Shammai disagreed about the duration of the prohibited period, as we see in the first mishnah in tractate *Shevi'it*.[114] Indeed, Bavli refers to this law as "תקנתא דבית שמאי ובית הלל".[115] Accordingly, R. Akiva's *derashah* was introduced later to support a practice which had emerged during the Second Temple period and was assumed within much tannaitic discourse.[116] This was, in short, a "reinforcing *asmakhta.*"

---

[112] The basic ideas of this *derashah* (according to some texts and manuscripts, with the term דתנן), is quoted in b*Rosh Hashanah* 9a (regarding the broader notion of *tosefet shabbat*), b*Makkot* 8a, and b*Mo'ed Katan* 3b–4a, and is directly attributed to R. Akiva.

[113] See *Mekhilta de-Rebbi Shimon bar Yoḥai*, *Shemot* 34:21. In the context of discussing the notion of *tosefet Shabbat*, *Mekhilta R' Yishmael* to 35:3 also records a similar *derashah* to 34:21 that would assume the notion of *tosefet shevi'it*. This is surprising given that R. Yishmael does not affirm this *derashah* in m*Shevi'it* 1:4 and b*Mo'ed Katan* 4a. Classic commentators to this passage, however, note that this is indeed a *derashah* connected to R. Akiva and is possibly an interpolation from elsewhere.

[114] m*Shevi'it* 1:1 and Felix, *Masekhet Shevi'it*, Vol. 1, pp. 84–87. See Safrai, *MEY: Shevi'it*, p. 6 and p. 29, who affirms that the notion of *tosefet shevi'it* was widely accepted in the tannaitic period.

[115] b*Mo'ed Katan* 3b.

[116] As noted previously, the *mishnah* records a different *derashah* of this verse in the name of R. Yishmael. Does this mean that he did not accept the entire notion

A few generations later, however, this law was no longer viable or had become counter-productive, leading Rabban Gamliel and his court to nullify it. How could they make such a change, given the antiquity of this practice and the *ein bet din* rule? One possibility was to utilize the "revisionist *asmakhta*" strategy that R. Akiva himself employed elsewhere to support halakhic changes. As R. Yonatan continues to explain in the Yerushalmi, Rabban Gamliel based the new law on Biblical exegesis, in this case an alternative interpretation of the same verse (Exodus 34:21) that had previously supported *tosefet shevi'it*.

רבי אחא בשם רבי יונתן בשעה שאסרו למקר' סמכו ובשעה שהתירו למקרא סמכו. בשעה שאסרו למקרא סמכו בחריש ובקציר תשבות בחריש שקצירו אסור ואי זה זה חריש של ערב שביעית שהוא נכנס לשביעית ובקציר שחרישו אסור ואי זה זה קציר של שביעית שהוא יוצא למוצאי שביעית. ובשעה שהתירו למקרא סמכו ששת ימים תעבוד ועשית כל מלאכתך מה ערב שבת בראשית את מותר לעשות מלאכה עד שתשקע החמה אף ערב שבתות שנים את מותר לעשות מלאכה עד שתשקע החמה[117]

Through a new interpretation of this verse, the *derashah* of R. Akiva is nullified—and so is the legal norm that pre-dated R. Akiva! Or to put it another way, the "reinforcing *asmakhta*" of R. Akiva gets nullified by the "revisionist *asmakhta*" of Rabban Gamliel. This, in fact, was exactly the strategy regularly utilized by R. Akiva and others that we have seen in this chapter. Once attached to a Biblical verse, the law becomes tied to the fate of that interpretation. An alternative *derashah* provides sufficient authority to make innovative changes to the pre-existing law, even against retentionist notions like the *ein bet din* rule.

Do *Asmakhtot* Produce Legal Stability? Authority, Continuity, and the Power to Change

We must now ask why laws rooted in textual exegesis are more pliable for change and nullification. As we previously saw, Rambam asserted that laws based on rules of exegesis may be changed by a lesser court, while an

of *tosefet shevi'it?* Such an opinion is recorded in *Melekhet Shlomo* to m.*Shevi'it* 1:4 at the end of *d.h. R. Yishmael.* More likely, however, is that he believed this was an ancient tradition not linked to Torah verses. This, in fact, is the opinion that is attributed to him in b*Mo'ed Katan* 4a, as discussed previously.

117 y*Shevi'it* 1:1, 33a. See Felix, *Masekhet Shevi'it*, Vol. 1, pp. 24–25. This *derashah*, of course, has implications for our understanding of the historical development of the notion of *tosefet Shabbat*, which this text seems to deny or greatly minimize. See Gilat, *Perakim*, pp. 315–320 and Safrai, *MEY: Shabbat*, Vol. 1, pp. 31–36.

act of independent legislation (a *gezerah* or *takanah*) requires a greater court, as demanded by the *ein bet din* principle. An explanation for this position was developed by Rabbi Yehuda Heschel Levenberg (d.1938), a rosh yeshivah in New Haven, Connecticut, and Cleveland, Ohio.[118] Levenberg asserts that the difference between hermeneutics and legislation lies in the fact that the former does not create a new, independent legal norm.[119] The Torah's words existed beforehand, with their legal meaning subject to interpretation. As such, a given interpretation does not represent a judicial pronouncement ("*shem hora'ah*") that becomes a part of the Oral Law because nothing new was introduced. Instead, Levenberg asserts, it is a mere explanation or extraction of the intent of the Torah ("*gilui kavanat ha-Torah*"). While binding in its period, it remains subject to review by later scholars, who also retain interpretive authority. Decrees, however, become new entities within the corpus of Torah. They represent substantive additions to the Oral Law, and when challenged, represent nullifications of the law (*bitul ve-akirah*) which require the sanction of a greater court. [120] Alternative interpretations, in short, preserve continuity

---

[118] For more on R. Levenberg, see Moshe D. Sherman, *Orthodox Judaism in America: A Biographical Dictionary and Sourcebook* (Westport, CT, 1996), pp. 131–133.

[119] See his *Imrei Ḥen, Hilkhot Mamrim*, p. 54, also found in Ḥanina Ben-Menaḥem, *Ha-Maḥloket Ba-Halakhah*, Vol. 2, pp. 635–6.

[120] A different approach to the distinction in Maimonides and the role of hermeneutics was taken by R. Avraham Yitzḥak Kook. In the course of his defense of the temporary sale of Israeli territory during the agricultural Sabbatical year (*heter mekhirat karka'ot*), R. Kook affirmed that the *ein bet din* principle did not apply to laws derived from *derashot*, as stated by Rambam. He then went further to state that even in cases of bona fide *gezerot*, a greater *bet din* is not required if the later *bet din* finds an *asmakhta* to prove that the given law was not Biblical. In this case, an *asmakhta* is not coming to buttress the legitimacy of a rabbinic decree by showing that the Torah hinted toward this rabbinic law. Rather, the *asmakhta* highlights the fact that the Torah itself did not forbid this action, and therefore one may argue that the Torah itself implicitly states that such an action should be permissible. While the Sages were allowed to nonetheless prohibit the action, the rules for nullification are relaxed should scholars in a later era deem it necessary to overturn that decree, since their opinion is buttressed by the *asmakhta* which indicated the Torah's permissive stance on the matter. To prove the legitimacy of this method, R. Kook cited the famous position of the Tosafists (*Yevamot* 68a *d.h. mitokh*) that the rabbis may dictate non-observance of Torah law, even by acts of commission (*kum ve-aseh*), if there exists a compelling reason and *asmakhta* for this decision. All the more so, R. Kook contends, the rabbis, when compelled, may undermine earlier rabbinic laws with the support of an *asmakhta*. See chapters 2–3 of the introduction to Kook, *Shabbat Ha-Aretz im Tosefet Shabbat*, Vol. 1, pp. 86—92 and the commentary of Hagi Ben-Artzi, *He-*

by affirming the authority of the text. Repeal of legislation, in contrast, terminates a law entirely and therefore requires a greater court to authorize such an act of discontinuity.

Rabbi Levenberg, I believe, is touching upon a larger question of why many legal systems prefer changes through new interpretation of texts rather than writing the law anew. In a wide-ranging essay, the legal scholar Joseph Raz asked the fundamental question, "Why interpret?"[121] That is to say, why do we seek to determine the law by interpreting an authoritative text, as opposed to simply stating what we think is politically appropriate or morally correct in the given circumstance, irrespective of other positions, texts, or precedents. Legal systems require intervention to improve the law, address changing conditions, and provide equity for the citizens impacted by the law. To achieve that goal, it would be much easier for judges, for example, to employ moral and legal reasoning like that done by the legislators who first enacted the law. Nonetheless, they feel bound to the constraints of the authoritative text of the legal code. Why?

Raz's answer is both simple and elegant: authority and continuity.[122] We interpret legal texts because we consider the original law to have undergone an authoritative process which makes it valid and binding. Furthermore, we affirm the text's ongoing authority since the sustained observance of this law creates continuity that provides stable guidance for a political society.[123]

Analogously, *mutatis mutandis*, one can say that the Torah certainly held primary stature as an authoritative legal text. As new laws needed to be created over time, many Sages felt it was critical to connect laws to Biblical

---

Ḥadash Yitkadesh, pp. 157–159. R. Kook further defended his claim in *Shu"t Mishpat Kohen* # 68.

[121] Raz, *Between Authority and Interpretation* (Oxford, 2009), pp. 223–240.

[122] Ibid., pp. 235–237.

[123] A similar phenomenon exists in many common-law systems. As legal philosophers have noted, courts tend to eschew overt challenges to precedent rulings, preferring methods that allow for legal change without stirring legal quarters. It softens the potential harm to institutional authority by not directly challenging the wisdom or stature of the earlier judges. It provides, therefore, an important method for legal change while, relatively speaking, preserving institutional stability by maintaining a sense of continuity with the original authoritative text. The same, moreover, could be said about many legal changes that are made in terms of constitutional interpretation. See, for example, David Strauss, "Common Law Constitutional Interpretation," *University of Chicago Law Review* 63 (1996), pp. 913–916 in particular. Similarly, by obviating the *ein bet din* principle, hermeneutics prevent many of the problems caused by direct legal repeals.

words or verses. Accordingly, the process of "re-scripturalizing" gave rabbinic law the imprimatur of exegetical authority while at the same time maintaining a sense of continuity with the ancient tradition. Laws developed in consonance with the authoritative text gave a feel of consistency with the tradition.[124] This was the support offered by an *asmakhta*, whether it was buttressing a new norm or altering an existing practice ("reinforcing *asmakhta*").

Yet once that process was introduced, an attempt to further adapt the law would also need to be rooted in the Biblical text. Accordingly, changes to previous rabbinic proclamations which were portrayed as alternative interpretations ("revisionist *asmakhot*") helped maintain a sense of authority and continuity. After all, the revised law made the same claim to the

---

124 The notion of an *asmakhta* being used to support the authority of legal rulings is discussed by a few medieval commentators. Many medieval commentators believed that *asmakhtot* were divorced from the simple meaning of the text; instead, the laws were based on tradition and the *asmakhtot* employed as mere memory tools for Oral Law teachings. See, for example, Yehudah Halevi, *Kuzari* 3:72–73 and Ibn Ezra's abridged commentary to *Shemot* 21:8. More significantly, the Maharil (R. Yaakov ben Moshe Halevi Moelin, *Sefer Maharil*, Likutim, #70) argued that an *asmakhta* was meant to prevent the masses from denigrating the significance of rabbinic laws. אמר: כל היכא דאיתמר מדרבנן הוא וקרא אסמכתא בעלמא, הכי פירושו ודאי תקנתא דרבנן הוא והם יצאו ובדקו ומצאו להם סמך מקרא, **וסמכו דבריהם עליו כדי להחזיקם שיהיו סבורים דהוא מדאורייתא ויחמירו בו, ולא אתו לזלזל ולהקל בדברי חכמים.** This position of the Maharil was severely criticized by the Maharal (R. Yehudah Loew ben Bezalel of Prague), who deemed it unfathomable that the Sages would trick the masses (*geneivat da'at*). See his *Gur Aryeh* to *Shemot* 19:15. (For his own theory and the broader debate, see Maharal's *Be'er Ha-Golah*, *Be'er Rishon*, Chapter 1 and the discussion in Gafni, *Peshutah shel Mishnah*, pp. 246–248 and Ariel, *Nata Betokheinu*, Vol. 2, pp. 239–250). Nonetheless, the larger point made by the Maharil is that an *asmakhta* creates continuity with the Biblical text which creates a sense of continuity, thereby preventing people from dismissing the rabbinic inventions. This claim, in fact, was also made by Rabbenu Asher (Rosh *Mo'ed Katan* 1:1) regarding the *derashot* to support work prohibitions on *Ḥol Ha-Mo'ed*. אבל מלאכה לא נאסרה כי אם בראשון ובשביעי אלא ודאי ק"ו ליתא **אלא אסמכתא בעלמא לחזק דברי חכמים** שאסרו מלאכת חוה"מ אבל התירו דבר האבד כדתנן. See also the statement of Ramban, *Hasagot Le-Sefer Ha-Mitzvot* (ed. Chavel), p. 8, and other statements of his cited by R. Ariel, *Nata Betokheinu*, p. 241 fn. 48. Moreover, it could be that in fact, scholars themselves (not just the masses) would treat rabbinic laws that were supported with an *asmakhta* more severely, as claimed by R' Yosef Teumim (*Pri Megadim*, Introduction to *Oraḥ Ḥayyim*, Section 1.) משמע אסמכתא חשובה שיש לה כעין רמז בקרא הוה כדין תורה ממש... הא כל היכא דאסמכוה אקרא באסמכתא חשובה דעתם להיות ממש כדין תורה, ולא מקילין בספיקו וגוזרין גזירה לגזירה באפשר וכדומה.

canonical text. In essence, the legal text, as understood by the Sages, maintains its authority and continues to remain in force. In practice, Scripture's legal implications have shifted in light of its new interpretation. A lower court cannot overturn the authoritative teaching of its greater predecessor. Yet alternative interpretations, as Rav Levenberg asserted, do not uproot an earlier teaching; they merely redefine it.

Alternative interpretations, by their nature, do not directly call for normative reform. Their overt aim seeks to understand the text, with legal ramifications a secondary consequence. The normative impact, however, remains enormous, and thereby allows for evolution within the law, without explicit challenges to the authority of earlier texts or figures. [125] That is precisely what happens in cases of direct repeals, which directly nullify or uproot the original law. The Sages believed that such actions require the *gadol mimenu* clause, whereas more subtle changes based on exegesis

---

[125] As many have shown, in different ways, textual interpretation remains a central method for the law's evolution, whether we are dealing with a Biblical text, a tannaitic work, or a legal practice. See, for example, Moshe Halbertal, *Mahapekhot Parshaniot Be-hithavutan;* Shai Wosner, *"Atzma'ut u-Mehuyavut Parshanit,"* *Akdamot* 4 (Shevat 5758), pp. 9–28; and R. Michael Broyde, *Innovation in Jewish Law.* This is certainly true regarding many cases of *ukimtot* in which *amoraim* interpret earlier rabbinic statements in ways which can deeply affect halakhic norms. In this respect, it pays to note that statement of R. Shlomo Fisher, contemporary head of the Itry yeshivah, in his *Derashot Beit Yishai, Siman* 15, p. 114. ובזה תבין עניין דוחקים והאוקימתות שעושים האמוראים כשמקשים עליהם מדברי התנאים, שרבים תמהו על זה. דהואיל והאמוראים יודעים שהאמת עמהם ורק האיסור לחלוק הוא העומד בפניהם, לכן דוחקים בלשון התנאים להתאים את דבריהם עם האמת... וכך נוהג החזו"א בעצמו עם לשונות הראשונים. Fisher's comments follow the spirit of a statement he briefly cites that is attributed to the R. Ḥayyim Soloveitchik of Brisk by R. Elchanan Wasserman in *Kovetz Shiurim*, Vol. 1, *Siman* 633, p. 326 (commentary to *Bava Batra* 170b). The Talmud (*Bava Batra* 170b) records a statement in the name of Rav in which he explicitly chooses to disagree with the two positions of *tannaim* stated in the mishnah. The medieval commentators, like Rashbam and Ritva, discuss why he had such powers, with the former arguing that Rav was sometimes treated like a *tanna* and the latter asserting that Rav was transmitting a third tradition that he had from his tannaitic teachers. Rabbi Soloveitchik, on the other hand, simply claimed that *amoraim* had the authority to disagree with *tannaim*, and if they knowingly chose to disagree with a *tanna*, the law could indeed follow their position, as it does in this specific case. R. Wasserman added that proof for R. Soloveitchik's claim may be found in the fact that sometimes the *amoraim* will dismiss an alleged tannaitic statement by stating that it is אינו משנה. R. Wasserman than goes on to suggest that perhaps there is a distinction between tannaitic statements made in mishnayot, which would have authoritative stature since this text was accepted as canonical, as opposed to tannaitic statements quoted elsewhere, which did not garner such acceptance.

do not, even if they may have the same effect on the bottom-line normative law.

R. Yehoshua congratulated R. Akiva for his methodology because he
believed that a law would be buttressed through scriptural support. That
strategy works, we saw, until a different scholar emerges with a new exegesis to help change the law.

Our exploration of the nullification of the prohibitions of *tosefet shevi'it*
have thus revealed much more than the history of a particular law. They
have also highlighted different strategies taken by *amoraim* and later commentators to explain various developments in the history of halakhah. I
hope to explore other fascinating examples in future studies. ◌

Matan Torah: What Was Revealed to Moshe at Sinai?*

By: ARYEH LEIBOWITZ

Introduction

Matan Torah was a unique and unprecedented event. On Har Sinai, God revealed to Moshe Rabbeinu the entirety of Torah, as Chazal teach (*Yerushalmi Peah* 2:4, *Vayikra Rabbah* 22:1, and *Koheles Rabbah* 1:2): "The Torah, Mishnah, Talmud, and *aggadah*—even that which a seasoned student (תלמיד ותיק) would later teach in the presence of his teacher—was already stated to Moshe at Sinai." Similarly, in *Megillah* 19b: "God showed (הראהו) Moshe *dikdukei Torah*, *dikdukei Sofrim*, and that which the *Sofrim* would originate in the future."

However, this all-encompassing numinous revelation of the entirety of Torah was transmitted to Moshe in a germinal and non-explicated form. Much like a seed, which despite its small size contains within its seedcoat all the potential needed to become a towering tree laden with fruit, the revelation to Moshe contained within it the kernel from which all future Torah laws and teachings would later evolve.[1] All subsequent

---

* Thank you to R. Daniel Belsky and R. Reuven Isaacs for their contributions to this article. Thank you as well to R. Benzion Buchman, R. Yitzchak Goldstein, and R. Raphael Stohl for their time and assistance.

[1] Maharal (*Gur Aryeh*, *Shemos* 20:1 ד"ה מלמד) explains that the entirety of Torah was revealed to Moshe in one single utterance. Although Moshe was not able to fully grasp what he heard, this enigmatic divine utterance still revealed, on some level, the entirety of Torah to Moshe. Tosafos Yom Tov (Introduction) notes that *Megillah* 19b, quoted above, does not say that the entire Torah was *transmitted* to Moshe, rather it says that it was *shown* (הראהו) to him. This, he writes, is like "a person who shows something to his friend to see, but he does

---

Aryeh Leibowitz is a *Ra"m* at Yeshivat Sha'alvim and teaches at Ma'arava – Machon Rubin. He is the author of *Hashgachah Pratis: An Exploration of Divine Providence and Free Will* (2009), *The Neshamah: A Study of the Human Soul* (2018), and three introductory works on the transmission of the Masorah: *The Tannaim* (2022), *The Early Rishonim* (2015), and *The Later Rishonim* (2020). He received rabbinic ordination from Rabbi Isaac Elchanan Theological Seminary and his Ph.D. from Bernard Revel Graduate School.

divine revelations of Torah to Moshe, as well as all future Torah scholarship, were part of a divinely-designed explication process of the germinal form of the Torah that had been revealed to Moshe at Har Sinai.

This article does not directly address this all-encompassing germinal
revelation to Moshe Rabbeinu of the entire Torah. Moshe also received
an explicit revelation of Torah during his multiple ascents of Har Sinai,[2]
and it was this explicit revelation that he was charged to transmit to the
Jewish nation. This article addresses this explicit revelation and asks:
What elements of the Torah were revealed—in an explicit form—to
Moshe on Har Sinai?

Chazal's answer to this question is that God, on Har Sinai, transmitted to Moshe the 613 mitzvos (*Yalkut Shimoni Michah* #556, *Tanchuma
Shoftim* #10),

---

not fully give it to him." Indeed, Moshe was not commanded, or perhaps even
able, to further transmit this all-encompassing revelation to the Jewish nation
(*Megillas Esther, Shorashim* 1:4).
There was an additional aspect to this all-encompassing revelation to Moshe.
Chazal teach that our earthly Torah is a material manifestation of a more elevated, heavenly Torah. This supernal and primordial form of the Torah, in at
least one of its emanations, is described by Chazal as being written with "black
fire on white fire" (Ramban, Introduction to *Bereishis*). In fact, Radvaz (III:643)
suggests that it was this heavenly form of the Torah that the angels had in
mind when they protested God's transmission of the Torah to *Bnei Yisrael*
(*Shabbos* 88b–89a). God silenced the angels by informing them "that the [heav-
enly] Torah has an alternative—more material—form, which is manifest
through formed words dealing with human matters, such as ritual impurity and
purity, the prohibited and the permitted, the exempt and the obligated, and all
of [the material Torah's] other laws." When Moshe ascended Har Sinai, in addition to the revelation of the entire earthly Torah in its germinal form, God
also revealed to Moshe a conception of the elevated heavenly form of Torah
and its infinite depth. This even included some type of perception of the letters of the Torah (see *Chasam Sofer, Shabbos* 88b [ד"ה ואמר ר' יהושע]). There was
even a revelation of this more elevated form of the Torah on the original *Luchos*. For a non-esoteric elaboration on this, see *Moadim U'Zmanim* (*Shevuos,
Siman* 320). Certainly, the nature of that more elevated form of Torah, and
Moshe's conception of it, is far beyond the scope of our current work.
2   *Matan Torah* was not a single-day event. Moshe ascended Har Sinai on the sixth
or seventh of Sivan to receive the Ten Commandments, but he also reascended Har Sinai at later points to receive other mitzvos (*Shemos* 24:12 with *Rashi*).
Rashi in *Taanis* 21b (ד"ה אל מול) even suggests that the resting of the divine
presence on Har Sinai and the giving of mitzvos did not end until the *Mishkan*
was inaugurated on the first of Nissan (see later fn. 8).

R. Simlai taught: Six-hundred and thirteen mitzvos were said to Moshe at Sinai, 365 negative commandments correlating to the days of the solar year, and 248 positive commandments correlating to the limbs of a person.

Chazal additionally maintain that on Har Sinai Moshe also received a detailed commentary on the mitzvos. Both the mitzvos and their commentary were transmitted orally to Moshe. It was only years later that the text of the Torah—as we have it today—was committed to writing by Moshe.[3]

And yet, a careful reading of the Torah suggests that Moshe did not receive *all* the mitzvos on Har Sinai. Instead, it appears that he only received the Ten Commandments,[4] the laws of idolatry and altars that appear at the end of *Parashas Yisro*, the mitzvos and laws of *Parashas Mishpatim*, and the mitzvos of *Parashas Behar*, such as *shemittah* and *yovel*.[5]

Interestingly, *Makkos* 23b records the same teaching of Chazal quoted above in the name of R. Simlai, but there the word "Sinai" is omitted. *Makkos* simply reads, "Six hundred and thirteen mitzvos were said to

---

3   Portions of the Torah's text were revealed to Moshe at early points, and some of these portions were even immediately committed to writing (see *Shemos* 24:7). However, when and how the entire text of the Torah was compiled and recorded as a complete written text is a subject of dispute in *Gittin* 60a. Reish Lakish maintains that the complete text was written as a singular "sealed document" (תורה חתומה ניתנה) at the end of Moshe's life. See Ramban (Introduction to *Sefer Bereishis*) and *Tosafos* (*Gittin* 60a ד"ה תורה) for an analysis of Reish Lakish's opinion. However, Rav Banaah maintains that the text of the Torah was written down "scroll by scroll" (תורה מגילה מגילה ניתנה). The simple explanation of R. Banaah's opinion is that Moshe wrote down the text of the Torah section by section, as he received new passages from God. This process began after *Matan Torah* and was completed at Arvos Moav, at the end of the forty-year desert period. However, see Ramban above for a more literal reading of Rav Banaah's opinion.

4   Rashi (*Shemos* 24:12) cites R. Saadiah Gaon that all 613 mitzvos are contained in the Ten Commandments.

5   The beginning of *Parashas Behar* (25:1) states clearly that the laws of the *parashah* were taught at Har Sinai. The Ibn Ezra (see also Rashi) explains that even though these laws appear at the end of *Sefer Vayikra*, they were really given on Har Sinai along with the laws of *Yisro* and *Mishpatim*. Ramban agrees that the mitzvos of *Parashas Behar* were given on Har Sinai, but he argues that it was not during Moshe's initial ascent of Har Sinai. At that point, God only gave some of the mitzvos to the nation, as Ramban explains at the beginning of *Parashas Terumah* (*Shemos* 25:2). It was only when Moshe Rabbeinu ascended Har Sinai to receive the second *Luchos*, after the sin of the Golden Calf, that he received the mitzvos of *Parashas Behar*.

Moshe (שש מאות ושלש עשרה מצות נאמרו לו למשה).'' There is no mention of Sinai.

Were all 613 mitzvos given to Moshe *at Sinai*? If not, what was given there, and when were the rest of the mitzvos given?

This article will demonstrate that the simple reading of Chazal maintains that all the mitzvos, with an accompanying detailed explanation, were transmitted to Moshe on Har Sinai. However, we will also see that several prominent Rishonim considered the possibility that many of the mitzvos were first transmitted to Moshe at a later time, perhaps even decades after Har Sinai. Lastly, we will see that according to other Rishonim, many of the details of the Torah's laws were *never* transmitted to Moshe. God omitted these laws and empowered the *chachmei hamesorah* to address the lacunae through rigorous analysis of the Torah's text using the *middos* of *derashah* that were given to Moshe on Har Sinai.[6]

The 613 Mitzvos

We saw earlier that Chazal teach in the name of the Amora, R. Simlai, that all 613 mitzvos were transmitted to Moshe Rabbeinu at Har Sinai. This view of Chazal is first recorded in the *Sifra*, and quoted by Rashi, at the beginning of *Parashas Behar* (*Vayikra* 25:1). The Torah there records the laws of *shemittah* as they were "stated to Moshe at Har Sinai." The working premise of the *Sifra* is that all 613 mitzvos, like *shemittah*, were given at Sinai.

> "And God spoke to Moshe at Sinai saying" (*Vayikra* 25:1). What is the connection between *shemittah* and Har Sinai? Were not all the mitzvos said at Sinai? The answer is: just as *shemittah*—its general laws and fine points (כללותיה ודקדוקיה) —are from Sinai, so too all the mitzvos—their general laws and fine points (כללותיהם ודקדוקיהם)—are from Sinai.

---

6   To be clear, the explicit revelation of the mitzvos on Sinai or afterwards (according to those Rishonim that maintain that not all the mitzvos were given at Sinai) are all part of the explication process of the germinal all-encompassing revelation to Moshe. Moreover, the opinion of the Rishonim referenced above (and discussed later in detail) that many laws of the mitzvos were *never* revealed to Moshe is specifically referring to the laws in their explicated and developed form. Nothing was lacking from the original all-encompassing germinal revelation to Moshe. Moreover, the creation of new laws by the *chachmei hamesorah* using the *middos* of *derashah* (discussed later) is also part of the divinely-designed explication process referred to above.

Not only were all the mitzvos first transmitted to Moshe at Sinai, but Chazal also maintain that the mitzvos were transmitted there with an accompanying explanation. The Rishonim learn this from the end of *Parashas Mishpatim*, where the Torah states (*Shemos* 24:12) that after Moshe descended Har Sinai he was summoned again up the mountain to receive the "*Luchos*, the Torah, and the Mitzvah."[7] Rambam (Introduction to *Mishneh Torah*, cf. Ramban's Introduction to *Bereishis*) explains that the "Torah" refers to the 613 mitzvos and the "Mitzvah" refers to the *Peirush* (פירוש), a detailed oral explanation and elaboration of the mitzvos.

It emerges that by the end of the Har Sinai experience,[8] Moshe had received *all* the mitzvos of the Torah and the *Peirush*. This accompanying *Peirush* is also known as the Oral Law (Rambam, Introduction to *Mishneh Torah*).

It is important to note that during the process of *Matan Torah* both the mitzvos and the accompanying *Peirush* were transmitted to Moshe orally. Only the Ten Commandments, which were also originally transmitted orally to Moshe, were committed to writing on the *Luchos* when Moshe reascended Har Sinai.[9] Nonetheless, there was still a clear distinc-

---

7   Rashi and Ramban debate if the preceding *pesukim* (24:1–11) refer to Moshe's initial ascent of Har Sinai originally described in *Parashas Yisro* or if they refer to a second ascent. Yet, both Rashi and Ramban agree that the current *pasuk* (24:12) refers to an additional ascent and not the original one of *Parashas Yisro*.

8   Rashi in *Taanis* 21b (ד"ה אל מול) suggests that the Har Sinai experience of *Matan Torah* did not end until the *Mishkan* was inaugurated on the first of Nissan. For approximately ten months, "the *Shechinah* dwelled on the mountain," and from there "all the mitzvos were revealed with awesome sounds and flames, from the day the Ten Commandments were given until the first of Nissan when the *Mishkan* was erected." Once the *Mishkan* was completed, the divine presence left Har Sinai and move to the *Mishkan*. At that point, Rashi writes, the Torah was retaught, as per R. Akiva's opinion that the Torah was first taught at Sinai and then repeated a second time at the Ohel Moed and a third time at Arvos Moav.

9   Rambam in the introduction to his *Peirush HaMishnah* writes that both the mitzvos and the *Peirush* were transmitted orally to Moshe: "Know that every mitzvah that God gave to Moshe Rabbeinu, He gave to him with its explanation. God would *say* to him (אומר לו) the mitzvah and then He would *say* to him (אומר לו) its explanation and details." This also seems to be Rambam's intent in his introduction to *Mishneh Torah*: "All the mitzvos that were given to Moshe at Sinai were given with an accompanying oral explanation…. Moshe wrote down the entire Written Law before his death…"

tion between what was the "Written Law" (תורה) and would one day be written down, and what was the *Peirush* (מצוה) and would remain oral.

Mitzvos Seemingly Revealed After Har Sinai

After *Matan Torah*, the nation camped at the base of Har Sinai. There they erected the *Ohel Moed (Mishkan).*[10] Afterwards, as the nation travelled through the desert, the *Ohel Moed* stood in the center of the camp and served as the venue for Moshe Rabbeinu's continued communications with God.

The plain understanding of the Torah suggests that many of the mitzvos and their laws were first revealed to Moshe not on Har Sinai, but though the medium of the *Ohel Moed* during the nation's travels and encampments in the desert. For example, the commandments regarding sacrifices are recorded in the beginning of *Sefer Vayikra* and the text suggests that Moshe first received these mitzvos and laws at the *Ohel Moed* (*Vayikra* 1:1–2), "And He called to Moshe, and God spoke to him *from the Ohel Moed*, saying, 'Speak to *Bnei Yisrael*, and say to them: 'When a man from [among] you brings a sacrifice to God…'"

Other verses also seem to state that mitzvos and laws were only revealed after Har Sinai. For example, the very last verse in *Sefer Bamidbar* (36:13) states quite clearly, "These are the mitzvos and laws that God commanded *Bnei Yisrael* through Moshe at Arvos Moav, by the Yarden River at Yericho." The commentators (Ibn Ezra, Chizkuni, and Malbim) explain that "the mitzvos and laws" in this verse refers to many of the mitzvos and laws that appear in *Parashas Matos* and *Mas'ei*, including the laws of kashering vessels, vows, inheritance, and the punishment for a murderer. The Torah text suggests that these laws were only revealed to Moshe at a later point in the desert.

Additionally, *Sefer Devarim*, which records Moshe's words to the nation when they stood at Arvos Moav poised to enter the land of Israel after forty years of wandering in the desert, includes many commandments that do not seem to be recorded anywhere earlier in the text of the Torah. This suggests that these commandments were first given to Moshe at Arvos Moav, close to forty years after Moshe descended Har Sinai.

---

[10] The first *Luchos* were given to Moshe in Sivan, at the beginning of the summer. The second *Luchos* in Tishrei, after the summer. Then the nation began construction of the *Mishkan*, a process that extended over the entire winter and was completed on the first of Nissan.

There are also mitzvos and laws that are recorded in the Torah in association with specific events that occurred after Har Sinai. For example, the prohibition to accept a convert from Ammon or Moav (*Devarim* 23:4) is presented in the Torah as being on account of these nations' unwillingness to help *Bnei Yisrael* when the latter were wandering in the desert. The context and presentation of this law suggest that it was not given to Moshe on Har Sinai.[11]

Another mitzvah to consider is *Pesach Sheini*. The Torah's account of this mitzvah in *Bamdibar* 9 implies that *Pesach Sheini* was not even conceived as a mitzvah until the second year after the Exodus—when the nation was camped at the base of Har Sinai. At this time, months after Moshe descended Har Sinai, a group of individuals approached Moshe Rabbeinu in frustration, having been forced to miss the *korban pesach* due to ritual impurity. Moshe Rabbeinu turned to God for guidance. In response, God instructed Moshe about the mitzvah of *Pesach Sheini* – counted by Rambam as a distinct mitzvah (*Aseh* #57) from the regular mitzvah of *korban pesach* (*Aseh* #55)—taught to the Jewish nation. The Torah's description of the background to the mitzvah of *Pesach Sheini* certainly suggests that it was not given to Moshe at Har Sinai.

The Torah also records three instances where Moshe Rabbeinu was unaware of how to rule regarding an existent Torah law during the nation's travels in the desert. These laws are: The form of capital punishment for a Shabbos desecrator (the מקושש, *Bamidbar* 15:32–36), the appropriate punishment for one who curses God (the מקלל, *Vayikra* 24:10–16), and the laws of inheritance for Zelafchad's daughters (בנות צלפחד, *Bamidbar* 27:1–5). If Moshe, during the nation's travels in the desert, was unaware how to rule in these cases, seemingly the details of these laws were not given to him at Har Sinai.

Maintaining the Traditional View: All the Mitzvos were Given on Har Sinai

Despite the many aforementioned verses suggesting that mitzvos and laws were first given to Moshe after Har Sinai, the traditional view of

---

11 Note that the laws of kashering vessels are first recorded after the nation took home the spoils—including non-kosher cooking vessels—from their war with Midyan (*Bamidbar* 31:33). However, in this case it is clear that Moshe had already been given the laws earlier, as the verse explicitly states that it was Eliezer who taught the nation the laws "that God had commanded Moshe."

Chazal, recorded in the earlier-quoted *Sifra*, remains that *all* 613 mitzvos were given in an explicated form to Moshe at Sinai.[12]

Chazal's approach is supported by the verses that appear at the end of the earlier quoted section in the Torah regarding sacrifices. Although the sacrifices were introduced in the beginning of *Sefer Vayikra* as having been commanded by God at the *Ohel Moed*, the end of the Torah's discussion of the sacrifices states quite clearly that these very same laws were first given to Moshe at Har Sinai, "This is the body of law for the burnt offering, for the meal offering… and for the peace offering, *that God commanded Moshe on Har Sinai*" (*Vayikra* 7:37–38).

If it is the case that all the mitzvos were first given at Har Sinai, how are we to explain the fact that many mitzvos and laws appear from the text of the Torah to have first been given in the desert or at Arvos Moav?

Let us consider two approaches to addressing this question. The first is suggested by R. Akiva (*Chagigah* 6a, *Sotah* 37b, *Zevachim* 115b). He maintains that although all the mitzvos were first given at Har Sinai, they were regiven and retaught in the desert and then again at Arvos Moav.[13]

> Rabbi Akiva says: The general principles and fine details [of the mitzvos] were said at Sinai, repeated a second time (נשנו) at the *Ohel Moed*, and a third time (נשתלשלו) at Arvos Moav.[14]

The Malbim states this very point regarding the earlier quoted verse at the end of *Sefer Bamidbar* (36:13): "These are the mitzvos and laws that God commanded *Bnei Yisrael* through Moshe at Arvos Moav…" He writes that even though these mitzvos and laws appear from the text to have first been given and taught at Arvos Moav, according to Chazal they had already been given at Sinai. This means that God chose to record these mitzvos in writing for future generations based on when they

---

12 Maharal (*Gur Aryeh, Shemos* 21:1) explains that since the Torah is complete and perfect (תורת ה' תמימה), it was fitting that when the mitzvos were given at Sinai, they were *all* given, even those that were not immediately applicable.

13 This is ostensibly the intent of Rashi in *Berachos* 48b (ד"ה תורה) that Torah was "given (נתנה)" three times: Har Sinai, *Ohel Moed*, and Arvos Moav.

14 The Talmud continues, "R. Yishmael says: The general principles [of the mitzvos] were said at Sinai, and the fine details at the *Ohel Moed*." R. Yishmael agrees with R. Akiva that all the mitzvos were first given at Har Sinai. However, he disagrees regarding the details and argues that many of them were first given to Moshe at a later point. Therefore, when mitzvos themselves appear to be given for the first time in the desert or at Arvos Moav, R. Yishmael seemingly agrees with R. Akiva that these are instances of mitzvos being repeated.

were *retaught* at Arvos Moav.[15] The same explanation would also be necessary to explain the many new mitzvos that seem to first appear in *Sefer Devarim*.

Moreover, according to R. Akiva's approach, those mitzvos that appear in the Torah after Har Sinai and are associated with specific historical events—such as the prohibition against accepting converts from Ammon and Moav—were originally given at Har Sinai without historical context. However, God chose to have them recorded in the text of the Torah in the form that they were presented, which is, *when they were retaught* in association with a specific historical event.[16]

The mitzvah of *Pesach Sheini* can also be explained according to R. Akiva's approach. The *Sefer Marganisa Tava* on Rambam's *Sefer HaMitzvos* (*Shoresh* 1:3) argues that the mitzvah of *Pesach Sheini* was undoubtably given to Moshe Rabbeinu on Har Sinai. However, it was intended to only take effect once the nation entered and settled the land of Israel.[17] Thus, the Torah's record of Moshe's need to ask God is not because the mitzvah was not initially given on Har Sinai, but rather is a result of Moshe's doubt if the mitzvah could be performed before the land of Israel was entered and settled.[18]

---

[15] Malbim suggests that according to R. Yishmael, this verse is informing the reader that the details of these mitzvos were received now, at Arvos Moav.

[16] Chazal's approach highlights the distinction between when the mitzvos were given and when and how the official text of the Torah was composed and transmitted in its final form to Moshe. Although the mitzvos were all given at Har Sinai, the text of Torah—which is our written source today to the mitzvos—was transmitted at a later point in Moshe's life.

[17] The regular *korban pesach* was also intended to only take effect once the nation entered the land of Israel (see *Shemos* 12:25). However, a one-time exception was made for the first commemoration of the Exodus (see *Bamidbar* 9:1–5 with Rashi and Ramban on 9:1). Accordingly, the *korban pesach* was brought on the first Pesach in the desert, and it was at that time that Moshe questioned if *Pesach Sheini* could also be operative.

[18] According to this suggestion, it is well understood that Moshe responds to the nation and says (9:8), "Wait, and I will hear what God instructs concerning *you* (מה יצוה ה' לכם)." Moshe knew that there was a mitzvah of *Pesach Sheini*, but he wasn't sure if it was for them ("you"). Similarly, Moshe's statement afterwards is also well understood when he says, "Any person who becomes unclean from [contact with] the dead, or is on a distant journey, *whether among you or in future generations*, he shall make a *Pesach* sacrifice for God." It also explains why the law is also presented for those who were on a distant journey, something that was not the situation at this time. According to the *Margenisa Tava*, the law of *Pesach Sheini* for a ritually impure person or an individual on a distant journey was already revealed to Moshe at Sinai. It was only applied now due to the cir-

Regarding the three instances where Moshe Rabbeinu was unaware of how to rule, the Chazon Ish (*Orach Chaim* 125:4) notes that the actual mitzvos under discussion—Shabbos desecration, cursing God, and inheritance—had already been given at Sinai. He argues that in these three cases, God decided, for reasons not shared with us, to not transmit some of their details to Moshe on Har Sinai (See *Or HaChaim, Bamidbar* 27:5).

A second approach to explain the fact that many mitzvos and laws appear from the text of the Torah to have first been given in the desert or at Arvos Moav is that although *Moshe Rabbeinu* received all the mitzvos of the Torah at Har Sinai, he was not commanded to relay all of them immediately to *Bnei Yisrael*.[19] Hence, in regard to the laws of the sacrifices, it could be that Moshe received the laws at Har Sinai, but God told him to wait and only teach them to the nation at the *Ohel Moed*—when they would begin to bring sacrifices. Bolstering this suggestion is the fact that the verse in *Vayikra* introducing the sacrifices (1:2) does not focus on Moshe's receipt of the laws, but rather on his transmission to the nation, "Speak to *Bnei Yisrael*, and *say to them* (דבר אל בני ישראל ואמרת אליהם)." It is fair to surmise that Moshe had received these mitzvos and laws earlier at Har Sinai, but he was only relating them now to the nation, as per God's directive.

This approach also explains the mitzvos mentioned at the end of *Sefer Bamidbar* and all the new mitzvos of *Sefer Devarim*. They had already been given to Moshe at Har Sinai but were only transmitted to the nation—by directive of God—at Arvos Moav.

According to this approach, those mitzvos that appear in the Torah after Har Sinai and are associated with specific historical events, such as the prohibition against accepting converts from Ammon and Moav, were also given to Moshe at Sinai. However, Moshe was commanded to wait to teach them to *Bnei Yisrael* until an event occurred that would necessitate learning these laws.

This alternative approach helps us address the three cases noted earlier in which Moshe was unaware of how to rule. Perhaps these mitzvos had already been taught to Moshe at Sinai, but for whatever reasons,

---

cumstances of ritually impure people. Hence, when it was formally recorded, it was recorded with its full presentation, which includes those on a distant journey.

19   Ramban suggests a similar approach about the laws of *shemittah* at the beginning of *Parashas Behar*. They were taught to Moshe at Sinai, but they were not given over to the nation until a later point. See *Chazon Ish* (*Orach Chaim* 125:3) who also notes this approach as a possible way to account for the mitzvos that appear to be revealed at a point after Har Sinai.

Moshe was not immediately commanded to teach these laws to the nation. Therefore, when confronted with a question about these mitzvos, Moshe turned to God for instruction. Moshe knew the proper ruling in these cases, but he nonetheless turned to God to "clarify" the law because he had never been given permission to share these laws with the nation.[20]

This approach might also explain *Gittin* 60a–b that eight sections of the Torah were "said (נאמרו)" on the day of the inauguration of the *Ohel Moed*, which was after Har Sinai: "Eight sections were said on the day the *Mishkan* was erected. They are: The section of the *Kohanim* (*Vayikra* 21:1–22:26); the section of the *Leviim* (*Vayikra* 8:5–26); the section of the ritually impure (*Vayikra* 13:1–14:57)…" The simple explanation of this passage is that these laws were *first taught* to Moshe on the day of the *Mishkan*'s inauguration. But it could be that Moshe received these eight laws—just like all the laws of the Torah—on Har Sinai. However, he did not teach them to the nation until he was instructed to do so by God on the day the *Mishkan* was erected. R. Eliyahu Mizrachi (*Bamidbar* 11:10) writes: "Even though [these eight laws] were already taught to Moshe on Har Sinai, he did not relay them to *Bnei Yisrael* until *Rosh Chodesh* Nissan."

An Alternative View: Some Mitzvos were Given After Har Sinai

The earlier quoted verses in the Torah suggesting that mitzvos and laws were first given to Moshe after Har Sinai led some leading Rishonim and Acharonim to consider a broader perspective on this issue.

Ramban in a few locations suggests that some mitzvos were first revealed, through the medium of the *Ohel Moed*, after Har Sinai. For example, regarding the sacrifices, Ramban—after noting the traditional view of Chazal—suggests that the mitzvos and laws of sacrifices were first given to Moshe while the nation was camped at the base of Har Sinai, as the verse states (*Vayikra* 1:1), "And God spoke to him *from the Ohel Moed*, saying." Ramban writes (*Vayikra* 7:38),

> Our Sages teach that all the mitzvos were said to Moshe on Har Sinai, the general principles and the fine details… But the simple

---

20   It appears that this is how *Tosafos Rid* (*Bava Basra* 119b) understood the case regarding the inheritance of the daughter of Zelafchad. Chazon Ish (*Orach Chaim* 125:4) also raises this suggestion as a possibility regarding the cases of the מקושש and the מקלל, but he concludes that he is not convinced that this approach is correct.

reading suggests… that "on Har Sinai"[21] means at the current location, at the base of Har Sinai, which is the *Ohel Moed*… It was not on the mountain itself—the location of the divine glory, the spot where God spoke the Ten Commandments—and it was also not in the desert of Sinai after they had travelled from the mountain.[22] Rather it was in the desert of Sinai at the base of the mountain, in close vicinity [of the mountain], at the location of the *Ohel Moed*.

Ramban returns to this approach several times in his commentary on the Torah. In *Vayikra* 25:1 Ramban states that many mitzvos in the Torah were first taught at Sinai "or at the *Ohel Moed*" in close proximity to the mountain.[23]

Again, in his introduction to *Sefer Devarim*, Ramban writes that even though *Sefer Devarim*—which records the events that occurred when *Bnei Yisrael* stood at Arvos Moav after forty years of travel in the desert—includes many mitzvos that do not appear earlier in the Torah, these mitzvos were not first revealed to Moshe at Arvos Moav. They, states Ramban, had already been taught to Moshe on Har Sinai *or at the Ohel Moed* in close proximity to the mountain.[24]

---

21 Ramban is coming to resolve the verse in *Vayikra* 7:38, which states quite clearly that the mitzvos regarding sacrifices were originally given at Har Sinai (אֲשֶׁר צִוָּה ה' אֶת מֹשֶׁה בְּהַר סִינָי). Ramban's suggestion is that this later verse does not literally mean *on the* mountain when it says "*BeHar Sinai* (בְּהַר סִינָי)." Rather, it means *at the base of Har Sinai* and refers to the *Ohel Moed*. Ramban continues and notes that we find the same literary phenomenon in other places, such as the *korban tamid*: "Similarly, we find that the verse (*Bamidbar* 28:6) states, 'The daily burnt offering that was brought *on the mountain*,' but it does not really mean 'on the mountain,' for the daily burnt offering only started to be brought at the *Ohel Moed*…"

22 Ramban (*Vayikra* 7:38) seems to understand that the *Ohel Moed* was originally erected directly adjacent to the base of Har Sinai. Later, when the nation moved into their official desert-encampment formation (*Bamidbar* 1:48–54), the *Ohel Moed* was moved away from the mountain's base and into the center of the camp. Ramban here is suggesting that the laws of the sacrifices were revealed to Moshe while the *Ohel Moed* was still standing at the mountain's base.

23 Ramban in *Shemos* 40:2 and in *Vayikra* 7:1 states that all the *parshiyos* in the beginning of *Sefer Vayikra* were revealed to Moshe via the *Ohel Moed*. See also Ramban in the beginning of *Sefer Bamidbar* where he states that the narrative of *Bamidbar* and most of *Vayikra* was stated at the *Ohel Moed*. It is not clear if he means the formulations of the verses or the transmission of the mitzvos themselves.

24 Ramban here seems to add that the giving of new mitzvos via the *Ohel Moed* continued until the events of the spies, after the nation arrived at Kadesh. However, one could also interpret Ramban to mean that the giving of new

It is well known that this *sefer* is a repetition of the Torah. In it, Moshe Rabbeinu clarifies for the generation that is about to enter the land of Israel most of the mitzvos that they will need there… This *sefer* also includes many mitzvos that had not yet been mentioned at all, such as *yibum*, the law of a *motzi shem ra*, divorce, *zomemim* witnesses, and others. These mitzvos had already been stated at Sinai or at the *Ohel Moed* during the first year[25] before the event with the spies.[26] At Arvos Moav, only the covenant was renewed.

Ramban's opinion that some of the mitzvos were first revealed via the *Ohel Moed*, and not necessarily on Har Sinai, fits in well with his general perspective on the *Ohel Moed/Mishkan*. Ramban writes in the beginning of *Parashas Terumah* (*Shemos* 25:2) that the purpose of the *Mishkan* was to perpetuate the experience of Sinai. The *Mishkan*, which comes from the root "to dwell (שכן)," was to be an entity that would allow the divine presence to reside in the physical world—and specifically amongst the Jewish nation—as it did during the awesome revelation at Har Sinai. In this way, the *Mishkan* perpetuated the Har Sinai experience.[27] We now understand that this was not only in terms of the revela-

---

mitzvos was done only at the base of Har Sinai, and that there were no more mitzvos given once the nation left the immediate vicinity of Har Sinai (see fn. 22 above). Moreover, Ramban writes explicitly (*Devarim* 1:6) that both the mountain and its base are referred to as "Sinai," which would be consistent with the many locations that Chazal write that the mitzvos were first given at "Sinai," not "on Har Sinai."

25   This is likely a scribal error, as the *Mishkan* itself was not erected until the second year after the Exodus, and Ramban is seemingly not referring to Moshe's private tent, also called the *Ohel Moed*, mentioned in *Shemos* 33:7 (see Ibn Ezra there). In the commentary of the Tur on the Torah, Ramban is quoted with the words שנה שניה.

26   Ramban suggests that the reason these mitzvos were not recorded in the Torah's text until Arvos Moav, even though they were already revealed as Sinai, is either that their fulfillment is dependent on being in the land of Israel or that they are uncommon situations that never came up during the desert period.

27   Ramban, in his presentation of the purpose of the *Mishkan* (*Shemos* 25:2), stresses the role it played in facilitating the divine presence to dwell among the nation (השראת השכינה). Rambam, however, in presenting the *Mishkan*, stresses the aspect of the *Mishkan* being a place for service of God. In *Sefer HaMitzvos* (Positive, #20) and *Mishneh Torah* (*Beis HaBechirah* 1:1) he writes that the purpose of the *Mishkan* was to be a place for offering sacrifices and congregating for the festivals. In more simple terms, Ramban's main focus on the *Mishkan* is

tion of the divine presence, but also in terms of the revelation of the Torah. The *Mishkan* perpetuated *Matan Torah* and facilitated the continued giving of the mitzvos even after Har Sinai.[28]

Rabbinic scholars after Ramban went even further. R. Moshe of Trani, Mabit (d. 1580), in his work, *Beis Elokim* (*Shaar HaYesodos* 37), endorses Ramban's view that there are no new mitzvos in *Sefer Devarim* that had not been previously given to Moshe. However, Mabit raises the possibility that even according to Ramban, new mitzvos were given at Arvos Moav. Accordingly, Mabit suggests that the mitzvos and laws that appear at the end of *Sefer Bamidbar*, such as the laws of inheritance as they related to the daughters of Zelafchad, were indeed first given to Moshe at Arvos Moav and not at Sinai or at the *Ohel Moed* in close proximity to the mountain.

> It is possible that when Ramban wrote that only a new covenant was forged at Arvos Moav, but no new mitzvos [were given there], he only meant it regarding the new mitzvos mentioned in *Mishneh Torah*,[29] about which it says in the Torah, "Moshe began explaining," etc. However, those mitzvos that the Torah in *Parshiyos Pinchas*, *Matos*, and *Mas'ei* states explicitly were commanded at Arvos Moav were seemingly not taught at an earlier time. Accordingly, the generation of the desert did not engage in the entirety of Torah.[30]

---

as a place where God comes toward the nation, while for Rambam it is a place where the nation comes toward God.

[28] Perhaps this is also the intent of the Ibn Ezra who writes that "the purpose of the *Mishkan* was to build a resting place.... God would speak there with Moshe, and *he would not [need to] ascend the mountain.*"

[29] A passage in Ramban's *Hasagos* on Rambam's *Sefer HaMitzvos* (*Shoresh* 1) seems to support Mabit's approach. Ramban writes there quite clearly that many mitzvos were not necessarily first revealed at Sinai, but rather at a later point in the desert. Ramban states this in defense of the Behag, who counted some rabbinic commandments in his list of 613 mitzvos. Ramban argues that although Chazal state that 613 mitzvos were given *at Sinai*, their intent was to make a general statement, but not to be taken literally, for many mitzvos, says Ramban, were not actually given to Moshe at Sinai. However, note Ramban's *Hasagos* on Rambam's *Sefer HaMitzvos* (Negative Commandment 194), where he seems to express a view that is more similar to that which he states in his *Hakdamah* to *Sefer Devarim*.

[30] Mabit adds that it is still possible that the great scholars of the generation of the desert were able, on their own, to gain knowledge of those mitzvos that were not yet commanded. Accordingly, they studied and performed them, just as the *Avos* had done many years earlier.

Radvaz (d. 1573) goes even further. He disagrees (VI:2143) with Ramban and Mabit regarding the new mitzvos of *Sefer Devarim*; he argues that these mitzvos were first given to Moshe at Arvos Moav, at the end of the forty-year desert period.[31]

> I was asked to share my opinion regarding when the new mitzvos that appear in *Mishneh Torah* were first commanded... I think that all these new mitzvos were first commanded at Arvos Moav... and if you will ask me why God did not command these mitzvos at Sinai, like all the other mitzvos, I will respond and ask you why you are not asking about Shabbos and *dinim* that were commanded at Marah, or about those that were commanded at the *Ohel Moed*— why they were not commanded at Sinai? One who asks such questions is questioning God's will, which is beyond the ken of mankind... All the new mitzvos that appear in *Mishneh Torah*, God commanded to Moshe at Arvos Moav... as we learn in the *midrash*, "'You also did not know' (*Yeshayah* 48:8)—at Sinai; 'You also did not hear' (ibid.)—at Chorev; 'You also never opened your ear from then' (ibid.)—at Arvos Moav." We learn from here that at these three locations mitzvos were commanded [for the first time].[32]

It emerges that Ramban, Radvaz, and Mabit all entertained the possibility, based on a close and literal reading of the Torah's text, that many of the mitzvos were first revealed to Moshe after Har Sinai.

The Details of the Mitzvos

The Talmud (*Chagigah* 6a, *Sotah* 37b, *Zevachim* 115b) records a debate between two prominent Tannaim whether the mitzvos and *Peirush* that Moshe received on Har Sinai contained all the details of the mitzvos. The generally accepted view is that of R. Akiva, who states that indeed the "general principles and the fine details [of the mitzvos] were said at

---

[31] This might also be the opinion of Malbim who writes (*Torah Or, Devarim* 33:2), "Most of the Torah was given by Hashem at Sinai [which is] Horeb, [but] also much was given during the thirty-eight years [in the desert]. Many laws were added at the time of *Mishneh Torah* [i.e., *Sefer Devarim*] and many laws were given for the first time at the time of the covenant at Arvos Moav." Similarly, the Rashbam writes (*Shemos* 12:1, cf. Chizkuni) that "some of the mitzvos were given at Har Sinai, some at the *Ohel Moed*, and some at Arvos Moav." However, it is not immediately clear if the Rashbam is referring to when the mitzvos were given to Moshe or to when Moshe taught them to the nation.

[32] Radvaz states that he does not really feel adequate to argue with Ramban, but since there is no practical ramification in halachah, he feels he is justified in suggesting an alternate perspective.

Sinai (כללות ופרטות נאמרו בסיני)." This seems to also be the view of the *Sifra* in *Parashas Behar* quoted earlier that "all the mitzvos—their general laws and fine points (כללותיה ודקדוקיה)—are from Sinai." However, the Tanna R. Yishmael disagrees. He argues that many details of the mitzvos were only taught to Moshe later, through the medium of the *Ohel Moed*.[33]

According to both R. Akiva and R. Yishmael, all the actual mitzvos of the Torah were taught at Sinai with some degree of explanation and elaboration.[34] The Tannaim only argue regarding the details—were they all given to Moshe at Sinai or were some only given at later point? However, Rambam maintains a different perspective. He writes that many details of the mitzvos were *never* transmitted to Moshe, not on Har Sinai nor at any later point in his life. To properly understand Rambam's opinion, and how it relates to the above-quoted opinions of the Tannaim, we need to first survey the various components of the Oral Law transmitted to Moshe at Sinai.

The Components of the Oral Law Transmitted to Moshe at Sinai

Rambam, in the introduction to his *Peirush HaMishnah*, outlines multiple components of the Oral Law that were transmitted to Moshe on Har Sinai. The first component is the *Peirush*, an accompanying commentary to the mitzvos. Without the *Peirush* it would be impossible to understand or properly perform the mitzvos of the Torah, for the text of the Torah contains many uninterpreted terms and unexplained concepts. Moreover, many of the mitzvos are presented in the Torah in only the most

---

33 Rashi (*Chagigah* 6a and *Sotah* 37b), in explaining the opinion of R. Yishmael, cites the laws of the sacrifices. In this example, Rashi states that according to R. Yishmael the details were filled in at the *Ohel Moed* when it was stationed at the base of Har Sinai. Nonetheless, when R. Yishmael refers to the *Ohel Moed* he does not likely mean to limit this to when then *Ohel Moed* stood at the base of Har Sinai. Rather, he also means that some details were also first revealed at Arvos Moav, through the medium of the *Ohel Moed*. See *Chasam Sofer, Megillah* 2b ד"ה אלא and Malbim, *Bamidbar* 36:13.

34 It is possible that these Tannaim are not necessarily saying that *all* the mitzvos were given on Har Sinai. R. Akiva might simply mean that those mitzvos that *were* given on Har Sinai were given with all their details. Nonetheless, the simple reading of these Tannaim is that they do not disagree with the traditional view that all the mitzvos were given at Har Sinai. Note this same ambiguity in Rambam's introduction to *Mishneh Torah*: "All the mitzvos *that were given* to Moshe at Sinai were given with an accompanying explanation (כל המצוות שניתנו לו למשה מסיני, בפירושן ניתנו)."

general of terms. The *Peirush* elucidates the terse language of the Written Law and fills in many important details of the mitzvos and their laws.[35]

Rambam (*Peirush HaMishnah*, Introduction, and *Hilchos Mamrim* 1:3) writes unequivocally that there are no disputes in the literature of Chazal regarding the material that was transmitted in the *Peirush*. The interpretations and details of the laws that constitute the *Peirush* were received by Moshe at Sinai and then transmitted faithfully from generation to generation by the *Beis Din HaGadol*.

Rambam refers to the bulk of the *Peirush* as the *Peirushim Mekubalim MiSinai*, the "Received Teachings from Sinai." These interpretations and details of the law were transmitted to Moshe Rabbeinu as accepted fact, without any explanation or justification. In other words, neither the sources for these teachings, nor the logic behind them, were transmitted to Moshe. However, the *Peirushim Mekubalim MiSinai* can be independently derived through scholarly analysis of the Torah. In fact, many passages in the Talmud are attempts to uncover how the explanations and laws that were transmitted as a received tradition can also be deduced from the text of the Torah. Moreover, many of the disputes in the Talmud are not over the law itself, but rather over the sources of the law. This is because the sources—unlike the laws themselves—were not revealed to Moshe at Sinai.

But not all the interpretations and details of the laws transmitted to Moshe at Sinai can be post-facto derived through logic or analysis of the Torah's text. Some of the *Peirush* must always remain an accepted fact, forever a pure received tradition. This small group of non-derivable interpretations and details of the law are called the *Halachah LeMoshe MiSinai*, the "Laws of Moshe from Sinai." This title should not be misinterpreted to suggest that all the other interpretations and details of the law in the *Peirush* were *not* received by Moshe at Sinai. As we have seen, they too were received by Moshe at Sinai. Rather, this special title is reserved for laws that will always only be known due to their transmission

---

35   For instance, the Torah states that every individual must take on Succos a "*pri etz hadar*." Although the text of the Torah never identifies this term, God taught Moshe as part of the *Peirush* that this term refers to an *esrog*. The *Peirush* also provides details of the mitzvos and their laws. For example, the Torah records that certain sins are punishable by the death penalty. However, the Torah does not state explicitly the many legal conditions that need to be fulfilled to administer capital punishment, such as the issuance of an explicit warning before the act is committed (התראה), or the testimony of two witnesses who were present when the sin occurred and can withstand a very specific process of cross-examination.

to Moshe at Sinai and can never be post-facto derived using logic or scholarly analysis of the Torah's text.[36]

All the teachings in the *Peirush*—both the *Peirushim Mekubalim MiSinai* and the *Halachos LeMoshe MiSinai*—are considered to have the status of biblical law (דאורייתא), a similar status to those laws that appear explicitly in the Torah's text. Furthermore, the *Peirush* is absolutely binding. It is not open to debate, and it cannot be negated or altered by later generations. In this vein, Rambam (Introduction to *Peirush HaMishnah* and *Hilchos Mamrim* 1:3) writes unequivocally that there are no disputes in the literature of Chazal regarding the material that was transmitted in the *Peirush*.

Another component of the Oral Law that Moshe Rabbeinu received at Sinai is a collection of exegetical tools for analyzing the Torah. These tools are called the "*middos* of *derashah* (מידות שהתורה נדרשת בהם)," the "hermeneutic principles" for interpreting the Torah.[37] Although there is some discussion about the exact number of *middos* of *derashah*, Rambam (*Sefer Shorashim, Shoresh* 2) writes that there are thirteen primary *middos* of *derashah* plus the *derashah* mechanism of *riboi* (ריבוי).[38] Some examples of

---

[36] Since these laws are few in number—as most of the *Peirush* is comprised of *Peirushim Mekubalim MiSinai* and can be derived through logic and scholarly analysis—Rambam, in his introduction to his *Peirush HaMishnah*, attempts to list all of the known laws that fall into this small category of *Halachah LeMoshe MiSinai*. It should also be noted that sometimes the term *Halachah LeMoshe MiSinai* is borrowed and used for a rabbinic law that is very well established. See, for example, *Piskei HaRosh Mikvaos* 1 and *Peirush HaRash* on *Yedayim* 4:1.

[37] Rambam writes explicitly in the introduction to his *Peirush HaMishnah* that the *middos* of *derashah* were given to Moshe at Sinai. He writes, " במדות השלש עשרה הנתונות על הר סיני שהתורה נדרשת בהם." This is also stated explicitly by Radvaz (IV:232) and the *Sefer HaIkarim* (III:23).

[38] The early Tanna Hillel lists seven primary *middos* of *derashah*. However, the traditional list consists of the thirteen *middos* that were presented by the later Tanna, R. Yishmael. R. Akiva, a contemporary of R. Yishmael, basically agreed with R. Yishmael's list, but replaced the *middah* of כלל ופרט with ריבוי ומיעוט. An additional list of thirty-two *middos* was compiled by R. Eliezer b. R. Yosi HaGelili, but that list mostly pertains to analyzing Aggadah, while the list of seven and thirteen relate more to Halachah. If the *middos* were given at Sinai, how can there be a dispute about their number? R. Shimshon of Chinon, a French Rishon and author of the *Sefer Krisus*, argues that there is no dispute about the actual number of *middos* given at Sinai. He suggests that Hillel was known to generally use seven primary *middos*, but he also knew about, and accepted, the others on R. Yishmael's longer list. The 16th-century rabbinic scholar R. Aaron ibn Chaim, in his work *Korban Aaron*, offers a slightly different approach. He writes that the early Tannaim taught tersely and that R.

the *middos* are: *kal vechomer* (קל וחומר), *binyan av* (בנין אב), *kelal u'perat* (כלל ופרט), and *gezeirah shavah* (גזירה שוה).

The giving of the *middos* of *derashah* was vital for the future of Torah study and life. First, the *middos* were used by Chazal academically, as noted earlier, to post-facto derive many laws of the *Peirush* from the text of the Torah. Second, Rambam suggests, the *middos* served a vital role in the continued development of the Oral Law, as we will see shortly.

The Omitted Details of the Mitzvos

Rambam writes (Introduction to *Peirush HaMishnah*) that many non-essential details of the mitzvos were not included in the *Peirush* that was transmitted to Moshe. Additionally, the specifics of how to apply the mitzvos to non-standard situations was also omitted. When a question arose regarding a detail of a mitzvah or a novel application of a mitzvah, and the answer had not been taught to Moshe at Sinai, the Sages of the *Beis Din HaGadol* used the *middos* of *derashah* to analyze the Torah and fill in the missing details. Sometimes they even used their analysis of the Torah to create new laws entirely.[39]

This was a common occurrence in the years following *Matan Torah*. New situations arose that raised halachic questions that had not been directly addressed by the *Peirush*. The Sages turned to the Torah's text, and utilizing the *middos* of *derashah*, they reached halachically justifiable approaches to the situation or issue they were confronting.

That a body of laws exists that was created by the Sages through the analysis of the Torah's texts is stated clearly by Rambam in his introduc-

---

Yishmael's thirteen *middos* are all subsumed in Hillel's seven more general *middos*. He compares this to *Makkos* 24a that states that David HaMelech was able to subsume all 613 mitzvos into eleven primary principles, Yeshayah into six, Michah into three, Yeshayah again into two, and Chavakuk into one.

[39] Rambam notes that this process was one of rigorous intellectual analysis and did not utilize prophecy. Only the Torah and the *Peirush* were given to Moshe via prophecy. After Moshe's death, future generations never used prophecy, only interpretative analysis, to arrive at Halachah. Rambam explains that the inability to use prophecy as part of the process of developing new laws is learned from the verse in *Devarim* 30:12—"It is not in Heaven (לא בשמים היא)." This also seems to be the intent of *Temurah* 16a. However, the Ashkenazic Rishonim were not as opposed to the use of prophecy, after the death of Moshe, in determining Halachah. See *Rashi Succah* 44a ד"ה ויסדום, *Tosafos Bava Metzia* 59b ד"ה לא, and *Yevamos* 14a ד"ה רבי. For an explanation how the view of the Ashkenazic Rishonim would respond to *Temurah* 16a, see *Mishpat Kohen* #92.

tion to the *Mishneh Torah*. He describes these laws as "novel teachings that emerged every generation, laws not learned through tradition but rather derived using the thirteen *middos* of *derashah*." Similarly, Rambam very clearly differentiates in his *Mishneh Torah* (*Hilchos Mamrim* 1:3) between those laws that were "transmitted via tradition (מפי השמועה)" and those laws that the Sages "derived based on their own analysis (מפי דעתם) using the *middos* of *derashah* and that appeared proper in their eyes (ונראה בעיניהם שדבר זה כך הוא)."[40]

These new laws are another important component of the Oral Law, as Rambam states clearly in the introduction to his *Peirush HaMishnah*,

> The first component of the Oral Law is the collection of *Peirushim Mekubalim MiSinai*; these laws are rooted in the text of the Torah and can be deduced using analysis... The second component is the laws that are called *Halachah LeMoshe MiSinai*, these have no source in the text of the Torah... The third component is the collection of laws that were created by the Sages using analytical study.[41]

When the Sages of the *Beis Din HaGadol* confronted situations that had not been directly addressed by God at *Matan Torah* and applied the *middos* of *derashah* to determine the proper law, sometimes the relevant rabbinic analysis was clear and undisputable. In such cases, the new rul-

---

[40] In the *Kuzari* (3:39), R. Yehudah HaLevi refers to these laws as "laws that come from the place chosen by God (מן המקום אשר יבחר ה')," a reference to the Sages of the *Beis Din HaGadol* who used the *middos* of *derashah* to create new laws and details of laws.

[41] Rambam writes in his *Sefer HaMitzvos* (*Shoresh* 2) that the "*majority* of the Torah's laws are derived using the thirteen *middos* of *derashah* (רוב דיני התורה יצאו בשלש עשרה מידות שהתורה נדרשת בהם)." From Rambam's context there it is not clear if Rambam is saying that the new laws are the "majority of the Torah's laws" or if he is also including the *Peirushim Mekubalim MiSinai*, which can post-facto be derived from the Torah using the *middos* of *derashah*, when he refers to the "majority of the Torah's laws." However, *Gittin* 60b records a debate: What constitutes the bulk of the Torah—the Written Law or the Oral Law? The *Sefer Be'er Sheva* suggests that this debate primarily revolves around the many new laws and details of laws that were created by Chazal using the *middos* of *derashah*. Are they considered part of the Written Law, since they were derived from the text of the Torah, or are they considered part of the Oral Law, since they are not explicitly written in the Torah? Seemingly, the *Be'er Sheva* assumes that the number of new laws derived by the *middos* of *derashah* is very great. In fact, they are so numerous that their status as either the "Written Law" or "Oral Law" will be the factor that determines which category is the bulk of the Torah.

ing was immediately canonized into the corpus of the Oral Law. Yet sometimes the correct application of the *middos* of *derashah* was not immediately clear. In such cases, the proper application of the *middos*, and the resulting conclusions, became a subject of rabbinic debate. The *Beis Din HaGadol* debated the issue and eventually ruled based on majority vote. The newly created law was then canonized into the corpus of the Oral Law.

Ramban writes (*Hasagos* on *Sefer HaMitzvos, Shoresh* 2) that the new laws developed through the *middos* of *derashah* are considered biblical laws (דאורייתא), since they are derived directly from the text of the Torah. That is, the new laws are not mere inventions of the Sages' creativity. Rather the Sages' scholarly analysis, utilizing the *middos* of *derashah*, reveals that these laws are embedded in the text and part of its deeper meaning. However, Rambam's view on the status of these new laws is less straightforward. Although he writes in his *Sefer HaMitzvos* (*Shoresh* 2) that the new laws are "from the Rabbis (דרבנן)," there are strong indications that Rambam agrees that they are biblical in nature.[42]

Even if these new laws are biblical, they are still significantly distinct from the biblical laws transmitted as part of the *Peirush*. First, the new laws created through the *middos* of *derashah* are debatable. Unlike the teachings of the *Peirush*, which are not up for debate or discussion and must simply be accepted as fact, the laws that emerge from scholarly analysis of the Torah's text can be, and often are, the subject of rabbinic debate. One scholar or academy might arrive at one conclusion through the utilization of one *middah* of *derashah*, while another scholar or academy might arrive at a different conclusion as he applies a different *middah* or applies the same *middah* in a different way. As mentioned earlier, when the *Beis Din HaGadol* functioned, the debates were generally resolved through a formal vote.

---

42 Rambam begins that very passage stating that "the majority of the *Torah's laws* are from the scholarly analysis of the Torah using the thirteen *middos* of *derashah* (רוב דיני התורה יצאו בשלש עשרה מידות שהתורה נדרשת בהם)." Calling these laws "Torah laws (דיני התורה)" certainly suggests that these laws are considered biblical (see previous footnote). Similarly, several of Rambam's commentators (*Megillas Esther* and *Zohar HaRakia*) argue that all Rambam meant when he wrote that the laws derived using the *middos* of *derashah* are "from the Rabbis" is that the Rabbis are the ones who derived these laws from the Torah. Rambam's intent is that although these laws are considered biblical laws, they should still not be counted on the list of 613 mitzvos since they are not explicit in the words of the Torah (מפורש בקרא). See also, *Ohr Sameach* (*Mamrim* 2:1).

Second, the new laws created through the *middos* of *derashah* are not eternally binding. Meaning, a *Beis Din HaGadol* of a future generation can offer a reinterpretation of the Torah's text—by applying the *middos* of *derashah* differently—and thereby change, or even abolish, a created law. This is true even if the later *Beis Din HaGadol* is not greater in number or wisdom than the original one (Rambam, *Mamrim* 2:1).[43]

Rambam's position that many details of the mitzvos were not formally given to Moshe at Sinai was not universally accepted. The Geonim, for example, operated with a different understanding.[44] They

---

43 In hundreds of locations in his *Mishneh Torah*, and to a lesser degree in his *Sefer HaMitzvos*, Rambam describes laws using the mishnaic term, "The teachings of the *Sofrim* (דברי סופרים)." The *Sofrim* were the early Sages and members of the *Beis Din HaGadol*—those entrusted with the mission of preserving and transmitting the Oral Law. But what does Rambam refer to when he uses this term, "The teachings of the *Sofrim* (דברי סופרים)"? One option: Rambam writes in his commentary on the *Mishnah* (*Keilim* 17:12) that "the teachings of the *Sofrim*" is a general term for the Oral Law. It can refer to the teachings of the *Peirush* or even to rabbinic laws. Indeed, Rambam does occasionally use this term when discussing rabbinic laws (see for example, *Chametz U'Matzah* chapters 1, 6, and 7). However, the commentators on Rambam note that he more commonly uses this term for biblical laws that are not explicit in the text of the Torah (מפורש בקרא). These biblical laws are attributed to the *Sofrim* because "without the tradition transmitted to us by the *Sofrim*, we would never have known these teachings" (*Kesef Mishnah*, *Ishus* 1:2). Yet, in his *Sefer HaMitzvos* (*Shoresh* 2), Rambam uses the term "*Divrei Sofrim*" to refer specifically to the new laws derived from the text of the Torah using the *middos* of *derashah*. The *Maggid Mishnah* and *Kesef Mishnah* (*Ishus* 1:2) both suggest that despite the fact that the new laws learned from the *middos* of *derashah* have full biblical status, Rambam still calls them "the teachings of the *Sofrim*" and not "Torah law (דברי תורה)" because the laws needed to be derived via scholarly analysis and were not explicitly written in the Torah. The *Ohr Sameach* (*Mamrim* 2:1) concurs and posits that they are called "the teachings of the *Sofrim*" and not "Torah law" because of the rule quoted above that these new laws are subject to change, and even abolishment, if a reinterpretation is offered by a future *Beis Din HaGadol*, i.e., by later *Sofrim*.

44 This view is ascribed in general to the Geonim and appears to be the intent of R. Sherira Gaon in *Iggeres of Rav Sherira Gaon* (ד"ה והכי הוי מילתא). It also appears to be the view of R. Avraham ibn Daud in the introduction to his *Sefer HaKabbalah*. Some have noted that Rashi in one location, *Succah* 31a ד"ה לא מקשינן, states that besides *kal vechomer*, all the other *middos* of *derashah* require a received tradition to interpret the verse with a specific *middah*. This would seemingly mean that except for the logical applications of *kal vechomer*, there were no new laws after Moshe received a tradition of interpretations. However, Rashi in *Kiddushin* 17a ד"ה מיכה implies otherwise. Nonetheless, there are

maintained that all the details of the mitzvos—both essential and non-essential minutiae of the law—were included in the *Peirush* that was transmitted to Moshe at Sinai. It was also transmitted to Moshe at that time how to apply the mitzvos to all non-standard situations. According to the Geonic perspective, the *middos* were only used by Chazal academically, as noted earlier, to post-facto derive the *Peirushim Mekubalim MiSinai* from the text of the Torah. No law or detail was omitted at Sinai, and therefore nothing was left to future generations to originate or derive using the *middos* of *derashah*.

Indeed, Rambam's position appears to be against the statement of Chazal in the *Sifra* in *Parashas Behar*, quoted earlier, that all the details of the mitzvos (כללותיה ופרטותיה ודקדוקיה) were given at Sinai. It also appears to be against the opinions of R. Akiva and R. Yishmael that all the details of the mitzvos were transmitted at some point—whether at Sinai or later at the *Ohel Moed*—to Moshe. Rambam addresses this by offering a novel interpretation of Chazal's uncommon expression: כללותיה ופרטיה. Rambam suggests that this expression does not actually refer to *all* the mitzvos and their laws. Rather it refers specifically to the *Peirushim Mekubalim MiSinai*, i.e., those teachings of the *Peirush* that can be independently derived using the *middos* of *derashah*, such as "*kelal u'perat* (כלל ופרט)"—hence the term (כללותיה ופרטותיה).

> There are no disputes whatsoever regarding the *Peirushim Mekubalim MiSinai*... for they are all received traditions from Moshe. Regarding them, and things like them, Chazal state: "The entire Torah—*kelalosehah* (כללותיה), *peratosehah* (פרטותיה), and *dikdukehah* (דקדוקיה)—are from Sinai." Now, despite the fact that the *Peirushim Mekubalim MiSinai* were received as a tradition, and there are no disputes regarding them, we can nonetheless use our received Torah knowledge to derive these interpretations and laws from the Torah's text using various forms of logic and analysis... And this is what is meant when Chazal refer to *kelalosehah* (כללותיה) and *peratosehah* (פרטותיה). They mean those laws that can be [post-facto] derived using *kelal u'perat*, and the other thirteen *middos* of *derashah*.

According to Rambam's novel interpretation, Chazal only meant to say that all the *Peirushim Mekubalim MiSinai* were given with their details

---

indications in *Rashi* and *Tosafos* that they subscribed to the view of the Geonim. For a more modern presentation that seems to reflect this view, see the *Collected Writings of Rabbi Samson Raphael Hirsch*, Vol. V, starting on page 39.

at Sinai, but they never meant to suggest that *all the details* of *all* the mitz-vos were given at Sinai.

It thus emerges, according to Rambam (see also *Sefer HaIkarim* III:23), that even Chazal's opinion is that many details of the mitzvos were not transmitted to Moshe at Sinai. Therefore, many situations had to be addressed by later generations using the *middos* of *derashah* to ana-lyze and arrive at new rulings and laws.

Rambam's approach is well grounded. Firstly, the position that not all the details of the mitzvos were transmitted at Sinai is stated explicitly by a Midrash in *Shemos Rabbah* (41:6).

> Did Moshe really learn the entire Torah [at Sinai]? It says regarding the Torah, "Longer than the earth is its measure, and wider than the sea" (*Iyov* 11:9). Could Moshe learn it all in forty days? Rather, God taught Moshe the general principles (כללים).[45]

Besides clearly suggesting that Moshe did not receive the entire To-rah, this Midrash also states that in place of the entire Torah, Moshe was taught "general principle." The *Peirush Maharzu* on the Midrash (ד"ה ואיני) suggests that these "general principles" are the *middos* of *derashah*, which empowered Moshe and later generations to address situations that were not explicitly transmitted to him.

Second, the idea that the *middos* of *derashah* can be used to create new laws is attested to by the Torah itself. In *Vayikra* 10:16–20, a question arises about eating the meat of a *korban* after the death of a close relative but before burial, a status known as *aninus* (אנינות). Aaron HaKohen ana-lyzes the Torah using the *middos* of *derashah* and arrives at a conclusion that is ultimately accepted by Moshe Rabbeinu (see *Zevachim* 101a for Aaron's analysis). It seems from the Torah's narrative that this detail of the law of sacrifices had not been transmitted to Moshe at Sinai and came into existence as a "new law" through the scholarly analysis of Aaron.

The Talmud also records several cases of rabbinic analysis creating new laws. For example, *Yerushalmi Yevamos* (8:3, see also *Bavli Yevamos* 76b–77a) states that the law allowing marriage to a female *Moabite* (מואבי

---

[45] *Menachos* 29b teaches that God once gave Moshe Rabbeinu the opportunity to visit R. Akiva's academy. Once there, Moshe was unable to follow the discus-sion, something that caused him much distress (תשש כוחו). The simple inter-pretation of this passage suggests that the Torah being taught by R. Akiva was not something that Moshe had been taught by God. However, see Rashi there (ד"ה נתיישבה) for a possible alternate interpretation. See also *Or HaChaim*, *Vayikra* 13:37.

ולא מואביה) was not taught to Moshe but created through analysis of the Torah by the *Beis Din HaGadol*. It also appears from the Mishnah in *Berachos* 12b that there was no known law to mention the Exodus from Egypt every night until Ben Zoma's analysis of the Torah arrived at this conclusion.

Indeed, we find in the Talmud that great rabbinic Sages sometimes responded to a stated law with the expression, "If it is an accepted law, we will accept it; however, if it is a law based on rabbinic analysis, then there is a counter-argument to be made (אם הלכה נקבל ואם לדין יש עליו תשובה)." The speaker is seemingly saying that if the law under discussion was received by Moshe at Sinai as part of the *Peirush*, he will blindly accept it. But if it is a law that is being created through rabbinic analysis of the Torah, then he wishes to offer alternative analysis of the issue.

It emerges according to Rambam that even if Moshe Rabbeinu received all the mitzvos on Har Sinai, there were still many details that were purposely omitted by God. These details were not taught to Moshe along with the transmission of the mitzvos at Sinai nor were they taught to him at any later point via the *Ohel Moed*. Rather, God chose to never explicitly teach these details to Moshe. That is, Moshe never received, in an explicated form, an all-encompassing corpus that included every detail of every law or that addressed every single situation that would ever arise. It was God's will that these details be omitted from *Matan Torah* so that the leading rabbinic scholars of future generations could uncover, or even "create," new rulings and laws through their study of the Torah using the *middos* of *derashah*. It was God's desire that His nation would take an active role in the continued development of a living Torah.[46]

---

[46] This provides an important perspective on *machlokes*. Disputes in Chazal are not necessarily attempts to reconstruct what had originally been taught to Moshe at Sinai. If this were the case, the widespread existence of *machlokes* in the literature of Chazal suggests a severe breakdown in the transmission of Torah over the generations. Indeed, Rambam in his *Introduction to the Mishnah* censures one who suggests such a perspective on the origins of *machlokes* in Chazal. Rather, says Rambam, it is specifically the non-transmitted areas of the law that are the reason for *machlokes*. When rabbinic scholars confronted new situations or details of the law that had not been addressed at Sinai, they turned to the text of the Torah and used the *middos* of *derashah* to address the issue at hand. Differing methods of applying the *middos* of *derashah* led to different conclusions. Accordingly, we find (*Eruvin* 13b, *Gittin* 6b), "These and those (i.e., both opinions) are the words of the living God (אלו ואלו דברי אלקים חיים)," for both sides in a *machlokes* reflect valid applications of the *middos* of *derashah*.

Conclusion

This article has developed different perspectives on God's transmission of the mitzvos at *Matan Torah*. The most literal reading of Chazal suggests that all the mitzvos with all the details of their laws were given at Har Sinai. However, this article has shown that several rabbinic scholars maintained a more complex understanding of God's transmission of the mitzvos.

We have seen Rishonim and Acharonim who maintain that only some of the mitzvos were given at Har Sinai. Other mitzvos and the details of their laws were revealed at later points, be it at the base of Har Sinai or even at Arvos Moav at the end of the desert period. These scholars see *Matan Torah* not as a singular event, but as a process that extended over a longer period of Moshe Rabbeinu's life.

We have also seen Rishonim that assert that many details of the mitzvos were never transmitted to Moshe. In other words, even if a mitzvah itself was given at Sinai, its details were not always included. These scholars see an element of human involvement in a process of *Matan Torah* that extended beyond Moshe Rabbeinu's lifetime. Indeed, it was by divine design that details of the Torah's law would be creatively deduced through the study of Torah by the leading rabbinic scholars of future generations.[47] ଔ

---

[47] The giving of the mitzvos and their details directly to Moshe on Har Sinai, or at later points in his life, via prophecy, and the human deducing of new laws and details of the mitzvos via analysis of the Torah's text using the *middos* of *derashah* are all part of the divinely-designed explication process of the germinal form of the Torah that had been revealed to Moshe at Har Sinai, described in the introduction of this article.

Tax Ethics in Rashba's Responsa to Saragossa

By: DOV FISCHER*

Introduction

Consider the following questions on tax ethics and policy:

1. Should the tax code be applied based on its letter or its spirit?
2. Is it ethical for a taxpayer to take advantage of an unintended loophole?
3. Is a taxpayer ethically responsible when another party to a transaction engages in inappropriate tax evasion?

These questions, which are relevant today, were addressed by Rashba (Rabbi Shlomo ben Avraham ibn Aderet, 1235–1310). Rashba is arguably the greatest author of rabbinic responsa in history.[1] Like the Geonim and early Rishonim such as the Rif (Rabbi Isaac ben Jacob Alfasi ha-Cohen, 1013–1103), Rashba answers questions clearly and decisively. Unlike his predecessors, Rashba heralds a new style of responsa which persists to this day. Rashba's responsa frequently explore both sides in the manner of litigants in front of a judge. Rashba explores each argument before reaching his decision. By sharing his reasoning and thought process, Rashba's responsa can teach us much more than just the narrow decision of the case as presented.

---

*   The author dedicates this article to the continued good health of Shlomo Lev and other members of Cong. Kerem Shlomo (Rabbi Simcha Klahr). Opinions expressed and any errors in the article are those of the author only. This is an academic article and does not constitute tax, legal, or rabbinic advice.

1   In his podcast, Rabbi and historian Dovid Katz says that Rashba's responsa were the first that were consciously collected and intended for publication. ("The 'Rashba'—R' Shlomo ben Aderet (1235–1310): Baal HaBayis, Rosh Yeshiva, Posek and Royal Troubleshooter.")
https://anchor.fm/rabbi-dovid-katz/episodes/The-Rashba---R-Shlomo-ben-Adret-1235-1310-Baal-HaBayis--Rosh-Yeshiva--Posek-and-Royal-Trouble-shooter-eppbun/a-a9ka2n)

Dov Fischer is professor and department chair of accounting at Brooklyn College. He attended the Talmudical Yeshiva of Philadelphia, Yeshiva Torah Vodaath, Yeshiva University, and holds a Ph.D. from University of Colorado at Boulder.

Based in the Catalonian city of Barcelona, Rashba responded to thousands of questions from throughout Spain, Provence, North Africa, northern France, Germany, Bohemia, Sicily, Crete, and the Crusader city of Acre in Eretz Yisrael.[2] Among those that came from relatively near were questions from Saragossa, which lies two hundred miles inland from Barcelona.

Outside the confines of Torah scholarship, Rashba and his responsa are most famous for his ban on secular studies before the age of twenty-five. The ban was meant to quell a controversy that erupted in Languedoc and Provence to the east of Barcelona (see map).[3] Such sensational controversies notwithstanding, the majority of Rashba's responsa pertain to ritual observance and commercial disputes between individuals and between individuals and the Jewish community. Our focus is on a responsum pertaining to a tax question and specifically to internal Jewish tax administration to meet fixed levies imposed by the crown. Such responsa pertain to ethical and public-policy questions that are relevant beyond the narrow confines of Jewish law. Rashba himself notes that he does not base his tax rulings on Jewish law but on precedence and equity as seen through his own moral lens (III:412; IV:260).

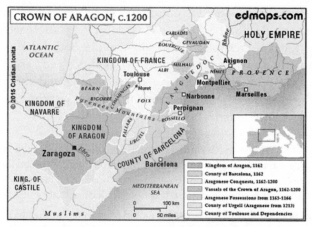

Map of the Crown of Aragon several decades before Rashba's birth. This map highlights that while both Barcelona and Saragossa (Zaragoza in Spanish) belonged to the Crown of Aragon, Saragossa was in the Kingdom of Aragon proper (unlike Barcelona) and was therefore subject to onerous taxation at the king's whim.

---

2   See: *Museu d'Història de Barcelona*, MUHBA. "Salomon ben Aderet, Barcelona 1230–1310: The Triumph of Orthodoxy."
http://www.bcn.cat/museuhistoriaciutat/docs/ProgramaSalomoANG.pdf

3   Buchman, A.B., "Avraham and Sarah in Provence," *Ḥakirah* 6.

This essay examines responsum III:406 (Machon Yerushalyim, 1997) addressed to the community of Saragossa, the capital of both the Kingdom of Aragon and the Crown of Aragon. In an interesting political arrangement, the Kingdom of Aragon and the County of Barcelona were united under a single sovereign in the Crown of Aragon. For much of Rashba's early life this Crown was held by James I, who reigned for a remarkable 63 years (born 1208; reigned 1213–1276). James I was an enlightened ruler, who ushered in a golden age for Barcelona and its Jews.[4] In Jewish history, James I is best known for officiating over the Disputation of Barcelona, in which Ramban (Moshe ben Nachman of Girona; Rashba's teacher) represented the Jewish position against an apostate who converted from Judaism to Christianity.[5]

While the Crown of Aragon reigned over both Saragossa and Barcelona, the two were subject to different administrations and institutions. Saragossa was the capital of the Kingdom of Aragon, and as such the king exercised direct powers of taxation (see map). On the other hand, Barcelona and Catalonia in general were given considerable autonomy in the exercise of their internal affairs, a historical anomaly within Spain that persists to this day in the Catalan separatist movement.

Being situated so close to royalty was a mixed blessing for the Jewish community of Saragossa. On the one hand, individual Jews were prominent in the financial administration of the Kingdom and Crown of Aragon.[6] On the other hand, the king was able to levy taxes on the Saragossa Jewish community at will. As with other pre-modern Jewish communities, the Saragossa community levied taxes on its own members to meet the required fixed payments to the king.

This background information explains why the responsa to Saragossa are especially interesting. The Saragossa Jewish community was subject to arbitrary tax levies by the king, and the community in turn had to devise creative ways to not only maximize tax revenue within its borders but also to expand the geographical range of its taxation powers and to prevent capital flight. This background information also sheds light on the nature of the tax questions posed by the Saragossa community to Rashba in Barcelona. Although they shared the same sovereign in the person of James

---

4   Assis, Yom Tov. *Golden Age of Aragonese Jewry: Community and Society in the Crown of Aragon, 1213–1327*. 1st edition. The Littman Library of Jewish Civilization in association with Liverpool University Press,1997, p. 3.

5   James I also had a close relationship with the father of the *Menorat Hama'or*, i.e., the father of Rabbi Isaac ben Abraham Aboab (https://www.jewishencyclopedia.com/articles/344-aboab Retrieved April 18, 2021).

6   See *Jewish Encyclopedia*, "Saragossa," by Richard Gottheil and Meyer Kayserling. https://www.jewishencyclopedia.com/articles/13192-saragossa

I and his successors, taxes in Saragossa were more onerous and capricious than in Barcelona. This was even more the case after the reign of James I, whose successors overstretched the treasury by embarking on expensive military campaigns to Sardinia and Greece.

Because of the heavy tax burden imposed on the Saragossa Jewish community, some of its members sought to emigrate. The community imposed a wealth tax which required members to annually self-assess their property values and to pay taxes on the estimated appreciation (III:407). Essentially, this is an unrealized capital-gains tax. The community also imposed a wealth tax on those who sought to emigrate.

Note that the responsum does not touch on the concept of primacy of temporal authority in fiscal matters (*dina d-malkhuta dina*), as the taxes in question were self-imposed by the community. The Crown was not directly involved in the administration of taxes within the community, though it enforced the decisions of community officials. The dispute centered on the fairness of the distribution of a fixed tax burden within the community rather than the overall legitimacy of these taxes.

Responsum III:406—Avoidance of Exit Tax Through Marriage

The Saragossa community instituted the following tax ordinance or *takanah* (III:406):

> A Jewish taxpayer who marries off a daughter or sister **out of the city to any man who is not subject to our taxes**, shall be responsible to pay an exit tax equal to the amount the taxpayer would have owed upon their exit from the city to permanently emigrate to another location, as is written in the emigration document.

The Question

The ordinance stipulates an exit tax for marriages which take place out of the city. The question arose when a father married off his daughter *in Saragossa*, after which the newlyweds emigrated without paying the tax. The father contended that the ordinance applies only if the marriage took place out of the city. Meanwhile the community maintained that the *purpose* of the ordinance was to prevent capital flight through marriage, regardless of the wedding's location.

While the father's argument seems trivial and based on a technicality in the language (see bolded quotes above), precedence supported his argument. The father cited previous instances of weddings which took place in the city before the newlyweds emigrated. In none of these cases was an exit tax levied. In fact, the dowry exit-tax had only been applied once before, and in that case the wedding took place outside the city.

Rashba's Response

Rashba rules in favor of the taxpayer, but not because of the taxpayer's assertion that the technical language of the ordinance supports his position. Rashba makes it clear that absent precedence, he would have disregarded the technical reading of the ordinance. While the technical reading appears to limit the dowry exit-tax to weddings outside the city, Rashba dismisses this as a "silly" argument (דברי הבאי). Rashba considers that the object of the ordinance was to prevent capital flight, regardless of where the wedding actually took place. In the absence of precedence, it would have been silly to differentiate between an in-town wedding versus an out-of-town wedding, so long as the newlyweds emigrated eventually.

Rashba notes that precedence sheds light that seemingly sloppy language of the ordinance was in fact intentional in limiting its application to in-city weddings. Rashba ruled that the father is not responsible to pay the exit tax because the community intended to levy the tax directly on the newlyweds rather than on the father. If the wedding took place in the city, then the exit tax obligation falls on the newlyweds rather than the father.

Rashba concludes that community officials were at fault for not detaining and collecting the exit tax from newlyweds prior to their departure from the city. Rashba's language implies that the father is not only legally blameless but also morally blameless for the evasion of the exit tax by the newlyweds, as the responsibility of enforcement lies elsewhere.

Lessons

1. Letter or spirit?

Rashba ruled in favor of the taxpayer, but at the same time he notes that his ruling is not due to the mere technical reading of the ordinance. Rashba specifically notes that were it not for precedence which corroborated the technical reading, he would have disregarded the technical language and would have supported the community's position. Rashba ruled in favor of the father only because precedence revealed that the dowry-tax ordinance was intentionally drafted to exclude in-town weddings even if the newlyweds subsequently emigrated.

Rashba teaches that the tax ordinances should generally be applied based on their spirit and intent. The question is how to determine that spirit and intent. If the ordinance is new and no precedence exists in its application, then we logically deduce the intent based on the ordinance itself. If, however, the ordinance had been applied differently than its perceived intent, then we deduce the intent based on preceding rulings.

Rashba is explicit that intent is determined first and foremost based on precedence rather than the assumed intent of the authors of the ordinance (III:409).

2. Are unintended loopholes ethical?

While it might appear that the taxpayer (i.e., Reuven, the father) did not act in good faith, Rashba does not condemn his actions. In the opening arguments, the taxpayer did not defend his position in that he expected that the newlyweds will pay the tax, which is the basis for Rashba's ruling in the taxpayer's favor. Rather, the argument was based on a technical reading of the ordinance, and Rashba rejected this argument.

The taxpayer insisted that the technical language of the ordinance exempts him from the tax and that precedence supports his position. Rashba rules in favor of the taxpayer, but only because precedence supports his position. Rashba then creates a new argument in favor of the taxpayer, but not because of the mere technical reading of the ordinance. Rather, Rashba combines the language of the ordinance and precedence to recreate an alternative argument to exempt the taxpayer. Rashba reasons that the ordinance did indeed intend to exempt weddings that take place in the city, as community officials would then have recourse to the newlyweds' finances should they decide to later emigrate. The father did not actually expect the newlyweds to pay the tax, but Rashba does not admonish him for being a party to tax evasion.[7] Instead, Rashba rebukes community officials for failing to exercise their responsibilities to detain the newlyweds until they paid the exit tax.

This lesson, which may come across as somewhat provocative or controversial, is that if an ordinance provides for an exception or exemption, it is ethical for the taxpayer to take advantage of it even in ways that were not originally intended. It is not the taxpayer's responsibility to understand the intent of the ordinance and to arrange his affairs in such a way as to maximize revenue for the community treasury. If the ordinance provides for an intentional exemption, the taxpayer may apply it in any way, even if its application does not conform with original intent of the drafters.

To explain the last statement, Rashba established that the exemption for in-city weddings was intentional. However, the intent was to levy exit taxes on the newlyweds when they leave the city. In this case, the city

---

7   Rashba would go beyond deciding a case and would add moral instructions to litigants when appropriate. For example, see end of responsum IV:315: "and he must calm his mind to accept what his Jewish colleagues instruct him so as to safeguard the matter and for the sake of heaven."

officials failed to levy the exit tax upon the exit of the newlyweds. Ultimately, the exemption of the dowry tax for the father did not conform with the ultimate expectation that the newlyweds will pay an exit tax. Still, Rashba reserves his admonition to the community officials, not the taxpayer for taking unfair advantage of a valid exemption to the dowry tax.

3. Responsibility if another party to the transaction cheats on taxes

This question builds upon the previous one. Suppose a transaction is structured in such a way that the taxpayer has good reason to believe that a counterparty to the transaction will take advantage of its structure to engage in illegal tax evasion. Does the taxpayer have a responsibility to avoid the transaction? Does the taxpayer have a responsibility to prevent the counterparty from evading taxes?

Before answering these questions, a distinction should be made between two types of transactions. In the first type, a transaction is structured in such a way that its only *conceivable* purpose is for the counterparty to evade taxes. In the second type, the transaction has other legitimate business purpose but also provides an opportunity for the counterparty to evade taxes.[8] Our discussion is reserved for transaction of the second type. In transactions of the first type, it is apparent that the taxpayer is essentially an accessory to the counter-party's tax evasion.[9]

Using the same general reasoning we used to answer the previous (loophole) question, Rashba's position is that the taxpayer is not responsible when a counterparty takes advantage of the structure of a transaction to evade taxes. In our responsum, it is apparent that the taxpayer fully expected that the newlyweds would not pay the required exit tax. In fact, the taxpayer supports his position by citing precedents of such cases.

Rashba implies that there were legitimate reasons for the community to encourage in-city weddings, even if the newlyweds were contemplating a later exit. Rashba states that it is not the father's responsibility to ensure that the newlyweds pay their required taxes after the wedding. The father

---

[8] Following the IRS on tax ethics, I use avoidance to connote tax minimization within the scope of the law, and evasion to connote illegal tax minimization. Note that in a quote from Judge Learned Hand below, he uses "evade" in the same sense we use "avoid."

[9] For more on the distinction between the two transaction types, see
(1) Fischer, D., Friedman, H.H. Tone-at-the-Top Lessons from Abrahamic Justice. *Journal of Business Ethics* 156, 209–225 (2019).
(2) Avi-Yonah, R. (2008). Corporate social responsibility and strategic tax behavior. In W. Schön (Ed.), *Tax and corporate governance* (p. 183). Berlin: Springer.

is not responsible for tax compliance by the counterparties to a transaction. In this case, the transaction is the dowry, and the counterparty are the newlyweds.

While such an ethical position may not be consistent with altruistic notions such as *lifnim mishurat ha-din*, it does recognize the realities of financial life. It is unreasonable for tax authorities to expect taxpayers to deduce original intent of complicated tax ordinances. To the contrary, it is the responsibility of the tax authority to draft tax laws in a way that is consistent with their aims and intentions.

Corollaries in U.S. Tax Law—Judge Learned Hand

Learned Hand (1872–1961), is one of the most cited U.S. judges.[10] In his most famous case, *Helvering v. Gregory (1934),* Hand answers our <u>second</u> (loophole) question that it is ethical for a taxpayer to take advantage of an unintended loophole:

> … a transaction … does not lose its immunity, because it is actuated by a desire to avoid, or, if one choose, to evade, taxation. Anyone may so arrange his affairs that his taxes shall be as low as possible; **he is not bound to choose that pattern which will best pay the Treasury**; there is not even a patriotic duty to increase one's taxes. (Helvering v. Gregory, 69 F.2d 809, 2d Cir. 1934)

Hand's choice of words, bolded in the above quote, also suggests a negative answer to our <u>third</u> question (tax cheating by counterparties): so long as there is a legitimate business purpose for a transaction, the taxpayer need not worry if its structure may lead to a loss of revenue to the Treasury.

In *Helvering v. Gregory*, the taxpayer (Evelyn Gregory) created a corporation to which he transferred appreciated stock. The corporation then sold the appreciated stock, and the taxpayer dissolved the corporation. Based on tax laws at the time, the taxpayer argued that these transactions avoid the capital-gains tax that would have applied if the taxpayer had sold the stock directly. The Internal Revenue Service (IRS) commissioner (Guy Helvering) argued that the law did not intend to exempt such a transaction from capital gains.

Hand echoes his views in a later case:

---

10 Stone, Geoffrey R. *Perilous Times: Free Speech in Wartime from the Sedition Act of 1798 to the War on Terrorism.* New York: Norton, 2004, p. 200.

Over and over again courts have said that there is nothing sinister in so arranging one's affairs as to keep taxes as low as possible. Everybody does so, rich or poor; and all do right, for nobody owes any public duty to pay more than the law demands: taxes are enforced exactions, not voluntary contributions.[11]

Judge Learned Hand apparently shared Rashba's legal philosophy on tax policy and ethics. In *Helvering v. Gregory*, Judge Hand did ultimately rule in favor of the U.S. Treasury because of the tax doctrine of substance over form. In this part of the opinion, Hand echoes Rashba's answer to our first question (letter or spirit) that in the absence of precedence to the contrary, we read the tax code based on its presumed intent rather than its technical wording:

> Nevertheless, it does not follow that Congress meant to cover such a transaction, not even though the facts answer the dictionary definitions of each term used in the statutory definition. ... the meaning of a sentence may be more than that of the separate words, ... and no degree of particularity can ever obviate recourse to the setting in which all appear, and which all collectively create. (*Helvering v. Gregory*)

Conclusion

Among Rashba's many responsa, some address questions of community taxation to meet the fixed levies set on the community by the Crown. Due to its proximity to the Crown, the Saragossa Jewish community was subject to high, arbitrary taxes. Consequently, the community was forced to enact draconian tax ordinances to raise revenue from its members and to prevent capital flight to cities with lower tax burdens. These measures included an exit tax on assessed wealth. Furthermore, the community enacted an ordinance to tax dowries if the recipients marry out of the city. The question in responsum III:406 related to a dispute between the community and taxpayer Reuven, whose daughter married an out-of-towner *within* the city but then subsequently emigrated without paying the exit tax. The community sought to recover an exit tax from Reuven, who in turn argued that the technical language of the ordinance exempts weddings that take place in the city even if the newlyweds later departed.

Rashba dismisses the purely technical argument, but ultimately rules in the taxpayer's favor because of precedence in the application of the ordinance. Previously, the community had indeed distinguished between weddings that took place within the city and those that took place out of

---

11   *Commissioner of Internal Revenue v. Newman*, 159 F.2d 848 (2d Cir. 1947).

the city. In the case of in-city weddings the community had not previously levied an exit tax on the father. Rashba thus deduces that the intent of the ordinance was to delay the tax levy until such time as the newlyweds departed. Rashba did not fault the father for the failure of community officials to detain the newlyweds before they left the city.

We derive three lessons on tax ethics and policy. First, the tax code should be applied based on its spirit, as determined by the application of precedence. Second, a taxpayer is blameless for taking advantage of a valid loophole, even if the application of the loophole does not conform with the intent of the drafters of the tax code. Third, a taxpayer is blameless when another party to a transaction engages in inappropriate tax evasion. This is the case even if the structure of the transaction contributed to the evasion so long as the transaction is not purely a tax evasion scheme. In the early 20th century, U.S. Judge Learned Hand reached similar conclusions on tax policy and ethics.

Responsum III:406 (Machon Yerushalyim, 1997) follows.

הרשב"א   שו"ת   ח"ג סימן תד—תו   רכ

אותן או מקילין מעליהם זמן כדי שיקבעו דירתן שם, ואדרבה
אין עושין כן אלא כדי שיקבעו דירתן עמהם ויהיה שותף
עמהם לסבול עול המס והמשׂחרורות מאותו זמן ואילך.

סימן תה
סרקוסטה

שאלתם ראובן שמעון לוי ויהודה היו דרים עם קהל
סרקוסטה ורצו להעתיק דירתם משם ולדור בקהל
אחר, ובאו לחשבון עם הקהל ופרעו כל חלקם בכל המסין
וההולאות והמוטות שנתחייבו הקהל עד היום ההוא, ועשו
להם הקהל שטר הודאה ופטרו מהכל והכל בידם להם. ועכשיו
נתחדש עניין שלוה המלך לכל עמי הארץ להשיב כל ריבית
שלקחו משום אדם, וכבא מלמו הוליאו הקהל סך ממון מיד
העטו"ס, ועכשיו באו ראובן ושמעון ותבעו מן הקהל לתת
להם חלקם מאותו ריבית שהחזירו להם העטו"ס, לפי שהם
פרעו חלקם מן כשהיו דרים עמהם כשנתחייבו עלמם מהם.
השיב הקהל שאינם חייבים שזה כענין מלאיתו הוא, שלא עלה
זה על דעת שום אדם. ועוד שמיים שנעשם מה משם הניעו
לקהל כמה הפסדים וההולאות ורביות מהמוטות שנתחייבו
עליהם ונפטרו הם מהם, והוחיל ולינם חייבים מזוק אין זין
בשם. וראובן ושמעון טענו שממחמת הרעים שפרעו הם כמו
שטענו הוליאו הקהל מה שהוליאו, הדין עם מי.

תשובה דברים ברורים אני רואה כאן שהדין עם אותן
ראובן ושמעון, שריבים זה בין שהשיבו אותו
העטו"ס מדעתם בין שהשיבאו בעל כרחם לא מלאיה היא זו
אלא שפשוט הריבית וסען השבת גזלה, ולמי מסלמין לאשר
גזל ולמקום שנטלו הם מחזירין, ואפילו גם חובם מן הקהל
נגמרי עוד מחמשבן עמהם ומחזירין מה שכבר גט וכבר נפרע
נגמרי, שאלו לא היו חייבין להשיב אלא כמה שהיו חייבין
הקהל עדין וינכו להם מן החוב כנגד הרעית, בזה היה כדי
לטעות ולומר אין זה אלא כמחמשמך עם בעל חובו ומנכה לו
ממה שהוא חייב לו, אבל העטו"ס הללו שממחמירין ושלא
מדעתם לבא לגים החמשן, ואפילו על רעים חובם שנפרעו,
זה דמחשבנא גזלה היא זו, וכל הנגזלין ופורעגן ברוים להם
מחזירין וכולן נטלין בו לפי משטן, כזה נראה לי פשוט.

סימן תו
סרקוסטה

עוד שאלו, לפי שקלא מבני העיר היו מערימין ונעתקקים מן
העיר לגור במקום אחר ולא היו פורעין כמוטות וכל מה
שנתחייבו הקהל קודם מן העיר, הוליכו הקהל לעשות

מקנה על המעתיק מן העיר שיפרע חלקו קודם העתקתו מן
העיר בכל מה שנתחייבו הקהל קודם לכן, לפי שגם הוא
מחוייב כאחד מהם, חה נוסח הפרק ההוא מהמקנה הנזכרת
וכו', וכמו כן כתוב פרק אחר בתקנתם חייבי פורע הממ, חה
לשונו, כל בר ישראל או בת ישראל שישיא מולה לעיר הזאת
בנו או אחותו הוא על אותו סך שנתן עמה כאלו הוא וגם יבא
ונעתק מן העיר לקטע דירתו במקום אחר, כמו שנכתב
כמכתב ההעתקה, ע"כ. עכשיו ראובן השיא את בתו לעירו
לשמעון ושמעון לא היה כן עיר ראובן ונתן לו סך ממון
בנדוניא, ולפי שכתוב בתקנה הנזכרת שכל מי שישיא את בתו
מולה לעיר טוען החולק ד"ף י דלראובן חייב לפרוע מם בעד
סך הנדוניא שנתן לבתו לפי שהשיאה למי שאינו חייב לפרוע
מם עמנו בכל שנתחייבו הקהל קודם לכן עד עם הנישואין,
ואעפ"י שלא היו הנישואין מן לעיר וכלשון התקנה, דאמר
הכוונה אזלינן, ולפי שלא פרע שמעון הוא עבריין על החרם
ועל קנם אותה התקנה. וראובן אומר דכין שלא השיאה מן
לעיר כלשון התקנה אין בכך כלום, דעקר לשון התקנה
בנשואין י הוא על פי ואחר לשון התקנה אזלינן. ועד אמר
ראובן שמעון שעשו בעלו התקנה הנזכרת שים לו זמן ארוך השיאו
אנשים רבים אם בנותיהם לעיר הזאת לאנשים שלא היו מבני
העיר שלא פרע אחד מהם המס הנגבע ממנו עכשיו עד שלא
השיאו אותם מולה, אבל נמלא איש אחד שהשיא את אחותו
מולה לעיר ופרע מם בתוך הנדוניא כלשון התקנה, הודיענו
הדין עם מי.

תשובה נראה לי שהדין עם ראובן. וכדי שיתבאר הדין יפה
לפי דעתי אכתוב לכם קלא בארוכה, ואומר אני
שאלו היה הכל תלוי במה שפלליהם אותו, דהיינו במה שכתוב
בפרק מיקומי החיוני כל בר ישראל שישיא בנו או אחותו
מולה לעיר לשום אדם שאינו מחוייב לפרוע מם עמנו, חה
טוען לא היו הנישואין מן לעיר, מה קרוב בעיר לאמרו על
זה, שלשון המשיא מולה לעיר אין במשמע שיהיו הנישואין
ממש כלומר החופה מן לעיר, אלא אפילו ישאנה למי שימענה
עמו שיוליאמנה מן לעיר ולהוליכה עמו לעירו, שזה משיאה
מן לעיר אעפ"י שהחופה בתוך העיר, ואין הכונה מה
למכניסי לחופה בתוך העיר למכניסה מן לעיר, שאלו דברי
הבאי דמה הקפדה לקהל מה.

אלא שאני רואה שכונת העניין עד אחר יש לו, והוא שהקהל
רצו לחייב עלמם לפרוע כל אחד ואחד חלקו במה
שלו ונתחייבו הקהל אלא שאחר מה אחר החיוני לא אחר גוזיינא,
לי גם אלמנו נתחמשבנו מה מלד אל נד עד שממונו נגד החיוב

תה. ע"ע להלן חתו.   1 ציל וכשהשתיקו.   2 ציל הם.   3 ציל
שהשיבו.   4 נרצ"ל מהשבת.

תו. 1 אולי ר"ל דבר פשוט.   2 אפשר שצריך להוסיף, חוץ לעיר.
3 נרצ"ל לחלק בין מכניסה.

וקבעו אותו לחק,' והיולא חייב בכל מה שחייבין הקהל
והנכנס פטור, ולזה היה עקר פרק הסעמסקה, וכן עקר פרק
מקנת החוזרין, שכל מי שישיא בתו או אחותו חוזה לעיר
ממה שיחמיר במזוני המעמקין עצמו, לפי שהמשיאן ממש הך
לעיר לא נודע לקהל מה נתן ומה יוליך עמו החתן ונמנאו
הקהל מפסידין, שאין להם מה שיפפטו ומי שיעכב. אבל
המשיא בתוך העיר הקהל יכולין לעכב ביד החתן המטי אללא
שלא להטמיק משם סך ממון הנדוניא, דלא עדיף החתן
מגברא דאתי מחמתיה, והרי הוא נכנס מחה נתן הנדוניא,
והחתן שנכנס' במזיב וילא הנותן, וממוני הקהל שלא עכבוהו
ולא הפפישו ממון הנדוניא הם הפקידו על נפשם. ועל זה
נראה לי שלשון חך לעיר דוקא, שהכוונה טדלא נראית ק
כמו שאמרת, ועוד' אם זה מה שטען ראוון אם האמת כמו
שטען שמעשים רמים היו במי שהשיאו בתוך העיר ולא חייטם
הקהל ואחד השיא מן לעיר וחייטהו. ועוד שהטוען כנגד
ראוון בא להוליא, והמוליא מחבירו עליו שיש לו שני פנים
עליו הראיה.

Criminal Proceedings Against a Jew in a Non-Jewish Court for Get Refusal: The Effect on the Validity of the Get

By: A. YEHUDA WARBURG

Part 5 of the U.K. Serious Crime Act 2015, entitled "Protection of Children and Others," contains a section on Domestic Abuse. Article 76 of that section which came into force on December 29, 2015, addresses coercive control or controlling behavior in an intimate or family relationship.[1]

In other words, violence perpetrated towards a spouse is not limited to physical violence and emotional and verbal abuse. Violence towards a spouse is also characterized by the attempts of the abuser to control the wife and to limit her actions. Manifestation of control in general, and prevention of the formation of contacts outside the family, criticism of the way a wife dresses, prevention of access to financial information and demanding that she account for herself in particular, cause tension, shouting, cursing, and trading insults at a higher rate than that typical of couples who live together without violence.

Controlling relationships are defined by Professor Evan Stark, as quoted in an English judgment, as follows:[2]

> In coercive control, abusers deploy a range of non-consensual, non-reciprocal tactics, over an extended period to subjugate or dominate a partner, rather than merely to hurt them physically. Compliance is achieved by making victims afraid and denying basic rights, resources and liberties without which they are not able to effectively refuse, resist or escape demands that militate against their interests.

---

[1]   In light of the above legislation on February 21, 2022, for the first time a man who refused to give his wife a *get* (i.e., a writ of Jewish divorce) has been convicted on a charge of coercive control. Despite the threat that he would be sentenced to imprisonment, the husband refused to give his wife a *get* and on April 1, 2022, he was sentenced to be imprisoned for eighteen months.
    A similar legislative proposal (A347) is pending in front of the New York Standing Committee on Codes.

[2]   Regina v. Challen (2019), EW CA 916, Court of Appeal.

Rabbi A. Yehuda (Ronnie) Warburg is director and *dayan* of The International Beit Din, NY, and author of *Rabbinic Authority: The Vision and the Reality: Beit Din Decisions in English*, Vols. 1–5.

Insofar as an English court decides in a particular case that *get* (i.e., a writ of Jewish divorce) refusal constitutes an instance of coercive control on the part of the husband, and sentences him to a set period of imprisonment in accordance with the above legislation, does the criminal process against the *get* refuser affect the validity of the executed *get*? In other words, seemingly the threat of prosecution would result in a coerced *get*.

The question emerges: is the execution of a *get* under these conditions deemed halakhically a coerced *get*?

It is well known that if a husband gives his wife a *get* under coercion, the *get* is void.[3] Therefore, if he is imprisoned until he gives the *get*, and he gives it in order to secure his release from prison, the *get* is void.[4] Apparently, on the basis of the above, if the court in England sentences a person to prison due to a conviction for the criminal offense of coercive control vis-à-vis his spouse and he then gives the *get*, the *get* will be null due to the coercion! In other words, the Jewish husband and Jewish wife must consent to divorce. Consequently, if a husband gives his wife a *get* against his will in order to be released from imprisonment (i.e., coercion) or if *he was threatened to be imprisoned* and gives the *get* to avoid incarceration, the *get* is null.[5]

The question arises: Is there a halakhic (a Jewish legal) basis for compelling a *get* by means of a criminal process of a non-Jewish court?

In accordance with the Biblical passage (*Devarim* 24:1), "…he writes her a bill of divorce and gives it in her hand, and sends her out of his house," the *Mishnah* (the restatement of Yehudah ha-Nasi, redacted about 200 C.E.)[6] and the authorities[7] state that a man may not divorce his wife except of his own free will. It is clear that the *get* must be given with the

---

[3]   *Mishneh Torah, Hil. Gerushin* 1:1; *Shulḥan Arukh, Even ha-Ezer* 134:7. For additional authorities, see this writer's *Rabbinic Authority*, vol. 3, p. 30, note 11.

[4]   *Resp. Rashba* 2:276; *Resp. ha-Rivash* 232; *Resp. Mas'at Binyamin* 22. There is a *mesorah* that if a *beit din* threatened to imprison him or threatened to extradite him to the government where there is a fear they will imprison him and he gave the *get* to avoid incarceration, the *get* is null and void. See *Resp. ha-Rashba*, op. cit.; *Arukh ha-Shulḥan Even ha-Ezer* 134:22; *Resp. Rabbenu Bezalel Ashkenazy* 15.
      A fortiori (*kal ve-ḥomer*) if the government would threaten to prosecute him if he doesn't give a *get*.

[5]   *Gittin* 88b; *Shulḥan Arukh, Even ha-Ezer* 134:7; *Beit Shmuel*, ad. loc. 13; *Rashba*, supra n. 4; *Resp. Rabbenu Bezalel Ashkenazy* 15; *Arukh ha-Shulḥan Even ha-Ezer* 134:22.

[6]   *M. Yevamot* 13:1.

[7]   *Mishneh Torah, Hil. Gerushin* 1:1–2; *Rashbam, Bava Batra* 48a, s.v. *ve-ken atah omer*.

agreement of the spouse, and that a *get* that is given without the husband's volition is void.[8]

On the other hand, the *Mishnah* expounds:[9]

> A *get* compelled by a Jewish court is valid, but by [if he was compelled by] gentiles [it is] invalid. But with regard to the gentiles, they may beat him [at the request of the *beit din,* a rabbinical court] and say to him, Do what the Jews are telling you, and it is a valid [divorce].

And the *Talmud* (the *Mishnah* and the discussion of the *Mishnah* by the scholars of Babylonia) states:[10]

> And similarly you find [this *halakhah*-norm of Jewish law] with bills of divorce, [that when the Jewish court rules that he must divorce his wife] they coerce him until he says, I want [to divorce my wife]. [The *Talmud* rejects this proof as well]. But perhaps there it is different, because it is a *mitzvah* (a religious duty) to listen to the instruction of the Sages.

In other words, although under certain conditions the husband is compelled to give his wife a *get,* his consent to accept the judgment of a *beit din* is effective for the purpose of considering the *get* to have been given "of his own free will."

Maimonides's explanation is well known and incisive:[11]

> When a man whom the law requires to be compelled to divorce his wife does not desire to divorce her, the *beit din* should have him beaten until he consents, at which time they should have a *get* written. The *get* is acceptable. This applies at all times and in all places.
>
> Similarly, if gentiles beat him while telling him: "Do what the Jews are telling you to do," and the Jews have the gentiles apply pressure

---

8   There is a controversy amongst the decisors as to whether a coerced *get* is biblically or rabbinically invalid. According to the majority of authorities a coerced *get* is null and void. See this writer's *Rabbinic Authority,* vol. 3, p. 30, note 11. However, there is a minority opinion, that *be-diavad* (ex post facto) the execution of the *get* under duress is valid. See *Mishneh Torah, infra* n. 11; *Ḥiddushei ha-Ran, Bava Batra* 48a; *Resp. Be'er Yitzḥak, Even ha-Ezer* 1:10(3); *Resp. Ḥatam Sofer, Even ha-Ezer* 2:174; *Resp. Ma'aseh Ḥiyah* 24.

   On the other hand, according to biblical law, a woman may be divorced against her will. See *Tosefta Ketuvot* 12:3; *Gittin* 78a. As is known, in pursuance to Rabbenu Gershom's medieval enactment, a wife may be divorced only if she consents. See *Resp. Rosh* 42:1.

9   *M. Gittin* 9:8.

10   *Bava Batra* 48b.

11   *Mishneh Torah, Hil. Gerushin* 2:20.

upon him until [he consents] to divorce his wife, the divorce is acceptable…

Why is this *get* not void? For he is being compelled—either by Jews or by gentiles—[to divorce] against his will [and a *get* must be given voluntarily].

Since the concept of being compelled against one's will applies only when speaking about a person who is being coerced and forced to do something that the Torah does not obligate him to do, e.g., an individual who was beaten until he consented to a sale or to give a present. If, however, a person's evil inclination persuades him to negate [the observance of] a *mitzvah* or to commit a transgression, and he was beaten until he performed the action he was obligated to perform, or he disassociated himself from the forbidden behavior, he is not considered to have been forced against his will. On the contrary, it is he himself who is forcing [his own conduct to become debased]. With regard to this person who [outwardly] refuses to divorce [his wife]—he wants to be part of the Jewish people, and he wants to perform all the *mitzvoth* (religious duties) and eschew all the transgressions; it is only his evil inclination that persuades him. Therefore, when he is beaten until his [evil] inclination has been weakened, and he consents [to the divorce], he is considered to have executed the divorce willfully.

It is emphasized in Maimonides's ruling that in a case in which the husband is compelled to give his wife a *get*, he must say, "I want it." Even though there are circumstances in which the halakhic system allows for the *get* to be coerced,[12] succumbing to the pressure is halakhically construed as consent to give a *get*.[13]

In short, a *get* compelled by a *beit din* is valid, but compulsion of the *get* by a non-Jewish court is invalid.

In the event that the *beit din* ruled to compel the *get* in a particular case, does compulsion of the *get* by non-Jewish courts invalidate it? *Tur, Even ha-Ezer* 134 cites a medieval dispute between his father (the Rosh) and Ramah dealing with the law in the case of a non-Jewish court that compels a man to give a *get*, when the *beit din* did not state, "Do what the Jews are

---

[12]   *M. Ketuvot* 7:9–10.

[13]   And others concur with Maimonides's ruling. See *Tosafot, Bava Batra* 48a, s.v. *alima maha; Rashbam, Bava Batra* 48a, s.v. *dilma; Resp. Or Zarua* 754; Resp. *Maharaḥ Or Zarua* 126; *Resp. Tashbetz* 2:68; *Resp. Yakhin u-Boaz* 2:21; *Resp. Mabit* 1:76; *Resp. Ein Yitzḥak* 2:46; *Resp. Ḥavot Yair* 55; *Shulḥan Arukh, Ḥoshen Mishpat* 205:1. Compare *Ḥiddushei ha-Ramban, Yevamot* 53b, s.v. *ho de-amar Rabbah; Ḥiddushei ha-Ritva, Ketuvot* 64a; *Resp. Ridvaz* 4:1228; *Resp. Maharik, Shoresh* 63.

telling you." Under such circumstances, is the *get* valid or not? Tur expounds:

> If a *beit din* compels him through the non-Jewish court, and they say to him, Do what the *beit din* tells you, and they compel him, then the *get* is valid, and Ramah wrote that they must use those words, but if the non-Jews compel him and say to him, Give a *get*, even though they have been told by a *beit din* to compel him, the *get* is invalid. And it is unclear to my father, the Rosh, that because the *beit din* instructs the non-Jewish court to compel him, even if the non-Jewish court says, "Give a *get*," the *get* is valid.

The focus of the disagreement between the Rosh and Ramah is elucidated by Dayan Uriel Lavi, presiding *dayan* of the Jerusalem Beit Din:[14]

> Ramah and Rosh were in disagreement concerning a case in which a *beit din* ruled that the husband is compelled to divorce, and subsequently the non-Jewish court compelled him to give a *get* by virtue of their law, doing so independently, and not in order to comply with the ruling of a *beit din*. Ramah opines that since the non-Jewish court is not compelling the husband as an agent of the *beit din*, the *get* is invalid. According to the Rosh, however, because prior to the compulsion the *beit din* had already ruled that he is to be compelled to divorce (in accordance with Jewish law—AYW), then whoever enforces the compulsion, including the non-Jewish court, will be considered the long-arm of the *beit din*, even if they have not said as much.

To state it differently, according to Ramah it is possible for a non-Jewish court to enforce the ruling to compel the *get* issued by a *beit din*, on the condition that the former says, "Do what the Jewish court rules." On the other hand, according to Rosh, it is sufficient that the non-Jewish court compel, on its own initiative and unrelated to the judgment of the *beit din*, provided that the *beit din* handed down a decision to compel the *get*.[15]

---

14   File 622918, Jerusalem Regional Beit Din, 4 Sivan 5777.

15   The position of Rosh dovetails with the general principle in *Ḥoshen Mishpat* (the restatement of the Jewish law of commercial relations) that it is permissible to enforce a judgment issued by a *beit din* via a non-Jewish court. See *Resp. ha-Ḥadashot* 204; Tur, *Ḥoshen Mishpat* 2; *Drishah* ad. loc.; *Sefer Me'irat Einayim, Ḥoshen Mishpat* 26:5; *Beit Yosef, Ḥoshen Mishpat* citing *Sefer ha-Terumot*; *Resp. Ḥatam Sofer, Ḥoshen Mishpat* 3; *Bi'ur ha-Gra, Ḥoshen Mishpat* 26:2; *Resp. Maharsham* 1:89; *Resp. Ha-Elef Lekha Shelomo* 4, *Ḥoshen Mishpat* 3; *Resp. Beit Avi* 4:169; *Kovetz Teshuvot* 1:180; File no. 846913, Haifa Regional Beit Din, 18 Sivan 5777 citing Rabbis

R. Yosef Karo, author of the *Shulḥan Arukh* (a classic restatement of Halakhah) resolved the controversy in the following fashion:[16]

> And if the *beit din* compelled him through the Cuthites (Samaritans) and the Cuthites whip him and say, 'Do what the court (*beit din*— AYW) tells you,' it is considered as if the *beit din* compelled him.

From the plain language of R. Yosef Karo, it appears that his ruling is in consonance with Ramah's posture.[17] However, the glossators of the

---

Elyashiv and Shlomo Zalman Urbach. In other words, a *hekesh* (an analogy) may be drawn between the halakhah relating to divorce and the halakhah concerning a civil matter. In other words, regardless if a *beit din* ruling is handed down regarding a matter of ritual law or a monetary matter, we may utilize the services of a non-Jewish court to enforce the judgment. See *Beit Yosef, Ḥoshen Mishpat* ad loc.; *Bi'ur ha-Gra, Ḥoshen Mishpat* ad loc. Cf. *Resp. Be'er Yitzḥak, Even ha-Ezer* 10. To state it differently, Halakhah distinguishes between employing an agent regarding the performance of a religious obligation, concerning the performance of an undertaking (*kinyan*) or a sale where one requires an agent and agency for the purpose of enforcing a *beit din* ruling such as *get* enforcement which is viewed like "the act of a monkey" (*ma'aseh kof*). See *Shulḥan Arukh, Ḥoshen Mishpat* 188:1; *Resp. Ḥatam Sofer, Oraḥ Ḥayyim* 201; *Resp. Ḥelkat Yoav* 3; *Resp. Iggerot Moshe, Even ha-Ezer* 1:256; *Kefiyah be-Get*, p. 99. Regarding the former type of agency, a non-Jew cannot serve as an agent for a Jew. See *Gittin* 23b, *Kiddushin* 41b; *Responsa ha-Ritva* 39. On the other hand, the second type of agency may be employed by a non-Jew for a Jew.

Consequently, we therefore can understand why R. Maharil Diskin and R. Shmuel Gartner argue that formally speaking, the non-Jewish court does not serve as an agent for the *beit din*. See *Resp. Maharil Diskin, Pesaḥim* 52(5); *Kefiyah be-Get*, pp. 96–99.

Alternatively, there is the opinion that the woman is the agent of the *beit din*. See *Kefiyah be-Get*, pp. 85–86, n. 54. Since agency may be established by verbal agreement between the principal and the agent (see *Shulḥan Arukh, Ḥoshen Mishpat* 182:1), in our situation there ought to be communication between the *beit din* and the woman concerning directing the non-Jewish court to address *get* coercion in accordance with its laws.

Finally, as R. Meir Arik notes, the non-Jewish court addresses the matter upon its own initiative and in effect becomes the agent of the *beit din*. It is as *if* the *beit din* directs the court to coerce the husband to give a *get*.

See *Kefiyah be-Get*, p. 85. The implicit premise of this position is that the principal, namely the *beit din*, may authorize the court to be its agent in its absence. See *Shulḥan Arukh, Even ha-Ezer* 120.

16   *Shulḥan Arukh, Even ha-Ezer* 134:9.

17   This is also the opinion in *Resp. Rabbenu Bezalel Ashkenazy, supra* n. 4; *Resp. Rid* 55; *Resp. Rashbash* 339; *Resp. Oneg Yom Tov* 128 citing several *Rishonim* (early authorities).

Shulḥan Arukh understood that R. Karo was in fact ruling in accordance with Rosh, and that his mention of the declaration of the Cuthites was not necessarily the ruling he adopted.[18]

The emerging question is whether according to the approach of Rosh, every compulsion of a *get* carried out by the non-Jewish courts by virtue of their governing law (i.e., that *get* refusal is an example of coercive control) will be considered as compulsion on the part of the *beit din*.

A reply to this question may be found in the words of R. Joseph Feigenbaum, who decided in accordance with the opinion of Rosh:[19]

> It is clear… according to the words of Rosh and those who support his view, the *get* is not valid. This is because the civil authorities compel him to divorce; this is not due to the laws of Israel (Jewish law—AYW) but is rather in accordance with their own conventional state law.
>
> Based upon the foregoing, if a *beit din* compels the husband to give a *get* to his wife, the *get* is not valid if the non-Jewish court compels him to do so by virtue of their own laws. Said conclusion applies even if the non-Jewish court says, "Do what the Jewish court orders according to Jewish law" and any ensuing *get* is invalid.

Disagreeing with R. Feigenbaum's position is R. Meir Arik, author of *Resp. Imre Yosher* and *Minḥat Pittim*, who argues:[20]

> If the wife wants to be judged in a *beit din* in accordance with Halakhah… and the husband refuses to appear, nevertheless, *the beit din* may say to him that he is obligated to appear in *beit din*… and he will be coerced to give a *get* by a *beit din*… Surely, the *beit din* may designate the wife herself to be an agent, who will compel the husband through the non-Jewish courts, and in that case, the *get* would be valid because she is an agent of the *beit din*, and what she does is as if the *beit din* did it. Therefore, the *beit din* should issue a ruling that the matter be considered by the state court, and if what she says is true, he is obligated to divorce her, and it is valid because the state compulsion is due to the wife being an agent of the *beit din*.

R. Yaʿakov Shor concurred with R. Arik and stated the following:[21]

---

18   *Beit Shmuel, Even ha-Ezer* ad loc. 15; *Sema, Even ha-Ezer* 26:5. In contemporary times, R. Shmuel Tzvi Gartner is of the opinion that "the decisive majority of *Rishonim*" endorsed the view of the Rosh. See *Kefiyah be-Get*, pt. 14, p. 145.

19   *Kovetz Shaʿarei Torah*, pt. 3, *kuntres* 11:63, pp. 173 ff.

20   *Kovetz Shaʿarei Torah*, pt. 4, *kuntres* 15, pp. 25 ff.; *Kovetz Shaʿarei Torah*, pt. 4, 34:2, pp. 68ff.

21   *Kovetz Shaʿarei Torah*, pt. 4, 34, pp. 68ff.

It is clear to me that in fact, as long as the *beit din* orders that he must divorce his wife, and they warn him that if he does not comply they will allow the wife to sue him under their [non-Jewish] laws to force him to divorce her, then even though their compulsion is not by virtue of the orders of the *beit din,* but by virtue of conventional state law, the *get* is a valid compelled *get* under Jewish law, and it is acceptable *ab initio* as if he divorced her in a *beit din*… And if he is coerced by a *beit din,* [the *get*] is kosher.

In accordance with the position of R. Arik and R. Shor, together with the adoption of Rosh's approach, prior to proceeding to a non-Jewish court to have a *get* coerced in accordance with the norms of state law, a *beit din* must examine the case and arrive at a judgment that there are grounds to compel a *get* in pursuance to Halakhah.[22] Given that in the Diaspora, a *beit din* is legally and therefore halakhically unable to engage in *get* coercion,[23] a *beit din* must arrive at the conclusion that there are grounds for *get* coercion, issue a decision of obligating a *get,* and acknowledge that the court is resolving the matter in accordance to their law in general and their norms of coercion in particular.[24]

In light of our foregoing presentation and in accordance to Rosh and his adherents and the contemporary views of Rabbis Arik, Shor, Gartner, Liebes, Lavi, Tam, and Malka,[25] in order to eliminate the possibility that a *get* that is given due to a criminal proceeding in a non-Jewish court will be deemed a coerced *get* and therefore void, bringing charges against a *get* refuser ought to be pursued only in the cumulative circumstances as described below:

1. From a procedural point of view, a *beit din* is permitted to decide on a matter of divorce with the participation of both spouses or in the presence of a wife alone, on condition that the husband

---

22   File no. 622918/19, Jerusalem Regional Beit Din, 4 Sivan 5777 (R. Uriel Lavi's opinion) in the name of Rabbis Arik and Shor.

23   *Kefiyah be-Get* in the name of Rosh, *Ketzot ha-Ḥoshen, Netivot ha-Mishpat* and *Ḥatam Sofer*, pp. 99, 105, 108.

24   Implicit in said conclusion is that handing down of a judgment of obligating a *get* fails to run afoul of the strictures of a *get me'useh* (a coerced *get*). See *infra*, note 27. Our conclusion is reflective in the *get* enforcement decisions handed down by the Israeli *battei din* under the Chief Rabbinate. As aptly noted by Israel's Chief Rabbi, R. Yitzhak Yosef, if it is clear in a particular case where the authorities determine that there are grounds for a divorce, it is proper to direct the husband that he is obligated to give a *get*. See *Resp. ha-Rishon le-Tzion Even ha-Ezer* 17 (end).

25   See *supra* notes 20–21; *Kefiyah be-Get*, pt. 14, *Resp. Beit Avi* 14, 169:14; *supra* note 22.

was summoned to the *beit din* and refused to appear at the proceeding.[26]

---

[26] *Resp. Rashbash* 46; *Resp. Maharashdam ha-Ḥadashot, Zikhron Aharon* ed., 5775; *Resp. Ramah me-Fano* 86; *Resp. Mabit* 1:76, 2:138; *Resp. Lev Mavin, Even ha-Ezer* 130; Resp. *Mishpatim Yesharim* 1:436; *Resp. Maharsham* 6:161; *Resp. Avnei Nezer, Even ha-Ezer* 238; R. Yo'ezer Ariel, *Laws of Arbitraton* (Heb.), p. 302; R. Dr. Eliav Shochetman, *Procedure in the Rabbinical Courts* (2 ed., Heb.) pp. 521–522; R. Abraham Debaremdiker, *Book of Procedure* (Heb.) 1:59; this writer's *Rabbinic Authority*, vol. 4, p. 216, note 2. Cf. the opinion of Rabbis Elyashiv and U. Lavi who contend that the convening of a *beit din* proceeding for matters of marriage and divorce require the presence of both parties. See R. Gartner, *Kefiyah be-Get, Introduction; Kovetz Teshuvot* 1:181, 3:202; File no. 865704/1, Safed Regional Beit Din, 12 Iyar 5777. A review of the above rulings will demonstrate that we can conduct a hearing in the absence of a husband for two reasons. First, in a matter of personal status (*ishut*), we may convene a hearing in the absence of a party. Secondly, in a situation of *igun*, we may conduct a *beit din* proceeding in the absence of the husband. See R. Lavi, *Resp. Ateret Devorah* 3:87.

Furthermore, in the absence of the husband at a hearing, a *beit din* may hear the submission of evidence by witnesses insofar as it relates to matters of personal status. See *Resp. Ohalei Ya'akov* 27 in the name of Meiri and Ridvaz; *Resp. ha-Rivash ha-Ḥadashot* 14 in the name of Ramah; *Resp. ha-Rashba* 4:200; *Resp. Tashbetz* 2:19; *Resp. ha-Rashbash* 46, 287; *Resp. Maharshal* 33; *Resp. ha-Ridvaz* 70; *Resp. Avnei Nezer Even ha-Ezer* 30, 123, 124; *Resp. Noda be-Yehudah, Mahadura Kamma, Even ha-Ezer* 72 (Cf. with no. 92); *Resp. Karnei Reim* 1:4; *Yeshuot Ya'akov Even ha-Ezer* 42; *Resp. Ḥelkat Ya'akov, Even ha-Ezer* 1:4; *Resp. Ḥatam Sofer, Even ha-Ezer* 1:84; *Resp. ha-Maharnah* 1:68; *PDR* 6, 266, 281.

In the event that one deals with an *agunah*, the situation characterized as "an hour of emergency" and as such is halakhically viewed ex post facto and therefore, evidence in matters related to personal status may be submitted in the absence of the husband. See Maharnah, op. cit.

Cf. *Rema, Shulḥan Arukh Even ha-Ezer* 11:4, *Ḥoshen Mishpat* 28:15; *Resp. ha-Rema* 17; *Beit Shmuel, Shulḥan Arukh, Even ha-Ezer* 11:16; *Resp. Maharshal* 11; *Resp. Mas'at Binyamin* 106; *Resp. Panim Meirot* 1, *Even ha-Ezer* 104; *Resp. Maharashdam Even ha-Ezer* 21, 27; *Resp. R. Akiva Eiger* 99. For further discussion, see S. Shilo, "Testimony in the Absence of a Party in Matrimonial Matters," (Hebrew) 5 *Shenaton Ha-Mishpat ha-Ivri* 321 (1978).

Whether it is essential to turn to a *beit din* or whether a scholar(s) who is an expert in *Even ha-Ezer* and *Ḥoshen Mishpat* may issue a ruling regarding marriage and divorce such as coercing and obligating a *get* is subject to debate amongst the authorities. See *Yam Shel Shelomo, Bava Kamma* 3:9; *Ketzot ha-Ḥoshen* 3:1–2; *Netivot ha-Mishpat, Ḥoshen Mishpat* 3:1; *Resp. Yehudah* (Gordin), *Even ha-Ezer* 51:2; *Resp. Ma'aseh Ḥiya* 24; *Resp. Ḥatam Sofer, Even ha-Ezer* 2:64–65, *Ḥoshen Mishpat* 177; *Resp. Avnei Nezer, Even ha-Ezer* 167:1; R. Z.N. Goldberg, *Lev Mishpat* 1:149–150; this writer's *Rabbinic Authority*, vol. 5, p. 232, note 1.

2. The lack of authority of rabbinical courts in the Diaspora does not prevent the *beit din* from arguing on theoretical grounds that there is a basis for coercing a *get*. In other words, a precondition for submitting a claim to civil court is contingent upon the beit din in the Diaspora arriving at the conclusion that there are grounds to coerce a *get*, issue a decision of obligating a *get* and acknowledge that the court will follow their law is general and their norms of coercion in particular. Given the legal and therefore halakhic impossibility to coerce a *get* in the Diaspora, the second precondition for submitting a claim to civil court is contingent upon the *beit din* in the Diaspora arriving at the conclusion that there are grounds to obligate a *get*.[27]
3. Assuming the above conditions have been obtained, if the husband gave the *get* in order to prevent an incarceration under the above law, the *get* is valid.

---

27 In the Diaspora where, generally speaking, rabbinical courts refrain from issuing a ruling of obligating the giving of a *get*, our presentation demonstrates the significance of a *beit din*'s acute need to issue this type of ruling in order to address the plight of the *agunah* who is seeking relief via the services of a non-Jewish court.

There is a minority of authorities who argue that rendering a judgment to obligate the giving of a *get*, similar to coercing a *get*, runs afoul of the strictures of a coerced *get* (a *get me'useh*). See *Ḥazon Ish EH* 99:2; *Teshuvot Yabia Omer* 2 *EH* 10; R, Shimshon S. Karelitz, *Teshuvot Ateret Shlomo* 1:32 (6) in the name of Rashba and Rivash; *Piskei Din Rabbanayim* (hereafter: PDR) 7:201, 204 (Rabbi Elyashiv in the name of Rosh); File no. 8211227/2, Jerusalem Regional Beit Din, December 12, 2013; File no. 1083672/1, Haifa Regional Beit Din, January 25, 2018.

However, the majority of authorities including but not limited to the majority of the Israeli rabbinical courts under the network of Israel's Chief Rabbinate issue decisions of obligating a *get*. Consequently, the rabbinical courts in the Diaspora should follow the procedure adopted by the above Israeli rabbinical courts as well as by numerous decisors. See *Tosafot, Ketubot 70a*, s.v. *yotzi* in the name of Rabbeinu Ḥananel; *Tosafot, Yevamot 64a*, s.v. *yotzi*; *Piskei ha-Rosh, Yevamot* 6:11; *Resp. Maharam of Rothenberg*, Prague ed., 946; *Ḥiddushei ha-Ran, Ketubot 77a*; *Resp. ha-Rashba* 7:477; *Resp. ha-Rivash* 127; *Resp. Tashbetz* 2:68; *Semag, Positive Mitzvah* 48 (end); *Ḥiddushei ha-Ritva, Ketubot 77a*; *Tur and Beit Yosef, Even ha-Ezer* 70, 154; *Shulḥan Arukh, Even ha-Ezer* 70:3, 154:3, 21; *Rema, Yoreh De'ah* 228:20, *Even ha-Ezer* 154:21; *Arukh ha-Shulḥan, Even ha-Ezer* 154:20; Shakh, *Gevurat Anashim* 29; *Pitḥei Teshuvah, Even ha-Ezer* 154:15; *Resp. Maharit* 1:113; *Resp. Noda be-Yehudah, Mahadura Tinyana* 90; *Resp. Nosei ha-Ephod* 32:18; *PDR* 1:141 (R. Elyashiv's opinion). See further, this writer's *Rabbinic Authority*, vol. 5, pp. 306–324.

In light of the above, on one hand, should a non-Jewish court work without the assistance of a *beit din*, the resulting execution of a *get* under these conditions would be invalid.[28] On the other hand, should the non-Jewish court operate according to their law, then any ensuing *get* is valid.[29]

To state it differently, a judgment issued by a *beit din* together with enforcement through the initiation of a criminal process in the English courts may save Jewish women living there from the state of *igun* (a chained woman in marriage) and may prevent serious violations of Halakhah pertaining to married women as well as preventing the proliferation of *mamzerim* (bastards under Halakhah) in our community.

May Hashem (God) save us!

---

[28]   *Mishneh Torah, supra* n. 11; *Tur, Even ha-Ezer* 134; *Shulḥan Arukh, Even ha-Ezer* 134:5.

[29]   See *Tur, Even ha-Ezer* 134; *supra* text accompanying notes 14, 20–21.

Addendum 1

A new law on coercive control (California Family Code 6320) became effective on January 1, 2021. According to the new law, among the remedies available to victims of domestic violence is that the courts may consider such behavior as a factor in determining child custody and visitation privileges as well as calculating the amount and duration of spousal support.[30] Prior to a court's determination that *get* recalcitrance is an example of coercive control; a *beit din* must have ruled that in theory the circumstances dictate that a *get* ought to be coerced. However, in practice, given that legally and therefore halakhically the imposition of *get* coercion is an impossibility, the *beit din* must have handed down a ruling that the husband is obligated to give a *get* and acknowledge that the court is following their law. In effect, with the existence of such a rabbinic judgment, a civil court order will not impact the integrity of any subsequent execution of a *get*. See R. Tobol, *Resp. Mar'ot Yesharim* 29. As we explained earlier, in effect the civil court is serving as a *shaliach,* an agent of the *beit din*. For further discussion, see *Kefiyah be-Get, supra* note 18, pp. 85, 87, 99–100.

Finally, whereas we are dealing with the halakhic validity of *get* coercion by a non-Jewish court, the NY *Get* Law stated that the party initiating a divorce proceeding in the civil courts must certify that he or she has removed any "barrier to remarriage" as defined in that law. However, this statute is limited, for it only withholds a civil divorce but cannot compel a *get*. As such, we have refrained from examining the NY *Get* Law in our presentation.

---

[30] Prior to adjudicating matters of spousal support, child support and parenting arrangements in a non-Jewish court, one is required to receive *"heter arkha'ot,"* permission to proceed to non-Jewish court to deliberate end-of-marriage issues. Whether one must receive halakhic permission from a *beit din* or whether a *hora'ah* (an instruction) of a scholar who is an expert in *Even ha-Ezer* and *Ḥoshen Mishpat* suffices in order to be permitted to litigate in a non-Jewish court is subject to debate. See *Shulḥan Arukh, Ḥoshen Mishpat* 26:2; *Resp. Maharil Diskin* 13; *Resp. Shevet ha-Levi* 4:183. See further, this writer's *Rabbinic Authority*, vol. 1, p. 154, note 160.

Addendum 2

Below is a sample *beit din* decision which can serves as a vehicle for a wife to file a claim pursuant to the coercive control legislation without running afoul of the strictures of a coerced *get*.

Avraham v. Miriam

Facts of the case

Avraham and Miriam were married on July 3, 2001. Since October 2018 the couple has been separated. To date, Avraham refuses to give Miriam a *get*. We convened a hearing with the parties.

Discussion

Based upon information submitted at the hearing, there are no prospects for *shalom bayit*, marital reconciliation. Given that Avraham and Miriam have been separated for more than 18 months, Avraham is obligated to give a *get* to Miriam. R. Pelaggi, a renowned Sephardic authority, rules:

> In general, … when *Beit Din* realizes that they are separated for a long time and there is no way… we have to make an effort to separate them from each other and he should give a *get* in order that they not sin grievously… And my time frame, in case of dispute [between] wife and husband… and 18 months have passed… *Beit Din*… should force him to give a divorce…

We concur with R. Pelaggi, that there are grounds to coerce a *get* (see also *Piskei Din Rabbaniyim* 9:145, 152). However, in contemporary times in the Diaspora we cannot coerce a *get*. **Therefore, we obligate Avraham to give a *get* immediately.** See also *Iggerot Moshe, Yoreh De'ah* 4:15(2).

Should Miriam file a claim against *get* recalcitrance as an example of coercive control in marriage under English law, in accordance to Rabbi Meir Arik, Rabbi Yaakov Shor and others, we acknowledge that the court in general is following their law and their norms of coercion in particular, and the ensuing *get* will be valid. See *Kovetz Sha'arei Torah*, Section 4, *Kuntres* 15, 34, pp. 69ff: File no. 622918/19, Jerusalem Regional Beit Din, May 29, 2017; File no. 846913/2, Haifa Regional Beit Din, June 12, 2017. ❧

Solomonic Wisdom vs. the Letter of the Law: A Midrashic Reading

By: SHLOMO ZUCKIER

Shemot Rabbah, in its opening to *parashat Va'era*, offers a beautiful meditation on the law: the letter of the law, the spirit of the law, and the laws of nature. In exploring that midrashic passage, I will first engage its rich intertextual, literary account of an error made by Shlomo ha-Melekh, and then consider what the broader polemical point of the midrash might be.

Unexpectedly, this midrash appears in the context of God's first revelation to Moshe with His true name, in *Shemot* 6:2.

וידבר אלקים אל משה ויאמר אליו אני ה', וארא אל אברהם אל יצחק, הה"ד
(קהלת ב) ופניתי אני לראות חכמה והוללות וסכלות כי מה האדם שיבא אחרי
המלך את אשר כבר עשוהו.

As *midrashim* often do, this midrash begins by citing a verse from elsewhere in Tanakh, which will be brought into conversation with the *parashah* by the end.[1]

Our midrash engages a verse narrating the long journey of Kohelet, where he turns to find "wisdom, madness, and stupidity; for which person can come after the king, after they [the king] already acted?" (Eccl. 2:12)

---

[1] This opening style is the opposite of the standard (and somewhat dull) sermonic opening line, "in this week's *parashah*." *Ḥazal* often go out of their way to start *not* in this week's *parashah* but elsewhere, in order to demonstrate the interconnectedness of Torah and to build anticipation for how the verses connect.

Shlomo Zuckier, a Research Associate at the Institute for Advanced Study in Princeton and a *musmach* of RIETS, recently completed studies in YU's Kollel Elyon and earned a PhD in Religious Studies at Yale University. Shlomo is a founder of *The Lehrhaus*, as well as a former director of OU-JLIC at Yale University, and has taught at Yale Divinity School, Yeshiva University (YC and Revel), and Touro's Graduate School of Jewish Studies. Shlomo has held the Flegg Postdoctoral Fellowship in Jewish Studies at McGill University, a research fellowship at the Notre Dame Center for Philosophy of Religion, the MFJC Advanced Torah Fellowship, and the Wexner and Tikvah Fellowships. He serves on the editorial committee of *Tradition*, and has edited two books on contemporary Jewish theology.

The verse's overall meaning is obscure, and it is especially confusing how these three categories—wisdom, madness, and stupidity—are conflated as areas of study, only to be rejected. Presumably, it would be reasonable to distinguish between them: to value wisdom and to reject madness and stupidity. Instead, Kohelet rejects them all, the reason being that it is not a person's place to reject that which the king already carried out. This obscure verse is the starting point and basis of this midrash's exegesis.

הפסוק הזה נאמר על שלמה ועל משה.

The midrash announces that it will offer two interpretations of this verse, one regarding Shlomo[2] and the other Moshe. Of course, the connection to *parashat Va'era*, involving Moshe, is reserved for last, in order to hold the audience in suspense for longer before returning to the *parashah*.

על שלמה כיצד כשנתן הקדוש ברוך הוא תורה לישראל נתן בה מצות עשה ומצות לא תעשה ונתן למלך מקצת מצות שנא' (דברים יז) לא ירבה לו סוסים וכסף וזהב וגו', ולא ירבה לו נשים ולא יסור לבבו, עמד שלמה המלך והחכים על גזירתו של הקדוש ברוך הוא ואמר למה למה אמר הקדוש ברוך הוא לא ירבה לו נשים לא בשביל שלא יסור לבבו אני ארבה ולבי לא יסור.

The king in this sense is a microcosm of the Jewish People. Just as the Jewish People received both positive and negative commandments, the king was given a focused subset of commandments as well (although they were primarily negative): not to increase his horses or wealth and not to have too many wives.

Shlomo ha-Melekh, however, thought that he could outsmart God's decree. Invoking the *ta'ama di-kra*, he reasoned that if the only problem with multiplying wives was that the king's heart would go astray, if he knew for certain that he would *not* veer from the proper path there would be no problem marrying multiple wives.

This presumption, and presumptuousness, that he would be exempt from the prohibition against marrying multiple wives "angered the *yud*" in the word ירבה, as the story continues:

אמרו רבותינו באותה שעה עלתה יו"ד שבירבה ונשתטחה לפני הקדוש ברוך הוא ואמרה רבון העולמים לא כך אמרת אין אות בטלה מן התורה לעולם, הרי שלמה עומד ומבטל אותי ושמא היום יבטל אחת ולמחר אחרת עד שתתבטל כל התורה

2   It is worth noting that there are several versions of this story about what Shlomo ha-Melekh got wrong and why, including a prominent one at *Yerushalmi Sanhedrin* 2:6. See also b.*Shab* 56b. The goal of this paper is to present a close reading of the midrash at hand, rather than to compare the versions of this teaching.

כולה, אמר לה הקדוש ברוך הוא שלמה ואלף כיוצא בו יהיו בטלין וקוצה ממך
איני מבטל.

The interplay in this passage features the relationship between the spirit and the letter of the law, in both of the latter's senses. First, Shlomo's rejection of the letter of the law in light of its spirit, his presuming to reject a consequentialist law given his self-assessed imperviousness to those consequences. But second of all, the *literal* letter of the law, the *yud*, is the one so offended that it goes knocking on Heaven's door with claims against King Shlomo. By presuming that the law did not apply to him, he was not only ignoring a law, but was effectively *erasing* that law from the Torah. Thus, Shlomo's offense was not only against the letter of the law as practiced, but also the *physical* letter of the law as it appears in the Torah. The midrash says that Shlomo attempted to outsmart God's *gezerah*, His decree. A *gezerah* is absolute as it represents a categorical, inflexible form of law; furthermore, it can also refer to a literal *gezerah*, something that is cut and chiseled—a letter! The fixedness of this teaching is reflected not only in the nature of the law but in the nature of the writing as well, the physical manifestation of the law etched into parchment (if not stone).

It is worth noting here the prevalence of the "slippery slope" argument, in different forms, as the Midrash extends the scope of this worry as well, as the *gezerah* is meant to forestall unexpected and unseemly consequences. The Torah expresses a concern that if the king has too many wives it will lead his heart astray, even if he is unconcerned. The Midrash commenting on this story raises the fear that erasing one letter of the Torah will lead to erasing the whole Torah, even if Shlomo is not worried in this vein. Following the rule, even if does not seem applicable, avoids these problems.

Why, of all letters, is it the *yud* that complains before God?[3] Some commentaries point out that, when added to the root ר.ב.ה, and accompanied by a negation, the *yud* provides imperative prohibitive force to the verb. Additionally, we could argue that, in subverting the Biblical command of לא ירבה with his own assertion that אני ארבה, Shlomo effectively erases the *yud*, replacing it with an *alef*. While this is true, the *yud* also symbolizes something else. As God says, a great king like Shlomo and a thousand more like him (note the resonance with האלף לך שלמה at *Shir ha-Shirim* 8:12) can be undone before God is willing to undo a *kotza*, a jot, a

---

3   There is a wonderful pun here, as the letter *yud* asks God why, if God committed not to erase letters, "you are erasing me." The word "me," אותי, could literally be translated as "my letter," or "my *ot*," a double entendre facilitated by granting speech to letters.

yud, from His Torah. It is precisely the fact that the *yud* is the smallest and most minor letter that makes the message of God's unwillingness to modify any letter of the law all the more powerful. Although kings may seem formidable in this world, representing actual power, and a minor *yud* and the mere, slippery slope argument it represents, seems much weaker, at best representing potentiality, God makes it clear that this is an incorrect assessment of reality. The Divine unbreakable word can never be undone, and the smallest letter from God outweighs the greatest human monarch. The letter of the law, both in the pure Halakhic rules without recourse to *ta'ama di-kra* and in the sense of *ot aḥat min ha-Torah*, will never be abrogated.

And thus, mighty Shlomo, for rejecting but a *yud*, faces the full force of the God's wrath.

ומנין שבטל אותה מן התורה וחזר לתורה שנאמר (בראשית יז) שרי אשתך לא תקרא שמה שרי כי שרה שמה, והיכן חזר (במדבר יג) ויקרא משה להושע בן נון יהושע.

We have proof that letters of the Torah, even the minor *yud*, cannot be erased. Even where a *yud* seems to disappear, such as with the shift from Sarai to Sarah, it simply reappears later in Yehoshua's reinforced name. And just to make the message clearer, the shift from Hoshea to Yehoshua introduces a theonym as Hoshea expands into *Ya-h yoshi'akha*, the Lord will save you, the erased *yud* preserved through Yehoshua. The Torah's *yud* will always be protected. But what about Shlomo?

ושלמה שהרהר לבטל אות מן התורה, מה כתיב בו (משלי ל) דברי אגור בן יקא, שאיגר דברי תורה והקיאן, נאם הגבר לאיתיאל, דבר זה שאמר הקדוש ברוך הוא לא ירבה לו נשים לא אמר לו אלא בשביל לא יסור לבבו, לאיתיאל שאמר אתי אל ואוכל, מה כתיב ביה (מ"א =מלכים א'= יא) ויהי לעת זקנת שלמה נשיו הטו את לבבו, אמר רשב"י נוח לו לשלמה שיהא גורף ביבין שלא נכתב עליו המקרא הזה.

For his thought to delete a letter from the Torah, Shlomo is not only expelled from his position (see *Gittin* 68) but is also insulted in his very own *Mishlei* 30:1. He is referred to as Agur ben Yakeh, understood as one who gathers words of Torah, only to spit them out. This describes Shlomo's failure to properly internalize the Divine command, and his preference to interpret it according to his own whims instead, and thus spitting out not just a *yud* but the law's application to his life as well. This was done with the false confidence of the one who hears the Divine word (נאם הגבר where God is the "גבר") of the prohibition and presumptuously responds איתי אל ואוכל, "God is with me and I will succeed," as that verse ends.

Damningly, Shlomo's greatest embarrassment, worse than being engrossed in the sewage cleaning business (where he might have come across the words of Torah he spat up), is the revelation that, in the end, his many wives did sway his heart away from God, giving the lie to the very confidence he placed in himself.

The rejection of Shlomo's path is thus double. First, he is incorrect for rejecting the Divine word, reasoning that it is inapplicable to him. Rejecting the letter of the Divine law is wrong in itself. Here, however, the midrash reveals another aspect to Shlomo's error. His very logic as to why the law should not apply in his case was disproven. Shlomo's insistence that he would never be led astray—used to "permit" his overly polygynous ways—was itself what did lead him astray in the end.

In fact, the midrash's formulation of Shlomo's original claim— אני ארבה ולבי לא יסור—is the bridge between *Devarim*'s prohibition— ולא ירבה נשיו הטו את לבבו—and Shlomo's ultimate failure—לו נשים ולא יסור לבבו. This formulation draws out what the verses already indicate, namely Shlomo's inability to appreciate that the "slippery slope" argument applies to the supremely wise Shlomo as much as to anyone else, and maybe even most of all. Far from being the exception to the rule, Shlomo becomes the very cautionary tale against kings having too many wives.

The verse in *Mishlei* 30 is invoked not only because of the brilliant wordplay regarding one who takes in Torah but spits some of it out, who hears the charge of the Divine גבר and presumes he can ignore it and succeed. The context in that chapter is also deeply connected to the very topic that the midrash is explicating.

The continuation features a sharp, flagellatory self-critique (*Mishlei* 30:2–3):

כִּי בַעַר אָנֹכִי מֵאִישׁ וְלֹא־בִינַת אָדָם לִי
וְלֹא־לָמַדְתִּי חָכְמָה וְדַעַת קְדֹשִׁים אֵדָע

The speaker (Shlomo, as the midrash tells us) calls himself a brute rather than a man, lacking basic human wisdom (בינה). He failed to learn wisdom (חכמה), lacking the knowledge (דעת) of the holy ones.

With the invocation of this passage about how Shlomo (in *Mishlei*, as Agur ben Yakeh-Itiel) fails to achieve חכמה ודעת, wisdom and knowledge, the midrash can return to its opening verse,[4] Shlomo's depiction (in his

---

4   This midrash appears to be conflating two different verses in *Kohelet*. While the citation at the beginning of the piece was that of וּפָנִיתִי אֲנִי לִרְאוֹת חָכְמָה וְהוֹלֵלוֹת וְסִכְלוּת, i.e., Eccl. 2:12, the citation here incorporates the word דעת, following Eccl. 1:17 (וָאֶתְּנָה לִבִּי לָדַעַת חָכְמָה וְדַעַת הוֹלֵלוֹת וְשִׂכְלוּת), while retaining the opening

Kohelet persona) of his failed attempt to achieve חכמה ודעת, wisdom and knowledge:

ולכך אמר שלמה על עצמו (קהלת ב) ופניתי אני לראות חכמה ודעת הוללות
וסכלות, אמר שלמה מה שהייתי מחכים על דברי תורה והייתי מראה לעצמי שאני
יודע דעת התורה ואותו הבינה ואותו הדעת של הוללות וסכלות היו.

Shlomo ha-Melekh's incorrect interpretation of the prohibition against monarchic polygyny is the failed attempt at wisdom and knowledge hinted at in this verse. The midrash here resolves the tension between the positive חכמה and דעת, on the one hand, and the negative הוללות וסכלות on the other. In fact, this was not true wisdom (חכמה) but rather an attempt to outsmart the Torah (מחכים על דברי תורה); this was not true knowledge (דעת) but a false self-impression of knowledge (הייתי מראה לעצמי שאני יודע). In truth, this "knowledge" was nothing more than a knowledge of madness and folly (אותו הדעת של הוללות וסכלות היו). This tension fits our case perfectly, as Shlomo adopted madness and folly, which presented itself under the guise of wisdom and knowledge.

What was the cause of his error? As noted above, Shlomo failed in multiple ways when he rejected this law by presuming its inapplicability to his situation. First, generally speaking, one must follow the letter of the law and not invoke the טעמא דקרא,[5] the reason or spirit of the law, in rejecting it. Second, one cannot reject the textual letter of God's law, the *yud*, and doing so has dire consequences. Third, the entire attempt was based on overconfidence and a failure by Shlomo to estimate his own character, as is demonstrated by his ultimate downfall.

The midrash adds another cause of Shlomo's error, one that is hiding in plain sight, in *Mishlei* 2:12:

למה כי מה האדם שיבא אחרי המלך את אשר כבר עשוהו, מי הוא שיהיה רשאי
להרהר אחר מדותיו וגזרותיו של ממ"ה הקדוש ברוך הוא דברים אשר הם חצובים
מלפניו, שכל דבר ודבר שיוצא מלפניו טרם הוא נמלך בפמליא של מעלה ומודיע
להם הדבר כדי שידעו ויעידו כולן כי דינו דין אמת וגזירותיו אמת וכל דבריו
בהשכל, וכה"א (משלי ל) כל אמרת אלוה צרופה ואומר (דניאל ד) בגזירת עירין
פתגמא שלפי שהרהרתי אחר מעשיו נכשלתי.

---

of ופניתי אני from 2:12. The inclusion of דעת (from 1:17) renders the connection to Proverbs 30 and its חכמה ודעת stronger, while the continuation of 2:12 features the very important reference to the impossibility of second-guessing the King, as we will see below: כִּי מֶה הָאָדָם שֶׁיָבוֹא אַחֲרֵי הַמֶּלֶךְ אֵת אֲשֶׁר־כְּבָר עָשׂוּהוּ. The conflation of the two verses may thus best serve the midrash's goals.

5   See b*BM* 115a and b*San* 21a.

The midrash focuses, in explicating Shlomo's confessed failure in *Kohelet*, on his improper questioning of the (Divine) King's decree. "Who can question the attributes and decrees of the King of Kings, the Holy One blessed be He, words that are chiseled before Him?"

This passage features the repeated theme of the Divine word as an implement that literally shapes the physical word. God's expressions are referred to multiple times as *gezeirot*, meaning decrees but carrying the further implication of something that is physically cut (ג.ז.ר) into the fabric of reality. God's words are referred to as חצובים מלפניו, "chiseled before Him," the words ingraining themselves in the physical world.

God's words are not only given expression in a physical dimension but are also defined by their aspect of truth. The midrash offers to the פמליא של מעלה, the Divine retinue, as it were, the role of affirming that every Divine utterance is true and wise (גזירותיו אמת וכל דבריו בהשכל). But the truth value of these statements is determined *before* they are heard by this Divine retinue, טרם הוא נמלך. God, of course, does not need advisors to weigh His opinions; these angelic beings are meant primarily to affirm the transcendent truth of the Divine utterances.

Thus, two verses are invoked, one of which returns us to that same chapter of *Mishlei* (*perek* 30):

(ה) כָּל־אִמְרַת אֱלוֹהַּ צְרוּפָה מָגֵן הוּא לַחֹסִים בּוֹ:
(ו) אַל־תּוֹסְףְ עַל־דְּבָרָיו פֶּן־יוֹכִיחַ בְּךָ וְנִכְזָבְתָּ:

Not only is verse 5, which is cited by this midrash and asserts the truth and perfection (צרופה) of God's statements, relevant, but so is the continuation. God's words are not only perfect but also protective of those who follow them, מגן הוא לחוסים בו. By contrast, those who attempt to diverge from God's word, specifically those who *add to* God's word, building in exceptions and the like, will find themselves rebuked and dismayed. This is a perfect description of Shlomo's attempt to add to the law, which results in his personal destruction.

The other verse cited is also significant, drawing as it does from one of Daniel's speeches to Nebuchadnezzar (Dan. 4:14):

(יד) בִּגְזֵרַת עִירִין פִּתְגָמָא וּמֵאמַר קַדִּישִׁין שְׁאֵלְתָא עַד־דִּבְרַת דִּי יִנְדְּעוּן חַיַּיָּא דִּי־שַׁלִּיט עִלָּאָה עִלָּאָה בְּמַלְכוּת אנושא אֲנָשָׁא וּלְמַן־דִּי יִצְבֵּא יִתְּנִנַּהּ וּשְׁפַל אֲנָשִׁים יְקִים עליה עֲלַהּ:

This verse features several of the points made in the midrash. It highlights the prospect of language affecting the world—the clause בגזרת עירין פתגמא ומאמר קדישין שאלתא features no fewer than four terms referring to speech, while also affirming that they determine what happens in the world, drawing upon the synonymy in Aramaic (as in Hebrew) between utterances and things (פתגמא). The goal here is also knowledge, but a particular type of knowledge, with the goal being that all creatures know (די וינדעון חייא) and recognize God's authority. Furthermore, while the decisive decree is made by God, the ruling is expressed by several angels (עירין קדישין), as it were, before being delivered unto the world. This depiction of an affirming Divine retinue is followed by our midrash. But most of all, the theme of God transferring power from the strong to the weak is central. Consider the midrash's earlier distinction between the powerful King Shlomo and the tiny letter *yud*; this verse reinforces the statement of God's ability to control the world and its power structures simply with His word.

Having concluded the account of Shlomo and his failed attempt to outsmart the Divine word, the midrash now turns to that parallel and more *parashah*-appropriate case of Moshe and his attempt to avoid the Divine word.

כיצד נאמר על משה לפי שכבר הודיע הקדוש ברוך הוא למשה שלא יניח אותם פרעה לילך, שנאמר ואני ידעתי כי לא יתן אתכם מלך מצרים להלוך ואני אחזק את לבו, ומשה לא שמר את הדבר הזה אלא בא להתחכם על גזירתו של הקדוש ברוך הוא והתחיל ואומר ה' למה הרעות לעם הזה התחיל לדון לפניו (כמו שכתוב למעלה).

Moshe had been warned from the beginning of his mission that he would face rejection at the early stages of his interactions with Pharaoh. Rather than wisely heeding this Divine caution, Moshe seeks to outsmart God's decree that he go to Pharaoh, instead critiquing God's path as one that worsens Israel's situation.

וע"ז נאמר שאותה חכמה ודעת של משה של הוללות וסכלות היו, כי מה האדם שיבא אחרי המלך, וכי מה היה לו להרהר אחר מדותיו של הקדוש ברוך הוא את אשר כבר עשוהו, מה שכבר גילה לו שהוא עתיד לחזק את לבו בעבור לעשות לו דין תחת אשר העבידם בעבודה קשה.

Here the midrash invokes that same verse in *Kohelet* asserting that a plan Moshe thought to be wise and knowledgeable turned out to be mad and silly. On this reading, Moshe's folly is twofold: not only is he trying to second-guess the King, but he does so after God already informed him of the plan to harden Pharaoh's heart! Despite the lack of new information, Moshe dares to question God, a move that is called silly. In this reading, as opposed to the one regarding Shlomo, את אשר כבר עשוהו denotes not just the general concept of Divine command, but specifically the fact that God foresaw and foretold the situation that Moshe is only now inappropriately responding to.

ועל דבר זה בקשה מדת הדין לפגוע במשה, הה"ד וידבר אלהים אל משה, ולפי שנסתכל הקדוש ב"ה שבשביל צער ישראל דבר כן חזר ונהג עמו במדת רחמים, הה"ד ויאמר אליו אני ה'.

Based on Moshe's error God wished to injure and punish him, as the *middat ha-din* is invoked at the beginning of *Va'era*, but God instead treated Moshe with mercy, and this explains the shift in both Divine names and speech verbs at the beginning of the *parashah* (*Shemot* 6:2), from the harsher ד.ב.ר and *Elokim* to the more merciful א.מ.ר and *Shem Havayah*.

***

It is clear that this midrash is masterfully built, with insightful invocations of verses to support its broader point. God runs the world, with a plan; God's decrees affect the very physical world and should not be questioned; God has the capacity to invert power hierarchies; the letter of the law must be preserved. What broader implications might this midrash hold, beyond those touching on the specific story at hand?

I would suggest that this midrash is making a specific point about the unchanging nature of Halakhah, polemicizing against those who would reject it. Shlomo's conceit was that the law's letter could be rejected in light of its spirit, with the proper understanding of the law's purpose permitting the erasure of its letter. Further, he thought he could understand his personal proclivities better than the undifferentiated law might have. This approach entails a rejection of both law as binding rather than suggestion and a rejection of the physical instantiation of the law, namely the law's body, the physical letter of the law, i.e., the *yud*. God's response to Shlomo is not just that God possesses superior wisdom, but also, possibly more importantly, that God has full control over the physical world. Erasing but a *yud* can trigger the downfall of a pluripotent monarch. God wishes the law to be followed as He set it out, and so it must be. There are multiple references here to God as Creator of the world, the King Who created and set everything into motion from the beginning. The law is not just some tepid suggestion; it is chiseled in stone, integrated into the fabric of the universe that God established. As Shlomo learns all too painfully, the letter of God's law is built into the world's very nature and it cannot be avoided.

One might more fully appreciate the significance of these powerful claims about the unchanging nature of the law as God's plan for the world in light of some philosophical movements that rabbinic Jews were confronted with. The claims of this *midrash* serve as strong responses to Platonism, a belief system stemming from the Athenian philosopher Plato that was influential in different iterations around the first few centuries CE, built upon by both Philo and Paul, and which influenced early Christianity (through Middle and Neo-Platonism) well into the Medieval period.

Although *Shemot Rabbah* is understood by scholars to have a fairly late date of final compilation, around the 11th or 12th centuries, there are several reasons why we might still look back to the first few centuries CE for helpful context. First of all, *Shemot Rabbah*'s final form may contain earlier materials responding to critiques from the Tannaitic and Amoraic periods. Even if the material in this *midrash* is itself of late provenance, it may very well still be responding to later incarnations of the concept that were raised (puns intended) by medieval Christians.

One of the central views of Middle Platonism was that words are not significant in themselves but serve only as repositories for the deeper, spiritual meanings that they contain. As Daniel Boyarin puts it:

> Language itself is understood as an outer, physical shell, and meaning is construed as the invisible, ideal, and spiritual reality that lies behind or is trapped within the body of the language.[6]

As Philo describes the views of the Therapeutae, a Greek philosophical sect adhering to Middle Platonism, the law is like a living organism, its words the body and its deeper, allegorical meaning the soul.[7] This is taken a step further by Paul in his critique of (Pharisaic) Judaism as incorrectly following the letter of the law rather than its spirit. Paul rejects the literal, and therefore physical, interpretation of laws such as sacrifice (I Cor 10) and circumcision (Gal 5).[8]

The now widespread English phrases "letter of the law" and "spirit of the law" originate with Paul, mediated through the King James translation.[9] Of course, Paul was not just presenting this lucid dichotomy for

---

6   Daniel Boyarin, *A Radical Jew: Paul and the Politics of Identity* (Berkeley: University of California Press, 1994), p. 15.

7   See *De Vita Contemplativa*, II.78.

8   For an extensive treatment of Paul's conceptual project, see Boyarin, *A Radical Jew*, at length.

9   For this reason, I often chuckle when I see these terms quoted by contemporary rabbis who would never knowingly quote the New Testament and who invoke this dichotomy as they argue that Judaism is *really* about the spirit of the law rather than its letter or that only *poskim* can appreciate the spirit of the law that

the purposes of intellectual exploration; he was participating in a polemic that delegitimized the traditional Jewish perspective of law. The stereotype of the Pharisee as the small-minded, legalistic hypocrite who fails to see the larger picture emerges directly from Paul and had major, negative implications for Jewish life (and Jewish lives) for centuries afterward. Paul's line that it is necessary to embrace a new covenant (also known as a new testament), because "the letter kills but the spirit gives life" (II Cor 3:6) led to a supersessionist movement with noxious implications for Jews and Judaism. This was animated not just by a rejection of legalistic formalism, but also by a claim about the very nature of law. Law in this view is not fundamentally comprised of the legislated material, but of the concepts behind it. This was animated by a metaphysical perspective on reality—the "real" world is not the physical world but the spiritual world. On this basis, building upon Middle Platonism and applying it to the law and its presumed limitations, generations of Christians attacked Judaism and the legalism it stood for.

Enter our midrash.

The midrashic passage studied in this article responds to each of these claims. It starts by asserting that the physical world that God created is of great value. Rather than see the existence of the physical world itself as insufficient or flawed in some sense (as many thinkers of the first few centuries CE did, to one degree or another[10]), Ḥazal emphasize that the Creator of the physical world is the one and true God. Not only that, but the world's existence itself had Torah law baked into it. The law is not some general or loose rule of thumb to be consulted or adopted voluntarily, but is chiseled and cut, and thus exceptionless. Not only is the law an essential part of the physical world, but the physical instantiations of the Law are essential, as well. If even one of the Torah's physical letters is out of place, God will invoke righteous indignation on its behalf, carry out justice, and impose punishment in this physical world.

The context utilized by the midrash further supports this idea that it is a polemic against Greek philosophy in a Christian guise. Consider the text around which this Midrash is constructed, namely *Kohelet*. Of course,

---

lies behind and animates its letter. The term *lifnim mi-shurat ha-din*, literally "within the line of the law," is all too often mistranslated as "beyond the letter of the law," again unwittingly invoking Pauline stereotypes.

10   The most extreme of these were the Gnostics, who believed that the physical world was inferior to the spiritual world, and human bodies inferior to souls. This could only be the case because (in their dualistic system) an inferior god created the physical world, one who could not measure up to the true god who created the spiritual world.

this is the most philosophical of all Biblical books, with its author questioning the meaning of life at every turn. Another text cited here, *Mishlei*, is also deeply philosophical in nature. It is no coincidence that both are attributed to Shlomo ha-Melekh's authorship, as he was known to be the wisest of all people. The moral of this story is that too much philosophy can lead one astray, as it did Shlomo. Sometimes, argues the *midrash*, what is necessary is not more philosophy but instead an absolute, unthinking commitment to God and God's law, to direct our conduct in this physical world. To that end, the midrash parodies Agur ben Yakeh, who plays the role of philosopher. He hopes to take in words of Torah and spit them out at will, presuming that God supports this endeavor. The attempt, however, to spit out Torah and reject the physical aspect of the law while asserting Divine support on account of following the spirit of the law, is a recipe for disaster. As Shlomo says, reflecting back upon his own experiences, what he thought would be wise and knowledgeable, revealed itself to be folly instead.

This midrash thus pits Middle Platonism, camouflaged as (disastrous) Solomonic wisdom, against the concept of the letter of the law, in both of its senses. Can we question the Torah's punctiliousness? Dare we reject its hold on our physical world? The midrash comes down very squarely against Shlomo ha-Melekh, building on his own expressed regrets at the end of his life. There is no second-guessing the primordial God, Who created the world, engrained the law within it, and encoded that law using the unchanging letter of the law. Questioning such a God can be nothing other than folly. CR

Sefer ha-Tappu'aḥ, The Book of the Apple: Aristotle Expresses an Interest in Jewish Concepts

By: MARVIN J. HELLER[1]

Now it came to pass, when the Philosopher had ceased speaking these words, that his hands grew weak, the apple dropped from his hand, his face changed color, and he died. His disciples fell upon him and kissed him; and they lifted up their voices together and wept bitterly, exclaiming: May He Who gathers the souls of the "Lovers of Wisdom" gather unto Himself thy spirit, placing thee among His secret treasures, as it beseemeth a perfect and upright man like thee![2]

Sefer ha-Tappu'aḥ (Book of the Apple) is an unusual and thought-provoking work. Attributed to Aristotle, the noted Greek philosopher (fourth century B.C.E.), *Sefer ha-Tappu'aḥ* is the reputed famed deathbed conversation between Aristotle and his friends and pupils, in which they engage in philosophical discussions, concluding with Aristotle's expressing a belief in Judaism and Jewish concepts. It was the opinion of Maimonides (Rambam, 1138–1204) that *Sefer ha-Tappu'aḥ* is a pseudo-Aristotle, an opinion widely accepted today.[3] *Sefer ha-Tappu'aḥ* is modeled on Plato's

---

[1]   I would like to express my appreciation to Eli Genauer for reading the article and his comments.

[2]   Hermann Gollancz, *Translations from Hebrew and Aramaic* (London, 1908), p. 117. All quotes from *Sefer ha-Tappu'aḥ* are from Gollancz's translation, pp. 91–117. That Maimonides was well versed in Aristotelian studies and philosophy is evident from numerous references and citations in Fred Rosner and Samuel S. Kottek, eds., *Moses Maimonides: Physician, Scientist, and Philosopher* (Northvale, NJ, 1993).

[3]   *Sefer ha-Tappu'aḥ* is not the only pseudo-Aristotelian work. Charles B. Schmitt and Dilwyn Knox record ninety-six such titles in Latin in their *Pseudo-Aristoteles Latinus: A Guide to Latin Works Falsely Attributed to Aristotle Before 1500* (Warburg

---

Marvin J. Heller is an award-winning author of books and articles on early Hebrew printing and bibliography. Among his books are the *Printing the Talmud* series, *The Sixteenth and Seventeenth Century Hebrew Book(s): An Abridged Thesaurus*, and several collections of articles.

Phaedo and, outside of Jewish studies, is best known by its Latin title, *Liber de Pomo*. Nevertheless, as we shall see, it was, at one time, a popular and reasonably well known work in Jewish circles.

Originally written in in Arabic in the 10th century as *Kitab al-Tuffaha*, although Greek too has been suggested as the original language, *Sefer ha-Tappu'aḥ* was translated into Hebrew in about 1235 by R. Abraham ha-Levi ibn Ḥasdai. *Sefer ha-Tappu'aḥ* was a text of considerable importance to several cultures in the Middle Ages and Renaissance. As Ioana Curut, referring to its Latin name, *Liber de Pomo*, informs that "*Liber de Pomo* is a privileged piece of work for at least three reasons. First of all, it circulated in at least four distinct medieval cultures: Arabic, Persian, Hebrew, and Latin." The other reasons are that its attribution to Aristotle "elevated the status of the opuscule to that of a text worth being read and commented upon in the medieval centres of knowledge," and lastly, that it was an important influence on Latin thought and influenced Christian dogma.[4] Our interest is restricted to the Hebrew editions, our subject matter is bibliographic, that is, describing the various early editions through the eighteenth century and giving an overview of the contents of *Sefer ha-Tappu'aḥ* .

R. Abraham ha-Levi ibn Ḥasdai (Ḥisdai, 13th century), resident in Barcelona, was responsible for the Hebrew translation and making *Sefer ha-Tappu'aḥ* available to the Jewish community. A noted translator and poet, his other translations into Hebrew include Algazali's *Moznei Ẓedek*; Isaac ben Solomon Israeli's *Sefer ha-Yesodot*; Maimonides's *Sefer ha-Mitzvot* and *Iggeret Teiman*; and *Ben ha-Melekh ve-ha-Nazir*.[5] Another ibn Ḥasdai translation is of *Barlaam and Josaphat*, an Indian romance, this in *maqāma* form, that is, a narrative in rhymed prose. Ibn Ḥasdai was a stalwart adherent of

---

Institute Surveys and Texts, 1985). This obviously does not include pseudo-Aristotelian works in other languages, such as our *Sefer ha-Tappu'aḥ*. There is at least one bilingual Latin-Hebrew work in our period, *librum De pomo Aristotelis ... ex Arabica lingua in Ebraeo-rabbinicam translatum a Abraham Levita, nunc Latine versum ... altera ostendit Consensum kabbalisticorum cum philosophia academica & peripatetica dogmatum*, printed in Giessen (1706), 20 cm. [8], 96, 52 pp. (NLI call no. 8909=R).

4   Ioana Curut, "Ad eruditionem multorum. The Latin Version of the Book of the Apple (Liber de Pomo) as a Philosophical Protreptic," *Philobiblon*, XXII, (1/2017), p. 22.

5   Mordechai Margalioth, ed., *Encyclopedia of Great Men in Israel*, I (Tel Aviv, 1986), cols. 55–56 [Hebrew]; for a discussion of several of these works, see Israel Zinberg, *A History of Jewish Literature*, translated by Bernard Martin, 1 (Cleveland, 1972–78), pp. 191–93.

Maimonides, defending the *Moreh Nevuchim*, communicating for that purpose with such sages as R. Judah ibn Alfakhar and R. Meir ha-Levi Abulafia, as well as community leaders who opposed that work.[6]

Sefer ha-Tappu'ah is not as well known today, perchance reflecting different cultural interests. As noted above, it has been translated into several languages, most notably Latin as *Liber de Pomo* (*Tractatus de Pomo et Morte incliti principis philosophorum* Aristotilis). This article, again primarily bibliographic in content, is intended to bring *Sefer ha-Tappu'ah* to the attention of a wider public, describing the various Hebrew editions of *Sefer ha-Tappu'ah* through the eighteenth century and interspersed with examples of its text.

I

Stylistically in dialogue form, *Sefer ha-Tappu'ah* has been described by Hermann Gollancz as a conversation between Aristotle and friends and disciples, on the immortality of the soul and, to a lesser extent, on the merits of philosophy and "the value of its study for the ends of investigating the Truth."[7]

The text begins with ibn Ḥasdai's introduction, in which he explains why he translated *Sefer ha-Tappu'ah* into Hebrew. He writes,

> When I reflected upon this book and its contents, composed by the Sages of Greece, I thought that it might be of service in the interests of our Faith to strengthen the hands of the weaklings among our people. By weaklings I mean those who meditate upon the words of the heretics, who aver that, after the dissolution of the body, man has no real existence, whereas, at his death, nothing remains. . . .
>
> It is for this reason that I have determined to translate this book from Arabic into Hebrew . . .[8]

Gollancz informs that the reason the book is so titled is due to the fact that Aristotle, conversing with his companions on his deathbed,

> in his last moments, in order to sustain himself in this exhausting effort, is represented as holding in his hand (in place of the more usual smelling-flask) an apple, the scent of which refreshes him so that he is able to complete his task.[9]

---

6 "Ibn Ḥasdai, Abraham ben Samuel Ha-Levi," *Encyclopaedia Judaica*, 9 (2007), p. 679.

7 Gollancz, p. 5.

8 Gollancz, pp. 91–92.

9 Gollancz, pp. 5–6

II

Sefer ha-Tappu'aḥ was well recognized and more popular in the Middle Ages and Renaissance than at present. A number of manuscripts are extant today and, as with the majority of printed works, it was most often combined with other works. The earliest recorded copy of *Sefer ha-Tappu'aḥ* in the extensive list in the National Library of Israel (NLI) catalogue is held in the British Library, that is, a manuscript written in Viterbo in Tuscany, Italy, by R. Solomon Jeidah ben Moses of Rome. The colophon (117a) dates completion to 18 Kislev 5073 (Friday, November 11, 1272). *Sefer ha-Tappu'aḥ* (below) is part of a 216 folio codex.

The text, described as a "collection of philosophical writings," is in two columns, 40 lines to a page. The manuscript consists of several of Maimonides's writings, among them his commentary on *Avot*, *Perek Ḥelek*, and *Igeret Teḥiyat ha-Metim*. Other authors represented are R. Solomon ibn Gabirol, R. Kalonymus ben Kalonymus ben Meir, as well as several other works by Aristotle.

1272, R. Shelomoh Yedidyah ben Mosheh of Rome
Courtesy of the British Library, Digitized Manuscripts, MS 14763

Sefer ha-Tappu'aḥ: When the way of truth was closed against those sages, and the path of equity hidden from these wise men of intellect and understanding, called in their own language Philosophers, the etymology of which expression is "lovers of wisdom," they all assembled together at one and the same time, and agreed to explain and to cause men to understand which was the right way in which men should walk, so that he might live by it.

The second manuscript in the NLI listing, written in 1282, is part of the collection of the Casanatense Library, Rome, Italy. The scribe for this copy of *Sefer ha-Tappu'aḥ* was R. Abraham ben Yom Tov ha-Kohen who completed his work on Friday, Rosh Ḥodesh Ḥeshvan, 5044 (October 22, 1282). Here too, *Sefer ha-Tappu'aḥ* is part of a much larger work, appearing on pp. 267–70. The text, also in two columns, is in square letters.

We note two additional manuscripts, the first written in Chania (Greece) in 1382 by R. Abraham ben Moses on 23 Adar 5142 (Sunday, March 17, 1382). It was written, according to the colophon, on folio 108b for R. Shabbetai ha-Rofei. The second manuscript was written only five years later, in 1387, in Mistra, Greece, by the youth R. Solomon ben Moses Phanglo on 17 Sivan 5147 (Sunday, June 12, 1387), this in Cambridge University Library, Cambridge, England. *Sefer ha-Tappu'aḥ* is on ff. 19b–23b.

These manuscripts, the first two written within a decade of each other, the second group a century later within five years of each other, are indicative of both the value attributed to *Sefer ha-Tappu'aḥ*, it being written several times within slightly more than a century, but also that it was not a primary work, it being included in each instance in collections of works and not as a leading entry. Numerous manuscripts of *Sefer ha-Tappu'aḥ* are extant, those recorded in the NLI catalogue being only a portion of them.

Sefer ha-Tappu'aḥ: Now there was a great and eminent sage, versed in all wisdom and knowledge, whose name was Aristotle. All the wise men of the time were wont to listen to his wisdom, and to gain instruction from him.

And when he was lying ill of his fatal disease, and his time came near to die, all the wise men assembled together and went to visit him in his illness. They found him holding an apple in hand, and this he was smelling: he was very weak in consequence of the force of the malady, and the pains of death made him very restless:

III

Turning to the printed editions, we see that *Sefer ha-Tappu'aḥ* was also a relatively popular work in the Renaissance.

1519, Venice. The first printing of *Sefer ha-Tappu'aḥ* was in Venice in 1519 at the renowned press of Daniel Bomberg, printed as a quarto (4⁰: 36ff.). It was included in *Likkutei ha-Pardes*, a collection of several works, most notably the collected *halakhot* and responsa attributed to Rashi (R. Solomon ben Isaac, 1040–1105).

The title page (below), typical of the Bomberg press at this time, brief and unadorned, makes no mention of *Sefer ha-Tappu'aḥ*. Rashi's responsa concludes on 22a, followed by *Refuot ha-Geviyah le-ḥakham Rabbenu Judah [ben Solomon al] Harizi* (22b–23b); then *Sefer ha-Tappu'aḥ* (24a–27a); *Sefer ha-Nefesh* (28a–32b), attributed to Galinus ha-Rofei, also translated from the Arabic by al-Harizi; the *Takkanot* of *Rabbenu Gershom* (33a–34b); *Misheli Ḥakhamim ve-Ḥidotam* ([34]); and *Aryeh Mesubach* (35a) by Berechiah ben Natronai ha-Nakdan, which is parable sixty-eight from his *Mishlei Shu'alim*.

Bomberg began to print in about 1515, some suggest even earlier, and was active for several decades. It is noteworthy, for our purposes, that *Sefer ha-Tappu'aḥ*, among the many other possibilities, was included in *Likkutei ha-Pardes*, an early Bomberg imprint. The text, excepting headers (below), is in rabbinic letters in two columns.

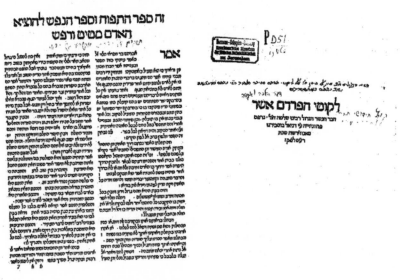

1519, *Likkutei ha-Pardes*
Courtesy of the National Library of Israel

Sefer ha-Tappu'ah: Now as regards the Intellectual faculties, which rule and guide us, and are not composed of the four elements, but of one simple element: of these there is the faculty which understands and recognizes the difference between good and evil, and grasps the axiom that things that are equal to the same thing are equal to one another. This is the faculty that understands that 3 is an odd number, and that 4 is even. It recognizes its Creator, and understands what He is: it is found in man alone, and in the rest of creation like him.

1562, Riva di Trento. The next edition of *Sefer ha-Tappu'ah* appeared as an appendage to R. Solomon ibn Gabirol's *Tikkun Middot ha-Nefesh* (The Improvement of the Moral Qualities) issued under the general title *Goren Nakhon*, that phrase appearing on the top of the page (below). Also included in the volume are R. Isaac ibn Honein's *Musrei Ha-Philosofim* (Maxims of the Philosophers). This edition of *Goren Nakhon* was published as a 19 cm. book; *Sefer ha-Tappu'ah* is on ff. 24–28 ff. (should say 26–30). *Tikkun Middot ha-Nefesh* was translated into Hebrew from the Arabic by R. Judah ibn Tibbon (1167) and had been published previously in Constantinople (1550).

The Riva di Trento press, located in the Tyrol, was active for four years only, from 1558 to 1562, issuing about thirty-five titles. The press was operated by R. Joseph Ottolenghi and R. Jacob Marcaria, a *dayyan* on the *bet din* presided over by Ottolenghi. Unusual, particularly given the situation (persecution) of Hebrew books at that time in Italy, the Riva di Trento press operated under the patronage and protection of Cardinal Cristoforo Madruzzo (1512–78), the Cardinal of Trent. A scholar and supporter of learning, he had argued at the Council of Trent (1562) for leniency and moderation in condemning books.[10]

---

10   Concerning the Riva di Trento press see David Amram, *The Makers of Hebrew Books in Italy* (Philadelphia, 1909, reprint London, 1963), pp. 296–302; Joshua Bloch, "Hebrew Printing in Riva di Trento," in *Hebrew Printing and Bibliography* (New York, 1976), pp. 93–110.

1562, *Goren Nakhon*
Courtesy of the National Library of Israel

Sefer ha Tappu'aḥ: I would furthermore, ask you this question: -
Do you know that death is but another name for the severance of
the soul from the body?
And they replied: - Yes, we know it.
He continued: - You rejoice when you attain some scientific truth
and take hold of it; you grieve when you are unable to gain and learn
more wisdom. Is it not so? And they assented.
Then he said unto them: - If this be the case, do you not observe
that it is not the body, of gross material, which sees and hears and
understands, but that it does so only by virtue of the soul, which is
united to it during the period of its existence?

1693, Frankfurt on the Oder. This edition of *Sefer ha-Tappu'aḥ* was
printed in Frankfurt on the Oder at the press of Johann Christoph
Beckman in a small octavo format (8⁰: [6] ff.). It was published together
with R. Isaac ben Solomon ibn Abi Sahula's *Meshal ha-Kadmoni*, a popular,
profusely illustrated collection of moral fables. In this volume, *Sefer ha-
Tappu'aḥ* precedes the *Meshal ha-Kadmoni*, the larger of the two works. *Sefer
ha-Tappu'aḥ* is not foliated and is set in a single column in rabbinic type.

Beckman, professor of Greek language, history, and theology at the
University of Frankfurt, operated a printing press from 1673. He obtained
a license to publish Hebrew books, on May 1, 1675, renewed on June 1,
1682. Beckman actually began publishing Hebrew works in 1677, issuing

five varied small books that year. By 1693, Beckman found that his responsibilities at the university left him with insufficient time to manage the press. He therefore contracted with Michael Gottschalk, a local bookbinder and book-dealer, to manage the printing-house, transferring all of the typographical equipment and material to Gottschalk. Among the works printed by Gottschalk is an edition of the Talmud (1697–99).

Sefer ha-Tappu'ah: *Meshal ha-Kadmoni*
Courtesy of the National Library of Israel

Sefer ha-Tappu'ah: Yes, all the stars together are but as servants appointed for a special purpose, to whom permission is not given to alter and vary, and whose movements and procedures are not dependent upon themselves or their own power; for it is in the upper sphere that restrains them in their course: and this power is resident in the first sphere; it comes from God, who formed and established things in His understanding. . . .

Now, mankind erred in this respect until there arose Noah, father of the wise men who excelled in the knowledge of the Creator; he perceived that all things must have a beginning and a head, that to Him belonged wisdom, a high degree of excellence and might.

IV

Our final imprints, two related editions, were both published in 1799, in Grodno and Vilna. They are, for bibliographic reasons, among the most interesting of the editions of *Sefer ha-Tappu'aḥ* discussed here, the relationship of the two articles being technically clear but otherwise unstated.

1799, Grodno. Grodno (Horodno), in Belorussia, is one of the oldest Jewish communities in Poland-Lithuania, dating to the fourteenth century. Hebrew printing in Grodno began in 1788 at the Royal press; a second press was established in 1793 by Barukh ben Joseph Romm, founder of the famed Romm press.

The Grodno edition, the fourth Hebrew printing of *Sefer ha-Tappu'aḥ*, is recorded as a duodecimo (12⁰: 16 pp.), the printer's name is lacking and the National Library of Israel catalogue states, concerning the Grodno edition, publisher unknown. The *Thesaurus of the Hebrew Book* records eleven Grodno titles for the period 1798–99, two only for the latter year. Of those eleven titles, four are attributed to Barukh ben Joseph Romm, the others have no attribution.[11] The National Library of Israel catalogue also only attributes four titles to the Romm press for this period. While it is not clear why the printer's name was omitted, there is no indication that the other books were printed by another press.

1799, Grodno
Courtesy of the National Library of Israel

---

11   Yeshayahu Vinograd, *Thesaurus of the Hebrew Book. Listing of Books Printed in Hebrew Letters Since the Beginning of Printing circa 1469 through 1863*, I (Jerusalem, 1993–95), pp. 156–57 [Hebrew].

What makes this edition of particular interest is that an identical edition was published (issued) in the same year in Vilna, the sole difference being the title-pages. The title-page of that like edition gives the printer's name as Aryeh Leib ben Jehiel. In both editions the title-page is followed by the front matter of the corrector, R. Abraham ben Eliezer Lipman, and the forward of ibn Ḥasdai, and then the text. It is clear that the editions are physically identical, employing the same font and layout; the Vilna *Sefer ha-Tappu'aḥ* was taken from Grodno and reissued with a new title-page in Vilna.

> *Sefer ha-Tappu'aḥ* : After Noah there was born Abraham, the Elder, who was a greater sage than the rest, and he learnt and understood that all the men of his generation were lost in the web of their own errors and vanities. It was then that God tried him and commanded him to offer up to Him his especial son: and he did so, for his heart was so perfect with God; he yearned to understand His attributes, and to grasp the ideas that the sun and moon had a First Cause that gave them motion.

1799, Vilna. Vilna is known in Jewish tradition as the "Jerusalem of Lithuania (*Yerushalayim de-Lita*)." The city's reputation stems from its yeshivot, being a center of Jewish learning, and from its prominent rabbis, most notably the Vilna Gaon (R. Elijah ben Solomon Zalman, 1720–1797). Jewish settlement in Vilna (Vilnius) dates to the fifteenth century, albeit in small numbers.

1799, Vilna

Courtesy of the Library of Agudas Chassidei Chabad Ohel Yosef Yitzhak

The first Hebrew press in that city dates to 1799 when the Romm press relocated a major portion of its printing press to Vilna from Grodno. As many as ten varied works are attributed to the Vilna press in its first year; among them a duodecimo (12^0: 16 pp.) edition of *Sefer ha-Tappu'aḥ*.

Why would a press reprint a work published in the same year in a neighboring city, and that on a subject of limited interest, that is, a philosophical work? More likely, indeed most certainly, when the Romm press relocated much of its activity to Vilna they brought uncirculated sheets of their edition of *Sefer ha- Tappu'aḥ*. Likely, they chose to add to their list of imprints in their new location. All that was required was to replace the title-page with a new title-page and then redistribute their copies.[12]

> *Sefer ha- Tappu'aḥ*: It was consequently necessary for the Creator, blessed be He, to bring into existence the man of wisdom and understanding, so as to instruct the boorish, and to enlighten those who have not the sense to understand and know their Creator, nor to attain to the knowledge of anything but what they have learnt from their childhood, whether it be good or evil.

V

One year after our subject period concluded, that limited to editions of *Sefer ha-Tappu'aḥ* from the Middle Ages through the eighteenth century, another edition of that work was published in Frankfort on the Oder in 1800, this edition also with *Meshal ha-Kadmoni*. Six years later, in 1806, yet another edition appeared, this in Lunéville, with *Goren Nakhon*. *Sefer ha-Tappu'aḥ* was published several times in the second half of the nineteenth century, including an 1872 Calcutta, India, edition (below) followed by an 1873 Lvov edition.

Later twentieth century editions, perhaps extant, were not noted. *Sefer ha-Tappu'aḥ* has been a moderately popular work, appearing in both manuscript and printed editions. A philosophical work, not the most popular subject for most, it has been relatively successful. That relative success may be attributed to the fact that it is a small work, ascribed to the eminent Aristotle, well written, readable, and does speak to the interests of many, all this hopefully evident from the examples of its text included with this article.

---

[12] For a somewhat similar case of a work being circulated with a new title-page, see Marvin J. Heller, "An enigmatic pseudo-edition of *Barukh She'amar*" Seforim.blogspot.com (February 2, 2020).

The popularity of *Sefer ha-Tappu'aḥ* and the reasons for its acceptance in Jewish circles is evident from the passages quoted here. The views reputedly expressed by Aristotle are consistent with Jewish beliefs, indicating (suggesting) Aristotle's acceptance of Jewish theological concepts, articulated on his deathbed.

> *Sefer ha- Tappu'aḥ*: Happy is the soul which has not been sullied by evil deeds, which has discerned its Creator and understood its Origin, and which returns to its habitation cheerfully and joyously after a strenuous life spent in noble deeds, and not after an existence spent in the enjoyment of low material aims!

1872, Calcutta
Courtesy of the National Library of Israel

◯ℜ

Shield of Abraham

By: ELIYAHU KHANIN

The Biblical word גן is understood to mean an "enclosed garden," though the very first garden in Tanakh, גן עדן, Paradise, is not surrounded by a wall or at least no wall is mentioned anywhere in the Creation story. Another word, מגן, shield, which is related to גן, implies a similar sort of protection by means of a physical barrier, and yet, as an epithet for God— for instance, in "Shield of Abraham"—it seems to be an unlikely metaphor for Divine protection. A protective physical barrier would imply that there is no control outside the protected area. In Tanakh, reliance on a physical barrier is disparaged as illustrated in the following verse:

If Hashem will not build the house, in vain do its builders labor on it; if Hashem will not guard the city, in vain is the watchman vigilant.[1]	אִם ה' לֹא יִבְנֶה בַיִת שָׁוְא עָמְלוּ בוֹנָיו בּוֹ אִם ה' לֹא יִשְׁמָר עִיר שָׁוְא שָׁקַד שׁוֹמֵר:

Instead of protection by means of a physical barrier, which separates a safe domain from an unsafe one, our tradition promotes the idea of Divine protection in which God controls both domains. How the alternative protection works can be inferred from the similarity between the concept of protection and the way meaning is delineated or delimited. Placing the protected domain all too easily behind a wall is tantamount to thinking in sharply defined categories taken from everyday experience. In Biblical Hebrew, however, most nouns can be traced back to an abstract verbal idea carried by the consonantal root. Understanding protection in terms of a physical barrier without first analyzing the verbal idea would therefore indicate an approach to meaning-making that is not characteristic of Biblical Hebrew. The very notion of Divine protection is an abstract idea and so is likely to reside at the level of the root that does not immediately refer to any ready-made concepts. Considering that the meaning of the root is

---

1   Psalms 127:1. Cf. also *Midrash Tanḥuma, Sh'lakh* 6, quoted by Rashi on Numbers 13:18: "If they dwell in camps, they are mighty and depend upon their strength; but if they are in strongholds, they are weak and have fearful hearts."

Eliyahu Khanin studied Jewish Studies and Semitology at the Jewish University of Petersburg, and worked as a lecturer and research associate. His areas of interest include Ancient Hebrew semantics, Midrashic and Talmudic logic.

not sharply delineated and often rather elusive, a closer reading is necessary in order to identify it and to understand how it is substantivized into
a noun.

Garden

The root of גן is גנן and its meaning can be inferred from the verse in
Tanakh where its only *Qal* form appears:

Like flying birds, so will Hashem, Master of Legions, protect Jerusalem, protecting and rescuing, passing over and delivering.[2] **RASHI: And delivering** — He will extricate Israel from the strait. This expression corresponds to *esmoucer* in Old French.	כְּצִפֳּרִים עָפוֹת כֵּן יָגֵן ה' צְבָאוֹת עַל יְרוּשָׁלָם גָּנוֹן וְהִצִּיל פָּסֹחַ וְהִמְלִיט: **רש״י: והמליט** — יוציא את ישראל מן הצרה לשון המלטה אישקמוציי״ר בלע״ז:

Protecting Jerusalem is compared to flying birds, but the implications
of this metaphor are not immediately clear. It is followed by two pairs of
infinitives, both consisting of one regular and one irregular infinitive vo-
calized as a finite verb. Let us start from the second pair featuring פסח,
here meaning "sparing," and המליט, meaning "causing to flee." The infinitives are coordinated: a person has to be spared before he can be caused
to flee. Rashi explains that the meaning of המליט is evident in the Old
French verb *esmoucer*. While *moucer* means "to cover," *esmoucer* with pre-
fixed *es* (*ex-*, i.e., "out") does not appear in major Old French dictionaries.
Nevertheless, it seems that *esmoucer* means "to take cover," especially because Rashi cites it elsewhere. Rashi's point is that המליט refers to taking
cover inside rather than escaping outside, as the verb is usually translated.
To prove this, let us look at another instance of the same verb explained
by Rashi using *esmoucer*:

Before she even feels her labor pains she will give birth; before any travail come to her she will deliver [וְהִמְלִיטָה] a son![3] **RASHI: Before she even feels her labor pains** — When Zion has not yet travailed with birth pangs, she has borne her children; that is to say that her children will gather into her midst, which was desolate and bereft of them, and it is as though she	בְּטֶרֶם תָּחִיל יָלָדָה בְּטֶרֶם יָבוֹא חֵבֶל לָהּ וְהִמְלִיטָה זָכָר: **רש״י: בטרם תחיל** — ציון חיל היולדת ילדה את בניה כלומר יתקבצו בניה לתוכה אשר הית' שוממה מהם ושכולה והרי הוא כאילו ילדתן עכשיו בלא

---

[2] Isaiah 31:5.
[3] Isaiah 66:7.

bore them now without birth pangs, for all the nations will bring them into her midst. **She will deliver a son** — Any emerging of an embedded [literally: swallowed] thing is called המליטה. [The verb] **והמליטה** corresponds to *esmoucer* in Old French.	חֶבְלֵי יוֹלְדָה כִּי כָּל הָעכו"ם יְבִיאוּם לְתוֹכָהּ: **וְהִמְלִיטָה** **זָכָר** — כָּל יְצִיאַת דָּבָר בָּלוּעַ קָרוּי הַמְלָטָה וְהִמְלִיטָה אישקמוצייי"ר בלע"ז:

Concerning the issue of inside and outside, Rashi's explanation is rather unexpected. The verse speaks of bringing Zion's children into her midst, i.e., inside, by leaving the nations which are outside. This process is metaphorically called "giving birth," despite the fact that the movement is from the outside to the inside. To emphasize this, Rashi cites the Old French *esmoucer*, i.e., "to take cover." His explanation will be clearer if we consider some relevant circumstances: When someone who is "swallowed" escapes outside, his escape will look more like taking cover in a shelter due to presumably poor conditions while being "swallowed." In the verse, Jews were "swallowed" by the surrounding nations that bring them back to Zion, as if to a shelter. Metaphorically, this is compared to giving birth by Zion. In reality, however, Zion becomes pregnant again, as it were. Rashi's explanation leaves no doubt that the verb המליטה denotes the movement from the outside to the inside and *esmoucer* is cited to strengthen that definition. Considering that the preceding infinitive פסח means "sparing," it speaks of fleeing inside, apparently to Jerusalem, which God promises to protect.

Back to the first pair of infinitives, גנון והציל. The infinitive הציל implies surviving without fleeing.[4] Whatever the preceding infinitive גנון means, the first pair speaks of a static situation. To fit together the pieces of the puzzle, let us consider the bird metaphor at the beginning of the verse. When in danger, birds flee to their nest built in an inaccessible location. Its protection is circumstantial rather than physical: nests are built to not interest predators. Jerusalem is not a nest but, like a nest, it enjoys circumstantial protection when potential invaders are busy with their own affairs or otherwise. This gives a clue to the meaning of גנון. Being parallel to פסח in the first pair of infinitives, גנון conveys a condition for the following הציל, i.e., something like "maintaining protective environment." Thus, the verse says the following:

Jerusalem will be [like a bird's nest] protected [יגן] by God who will save it [הציל] through maintaining its inaccessibility for the enemies [גנון] and will	כְּצִפֳּרִים עָפוֹת כֵּן יָגֵן ה' צְבָאוֹת עַל יְרוּשָׁלַ͏ִם גָּנוֹן

---

4   Cf. וַתִּנָּצֵל נַפְשִׁי, Genesis 32:31.

spare those outside [פסח] and cause them to take cover [המליט] in Jerusalem [like birds] flying [to their nest].	וְהִצִּיל פָּסֹחַ וְהִמְלִיט:

This meaning of גנון suggests that the garden, גן, itself protects, rather than it has to be protected with a surrounding wall. Like a bird's nest in the above metaphor, the garden is inaccessible to what it protects against, in particular, the parching heat of the sun. The foliage provides a natural barrier weakening and dispersing the sunlight: gardens (or oases) are meant to provide a refuge for environments where human life would otherwise be impossible.[5] That is the rationale for the Paradise [גן עדן]. Delicious and attractive fruits are a nice bonus that do not, however, turn it into an enclosed plantation for growing crops.

Shield

Though the noun מָגֵן [shield] and the root גנן are related, it is grammatically impossible to derive the former from the latter, because the vocalization of מגן is not attested in the derivatives of the ל"ל roots (i.e., roots with a duplicate last consonant). Considering that the vocalization of מגן is quite common in nouns or participles derived from the regular roots, e.g., זָקֵן ,חָבֵר, the מ in מגן can only be a part of the root. Incidentally, a *pi'el* verb מגן appears virtually next to the first instance of the noun מָגֵן in Tanakh and it seems reasonable to assume that they are related:

…and blessed be God, the Most High, who has delivered [מִגֵּן] your foes into your hand; and he gave [וַיִּתֶּן] him a tenth of everything. [6]	וּבָרוּךְ אֵל עֶלְיוֹן אֲשֶׁר מִגֵּן צָרֶיךָ בְּיָדֶךָ וַיִּתֶּן לוֹ מַעֲשֵׂר מִכֹּל:
Some time later, the word of Hashem came to Abram in a vision: "Fear not, Abram, I am a shield [מגן] to you; Your reward shall be very great."[7]	אַחַר הַדְּבָרִים הָאֵלֶּה, הָיָה דְבַר ה' אֶל אַבְרָם, בַּמַּחֲזֶה, לֵאמֹר: אַל תִּירָא אַבְרָם, אָנֹכִי מָגֵן לָךְ--שְׂכָרְךָ, הַרְבֵּה מְאֹד.

There are two more instances of the verb in Tanakh:

How can I hand you over [אֶתֶּנְךָ], Ephraim, or deliver [אֲמַגֶּנְךָ] you, Israel?	אֵיךְ אֶתֶּנְךָ אֶפְרַיִם אֲמַגֶּנְךָ יִשְׂרָאֵל אֵיךְ אֶתֶּנְךָ כְאַדְמָה

---

5   Cf. the clouds of glory, ענני הכבוד, in the desert.
6   Genesis 14:20.
7   Genesis 15:1.

How can I render you like Admah [or] make you like Zeboim? My heart has been overturned; My mercies have been kindled together.[8]

אֲשִׂימְךָ כְּצָבֹאִים נֶהְפַּךְ עָלַי
לִבִּי יַחַד נִכְמְרוּ נִחוּמָי:

It will set [תִּתֵּן] an adornment of grace upon your head; it will bestow [תְּמַגְּנֶךָּ] a crown of splendor upon you.[9]

תִּתֵּן לְרֹאשְׁךָ לִוְיַת חֵן עֲטֶרֶת
תִּפְאֶרֶת תְּמַגְּנֶךָּ:

Both of these instances are parallel to the verb נתן [to give], while the preceding one is more loosely coordinated with נתן in the next clause. Based on these verses, the rough meaning of the verb is "to make available," "to provide" for the benefit of the recipient. Thus, Abraham's adversaries are delivered into his hand, Jews are not delivered to their enemies, a crown is provided with entitlement to its wearer. How this translates into the notion of shield may be not immediately apparent, unless one takes into account that the shields mentioned in Tanakh were more sophisticated than a mere physical barrier. In particular, the shields were greased to deflect weapons. As follows from the following verse and Rashi's explanation, an ungreased shield would effectively be a mere physical barrier and considered a disadvantage, to say the least.

Setting the table, lighting the candelabrum, eating and drinking, Arise, O officers; anoint the shield.[10]

עָרֹךְ הַשֻּׁלְחָן צָפֹה הַצָּפִית
אָכוֹל שָׁתֹה קוּמוּ הַשָּׂרִים
מִשְׁחוּ מָגֵן:

RASHI: Anoint the shield — They were shields of boiled leather, and they would grease them with oil so that the weapons would glide off. The same is mentioned concerning Saul: "For there the shield of the mighty was rejected."[11] It rejected its grease and did not absorb it, and Saul's shield became as though it was not greased with oil.

רש״י: משחו מגן — מגיני
עור שלוק הן ומושחין אותן
בשמן כדי שיחליק את הזיין
וכך נאמר בשאול כי שם
נגעל מגן גבורים פלט את
משיחתו ולא קיבלה ונעשה
מגן שאול כאילו לא נמשה
בשמן:

The shield handles weapons in much the same way as the garden handles the parching heat of the sun. Technically, the shield must prevent weapons from hitting its owner, but from the perspective of the owner, his shield ensures his survival. As a physical barrier, the shield is a relatively small device, offering only partial protection and so, ultimately, it is

---

8   Hosea 11:8.
9   Proverbs 4:9.
10   Isaiah 21:5.
11   II Samuel 1:21.

of little use. That is why it was so important to have a shield that deflects incoming weapons, thereby providing [מגן] invulnerability to its owner, rather than one that merely protects a small area of the body. Similarly, the garden is not a place to merely unwind but rather, the only viable possibility to survive: no life is possible outside it. Thus, when God says that He is a "shield" to Abraham, it is much more about giving him something positive than protecting him from something negative:

After these events, the word of Hashem came to Abram in a vision, saying, "Fear not, Abram, I am a shield [מגן] for you; your reward is very great."[12]	אַחַר הַדְּבָרִים הָאֵלֶּה הָיָה דְבַר ה' אֶל אַבְרָם בַּמַּחֲזֶה לֵאמֹר אַל תִּירָא אַבְרָם אָנֹכִי מָגֵן לָךְ שְׂכָרְךָ הַרְבֵּה מְאֹד:
RASHI: After these events — Wherever אחר is used, it signifies immediately after the preceding event; whilst אחרי signifies a long time afterwards. "After these events" means: after this miracle has been wrought for him in that he slew the kings and he was in great anxiety, saying, "Perhaps I have already received, in this God-given victory, reward for all my good deeds" — therefore the Omnipresent said to him, "Fear not, Abram, I am thy shield against punishment, for you shall not be punished on account of all these people whom you have slain. And as for your being anxious regarding the receipt of any further reward, know that thy reward will be exceeding great."[13]	**רש"י: אחר הדברים האלה** — כל מקום שנאמר אחר סמוך, אחרי מופלג. אחר שנעשה לו נס זה שהרג את המלכים והיה דואג ואומר שמא קבלתי שכר על כל צדקותי, לכך אמר לו המקום אל תירא אברם אנכי מגן לך מן העונש שלא תענש על כל אותן נפשות שהרגת, ומה שאתה דואג על קבול שכרך, שכרך הרבה מאד:

To keep the symbolism of the shield, Rashi construes it as protection against punishment that Abraham may have feared. Receiving reward is viewed as a separate matter. Considering, however, that reward and punishment come from the same source, מגן as a participle meaning "providing," "making available" can accommodate both. Everything that comes upon Abraham comes from God, Who knows the overall balance of reward and punishment, so that Abraham's reward will not be jeopardized. Thus, מגן with reference to God implies providing everything one receives, both positive and negative, while keeping an overall positive balance. This is much like the garden that filters out excessive heat and lets through just enough sunlight.

---

12 Genesis 15:1.
13 Genesis Rabbah 44:5.

Shield of David

Another instance of the epithet מגן, which appears in connection with King David, provides an opportunity to confirm the above understanding. The blessing of the Patriarchs, which concludes with "Shield of Abraham," mentions, among other things, the promise to bring a redeemer to Abraham's descendants:

...and brings a Redeemer to their children's children, for His Name's sake, with love. O King, Helper, Savior, and Shield.[14] Blessed are You, Hashem, Shield of Abraham.	...וּמֵבִיא גוֹאֵל לִבְנֵי בְנֵיהֶם לְמַעַן שְׁמוֹ בְּאַהֲבָה מֶלֶךְ עוֹזֵר וּמוֹשִׁיעַ וּמָגֵן. בָּרוּךְ אַתָּה ה' מָגֵן אַבְרָהָם:

Ultimately, the redeemer must descend from David. It is hardly a coincidence that David too is associated with מגן, specifically in the blessing after the Haftarah that ends with מגן דוד, Shield of David. The Gemara teaches that this epithet is based on God's words that He gave David a great name:

Rabbah bar Sheila said: [While a blessing] in the prayer concludes with "He Who causes the horn of salvation to flourish," the blessing after the Haftarah concludes with "Shield of David." And I gave you great renown, like the renown of the great men of the world." Rav Yosef teaches: hence it is said, Shield of David.[15]	אמר רבה בר שילא: דצלותא מצמיח קרן ישועה, דאפטרתא מגן דוד. ועשיתי לך שם גדול כשם הגדלים, תני רב יוסף: זהו שאומרים מגן דוד:

In the verse quoted in the Gemara and used by Rav Yosef as a proof-text for the epithet "Shield of David," giving David a great name is accompanied by cutting down his enemies:

I was with you wherever you went—I cut down all your enemies before you and I gave you great renown, like the renown of the great men of the world.[16]	וָאֶהְיֶה עִמְּךָ בְּכֹל אֲשֶׁר הָלַכְתָּ וָאַכְרִתָה אֶת כָּל אֹיְבֶיךָ מִפָּנֶיךָ וְעָשִׂתִי לְךָ שֵׁם גָּדוֹל כְּשֵׁם הַגְּדֹלִים אֲשֶׁר בָּאָרֶץ:

There is a striking correspondence between this and the promise to Abraham above, in which מגן is mentioned. Both Abraham and David

---

14 Note that מגן appears in the blessing even before מגן אברהם in a group of participles and so is unlikely to denote a piece of military equipment.

15 *bPesaḥim* 117b.

16 II Samuel 7:9.

were given a great name[17] and both personally fought their enemies which potentially could have diminished or even canceled their chances to see that come true. When the uncertainty becomes an issue, the epithet מגן is used. In the case of David, God promises him that the Messiah will be of his lineage. This is, actually, what the blessing after the Haftarah is about:

Gladden us, Hashem, our God, with Elijah the prophet, Your servant, and with the kingdom of the House of David, Your anointed, may he come speedily and cause our heart to exult. On his throne let no stranger sit nor let others continue to inherit his honor, for by Your holy Name You swore to him that his lamp will not be extinguished forever and ever. Blessed are You, Hashem, Shield of David.	שַׂמְּחֵנוּ ה' אֱ-לֹהֵינוּ בְּאֵלִיָּהוּ הַנָּבִיא עַבְדֶּךָ וּבְמַלְכוּת בֵּית דָּוִד מְשִׁיחֶךָ. בִּמְהֵרָה יָבוֹא וְיָגֵל לִבֵּנוּ. עַל כִּסְאוֹ לֹא יֵשֶׁב זָר וְלֹא יִנְחֲלוּ עוֹד אֲחֵרִים אֶת כְּבוֹדוֹ. כִּי בְשֵׁם קָדְשְׁךָ נִשְׁבַּעְתָּ לּוֹ שֶׁלֹּא יִכְבֶּה נֵרוֹ לְעוֹלָם וָעֶד: בָּרוּךְ אַתָּה ה'. מָגֵן דָּוִד:

Elsewhere, the tradition indirectly confirms the similarity of מגן and גן, comparing Abraham and David, both of whom enjoyed having God as their "shield" [מגן], as it were, with Adam, who enjoyed the spiritual light in the Garden of Eden [גן עדן]. According to Midrash, Abraham was worthy to have been created before Adam,[18] while David received his seventy years of life from Adam who was supposed to live a thousand years but lived seventy years less.[19] ◙

---

[17] The promise to Abraham is given in Gen 12:2. Cf. also Alsheich on II Sam 7:9, "And I will make you a great name like that of the greatest men on earth." They are the Forefathers, since according to the Sages we say "Shield of David" just as we say "Shield of the Forefathers."

[18] Genesis Rabbah 14:6.

[19] Numbers Rabbah, *Naso* 14:12.

The Sanctity of Tefillin

By: ASHER BENZION BUCHMAN

תפילין של ראש, אין עושין אותה של יד, ושל יד, עושין אותה של ראש--
לפי שאין מורידין מקדושה חמורה, לקדושה קלה. וכן רצועה של תפילין של
ראש, אין עושין אותה לתפילין של יד. במה דברים אמורים, בשלבשן; אבל
תפילין של ראש שלא לבשה אדם מעולם, אם רצה להחזירה ליד, מותר.
(הלכות תפילין ג:יז)

A head *tefillah* may not be made into an arm *tefillah*, but an arm *tefil-lah* may be made into a head *tefillah*, because an article should not be lowered from a higher level of holiness to a lesser one. Similarly, the strap of a head *tefillah* should not be used for an arm *tefillah*. When does the above apply? After one has worn them. However, if head *tefillin* have never been worn, one may make them into arm *tefillin*. (*Hilchos Tefillin* 3:17)

Rambam gives no explanation as to why the תפילין של ראש has a higher level of holiness, קדושה, than תפילין של יד.[1] The standard explanation is that including the straps (רצועות), the של ראש has two letters of G-d's name, שד-י, while the של יד has only one.[2] However, the Brisker Rav points out that according to Rambam the knot of the ד in the straps of the של ראש is not meant to represent a letter but merely is in the form of a ד.[3] While the requirement of this knot as well as of the ש embossed in the של ראש is a *Halachah LeMoshe MiSinai*, the knot of the י was apparently instituted at a later date, and there is no Torah law[4] to make the שם שד-י with the body of the *tefillin*. Why then is the תפילין של ראש of a higher קדושה?

---

1   The Talmudic source is TB *Menachos* 34b.
2   See *Rabbenu Manoach* (*Hilchos Tefillin*, ibid.). The שם, שד-י is made up of the ש on the של ראש, the ד made of the knot on the של ראש and the י in the knot of the של יד.
3   *Chiddushei Maran Riz HaLevi, Hilchos Tefillin* 3:16.
4   Nor apparently even a Rabbinic law, but rather a Geonic custom.

Rabbi Asher Benzion Buchman, a *musmach* of RIETS, is the author of *Encountering the Creator: Divine Providence and Prayer in the Works of Rambam* (Targum, 2004) and *Rambam and Redemption* (Targum, 2005). He is the editor-in-chief of *Ḥakirah*.

To answer this question, we need to explore the nature of קדושת תפילין and קדושה in general.

The קדושה of Objects

Rambam speaks of קדושת תפילין in two other places:

חייב אדם למשמש בתפיליו, כל זמן שהן עליו, שלא יסיח דעתו מהן, אפילו
רגע אחד--שקדושתן גדולה מקדושת הציץ: שהציץ אין בו אלא שם אחד;
ואלו יש בהן אחד ועשרים שם של יוד הא בשל ראש, וכמותן בשל יד.

A person should touch his *tefillin* [from time to time] during the entire time he is wearing them, so that he will not divert his attention from them even for a single moment, for their holiness surpasses that of the *tzitz*. The *tzitz* has G-d's name [written] upon it only once, while the head *tefillin* and, similarly, the arm *tefillin,* contain the name י-ה-ו-ה 21 times. (ibid. 4:14)

Here we see that the source of קדושת תפילין is the שמות, the names of G-d, that are written in the *parshiyos*. Thus, in general, it would seem that קדושה pertaining to objects emanates from the presence of the שם, and *parshiyos* of the Torah in *mezuzos* and *tefillin* are the sources of their קדושה.

קדושה most prominently emanates from the actual Presence of השם, the Holy Presence. We are commanded to build a בית המקדש with the words "Make for me a *Mikdash* that I may dwell amongst them" ועשו לי מקדש ושכנתי בתוכם (שמות כה:ח). The *Beis HaMikdash* is to be perceived as a resting place for the שכינה, the Holy Presence. Rambam explains of our relationship to the *Mikdash*:

מצות עשה ליראה מן המקדש, שנאמר "ומקדשי תיראו (ויקרא יט:ל; ויקרא
כו:ב) ולא מן המקדש אתה ירא, אלא ממי שציווה על יראתו.

There is a positive commandment to hold the Temple in awe (ליראה), as [Leviticus 19:30] states: "And you shall revere my Sanctuary." Nevertheless, it is not the [physical building of] the Temple which must be held in awe, but rather, He Who commanded that it be revered. (*Hilchos Beis HaBechirah* 7:1)

While the fear of the *Beis HaMikdash* is an independent mitzvah, it is ultimately a command to experience fear of G-d. Since the *Mikdash* is identified as the resting place of G-d's Presence, the purpose of the mitzvah is to increase the awe of G-d; in fact, the קיום המצוה, the fulfillment of the mitzvah, is feeling that one is in the presence of G-d.

Likewise, the written שם serves as a representation of G-d's Presence and this is why קדושה emanates from it. Thus included in the prohibition of destroying the names of G-d[5] is the destruction of even a stone of the *Beis HaMikdash*, as Rambam[6] defines this *lav* of destroying the name of G-d as שלא לאבד דברים שנקרא שמו עליהם. "Do not destroy the things in which His name is associated." In addition, the Torah tells us בכל המקום אשר אזכיר את שמי אבוא אליך וברכתיך (שמות כ:כ) and *Chazal* interpret this to mean "where the שם is permitted to be said[7] there G-d's blessing will be felt."[8] The spoken name of G-d also has קדושה and ushers in the Presence of G-d.

The קדושה of Space

In the *Sefer HaMitzvos* (*lav* 65) Rambam describes this *lav* as שהזהירנו מנתוץ ומאבד בתי עבודת הקל ומאבד ספרי הנבואה ומלמחוק השמות הנכבדים והדומה לזה, "We are warned against destroying the houses of G-d, and the books of prophecy and from erasing the honored names or similar things." Significantly, in his *Sefer Mitzvos Katan*[9] Rambam explicitly includes בתי כנסיות ובתי מדרשות, and clearly this is his intent in the *Sefer HaMitzvos* in the term בתי הקל. There is much discussion and disagreement in the commentaries on what the source of קדושת בית הכנסת is. Rav Soloveitchik, ז"צל,[10] links it to *Sefer Yechezkel* where they are referred to as מקדש מעט. In turn he finds the source of קדושת מקדש and of all the encampments, מחנות, in the *luchos*:

> The Ark was placed on a stone in the western portion of the Holy of Holies. The vial of manna and Aharon's staff were placed before it. When Solomon built the Temple, he was aware that it would ultimately be destroyed. [Therefore,] he constructed a chamber, in which the Ark could be entombed below [the Temple building] in deep, maze-like vaults. King Josiah commanded that [the Ark] be entombed in the chamber built by Solomon, as it is said (II Chronicles 35:3): "And he said to the Levites who would teach wisdom to all of Israel: 'Place the Holy Ark in the chamber built by Solomon, the son of David, King of Israel. You will no [longer] carry it on

---

5   פרק ו מהל" יסדה"ת.

6   כותרת להל' יסדה"ת.

7   *I.e.*, where it can be said ככתבו, during ברכת כהנים and ודוי יום הכפורים.

8   See *Ḥakirah* 27 שם המפורש במקרא ובהלכה.

9   In the introduction to *Mishneh Torah*.

10   See *Morenu* Rav Hershel Schachter's *Eretz HaZvi, siman 12.*

your shoulders. Now, serve the L-rd, your G-d.' When it was en-tombed, Aharon's staff, the vial of manna, and the oil used for anointing were entombed with it. All these [sacred articles] did not return in the Second Temple. (*Hilchos Beis HaBechirah* 4:1)

Rambam implies that it is the presence of the *luchos* that invests the *Mikdash* with קדושה and that in the Second Temple the *luchos* were present but beneath the ground. In that case, in the *Beis HaMikdash*, it is actually the physical connection to the שם that creates קדושה in the space surrounding it. That is why the Holy of Holies, קדש הקדשים, has the highest קדושה and all other levels of קדושה emanate from this center. Likewise, the קדושה of the *beis haknesses* stems from the *Sefer Torah* which is present in the היכל [11] of the shul. Rambam makes the point that the sanctity of the *Sefer Torah* is akin to the קדושה of the *luchos*.

> It is a mitzvah to designate a special place for a Torah scroll and to honor it and glorify it in an extravagant manner. The words of the *Luchos HaBris* are contained in each Torah scroll. (*Hilchos Sefer Torah* 10:10)

Thus, the קדושה of *tefillin* is akin to the קדושה of the *Beis HaMikdash*, both stemming from the representation of G-d's presence, השם. The קדושה stems from the שמות in the *parshiyos* and extends to the בתים ורצועות.

While we speak of the שם, it is important to note that *Neviim* and *Kesuvim* are called כתבי קודש and this status is not dependent solely on the presence of the שם, as *Megillas Esther* does not have the שם. In the quote from the *Sefer HaMitzvos* above, Rambam refers to the prohibition of destroying *sifrei nevuah*. The word of G-d has קדושה; it too is a representation of G-d.[12]

The קדושה of Mitzvos

There is yet another source of קדושה. In *Mishneh Torah*, Rambam explains the naming of his *Sefer Kedushah* as follows:

> **The fifth book:** I will include within it all the mitzvos that involve forbidden intimate relations and those that involve forbidden

---

[11] Note that the terminology of היכל is taken from the בית המקדש.

[12] I believe this is a very important point. Trying to define exactly what the status of כתבי קודש is, is difficult. But here in the *lav* of אבוד השם we see that there is a Torah definition for it and Torah legislation about it.

foods. [I have grouped the two together] because it is in these two matters that G-d has sanctified us and separated us from the [other] nations. [The Torah mentions the concept of holiness] with regard to both these matters, stating [Leviticus 20:24, 27]: "[I am G-d, your L-rd,] who has separated you from among the nations... and I have set you apart among the nations." [Accordingly,] I have called this book *The Book of Holiness*. (Introduction to *Mishneh Torah*)

With regard to *arayos* and forbidden foods there are many prohibitions that extend over and above the seven Noachide principles of law, and this most clearly distinguishes us from other nations. קדושת ישראל is identified specifically with these mitzvos in which we exercise self-control and demonstrate that our focus is on satisfying the spiritual wants of man rather than his physical desires.

But more generally when the Torah states קדושים תהיו כי קדש אני ה' אלקיכם (ויקרא יט:ב), "Be Holy as I your G-d am Holy," Rambam interprets it as a command to keep all the mitzvos, as קדושה emanates from doing all of G-d's commands.

> And [others] have already erred in this principle, such that they counted, "You shall be holy" (Leviticus 19:2), to be included among the positive commandments. And they did not know that "You shall be holy," and "you shall sanctify yourselves and be holy" (Leviticus 11:44) are commands to keep the whole Torah. It is as if it said, "Be holy by doing everything I have commanded you and being careful about anything I have prohibited to you." And the words of the Sifra (*Sifra, Kedoshim*, Section 1:1) are, "'You shall be holy,' you shall be separated—meaning to say, separate from all the disgraceful things that I have prohibited to you." And in the *Mechilta* (*Mechilta d'Rabbi Yishmael* 22:30:1), "Issi ben Yehudah says, 'When the Holy One, Blessed be He, originates a commandment for Israel, He adds holiness to them'"—meaning to say this command is not a command in itself, but rather follows from the commands that they have been commanded. So, one who fulfills this command will be called holy. And there is no difference between it saying, "You shall be holy," or if it had said, "Do my commandments." (*Sefer HaMitzvos, Shoresh* 4)

Man attains קדושה by performing all mitzvos, and in performing each individual mitzvah he sanctifies himself. With regard to the mitzvos related to the *Beis HaMikdash*, the mechanism of this process is obvious:

> The object of the Sanctuary was to create in the hearts of those who enter it certain feelings of awe and reverence, in accordance with the command, "You shall reverence my sanctuary" (Leviticus

19:30). ... Our Sages, as is well known, said, "Even a clean person may not enter the Sanctuary for the purpose of performing Divine service, unless he takes previously a bath." By such acts the reverence [for the Sanctuary] will continue, the right impression will be produced which leads man, as is intended, to humility. (*Moreh Ha-Nevuchim* 3:47)

Upon entering the *Beis HaMikdash* one is commanded to feel in the presence of G-d and the experience of having been in the *Mikdash* elevates the character of a person and hence sanctifies the person. But even when the mitzvah seems of the most mundane nature and unrelated to what we consider קדושה, it is still a necessary part of what makes Israel holy.

The קדושה of Man

In addition, since קדושה is a characteristic of G-d, therefore the command of והלכת בדרכיו, "emulating G-d," specifically commands us to be קדוש as Rambam explains in *Hilchos Deos*:

ומצווין אנו ללכת בדרכים אלו הבינוניים, והם הדרכים הטובים והישרים, שנאמר "והלכת בדרכיו" (דברים כח:ט). כך לימדו בפירוש מצוה זו: מה הוא נקרא חנון, אף אתה היה חנון; מה הוא נקרא רחום, אף אתה היה רחום; **מה הוא נקרא קדוש, אף אתה היה קדוש.**

We are commanded to walk in these intermediate paths—and they are good and straight paths—as [Deuteronomy 28:9] states: "And you shall walk in His ways." [Our Sages] taught [the following] explanation of this mitzvah: Just as He is called "Gracious," you shall be gracious; just as He is called "Merciful," you shall be merciful; just as He is called "Holy," you shall be holy. (*Hilchos Deos* 1:5–6)

Later in *Hilchos Deos*, Rambam refers to the concept of קדושה in two places; once with regard to balancing carnal desires in accordance to what he stated with regard to the naming of *Sefer Kedushah*:

Although a man's wife is permitted to him at all times, it is fitting that a wise man behave with holiness. He should not frequent his wife like a rooster. (*Hilchos Deos* 5:4)

In the other place he mentions it, it is with regard to the content of one's speech:

One should always cultivate silence and refrain from speaking, except with regard to matters of knowledge or things that are necessary for his physical welfare. It was said that Rav, the disciple of *Rabbenu HaKadosh*, never uttered an idle word in all his days—

which is what the conversation of most people consists of. One should not speak at length even about matters involving one's physical needs. On this point, our Sages commanded us and said: "Whoever speaks at length brings on sin." They also said: "I have found nothing better for one's person than silence." (*Hilchos Deos* 2:4)

By referring to Rebbe as *Rabbenu HaKadosh*, Rambam links the concept of קדושה to the content of one's speech, hence the content of one's thoughts.

Accordingly, in the second place Rambam speaks of קדושת תפילין, there is a different slant from the first place.

קדושת תפילין, קדושה גדולה היא: שכל זמן שתפילין על ראשו של אדם, ועל זרועו--הוא עניו וירא, ואינו נמשך בשחוק ובשיחה בטילה, ואינו מהרהר במחשבות רעות, אלא מפנה ליבו לדברי האמת והצדק. לפיכך צריך אדם להשתדל להיותן עליו, כל היום--שמצותן, כך היא. אמרו עליו על רב תלמיד רבנו הקדוש, שכל ימיו לא ראוהו שהלך ארבע אמות בלא תורה, או בלא ציצית, או בלא תפילין.

The holiness associated with *tefillin* is very great. As long as a person is wearing *tefillin* on his head and arm, he will be humble and God-fearing and will not be drawn to frivolous behavior or empty speech. He will not turn his thoughts to evil matters, but rather will direct his heart to words of truth and justice. Accordingly, a person should try to wear [*tefillin*] throughout the entire day, for this is the mitzvah associated with them. Among the praises conveyed upon Rav, the student of *Rabbenu HaKadosh*, was that he was never seen walking four cubits without [reciting words of] Torah, without *tzitzit*, and without *tefillin*. (*Hilchos Tefillin* 4:25)

Rambam does not mean that the *tefillin* will automatically have this magical effect on the person wearing them,[13] but rather psychologically wearing the *parshiyos* has this effect and more precisely שמצותן כך היא "that one is obligated to act this way while wearing them." The קדושה comes from the fact that when one wears *tefillin* he is obligated to act with קדושה, to feel G-d's presence. Rambam ends by referring again to "Rav, the student of *Rabbenu HaKadosh*," just as he did in *Hilchos Deos*, who "never uttered an idle word in all his days." The conduct and the attitude of the wearer injects the קדושה into the *tefillin*. The performance

---

13   As this runs counter to the philosophy of the Torah he expounds most clearly in *Moreh HaNevuchim*.

of the mitzvah of wearing *tefillin* is מקדש the wearer and he in turn is מקדש the *tefillin* themselves.

In general, the act of being מקדיש an object means designating an item for use in the *Beis HaMikdash* for the service of G-d. So clearly, man can create קדושה with his speech. Man builds the *Beis HaMikdash* and sanctifies its space. Man is also in charge of the calendar and hence is מקדש the *yamim tovim* via his דעת, his thoughts, and it is a mitzvah for him to do so. Mitzvos were given to us because in their performance we become קדוש and conversely in our performance of these mitzvos we sanctify time, space, and matter.

של ראש ושל יד

In this halachah, Rambam characterizes one's being, while wearing *tefillin*, as being composed of two parts: "(1) He will not turn his thoughts to evil matters, but rather (2) will direct his heart to words of truth and justice." There is an element of the mind and of the heart. The תפילין של ראש are placed next to the brain and the של יד next to the heart.

> The arm [*tefillin*] should be tied to one's left arm at the muscle, i.e., the bulging flesh of the arm between the shoulder and the elbow. Thus, if one presses his arm to his ribs, the *tefillah* will be opposite his heart, thus fulfilling the directive [Deuteronomy 6:6], "And these words... shall be upon your heart." (*Hilchos Tefillin* 4:2)

The תפילין של יד is meant to impact the emotions and the character of the wearer which are related to the heart, the seat of one's emotions. This corresponds to perfection of the body (*shlemus haguf*), the central theme of *Hilchos Deos*.[14] The של ראש is placed next to the brain "the place where a child's brain [can be felt] to pulsate" (*Hilchos Tefillin* 4:1), in order to impact one's intellect (*shlemus hanefesh*), the central theme of *Hilchos Yesodei HaTorah*. Or from another vantage point, the של יד gets its קדושה from the heart and של ראש from the head. Thus, the תפילין של ראש are on a higher level than של יד because it is placed on the head, the intellect being superior to emotion.[15] This also explains why this higher קדושה only emerges once the *tefillin* have been worn, with the תפילין של

---

[14] See *hakdamah* to *Perush HaMishnah*. The purpose of the mitzvos is to create a man with שלמות הגוף ושלמות הנפש with the שלמות הנפש being the highest attainment and ultimate goal.

[15] This is why *Hilchos Yesodei HaTorah* precedes *Hilchos Deos* in *Mishneh Torah*.

ראש getting its added קדושה from actually having been placed on the head.[16]

The halachic relationship between the של ראש and the של יד is unique. Each is a separate mitzvah in the *taryag* and each can be performed without the other and has a distinct *nusach* for its *berachah*. The Torah dedicated one mitzvah for binding the heart and another mitzvah for the binding of the mind.

> The [absence of the] head *tefillah* does not preclude [wearing *tefillin*] on the arm, and similarly, the [absence of the] arm *tefillah* does not preclude [wearing *tefillin*] on the head. They are two mitzvos, each one to be considered independently. What blessings are recited? On the head *tefillin*, one recites: "[Blessed are You...] Who has sanctified us with His commandments and commanded us concerning the mitzvah of *tefillin*." On the arm *tefillin*, one recites: "[Blessed are You...] Who has sanctified us with His commandments and commanded us to put on *tefillin*." (*Hilchos Tefillin* 4:4)

Yet when worn together as is the norm they are to be put on with only one *berachah* covering both and must be donned in the proper order of של יד before של ראש. Moreover, the unusual halachah exists, that there is an order in which the *tefillin* must be removed—the reverse order from how they are put on, with the של ראש being removed first.[17,18]

One other halachah is especially intriguing. There must be no speech between the donning of the של יד and the של ראש and Rambam refers to it as the Gemara does, as a sin, עבירה, to speak.[19] The Talmud singles it out as a sin that should cause a soldier at war to leave the front lest he perish because of it.[20] There must be a continuous progression from the connection to the Creator with one's heart to that of the mind. Perfection of character is a prerequisite for perfection of knowledge as Rambam explains in the introduction to *Perush HaMishnah*.

---

[16]   This is independent of whether הזמנה מילתא.

[17]   במה דברים אמורים, בשהניח אחת מהן; אבל אם הניח שתיהן--מברך ברכה אחת, להניח תפילין, וקושר של יד תחילה, ואחר כך מניח של ראש. וכשהוא חולץ, חולץ של ראש תחילה, ואחר כך חולץ של יד (ד:ה).

[18]   We will return to this point later.

[19]   מי שבירך להניח תפילין וקשר תפילין של יד--אסור לו לספר, ואפילו להשיב שלום לרבו, עד שיניח של ראש; ואם שח, הרי זו עבירה, וצריך לברך ברכה שנייה על מצות תפילין, ואחר כך מניח של ראש (ד:ו).

[20]   Whereas there are several explanations of what the sin is, the fact that the sin is only for speaking and that this halachah is comparable to the language of interrupting in *tefillah* and *Krias Shema* indicates our understanding.

Rambam does not bring this halachah of the Talmud that one should not engage in battle if he has committed the sin of speaking between putting on the two *tefillin*, but rather ends the chapter on engaging or refraining from battle with these words that reflect the concept that the Gemara formulates with this halachah:

> To whom does the phrase "Is there a man who is afraid or faint-hearted?" refer? The phrase should be interpreted simply, as applying to a person whose heart is not brave enough to stand in the throes of battle. Once a soldier enters the throes of battle, he should rely on the Hope of Israel and their Savior in times of need. He should realize that he is fighting for the sake of the oneness of G-d's Name. Therefore, he should place his soul in His hand and not show fright or fear. He should not worry about his wife or children. On the contrary, he should wipe their memory from his heart, removing all thoughts from his mind except the war. (*Hilchos Melachim* 7:15)

The heart must propel the soldier forward and his intellect must grasp that he is fighting for ייחוד שמו, "for the sake of the oneness of G-d's Name." The wearing of *tefillin* is meant to create soldiers with this make-up.

Tefillin and the *Beis HaMikdash*

We have drawn an analogy between *tefillin* and the *Beis HaMikdash* in that their קדושה stems from the representation of G-d's presence. And, in fact, *parshiyos* of the Torah are at the core of each structure. With regard to the *Beis HaMikdash* there is a specific mitzvah of *yirah*— מורא המקדש—which in reality is a mitzvah to be in a state of *yirah*, feeling the presence of G-d. So too, for one wearing *tefillin* Rambam describes the state of *yirah* to which one must aspire. While no separate mitzvah is defined, this *yirah* is a part of the mitzvah itself.

With regard to *Mikdash,* there are laws related to physical conduct. "How is reverence for it manifest? A person should not enter the Temple Mount holding a staff, or with sandals on his feet, or wearing only underwear, with dust on his feet, or with money wrapped in his kerchief" (*Hilchos Beis HaBechirah* 7:1). These halachos parallel the concept that the body must be physically pure, גוף נקי, while wearing *tefillin*.[21]

---

21   תפילין צריכין גוף נקי כאלישע (ד:ו).

Laws governing the state of mind while in the *Mikdash*,[22] are paralleled by laws governing the state of mind one must have while wearing *tefillin*.[23]

There is a prescribed way for entering the *Mikdash* and leaving it:

All who enter the Temple Mount should [face] the right side, walk around [in that direction], and leave on the left side. ... Anyone who has completed his service [in the Temple and desires] to leave, should not [turn around and] leave with his back to the Temple. Rather, he should walk backwards slightly and [then], walk slowly, and [turn] to his side until leaving the Temple Courtyard. Similarly, the members of the priestly watch, the representatives of the Jewish people, and the Levites [when they descend] from their platform, should leave the Temple in this manner, similar to one who steps backwards after his prayers. All these [are expressions of] reverence for the Temple. (*Hilchos Beis HaBechirah* 7:3–4)

This parallels the requirement, that we noted earlier, that the תפילין של יד be placed first while the reverse order should be followed while removing *tefillin*. One proceeds from a lower state to a higher state of קדושה by putting on the של ראש and then backs away from it by removing the של ראש before the של יד.

The Zohar, in fact, states (1:129) that when we wear *tefillin* we create a *Beis HaMikdash* in our own bodies. Perhaps the term בית was chosen by *Chazal* to describe the containers of the *parshiyos* of *tefillin* because of this parallel. We noted earlier that the קדושה in the *Beis HaMikdash* emanates out from its core, the *luchos* in the Holy of Holies, קודש הקדשים. The outer areas have reduced levels of קדושה extending throughout *Yerushalayim*. With *tefillin* as well, the קדושה from the *parshiyos* extends to the בתים ורצועות. But more than that, halachos govern the storage of *tefillin*[24] and the containers that the *tefillin* are stored in also attain a level of קדושה, from the time they are prepared to be used for *tefillin*.[25]

---

22 לא יקל אדם את ראשו כנגד שער מזרחי של עזרה, שהוא שער ניקנור, שהוא מכוון כנגד
קודש הקדשים. וכל הנכנס לעזרה--יהלך בנחת במקום שמותר לו להיכנס לשם, ויראה עצמו
שהוא עומד לפני האדון ה' שאמר "והיו עיניי וליבי שם, כל הימים" ומהלך באימה ויראה
ופחד ורעדה, שנאמר "בבית אלוקים, נהלך ברגש" (תהילים נה,טו) (הל' בית הבחירה ז:ה).

23 שכל זמן שתפילין על ראשו של אדם, ועל זרועו--הוא עניו וירא, ואינו נמשך בשחוק ובשיחה
בטילה, ואינו מהרהר במחשבות רעות, אלא מפנה ליבו לדברי האמת והצדק.

24 See *Hilchos Tefillin* 4:8–9

25 This halachah of תשמישי קדושה applies as well to *Sefer Torah* but not to *mezuzah*.

Guarding the *Mikdash*

A separate mitzvah in the *taryag* calls for the guarding of the *Mikdash*:

> There is a positive mitzvah to guard the Temple. [This mitzvah ap-
> plies] even though there is no fear of enemies or thieves, for the
> guarding [of the Temple] is an expression of respect for it. A palace
> with guards is [much more impressive] than a palace without
> guards. The mitzvah of guarding [the Temple] applies throughout
> the night.
> The priests and Levites shall serve as guards… The priests on
> watch did not sleep in the priestly garments. Instead, they folded
> them, placed them at their heads, and wore their own clothes. They
> slept on the ground. It is customary for all those who stand watch
> over the courtyards of kings not to sleep on beds… If one of them
> had a seminal emission [in his sleep], he would proceed down the
> winding underground stairwell. [There was no prohibition in-
> volved], because the underground passageways that opened up to
> [the portion of] the Temple Mount [outside the Courtyard] were
> not consecrated. [There,] he would immerse himself. [He would
> then] return and sit among his fellow priests until the gates were
> opened in the morning. [At that time,] he would leave and proceed
> [to his own affairs]. (*Hilchos Beis HaBechirah* 8:1–7)

The mitzvah of guarding, שמירה, is at night. And interestingly, while
the Leviim who watched outside the *Mikdash* were disciplined if they fell
asleep, the Kohanim actually slept at night and apparently were still considered to have been engaged in the mitzvah of שמירה.

Tefillin, as well, has a mitzvah of שמירה:[26]

> The time for wearing *tefillin* is the day and not the night, as [Exodus
> 13:10] states: "And you shall observe this statute in its appointed
> time, from day to day." "This statute" refers to the mitzvah of *tefil-
> lin*. Similarly, Sabbaths and holidays are not days on which *tefillin*
> [are worn], as [Exodus 13:9] states: "And they shall be a sign for
> you." Since the Sabbaths and the holidays are themselves signs, [the
> sign of *tefillin* is unnecessary]. When does the time to put them on
> begin? When one can see a colleague standing four cubits away and
> recognize him. [It continues] until sunset. It is permitted for a per-
> son who put on *tefillin* before sunset to continue wearing them after
> nightfall. They may even remain upon him the entire night. This

---

[26] As with its mitzvah of יראה it is not an independent mitzvah but a part of the
mitzvah of *tefillin*.

law, however, is not to be taught in public. Instead, everyone should be taught not to wear *tefillin* at night and to remove them before sunset. A person who puts on *tefillin* after sunset transgresses a Scriptural prohibition, as [implied by Exodus 13:10]: "And you shall observe (ושמרת) this statute... from day to day." (*Hilchos Tefillin* 4:10–11)

Here we have another parallel to *Mikdash*. Firstly, just like *avodah* cannot be done at night, so too the *mitzvas tefillin* cannot be done at night. Secondly, in place of *avodah*, the mitzvah pertaining to *Mikdash* at night is שמירה. Likewise, by *tefillin*, there is a concept of שמירה of *tefillin* at night.[27] It would seem that leaving the *tefillin* vulnerable at night is a violation of *mitzvas tefillin*. That this is the proper interpretation is made clearer in the next halachah.

When a person is wearing *tefillin* in the midst of a journey and the sun sets, marking the commencement of the Sabbath, he should cover them with his hand until he reaches his home, and then remove them. If he is sitting in the house of study and the sun sets, marking the commencement of the Sabbath, he should cover them with his hand until he reaches his home, and then remove them. If there is a house located near the wall [of a city] where they would be safe, he should place them there. If, however, he did not remove his *tefillin* after sunset because he did not have a place where they would be safe, it is permissible for him to continue wearing them in order to protect them. (*Hilchos Tefillin* 4:12)

Our concern is for the physical safety of the *tefillin*.[28] Just like the *Beis HaMikdash* needs protection at night which is not the time of the mitzvah of *avodah,* so too *tefillin* need protection at that time when there is no fulfillment of the mitzvah of wearing them. Ideally, the שמירה is done by storing the *tefillin* in a safe place when it is not worn, but if there is no safer place than remaining on one's body this option is to be taken. The fact that we legislate how the *tefillin* are stored also suggests that this is the proper interpretation.[29]

---

27 An actual קיום מצוה.

28 This is how the Brisker Rav learns while others explain these *halachos* differently.

29 See *Hilchos Tefillin* 4:9. כלי שהכינו להניח בו תפילין, והניחן בו--נתקדש, ואסור להשתמש בו בדברי חול... ואסור לתלות את התפילין, בין ברצועה בין בתפילה עצמה; אבל תולה הוא את הכיס שהתפילין מונחין בו.

The mere fact that the *tefillin* are presumed to be in a כלי is evidence that there is a physical requirement of שמירה of the *tefillin*.

The Public *Mikdash* and the Private *Mikdash*

All those who are exempt from the obligation to recite the *Shema* are exempt from the obligation to wear *tefillin*. If a minor knows [the importance of] guarding his *tefillin*, his father should obtain *tefillin* for him, to educate him regarding the performance of mitzvos. A person with stomach problems and anyone who can contain his excretory functions only with difficulty are exempt from the obligation to wear *tefillin*. [In contrast,] all those ritually impure (טמא) are obligated to wear *tefillin* like one who is pure. A person who suffers discomfort, or someone who is disturbed and cannot concentrate his thoughts, is exempt from the obligation to wear *tefillin*, since a person who wears *tefillin* is forbidden to divert his attention from them. Priests who are in the midst of [the Temple] service, Levites who chant on the platform, and Israelites while they are attending the Temple [ceremonies] are exempt from the obligation to pray and to wear *tefillin*. (*Hilchos Tefillin* 4:13)

Despite the strong similarity between the mitzvos of *tefillin* and *Mikdash*, there are also some surprisingly major differences. Let us begin with the statement at the end of this halachah. The act of *avodah* need not be done with *tefillin*.[30] Would not these two mitzvos be especially compatible and reinforcing, just as we find that *tefillin* is especially compatible with *tefillah*? As Rambam explains: "Although it is a mitzvah to wear [*tefillin*] throughout the entire day, it is most important during prayer. Our Sages declared: "Whoever recites the *Shema* without *tefillin* is considered as if he is giving false testimony." (*Hilchos Tefillin* 4:26)

Rambam addresses this anomaly in this very same halachah. Seemingly out of place, he tells us that while engaged in *avodah* or ancillary functions in the *Mikdash*, one is also excused from *tefillah*. There is the physical, public *Mikdash* which has a physical form of *avodah* and a spiritual, private *Mikdash* of the heart, whose *avodah* is *tefillah*, worship of the

---

[30] In fact, the יד של cannot be worn because it makes a הפסק to the בגדי כהונה but why not the של ראש? Actually, a Kohen may wear *tefillin* של ראש but there is no mitzvah to do so. This is comparable to the halachah that one who has worn *tefillin* during the day may continue to wear them at night, yet this halachah was not publicized and was limited to the *chachamim*. Here, too, the Kohanim in the *Mikdash* were at a level where the *avodah* of *tefillin* could be done outside of its time (הל' כלי המקדש י:ו). In fact, the Kohen Gadol wears the של ראש, which we will discuss later.

heart— עבודה שבלב.[31] Each operates in a separate realm. Thus, as we now turn to the beginning of this halachah we see that Rambam starts by tying the obligation of *tefillin* with *Krias Shema*, a form of inner intellectual *avodah*—*Yichud Hashem*. *Tefillah* and *Krias Shema*, mitzvos of the heart and the mind, are to be facilitated with the wearing of *tefillin* של יד and של ראש.

The halachah continues by stating that attaining the ability to guard, שומר, *tefillin* qualifies a child to wear them.[32] With regard to *Mikdash* the father is to bring his son there as soon as he is physically able to hold his father's hand and ascend *Har HaBayis;* the experience of *Mikdash* and the fulfillment of the mitzvah of coming to the *Beis HaMikdash,* ראיית פני הבית, is a physical and experiential one. *Tefillin* is an experience of the mind and requires the maturity and intellectual capability to perform שמירה.

Next comes another contrast. In *Mikdash* there is always a requirement of being ritually pure, טהרה. The Kohanim doing שמירה had to leave immediately with a seminal emission.[33] But by *tefillin* it is not a requirement at all, just as it is not a concern with *Krias Shema* or *tefillah*.[34] Instead, control of bodily functions is the measure. And this requirement goes past anything found in the *Beis HaMikdash*. Rambam explains "*Tefillin* require a clean body (גוף נקי); i.e., that one should be careful not to release gas while wearing them. Accordingly, it is forbidden to sleep while wearing them, neither a long sleep nor a nap." (*Hilchos Tefillin 4:15*)

This requirement does not exist by *Mikdash*, and as we have noted above, even the mitzvah of שמירה can be performed while sleeping and there is no mention of the issue of גוף נקי. It is only an issue for the pri-

---

31 תפלה is referred to as עבודה שבלב. See *Sefer HaMitzvos, Aseh 5* and *Hilchos Tefillah* 1:1.

32 Based on what we have established above, this is not שומר נקביו but שומר תפילין.

33 See *Hilchos Beis HaBechirah* quoted above, where Rambam makes this point in discussing the physical מעשה שמירה.

34 כל הטמאים--חייבין בקריאת שמע, ומברכין לפניה ולאחריה והן בטומאתן, אף על פי שאפשר להן לעלות מטומאתן בו ביום, כגון הנוגעים בשרץ או בנידה וזבה ומשכבן וכיוצא בהן. ועזרא ובית דינו תיקנו שלא יקרא בעל קרי לבדו משאר הטמאים, עד שיטבול; ולא פשטה תקנה זו בכל ישראל, ולא היה כוח לרוב הציבור לעמוד בה--לפיכך בטלה. וכבר נהגו כל ישראל לקרות בתורה ולקרות קרית שמע, והן בעלי קראין, לפי שאין דברי תורה מקבלין טומאה, אלא עומדין בטהרתן לעולם (הל' ק"ש ד:ח).

vate *Mikdash.*[35] While in the outer *Mikdash* the concern is with how the body interacts with the physical *Mikdash*, in the inner *Mikdash* our concern is with the inner workings of the body. Thus, the halachah continues that those in a state of pain or bewilderment may not enter the *Mikdash* of *tefillin*. It is the mind and heart that enters the *Mikdash*, thus, "it is forbidden to divert his attention from them," אסור לו להסיח דעתו, as the mitzvah of מורא requires a constant state of consciousness.

Shabbos and *Tefillin*

Once we understand that the *avodah* designated for the *Beis HaMikdash* is irrelevant to *tefillin*, we can understand as well why *tefillin* are not worn on Shabbos. The *Mikdash* is sanctified space, קדושת מקום, and the *avodah* done there is physical and engages the body. On Shabbos one enters yet another *Mikdash*, the *Mikdash* not of space but of time, and here, too, as in the *Beis HaMikdash*, the major participant is the body. The *avodah* done on Shabbos is with "rest from work," שביתה ממלאכה, coupled with acts of "honor and enjoyment," כבוד ועונג, enjoyment of the body. In contrast, as we have explained, when one wears *tefillin*, he enters the *Mikdash* of the mind and all the *avodah* done there is with the mind.

> Four things have been enjoined regarding the Sabbath: two on Biblical authority, and two on the authority of the Sages and clearly expressed by the Prophets. The Torah says: *Remember* (Exodus 20:8) and *Observe* (Deuteronomy 5:12); the Prophets clearly speak of *honor* and *enjoyment*, as it is written: "Call the Sabbath a delight, and the L-rd's sacred day an honor" (Isaiah 58:13). What is meant by *honor*? The Sages explained this by declaring that each person should wash his face, hands, and feet with hot water on Friday in honor of the Sabbath, and then enwrap himself in a fringed garment and be seated with dignity in expectation of the Sabbath, receiving it as if he were coming out to meet the king. The ancient Sages used to assemble their disciples on Friday, put on their best clothes, and say: "Come, let us go out to meet King Sabbath." We honor the Sabbath by wearing clean clothes. One must not wear weekday apparel on the Sabbath. But if he does not have [an additional set of clothing] to change, he should lower his garment, so that his [style of] dress is not like that of the week. And Ezra or-

---

[35] Probably no smell could be detected in the *Mikdash* where the strong smell of the *ketores* was meant to cover the less pleasant odors of animals being slaughtered as Rambam points out in the *Moreh HaNevuchim*.

dained that the people should wash their clothes on Thursday, on account of the honor of the [coming] Shabbos... What is meant by Sabbath enjoyment? The Sages explained this by declaring that one should prepare rich food and fragrant beverages for the Sabbath as much as he can afford. The more anyone spends for the Sabbath and the preparation of varied tasty food, the more praise he deserves. (*Hilchos Shabbos* 30:1–7)

Shabbos has a physical presence within time that Israel waits for after having prepared and adorned the body outwardly. The mitzvos with which we sanctify it are also related to the physical world. Although in refraining from work, it might seem that one is withdrawing from the physical world, this is not so. Refraining from work is coupled with enjoyment of the world and of the gifts of nature. Rest from work is a form of governing and directing the body away from toil and towards rest and enjoyment. The *kedushah* of Shabbos is similar to that of the *Beis HaMikdash* and wearing *tefillin* is not suitable for the *avodah* of either.

Kohen Gadol and *Tefillin*

Yet with regard to one halachah, the distinct domains of the *Beis HaMikdash* and *tefillin* converge. Whereas Kohanim in general did not wear *tefillin*, the clothes of the Kohen Gadol were specifically designed so that he would wear תפילין של ראש.

What is the order in which the priestly garments should be put on? [The priest] should put on the leggings first... Afterwards, he winds the headgear like a turban. He ties the forehead plate ציץ [behind his head,] above the turban. His hair was visible between the forehead plate and the turban and it is in that place that he would wear his *tefillin* between the forehead plate and the turban. (*Hilchos Klei HaMikdash* 10:1–3)

It is understandable that the Kohen Gadol wore *tefillin* because his daily function was not primarily that of physical *avodah*. To a certain extent his *avodah* was merely to be in the *Mikdash*.

Just as the priests are not warned against drinking wine except at the time they enter the Temple, so, too, they are forbidden to grow their hair long only at the time they enter the Temple. To whom does the above apply? To an ordinary priest. A High Priest, by contrast, is forbidden to let his hair grow long and rend his garments forever, for he is in the Temple at all times, תמיד הוא במקדש (*Hilchos Beis HaMikdash* 1:10). There was a chamber prepared for him in the Sanctuary which was called "the Chamber of the High Priest." The glory and the honor of [the High Priest] would be to remain in the Sanctuary the entire day and to go to his private home only at night or for an hour or two during the day. His home should be in Jerusalem and he should never depart from there. (*Hilchos Klei HaMikdash* 5:7)

The Kohen Gadol is halachically viewed as always being in the *Mikdash*, no matter where he is physically. He carries the *Mikdash* within himself wherever he goes. In addition, his wearing of the *bigdei kehunah* is itself an *avodah*. When the Kohen Gadol wears the *tzitz* he ratifies the sacrifices that were brought in *tumah*. "The *tzitz* does not bring about appeasement unless it is on the High Priest's forehead, as [the above verse] continues: 'It will be on his forehead at all times, for appeasement before G-d.'" (*Hilchos Beis HaMikdash* 4:8)

The *tzitz* on his head and the breastplate, חושן, on his heart parallel the two *tefillin* and he does *avodah* in his heart and mind throughout the day. Yet he still is to wear תפילין של ראש. From Rambam's presentation we might judge that it is the crowning garment of the Kohen Gadol. The explanation for this is not given in *Sefer Avodah* but in *Hilchos Tefillin*. Let us refer back to a halachah we studied earlier in this essay:

A person should touch his *tefillin* [from time to time] during the entire time he is wearing them, so that he will not divert his attention from them even for a single moment, for their holiness surpasses that of the *tzitz*. The *tzitz* has G-d's name [written] upon it only once, while the head *tefillin* and, similarly, the arm *tefillin* contain the name י-ה-ו-ה 21 times. (*Hilchos Tefillin* 4:14)

Only in *Hilchos Tefillin* does Rambam imply that the Kohen Gadol should not divert his attention from the *tzitz*. This halachah is a detail in *Hilchos Tefillin*, a halachah pertaining to man's inner *Beis HaMikdash*. ೞ

Jews Not Allowed on the Temple Mount After the British Capture of Jerusalem:
Tracing the ever-changing status quo, 1917-1927

By: F. M. LOEWENBERG

In November 1917, the British government issued the Balfour Declaration, proclaiming its support for the establishment of a "national home for the Jewish people" in Palestine. This decision was greeted with great enthusiasm by Jews throughout the world and especially by the small Jewish community of Eretz Yisrael. This optimism was still evident when a month later the British army occupied Jerusalem.

The Turkish Army retreated from Jerusalem on Friday, December 7, 1917, after the British army had been shelling some Jerusalem neighborhoods for the previous two days. Before the Turkish governor departed from the city that Friday evening, he handed a surrender document to Hussein Salim al-Husseini, the Arab mayor of Jerusalem, and asked him to deliver it to the British army the next day. That day, Saturday, December 8, was a cold, rainy, wintery day. Mayor al-Husseini, accompanied by his family and a delegation of ten dignitaries, as well as a photographer, repeatedly tried to deliver the governor's letter of surrender and the keys of the city to the British army. Before the day was over, the mayor had handed over the letter four or five times. Legend has it that just outside the city he came across two army cooks who were looking for eggs to serve for breakfast. They inadvertently became the first British soldiers to see the surrender document but they refused to receive it. Next were two British sergeants who encountered the Jerusalem delegation at the western end of Jaffa Road. They also refused to accept the surrender document and instead called their officers, who were prepared to receive it, but a higher-ranking officer, Brig. Gen. C.F. Watson, decided that the surrender of Jerusalem was so important that it required his accepting the letter

F. M. Loewenberg is professor emeritus at the School of Social Work of Bar-Ilan University. He received his academic degrees from Harvard (AB), Columbia (MS), and Wayne State (PhD). Since his retirement in 1993 he has been involved in research on the history of Jerusalem, especially the history of the Temple Mount and the Western Wall. His recent publications have appeared in *Ḥakirah, Middle East Quarterly, Segula*, and other publications. An earlier draft of a summary of this research appeared in *Mekor Rishon,* July 3, 2021 (Hebrew).

of surrender again. When the sector commander, Maj. Gen. John Shea, arrived in Jerusalem later that morning, he ordered Watson to return the letter to the mayor so that he, Maj. Gen. Shea, could receive it in a proper manner. When General Sir Edmund Allenby, the commander-in-chief of the British army in the Middle East, heard what had happened, he demanded that the official surrender ceremony be conducted in his presence. This final surrender ceremony took place on Tuesday, December 11, at noon, near Jerusalem's Jaffa Gate. Unfortunately, Mayor al-Husseini could no longer attend this ceremony since he died a day earlier.

When General Allenby entered the Old City of Jerusalem on foot that Tuesday for the official surrender ceremony, he became the first Christian conqueror of the Holy City since the days of the Crusaders. He was very much aware that this was an historic event. For over seven hundred years, the city had been living under Muslim rulers. Now everyone was anxious to find out what changes this new Christian ruler would introduce. Standing on the steps of the Citadel (today's Migdal David Museum), Allenby announced that for now a military government would rule Palestine. He assured all religious communities that the *status quo* would remain in effect so that everyone could continue to utilize their traditional rights at all of their holy sites. He said,

> … every sacred building, monument, holy spot, shrine, traditional site, endowment, pious bequest, or customary place of prayer of whatsoever form of the three religions will be maintained and protected according to the existing customs and beliefs of those to whose faith they are sacred.[1]

He did change, however, the rules of access to the Temple Mount that had been in place for more than seventy years. In a cable to the War Cabinet in London, General Allenby spelled out what had been decided with respect to the Temple Mount.

> Guards have been placed over the holy places… The Mosque of Omar and the area around it have been placed under Moslem control, and a military cordon of Mohammedan [Indian Muslim] officers and soldiers has been established around the mosque. Orders have been issued that no non-Moslem is to pass within the cordon without permission of the Military Governor and the Moslem in charge.[2]

---

1   "Proclamation of General Allenby," in Charles F. Horne (ed.), *Source Records of the Great War*, Vol. 6 (Stuart Copley Press, 1923), p. 417.

2   *Source Records of the Great War*, Vol. 6, pp. 416–417. The use of the term "Mosque of Omar" to designate the entire Temple Mount was a common usage at that time in British government documents. Most probably it was an attempt to be

The decision to close access to the Temple Mount to all but Muslims was a major change in the arrangements that had been in effect since the middle of the previous century. This change was most astonishing in view of Great Britain's traditional role of keeping this holy site open for both Christians and Jews. In fact, three months later the War Cabinet in London responded to the pressures of a number of English Protestant groups who demanded the restoration of the *status quo* that permitted all non-Muslims access to the Temple Mount. Allenby was forced to countermand his order and non-Muslim visitors once again flocked to the Temple Mount according to the rules that were in place prior to the British occupation. Although non-Muslims now were once again allowed on the Temple Mount, the day-by-day management of the site remained in the hands of Muslim religious authorities. Muslim control of the site was strengthened in 1922 when Haj Amin al-Husseini, Grand Mufti of Jerusalem and President of the Supreme Muslim Council, moved his office from a government building in downtown Jerusalem to the Temple Mount. From that time on, there were many instances when Jews and Christians were prevented from entering the holy site. The British authorities tacitly or actively agreed to their exclusion. For example, when Lord Arthur Balfour (a Christian)—the author of the famous Balfour Declaration and currently a senior member of the British Cabinet—was visiting Palestine in the spring of 1925 to participate in the inauguration of the Hebrew University, the Muslim authorities prevented his going on the Temple Mount by barricading all entrances to the site. They did this as part of a nationwide protest ordered by the Executive Committee of the Palestinian Arab Congress in protest against Balfour's visit to Palestine. The Mandatory police took no action to keep the site open for his visit, claiming that many threats on his life had been received.[3] In 1929, the *waqf* authorities closed the Temple Mount hermetically to Jews and this closure remained in effect until 1967.

The question is whether personal prejudices of General Allenby and, in later years, of leading officials of the Mandatory government were responsible for the closure of the Temple Mount to non-Muslims, and especially to Jews. Were they anti-Semites? Did they hold pro-Arab views? Or were there other reasons that led to this new policy?

neutral by avoiding the use of the Hebrew *Har Habayit* or the Arab *Haram al-Sharif.* See also p. 5.

3   Ronald Storrs, *The Memoirs of Sir Ronald Storrs* (NY: Putnam's Sons, 1937), p. 457; "Lord Balfour's Visit to Jerusalem," *The Times* (London), February 27, 1925, p. 11.

British government archives from the First World War suggest that the idea to restrict entry on the Temple Mount or turning over the management and complete control of it to the Muslim authorities was not the decision of one general or of one bureaucrat but reflected a change in policies and priorities at the highest levels of government. Once the Ottoman Empire entered the First World War in November 1914 on the side of Germany, the British government made great efforts not to displease their Muslim subjects in any way. In the war against the Islamic Ottoman Empire, the British Empire depended particularly on the support of the very large number of Muslim troops from India. Decision-makers on the highest levels believed that no Muslim would ever forgive Britain if any damage or disruption occurred to one of the Muslim holy sites in areas under their control.

Momentous decisions that impacted on the future of the Temple Mount were made during the four war years. These decisions were made in pursuance of the primary aim of all military and diplomatic activities to defeat the German Empire and its Eastern ally, the Ottoman Empire. Fostering Arab nationalism became a major strategy to weaken the thrust of the Ottoman army. Negotiations with the Arabs were conducted to encourage their revolt against the Ottoman Empire and their joining forces with the British Eastern army.

All of Britain's policies in Palestine during and after the war were also rooted in British geopolitical aims. Palestine could provide a foothold for Great Britain in the Eastern Mediterranean. It could serve as a buffer between the Suez Canal and Britain's enemies to the north. This would guarantee the security of the Suez Canal and keep the road to India open. Palestine could provide a reserve base near Egypt that was independent of Anglo-Egyptian relations. It would also provide an overland route to Iraq and its all-important oil reserves.

Ottoman Caliph Mehmet V, immediately after entering the war, proclaimed a *jihad* against the Allies and urged all Muslims to support the struggle against Great Britain and her allies. The immediate British response to this *jihad* was to encourage Arab nationalism by promising independence to all Arabs in Ottoman-occupied lands once they had been liberated from Ottoman rule. For example, after a long exchange of correspondence between Sharif of Hejaz King Hussein ibn Ali and Sir Henry McMahon, the British high commissioner in Cairo, Great Britain agreed in October 1915 to support an independent Arab nation in reward for King Hussein's joining a joint British-Arab uprising.[4]

---

4   Palestine Royal Commission (Peel Commission) *Report*. London, 1937, 17. The full report is available at https://ecf.org.il/media_items/290.

This promise to King Hussein reflected one of the recommendations of the De Bunsen Committee, an inter-departmental committee established by the British government in 1915 to formulate British objectives for the war in the Near East. Its final report was issued in June 1915, but was kept secret for over fifty years. The British government followed many, but not all, of the committee's recommendations when in the following years it entered into a number of conflicting agreements with the Arabs, the French, and the Zionists. One of the questions extensively discussed by the De Bunsen committee was whether Great Britain should take into account the strong feelings in the Muslim world that Islam should have a political as well as a religious base. The committee formulated nine objectives for the region for the period following Turkey's defeat. The seventh stated that Arabia and the Muslim holy places should "remain under independent Muslim rule."[5]

Several weeks *before* Gen. Allenby's army conquered Jerusalem, the War Cabinet received a suggestion to proclaim "throughout the Moslem world ... that we are the protectors of the Moslem religion and would pay every respect to the Moslem Holy Places." It was noted that this applied especially to the "so-called Mosque of Omar" which all Muslims regard as the third most holy spot after Mecca and Medina. The preparation of a proclamation along these lines was approved by the War Cabinet at its meeting on November 19, 1917.[6]

Early in 1918, a few weeks after General Allenby had conquered Jerusalem, the War Cabinet in London discussed King Hussein's concerns about the future of the Arab people. Lord Balfour, the Foreign Minister, suggested a three-point reply. The first point suggested an international regime to deal with the shrines, *waqfs*, and holy places, sacred to Christians, Moslems, and Jews. He added that "the mosque of Omar would be considered as a Moslem concern alone and would not be subjected, directly or indirectly, to any non-Moslem authority."[7] This message was cabled to

---

5   Asiatic Turkey: Report of de Bunsen Committee, June 1915, TNA: CAB 43/3/12, par. 12, p. 3. See also Aaron S. Klieman, "Britain's War Aims in the Middle East in 1915," *Journal of Contemporary History*, July 1968, v.3 (3), pp. 237–251.

6   TNA [The National Archives]: CAB/23/4/51, War Cabinet, Meeting Minutes, Nov. 19, 1917. See also the communication of the War Office to Headquarters Cairo, Nov. 21, 1917, concerning the policies adopted for the occupation of Jerusalem, TNA: PRO FO 371/3061.

7   TNA: CAB24/144/25, Eastern Report no. 50, January 10, 1918, p. 5. The second point dealing with giving the "Arab race" an opportunity to form a nation, provided the Arabs achieve unity. The final point reiterated Britain's policy on encouraging a Jewish homeland in Palestine, compatible with the economic and political freedom of the country's existing population.

King Hussein and evidently also communicated to General Allenby. Before long it became the unwritten policy guideline for the military government and, later, for the civilian Mandatory government of Palestine.

Even though Allenby's closure of the Temple Mount in December 1917 was cancelled within three months, subsequent events indicate that this new British policy that viewed this site as an exclusive Muslim holy site was not abrogated. The Council of the League of Nations endorsed this general policy when it assigned the Palestine mandate to the British government in 1922 by stating specifically that,

> ... nothing in this mandate shall be construed as conferring upon the Mandatory authority to interfere with the fabric or the management of purely Moslem sacred shrines, the immunities of which are guaranteed.[8]

As a result of this policy, the Mandatory government lost control of the Temple Mount within a few years. No one contradicted the Grand Mufti, Haj Amin al-Husseini, when he testified before the Shaw Commission on December 4, 1929, that the Muslim community had full autonomy and authority over its holy sites, including the Haram (Temple Mount) and the Buraq (Western Wall). He, and not the British government, had the power to exclude whomever they wished from these sites. As the leader of the Muslim community, he exercised sole jurisdiction. He decided who was permitted and who was not permitted to enter the Temple Mount.[9]

It seems clear that this new policy of denying access to the Temple Mount to non-Muslims was the result of policy decisions by the London government that were reached after lengthy deliberations. How was this decision received by the various groups in Palestine?

Reactions of the Arabs

The British troops that conquered Jerusalem were greeted warmly by Moslems, Christians, and Jews alike. They were received as liberators, not as conquerors, because all sections of the population had suffered extreme deprivations at the hands of the Turkish soldiers during the four years of war. The initial ambivalence of the Moslems about what life would be like under a Christian ruler was quickly replaced by a sense of euphoria when

---

[8]   Paragraph 13, League of Nations Mandate for Palestine (adopted 12 August 1922), Document C. 529. M. 314. 1922. VI., archived at https://ecf.org.il/media_items/291.

[9]   Great Britain. Commission on the Palestine Disturbances of August 1929 (Shaw Commission) *Report,* London, 1930, p. 534.

they heard Gen. Allenby's declaration that the *status quo* would be maintained at all the holy places and that the Temple Mount would be protected by Indian Muslim soldiers with orders not to permit access to any non-Muslims.

Soon, however, this sense of euphoria was replaced by skepticism and even anger, especially when three months later Allenby cancelled his original order and replaced it with instructions that permitted access to the Temple Mount to non-Muslims, as had been the practice for the previous seventy years. The issue of non-Muslim access to the Temple Mount did not seem to be of major concern as long as the site was under Muslim control, but it became a major issue once it was joined to the quest for Arab nationalism. Already in 1919 Emir Feisal, son of the Sharif of Mecca and leader of the Arab independence movement, presented a document to the British Chief of the General Staff of the Egyptian Expeditionary Force, stating, "every Mohammedan believes that his Holy Places should be under the protection of a Caliph or an independent ruler ..."[10]

Reactions of the Jews

The Jewish population of Palestine at the end of the First World War was estimated at 56,000 adults. Four years earlier the number had been 85,000; the drastic decline was due to epidemics, starvation, emigration, and deportation by the Turkish government. By 1922, the official census listed 83,970 Jews (12.9% of the total population). The *yishuv*, though small in number and proportion, was further divided into two entirely different groups, known as the Old Yishuv and the New Yishuv. The Old Yishuv generally refers to the descendants of the Jewish community that had lived in Palestine prior to the beginning of the Zionist-inspired immigration. These Jews continued a traditional way of life, were strictly observant, and resisted any modernization efforts in their way of life. Most males of the Old Yishuv spent their entire life studying Torah and Talmud, supported by the charity-*halukah* that was donated by overseas Jewry. They lived mainly in the "Four Holy Cities" (Jerusalem, Safed, Tiberius, and Hebron), with smaller communities located in Jaffa, Haifa, Acre, and Nablus. In contrast, the New Yishuv consisted primarily of nationalist-motivated immigrants from Eastern Europe, generally secularists, who settled in the communal settlements that were established beginning in the 1880s in the coastal plain and the Galil, or in the urban areas around Tel Aviv and

---

10   *Documents on British Foreign Policy*, 1st Series, Vol. IV, 1952, p. 388.

Haifa. Emphasizing work and self-sufficiency, many identified with so-cialist movements. All were motivated to establish a vibrant Jewish pres-ence in Eretz Yisrael.

Though the *Weltanschauung* of these two groups was completely diver-gent, their response to the Temple Mount closure was remarkably similar, even if based on disparate reasons. Neither group expressed any desire for Jews to visit the holy site. The Old Yishuv strictly prohibited Jews from going up on the Temple Mount. Though they prayed daily for the rebuilding of the Holy Temple and the restoration of sacrificial services, they declared that at the present time no Jew was in the state of ritual purity necessary for approaching the Temple Mount. In 1921, Chief Rabbi A. Kook wrote a response that confirmed the ban on entering any part of the Temple Mount, as had been proclaimed by the Jerusalem rabbis in the 1850s when non-Muslims were first permitted to enter the site.[11] Placards prohibiting going on the Temple Mount were posted annually in his name, both in Hebrew and in English.[12]

The strategy of the Zionist leaders was based on different premises. They relinquished any claim to the site because they thought that the Tem-ple Mount might become a point of contention between Arabs and Jews. This was made explicit in documents such as the agreement between Chaim Weizmann, president of the Zionist Organization, and Emir Fei-sal, which stated that Muslim holy places shall be under exclusive Muslim control (January 3, 1919 Agreement, par. 6). This agreement was limited to the area of the Temple Mount and did not include the Western Wall or the city of Jerusalem. As early as December 1917 Chaim Weizmann had written a letter to Herbert Samuel, a member of the British Cabinet who would later become the first British high commissioner for Palestine, re-futing the rumors that the Zionists had decided to relinquish any claim on Jerusalem.[13] Instead, Weizmann moved the "Temple" from Mount Mo-riah to Mount Scopus, the next mountain, where he was instrumental in

---

11   Abraham Isaac Kook, *Shu"t Mishpat Cohen, Hil. Bet Haheḥirah* (Jerusalem, 1966), pp. 182–192. (Hebrew). Archived at https://www.hebrewbooks.org/22302.

12   Poster archived at
      https://he.wikipedia.org/wiki/%D7%9B%D7%A0%D7%99%D7%A1%D7
      %94_%D7%9C%D7%94%D7%A8_%D7%94%D7%91%D7%99%D7%AA
      _(%D7%94%D7%9C%D7%9B%D7%94).

13   Chaim Weizmann, *Letters and Papers* (Jerusalem: Israel Universities Press) Vol. 8, edited by Dvorah Barzilay and Barnet Litvinoff, 1980, Letter 25.

founding the Hebrew University. In a letter to his wife, he called the university "the Third Temple."[14]

Response of British Military and Civilian Personnel in Palestine

Policies made by the highest levels of government in London needed to be implemented on the ground in Palestine. There are examples in history where such policy directives from the central government were ignored and not implemented because local personnel for one reason or another disagreed with the policy. Other such policies were enthusiastically implemented because they matched the local personnel's political or socio-cultural views.

As noted earlier, Great Britain's primary concern in Palestine was the protection of the Suez Canal and the sea route to India—not the creation of a Jewish National Home or the strengthening of Arab nationalism. The Balfour Declaration already stated that "nothing shall be done which may prejudice the civil and religious rights of existing non-Jewish communities in Palestine." This permitted British officials to follow the "dual obligation" doctrine and thus demonstrate their fairmindedness to both communities. In practice, however, this doctrine permitted British officials to switch their support consistently from one side to the other, resulting in anger from both sides.

The apparent anti-Zionism of key members of the military administration resulted in deteriorating relations between the military administration and the Zionist Commission in Palestine. An official Court of Enquiry into the April 1919 riots in Jerusalem found that the majority of officers in the military administration were pro-Arab.[15] In March 1920, Chaim Weizmann, as chairman of the Zionist Commission in Palestine, wrote to the Zionist Executive in London that "relations between the Jews and the Administration have gone from bad to worse."[16] The relationships became so bad that the Cabinet in London, especially Foreign Minister Balfour, became convinced that it was necessary to replace the military government with a civilian government.[17]

---

[14] Paz, Yair. "The Hebrew University on Mt. Scopus as a Secular Temple," in *The History of the Hebrew University of Jerusalem: Origins and Beginnings*, ed. Shaul Katz and Michael Heyd (Jerusalem, 2000), pp. 281–308.

[15] TNA: PRO WO 32/9614, April 1920.

[16] Letters and Papers of Chaim Weizmann, Weizmann to Zionist Executive, 25 March 1920.

[17] Bernard Wasserstein, *The British in Palestine: The Mandatory Government and the Arab-Jewish Conflict* (Oxford, 1991), pp. 58–72.

General Money, who was the chief military administrator immediately after the British occupation of Jerusalem, was highly critical of Great Britain's support of the Zionist effort to build a Jewish homeland in Palestine. He was not the only member of General Allenby's staff who was opposed to the work of the Zionist Commission headed by Weizmann when it arrived in 1918. This same General Money prohibited the soldiers of the Jewish Legion from entering the Old City of Jerusalem during Passover 1918. Their commanding officer, Col. J. H. Patterson, a Christian and a professional soldier, wrote, "I cannot conceive a greater act of provocation to Jewish soldiers than this, or a greater insult."[18] Brigadier General Sir Gilbert Clayton, the military governor of the Occupied Enemy Territory Administration South thought "the Balfour Declaration represented a policy not compatible with acceptance of a British mandate by the Arabs of Palestine." He refused to treat the Balfour Declaration as Government policy until he was specifically instructed to do so in August 1918.[19]

In summary, British military and civilian personnel in Palestine had no difficulty in implementing London's policy concerning the Temple Mount.

Ronald Storrs and the Grand Mufti

General Bill Borton was the first military governor of Jerusalem, but because of his poor health, he resigned this position after being in office only a few weeks. He, as well as his successor, Ronald Storrs, who previously had been the Oriental Secretary to the British Residency in Cairo, continued the Ottoman practice of relying on prominent local families to fill senior positions in the local government. General Allenby also confirmed this policy. He advised the War Office in London that the "Turkish system of government will be continued and the existing machinery utilized."[20]

During the First World War Ronald Storrs, as a member of the Arab Bureau,[21] had participated in the negotiations between Sharif Hussein and

---

[18] J. H. Patterson, *With the Judæans in the Palestine Campaign* (London: Hutchinson & Co., 1922), p. 195.

[19] Ronald Sanders, *The High Walls of Jerusalem: A History of the Balfour Declaration and the Birth of the British Mandate for Palestine* (NY: Holt, Rinehart and Winston, 1983), p. 651.

[20] TNA: PRO FO 371/3384, 23 October 1918. See also B. Wasserstein, *The British in Palestine* (Oxford: Blackwell, 1991), p. 20.

[21] The Arab Bureau was a section of the Intelligence Department established by the British in Cairo in 1916 for the purpose of collecting and disseminating propaganda and intelligence about the Arab regions in the Middle East. It was actively involved in providing logistic support for the Arab revolt. See Samir

the British government and was among those who were instrumental in organizing the Arab Revolt against the Ottoman Empire. In 1917, he was appointed as a political officer to represent the Egyptian Expeditionary Force in Mesopotamia (EEFM) in Baghdad and Mesopotamia. Later that year General Allenby appointed him as the military governor of Jerusalem, for which purpose he was given the army rank of lieutenant colonel even though he had had no previous military experience. He was meant to serve as a bridge between the military administration in Palestine and the political establishment in London. He served as military governor of Jerusalem from 1918 to 1920 and as its civilian governor from 1920 to 1926.

Soon after Storrs's arrival in Jerusalem, a new mayor for Jerusalem had to be appointed. Storrs's choice was Musa Kazim, one of the most prominent members of the Husseini family. Even though he was known as an activist for Arab independence, as mayor he initially muted his opposition to the British administration and the Zionist cause. However, before long Storrs was forced to dismiss him from office because of his role in fermenting the 1920 Nebi Musa riot.[22]

When the British Military Government of Palestine was replaced by a civilian government in 1920, Sir Herbert Samuel was appointed as its head with the title "high commissioner of Palestine." The Arab population of the country received this appointment with anger because they were convinced that this Jewish high commissioner who had been active in Zionist activities had now come to Palestine to establish a Jewish homeland. When Samuel arrived in Jaffa on June 30, 1920, he was greeted by a general boycott by most Arabs. Nevertheless, in both Jaffa and Jerusalem some Arab officials did welcome him. In Jerusalem, the city's current mayor, Ragheb al-Nashashibi, was on hand to greet him.

Within a year of his arrival, Sir Herbert Samuel was instrumental in appointing Haj Amin al-Husseini as Grand Mufti of Jerusalem and as president of the Supreme Muslim Council. By continuing the traditional policy of appointing a member of one of the city's prominent families, he most probably thought that he was making the best decision for the welfare of the country. Who was Amin al-Husseini?

Seikaly, "Arab Bureau" in *1914-1918-online International Encyclopedia of the First World War*, ed. Ute Daniel et al., Berlin, 2016. Archived at https://encyclopedia.1914-1918-online.net/article/arab_bureau.

22   Roberto Mazza, "Transforming the Holy City: From Communal Clashes to Urban Violence: The Nebi Musa Riots in 1920," *Urban Violence in the Middle East; Changing Cityscapes in the Transformation from Empire to Nation State,* Nelida Fuccaro et al., eds. (NY: Berghahn, 2015), pp. 179–94.

Amin al-Husseini was born in Jerusalem, probably in 1893. The Husseinis were one of the two most prominent Arab families in Jerusalem. They claimed descent from the Prophet Muhammad. The position of mufti of Jerusalem was held by members of the Husseini family from the end of the eighteenth century onwards. In 1840, Muhammad Tahir Effendi al-Husseini became the mufti of Jerusalem.[23] In 1865, the Ottoman Government had bestowed the title of mufti upon Amin's father, Mohammed Tahir al-Husseini. The title at that time signified that the bearer was an elder religious leader in the community. After his father's death in 1908, Amin's older half-brother, Kemal, was similarly honored.

Amin al-Husseini attended St. George's School in Jerusalem, and later studied at the al-Azhar University in Cairo. After he made the pilgrimage to Mecca he added the title of Haj to his name. During World War I, he served in the Turkish Army. Following the collapse and capitulation of the Ottoman Empire in 1918, he was attached to the British Public Security Service in Palestine, changing over later to work for the French Secret Service in Damascus. His services were in high demand by the English and French conquerors because he spoke fluent English, French, and Turkish, in addition to his native Arabic.

On April 4, 1920, when three religious holidays (the Jewish Passover, the Christian Easter, and the Muslim Nebi Musa) overlapped, Arab rioters took to the streets of Jerusalem and randomly attacked Jews, killing five and injuring many others. One of the leaders of the Arab mob was Amin al-Husseini. He was generally identified as the main inciter of the violence, though some have suggested that he tried to restrain the mob. After the riots he fled to Trans-Jordan. He was sentenced in absentia by a British court martial to ten years of imprisonment for incitement. At the behest of Ronald Storrs, the military governor of Jerusalem, Herbert Samuel, the newly appointed high commissioner of Palestine, soon pardoned him.[24]

Kāmil al-Husseini (1867–1921), Haj Amin al-Husseini's stepbrother, had been mufti of Jerusalem from 1908 until his death on March 31, 1921. The British had changed his title to "Grand Mufti" in 1919 in reward for his "underground" services to Great Britain during World War I. The Ottoman authorities had failed to have him removed from office during the

---

23 Butrus Abu Manneh, "The Husaynis: The Rise of a Notable Family in 18th Century Palestine," in David Kushner (ed.), *Palestine in the Late Ottoman Period* (Brill Academic Publisher, 1997), p. 95; Vincent Lemire and Angelos Dalachanis (eds.), *Ordinary Jerusalem 1840–1940*. Vol. 1. (Leiden and Boston: Brill, 2018) p. 193.

24 Boris Havel, "Haj Amin al-Husseini: Herald of Religious Anti-Judaism in the Contemporary Islamic World," *The Journal of the Middle East and Africa*, 2014 (5:3), pp. 221–243; *Encyclopaedia of Islam, New Edition* (Leiden: E. J. Brill, 1986–2004), 12:67.

war even though they had suspected that he was collaborating with the British.

Although the position of mufti is not hereditary, immediately after the death of his stepbrother Kamil al-Husseini, Haj Amin began to grow a beard, wear a turban, and conduct himself as though the position was already his. Apparently, this strategy was successful. When the high commissioner, Sir Herbert Samuel, made a mourning visit to the family, he implied that he would be the next mufti.[25] Haj Amin al-Husseini was appointed as Grand Mufti of Palestine on May 8, 1921.

The British Palestine government had reshaped and redefined the office of mufti of Jerusalem so that it bore little resemblance to the position of the same name that existed for centuries in the Ottoman Empire. Originally, this office was geographically limited to the city or district of Jerusalem. The mufti then had no power over any other local mufti, nor was he superior to the *qadi* (Muslim judge who makes decisions following Sharia law). The British restructured the office, making the mufti of Jerusalem the Grand Mufti of Palestine and placing him above all other Muslim religious officials in the country. Traditionally, the mufti's power and prestige were subordinate to that of the *qadi*. The *qadi* was chosen from the ranks of the centralized official Ottoman religious establishment and almost never came from a local family. The mufti, on the other hand, was always chosen from one of the foremost local families.[26]

According to Ottoman law (which prevailed in British Palestine in the absence of any other relevant Mandatory law), the governor of Jerusalem (whose authority the high commissioner had inherited) selected the new mufti from a short list of three candidates who had been elected by a council of religious leaders and local notables. When Mufti Kamil al-Husseini died in 1921 this council considered four candidates. Three candidates had more experience and a superior education than Haj Amin; these three received 19, 17, and 12 votes respectively, while Haj Amin received only 9 votes and thus was ranked number 4 on the list. He should have been automatically excluded from the short list of the three top contenders from which the final choice was to be made. Herbert Samuel was convinced, however, that from the British point of view, Haj Amin was the most desirable candidate. He therefore persuaded the top contender to withdraw by offering him another more prestigious appointment. This made it possible for Samuel to choose his favorite candidate from the revised short list.

---

[25] Lorenzo Kamel, "Hajj Amīn al-Husaynī, the 'creation' of a leader," *Storicamente* 9, 2013, pp. 4–5.

[26] Kamel (2013), 4–5.

Haj Amin al-Husseini was neither a *sheikh* (an accredited religious leader or judge) nor an *'alim* (a religious scholar). He never completed an accredited program of religious studies, nor did he have the religious qualifications which would qualify him to hold this office. He did, however, impress the high commissioner with his charisma and appeared to be reliable to further the interests of the Mandatory power—even though earlier a British government intelligence report had labeled him a "deep-seated enemy of Great Britain."[27] Samuel, as well as the senior echelon in the Mandatory government, thought, however, that they could easily manage this young and inexperienced person. Their choice of Amin was motivated primarily by underlying political and strategic factors. Years later, Samuel's great-granddaughter recalled that he once told her that the only thing he regretted about his term as high commissioner of Palestine was his appointment of Haj Amin al-Husseini as mufti of Jerusalem.[28]

The Establishment of the Supreme Muslim Council

A conference of muftis, *ulema*,[29] and other Moslem notables was summoned by the Mandatory government in November 1920 to consider questions relating to the long-term management of the Muslim religious courts and the administration of Muslim *waqfs*. This conference appointed a committee that advised the government on the establishment of a Supreme Muslim Council, an official government body that had never existed before. There was no precedent in the history of Islam or of the Ottoman Empire for such a Supreme Muslim Council, but, nonetheless, it was officially recognized by the high commissioner in December 1921. This new body was seen as a balance to the Zionist Commission which had been representing the interests of the Jewish community of Palestine. Note that the Mandatory government chose to relate to the local non-Jewish population not as Arabs but as Muslims.

Later that year, after certain modifications to the regulations were accepted by the Mandatory government, an assembly of Muslim representatives was elected. This assembly appointed a general committee to draw up the constitution of the Supreme Muslim Council and regulations for the administration of Muslim *waqfs* and Sharia affairs. The constitution

---

27 CZA – L35/50-1. William Ormsby-Gore (1885–1964), House of Lords, 8 December 1938.

28 Maya Polak, "Governor in the Service of the State," *Mekor Rishon-Dikon,* 26 June 2020, 25–31 at 26.

29 A body of Muslim scholars recognized as having specialist knowledge of Islamic sacred law and theology.

and the regulations were ultimately approved by the high commissioner in 1927.[30] The Council consisted of a president and four other officials. Its official functions included administering and controlling the *awqaf*,[31] approving the *waqf* budgets, nominating judges and inspectors for the *sharia* courts, and appointing muftis and administrative officials.

Haj Amin al-Husseini was elected to serve as president of the Supreme Muslim Council on January 2, 1922, by 56 electors, all of whom had been elected deputies of the last Ottoman parliament. Some prefer to call this an "appointment" rather than an "election" because in fact Haj Amin was selected by the Mandatory government. When Sir Herbert Samuel during his first month in office had called a meeting of local notables to discuss the establishment of a Supreme Muslim Council, Haj Amin was the designated leader and spokesman of this group. The same group of 56 persons who attended that preliminary meeting subsequently elected him. According to Kupferschmidt, Haj Amin's election was a foregone conclusion since by this time he already held the position of Grand Mufti.[32]

By law, the Council was established as an organ of the British government and its members received a government salary. The Council members, however, had a different perspective. They saw the Supreme Muslim Council as an organ of an independent Arab government. This became clear to the British Mandatory Government only after it received a secret intelligence report that the mufti

> was genuinely surprised at the theory proposed to him that he and the Supreme [Moslem] Council are in any way a branch of the Administration. He honestly regards himself as the elected millet-bashi of the Moslems of Palestine for all purposes.[33]

---

30   Andrews, Fannie Fern. *The Holy Land Under Mandate*, v. 2 (Cambridge: Riverside Press, 1931), p. 190. See *Official Gazette* of May 15, 1921 and *Official Gazette* of December 20, 1927.

31   A *waqf* (pl. *awqaf*) is a charitable endowment established under Islamic law in which a person endows their property and reserves its profit in perpetuity for charitable purposes.

32   Uri M. Kupferschmidt, *The Supreme Muslim Council: Islam under the British Mandate for Palestine* (Leiden: E.J. Brill, 1987), p. 20.

33   Secret Political Report for Jerusalem District, June 17, 1922. Storrs Papers, Pembroke College, Cambridge, Box III/2, cited by Robert W. Nicholson, "Managing the Divine Jurisdiction: Sacred Space and the Limits of Law on the Temple Mount (1917–1948)," Syracuse University thesis, 2012, p. 40. Archived at http://surface.syr.edu/hst_thesis.

Haj Amin al-Husseini, as president of the Council, was assigned an office in a British government building in downtown Jerusalem. A short time after his election, however, he moved his office to the Temple Mount. This move was much more than a mere geographic relocation of an office. Though this move was ignored by the government, it represented a major turning point for Palestine's Muslim community. Now, for the first time since the British had conquered the country, Muslims held effective and exclusive control over Palestine's most important Muslim space. They had regained a territorial center, a source of legitimacy, and a means for mobilizing international Islamic solidarity.[34]

Even though Great Britain was the country's sovereign power, actually the Temple Mount was no longer under its control. As Haj Amin al-Husseini testified before the 1929 Shaw Commission, he as the leader of the Muslim community decides who was permitted and who was not permitted to enter the Temple Mount.[35]

The British did not respond to Haj Amin's move to the Temple Mount because they were fearful of upsetting the worldwide Muslim community. In this manner, they handed complete and undisputed control of the Temple Mount to a Muslim administration. Nicholson has suggested that this policy of "affirmative deference" allowed Muslim leaders to carve out on the Temple Mount a sphere of *de facto* sovereignty and create there the center of a would-be independent Arab state in Palestine. By refusing to enforce the rule of law on this site, the Mandatory government effectively created a zone of lawlessness in the center of Palestine that was bound to undermine the entire regime. It is widely believed that the British adopted this new policy because they were fearful that any forceful reaction to Haj Amin al-Husseini's move would upset Muslims everywhere, but in time, this inaction resulted in undermining the very basis of the Mandatory regime.[36] For example, years later in 1937, when the British police wanted to arrest Haj Amin al-Husseini for his part in the Arab rebellion, he managed to escape and take refuge in the Haram al-Sharif where the British police did not dare to arrest him since he was protected by his bodyguard. He stayed there for three months, directing the revolt from within.

---

[34] Nicholson, 2012, p. 40; Kupferschmidt, 1987, pp. 26–27, 58.
[35] Great Britain. Commission on the Palestine Disturbances of August 1929 (Shaw Commission) *Report*, London, 1930, 534.
[36] Nicholson, 2012, pp. 3–4.

Summary

The Jewish response (or lack of response) to the changing *status quo* on the Temple Mount during the decade after the British occupation of Jerusalem made it easy for Great Britain to deal with the Arab demands for control of the Temple Mount. Even though the military administration was accused by most Jewish and non-Jewish Zionists of being anti-Zionist and/or anti-Semitic, in the case of the Temple Mount this charge is hardly relevant because Arab demands and British decisions coincided more or less with the Jewish positions.

At a 1939 cabinet meeting that discussed the general Palestine situation, not specifically the Temple Mount, Prime Minister Neville Chamberlain summarized the situation by pointing out the "immense importance" of having "the Moslem world with us. If we must offend one side, let us offend the Jews rather than the Arabs."[37] It appears that this summary guided the policy decisions of both the military government and the civilian Mandatory government since the first days after the occupation of Palestine in December 1917. ❧

---

[37] TNA: CAB/24/285/11 p. 18.

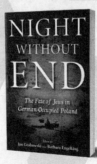

Academic Studies Press

Recent publications

Leibowitz or God's Absence
Daniel Horowitz
2022 | 9781644697948 | HB

This Was America, 1865-1965
Unequal Citizens in the Segregated Republic
Gerd Korman
2022 | 9781644696378 | HB

Leibowitz and Levinas
Between Judaism and Universalism
RABBI DR. TAL SESSLER | *Translated from the Hebrew by* EYLON LEVY
2022 | 9781644698532 | HB

Siddur Hatefillah
The Jewish Prayer Book. Philosophy, Poetry, and Mystery
ELIEZER SCHWEID | *Translated from the Hebrew by* GERSHON GREENBERG
2022 | 9781644698655 | HB

A unique opportunity to own this rare 1612 Kabbalah sefer

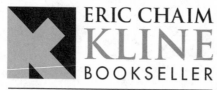

Sefer Shefa Tal

Hannoviyah [Hanau]: Hans Yakop Hena, [1612]. First edition of this compendium of Kabblistic topics, by Prague rabbi Shabtai Sheftel ben Akiva Horowitz (1565-1619). 92 leaves. Illustrated throughout with a total of 15 prominent and intriguing Kabbalistic woodblock diagrams and charts in black, as well as some small tables.

Among the specific subjects, the work provides commentary and analysis of the work of previous Kabbalists including "Iggeret ha-Te'amim" (Letter on the Accents) by 16th century rabbi Aaron Abraham ben Baruch Simeon ha-Levi, the writings of Rabbi Moses ben Jacob Cordovero (aka the RAMAK, 1522-1570), Sefer Yetzirah, and the Zohar.

Rebound in modern dark brown leather boards, with gilt lettering, red label and raised bands on the spine. Title page illustrated with historiated woodblock lettering at the top, and encircled by text borders.

Binding in very good+, interior in very good- condition overall. vg- to vg+.

Item #49853   10% promo code **HAK32**

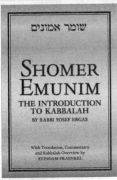

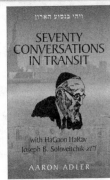
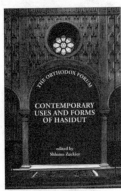

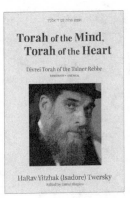

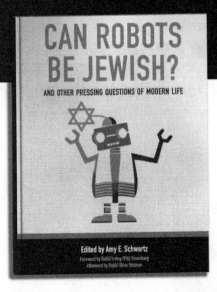

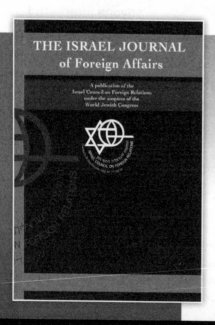

יו"ט הוא יום של שמחה ואין מקום לאבילות כלל, ולכן דברים שבפרהסיא מותרים. ואילו במימד הפרטי, אינו כן, ודברים שבצנעה נוהגים.

ונראה לנמק חילוק זה על פי דברי הגמרא בעירובין (יח.):

דרבי אבהו רמי כתיב זכר ונקבה בראם וכתיב (כי) בצלם אלהים ברא אתו בתחלה עלתה במחשבה לבראות שנים ולבסוף לא נברא אלא אחד.

נראה שרמוז כאן שיש שני פנים למהות האדם- כיחיד וכחלק מן הכלל. ביו"ט אותו אדם יכול להיות אבל כיחיד ואינו אבל כחלק מן הציבור, ואין כאן מקום להאריך בזה. ଓଃ

אין הלכות אבילות שייכים לו כלל. לעומת זאת ברגל, האדם הוא אבל בהגדרה, אלא שאינו אבל בפועל מכוח הזמן שבו הוא נמצא באותה עת. לכן ברגל אסור בתשמיש המיטה, כמו שביארנו.[33]

כל זה מובן על דרך האחרונים, ביניהם הערוך השולחן[34] שכתב (יורה דעה סימן שצ"ט סעיף ג) שהאיסור בצנעא ברגל הוא רק איסור של תשמיש המיטה (ולא שאר איסורים). וז"ל הערוך השולחן:

אבל להרא"ש והטור והש"ע שפסקו דגם ברגל דברים שבצנעא נוהג כמו שיתבאר לא שייך טעם זה והיה נלע"ד דברגל אינו נוהג כל דברים שבצנעא רק בתשמיש בלבד ...

נותר לנו להסביר את ענייננו לפי הסוברים שגם שאר איסורי אבילות נוהגים בצנעה ביו"ט.

ז. נספח (המשך) - אבילות בצנעה ובפרהסיא

בשיטה לתלמידו של רבינו יחיאל מפריש למועד קטן (כד.) מבואר שלדעתו כל דבר שבצנעה נוהג ביו"ט, ולא רק תשמיש המיטה:[35]

הכי אמר ר' יוחנן דברים שבצנעא נוהג. דמאי דעביד איניש בביתיה כי ליכא אינשי גביה צנעא הוא... אם מת לו מת ברגל דנוהג דברים שבצנעא... ויליך בגלוי הראש אפילו בתוך ביתו ... והוו להו דברים שבצנעא. וכן אסור לו לצאת מפתח ביתו...

לפי זה נראה לכאורה שלדעתו באמת יש אבילות ביו"ט (בניגוד למה שביארנו למעלה). וכן משמע ממה שכותב (שם יד:):

... ומיהו אע"ג דלא חייל ברגל היינו דוקא לדברים שבפרהסיא אבל לדברים שבצנעה ודאי חייל... וא"ת הא אמרינן הכא דלא אתי עשה דיחיד חייל על עשה דרבים, וי"ל דלא מקרי מועד עשה דרבים אלא לדברים שבפרהסיא דהוי מילי דרבים.

אבל צריך עיון, שהרי ראינו למעלה שסובר שבניגוד לשבת, אין אבילות ביו"ט כלל. אמנם האמת יורה דרכו, ממה שכתב עצמו שזה דוקא לעניין דברים שבפרהסיא. זאת אומרת שיש שתי פנים ליו"ט- אחד במימד הציבורי ואחד במימד הפרטי. במימד הציבורי,

---

33 וע"ע כעין חילוק זה בהקשר אחר בהסבר הנצי"ב (בהעמק שאלה שם) לדברי הרמב"ן שהזכרנו בהע' 19.

34 וע"ע בהעמק שאלה (שם).

35 שלא כמו שכתב הנצי"ב בהעמק שאלה (קנח:ג) בדעתו.

זה, ויסוד הדבר מובן דווקא על ידי שילוב שתי הנקודות, ובאמת הם ב' פנים של דבר אחד, כמו שנסביר בע"ה.

אף שגם הגאונים וגם הירושלמי דנים בטעם החילוק בין שבת ויו"ט, הדגש שונה. אם הגאונים הסבירו בעיקר למה יו"ט **מפסיק** (ולא שבת), הירושלמי מתמקד בשאלה למה שבת **עולה** (ולא יו"ט).

הירושלמי שואל איך אפשר לחלק בין שבת ויו"ט, הרי יש ניהוג אבילות של איסור תשמיש המיטה ביו"ט כמו שיש בשבת? אם משום כך שבת עולה, למה לא יו"ט?

הירושלמי ממשיך ומסביר שאף שיש שיש דמיון בדינם, יש הבדל יסודי במהותם.[30] מאחר שאבילות מוגדרת כשבוע, הרי אבילות נתקן מעיקרא לכלול גם אבילות של חול וגם אבילות של שבת. ואם כן מוכח שאיסור תשמיש של שבת הוא אבילות ממש ומשקף את זה שהוא באמת אבל (אלא שהאבילות מוגבלת כדי שלא יפגום בקדושת השבת) ולכן שבת עולה. בניגוד לזה, ביו"ט אין אבילות בפועל כלל וכלל,[31] אלא שאסרו לו תשמיש המיטה משום שאין ראוי שישמש מטתו במצב כזה.[32] לכן אין יו"ט עולה.

זאת אומרת שאין אבילות במועד כלל, אף שיש איסור תשמיש. וכן מפורש בהלכות גדולות (סימן כא - הלכות אבל):

ואף על גב דליכא אבילות במועד, אבל דברים שבצינעה נוהג, כגון תשמיש המיטה.

וכן אנחנו מוצאים בדברי הראשונים, כגון בתוספות (מו"ק כג:) ד"ה מאן דאמר וכו':

ומתרץ אף על גב דשבת עולה רגל אינו עולה הואיל ואין אבילות כלל משום דכתיב בהן שמחה שבת מיהא לא כתיב שמחה אפילו הינה נוהגת בירושלמי מפרש טעמא דשבת דאין אבילות נוהג בו משום דכתיב (משלי י) ברכת ה' היא תעשיר ולא יוסיף עצב עמה ושבת כתיב ביה ברכה.

יש להבהיר שמצד אחד, הדין שיו"ט מפסיק ואינו עולה (וההסבר של הירושלמי ושל הגאונים וראשונים שהבאנו) והדינים של אי-אבילות במקום שאין צער (שהבאנו מהראשונים) נובעים מיסוד אחד (שביארנו על דרך המהרש"ל). מצד שני, יש הבדל חשוב באיך יסוד זה מתבטא. במקרים של אי-אבילות שהבאנו, אין האדם מוגדר כאבל כלל, ולכן

---

30 עיין כעין זה בדברי המהר"ם מרוטנבורג בהל' שמחות (סי' קיב) [ווע"ע בב"י יו"ד סוס"י תב] "... ונראה דכיון דתנן השבת עולה ואינה מפסקת הרגלים מפסיקין ואינן עולין אף על גב דתרווייהו שוין לענין ניהוג אבלות דבתרווייהו דברים של צינעא נוהג ולא דברים של פרהסיא, ואפ"ה קתני השבת עולה והרגלים אינם עולין, א"כ עולה לכל דבר ולקולא אמר עולה ולא לחומרא..." זאת אומרת שהמהר"ם מפרש שאף ששבת ויו"ט שווים באיסורים לעניין צנעה ופרהסיא, שונים לעניין מהותם, כמו שכתבנו.

31 עיין תורת האדם (מה' שעוועל עמ' קצח) שאין ימי יו"ט ימי אבילות כלל. [ואכמ"ל להאריך במה שנראה סתירה לעניינים נהוגי שלושים ברגל שם (עמ' רכז-רכח) ושם (עמ' רלד). עיין בהע' שם ובנצי"ב בהעמק שאלה (טו:ז)].

32 עיין דברי הרמב"ן בתורת האדם (מה' שעוועל עמ' עד).

פי בקיאין אמר רבי ינאי חולה אומר צריך ורופא אומר אינו צריך שומעין לחולה מאי
טעמא לב יודע מרת נפשו פשיטא מהו דתימא רופא קים ליה טפי קא משמע לן." אנן סהדי
איך רוב אנשים מרגישים מצפון (ואפילו ברוב המקרים שהיה יחס רע בין האבל והנפטר
או לא היה יחס כלל) להתאבל על קרוביהם. ברור שאם מישהו אומר "איך אתאבל על
נפטר זה", שזאת המציאות בשבילו, אף אם יש להבין הדברים אחרת באופן אובייקטיבי.
עדיין הדין עם ה"אבל" שאין לחייבו מאחר שבעומק נפשו מרגיש ככה.
נסיים פרק זה במה שנפסק[29] ביו"ד (סי' שלז):

> חולה שמת לו מת, אין מודיעין אותו, שמא תטרף דעתו עליו. ואין קורעין חלוקו,
> ואין בוכין ואין מספידין בפניו, שלא ישבר לבו; ומשתיקין את המנחמין מפניו.

ויש ללמוד מזה ק"ו לעניינינו. ההלכה מלמדת אותנו למנוע ניהוגי אבילות ממי
שבאמת חייב כעיקרון להתאבל, כדי שלא נגרום נזק וצער לאבל. כל שכן בשאלה שלנו,
שנראה שאין דין אבילות חל עליה כלל, ודאי אין להחמיר עליה ולגרום לה נזק במה
שתצטרך להתאבל על הורים שהזיקו לה ככה.

ו. נספח- אבילות בשבת ויו"ט

כעת נחזור לעניין של אבילות בשבת ויו"ט. על פי מה שהקדמנו, ניתן להבין את דברי
הגאונים והראשונים בחילוק שבין שבת ויו"ט לעניין אבילות שהזכרנו למעלה. אדם יכול
להיות בצער על מתו בשבת, ולכן ניתן להגדירו כאבל, משא"כ ברגל. מאחר שבעיקרון אין
אדם נחשב כמצער על מתו ביו"ט, אין מקום אבילות כלל. משום כך רגל מבטל אבילות,
משא"כ שבת. לפי דרכינו הדבר מובן היטב.
אמנם לכאורה הירושלמי במועד קטן (פרק ג הלכה ה) מסביר את החילוק בין שבת
ויו"ט אחרת:

> דאמר ר' סימון בשם ריב"ל והלא אמרו אין אבל ברגל אלא שהרבים נוהגין בו
> בצינעה. מהו בצנעה שהוא אסור בתשמיש המיטה התיבון הרי הרגל הרי הוא אסור
> בתשמיש המיטה ואינו עולה אף השבת הואיל והיא אסורה בתשמיש המיטה לא
> תעלה. אמר ר' בא איפשר לשבעה בלא רגל אבל אי אפשר לשבעה בלא שבת:

ואכן הנצי"ב [העמק שאלה (טו:ז)] מפרש שיש מחלוקת בין הסבר זה של הירושלמי
ובין ההסבר שהבאנו למעלה מהגאונים (והוא מפרש שהגאונים פירשו ע"פ הבבלי בניגוד
לירושלמי). אבל לע"ד אין צורך לזה, ובאמת ניתן לפרש שב' ההסברים משלימים זה את

שאין פטירתו צער ומרירות כלל.

ויש להעיר שאין לחלק בין אבילות על אב ואם ואבילות על שאר קרובים לענייננו.[23]
אף שיש פן נוסף של כבוד אב ואם בניהוגי אבילות עליהם כידוע, ויש בזה כמה חומרות
למעשה. מכל מקום, אין נ"מ לנדון שלנו. שהרי פשוט שאין חיוב נפרד לנהוג אבילות על
או"א, אלא הרחבה של האבילות. במקום שיש אבילות על או"א מחמירים בה יותר
מבשאר קרובים. אבל במקום שאין אבילות (מפני שאין צער ואין זה יום מר) אין מה
להרחיב ואין כאן חיוב לנהוג אבילות של כבוד או"א.

ויש לדייק ככה מדברי הרמב"ם. הרמב"ם מביא כל דיני אבילות על הורים בהלכות
אבל, ואינו מרמז כלל להלכות אלו בהלכות של כבוד אב ואם שבהלכות ממרים- אף
כשכותב שם על כבוד או"א שלאחר מיתתם.[24] ואין כאן מקום להאריך בכל זה כאן.

ולע"ד ראוי להורות כמו שביארנו על פי דרכי התורה בכלל ויסודי הלכות אבילות
בפרט:

כן ראוי להיות לפי דרכי התורה: מאחר שכל דרכיה דרכי נועם,[25] איך יתכן להכריח
לעלובה זאת להתאבל על מי שהתעלל בה? הרי זה אכזריות נוראה להוסיף על כאבה ככה!
ועל פי יסודי הלכות אבילות: איך יתאבל על מי שאין לה שום צער באבדו והרי אינה
מוגדרת כאבל? וכן מאחר שהלכות אבילות אמורות לצמצם את ביטוי הצער הטבעי, לא
להוסיף עליו, איך יתכן לחייבה בניהוגי אבילות? הרי זה מתנגד לכל היסוד של אבילות
כמו שביררנו בע"ה.

טעם נוסף לפיו אין ראוי לנהוג אבילות במצב שלנו הוא משום שהדבר נראה כצחוק
ומביא ללעג. אין לנהוג ניהוג אבילות אפילו כשבאופן עקרוני יש חיוב בדבר במקום
שיביא ללעג[26] כידוע, וכל שכן במקרה שלנו שיש לפוטרה מעיקר הדין, ואכמ"ל.

וכן יש להוסיף שאבילות אמורה לתת מרגוע לאבל, על דרך מה שכתב הרמב"ם[27]
ואם נחייבה להתאבל על הורים כאלו, נהפוך את החסד של התורה לאכזריות ח"ו.

ויש להעיר שאין מקום לחקור על סיבת אי-הרגשת האבל או לדון מי צודק או מה
מידת הפגיעה וכדומה. אין הלכה זו תלויה בפטור משום שהנפטר פגע באבל, אלא במה
שבשביל האבל אין הרגשה של צער ואינו יום מר בשבילו, ולכן אין חילוקים אלו משנים
כלום. ויש לבסס הגישה הנכונה להלכה זו על פי דברי הגמרא:[28] "חולה מאכילין אותו על

---

23 כמו שלא חלקו בשו"ת במראה הבזק (שם).

24 הל' ממרים (פ"ו ה"ה).

25 סוכה (לב. לב:); יבמות (טו. פז:); חי' הרמב"ן יבמות (קיט.); חי' הרשב"א יבמות (טו.);
מרדכי גיטין פ' המגרש (רמז תמו) ועוד, ואכמ"ל.

26 עיין הל' שמחות (סי' מ) וב"י יו"ד (סי' שעד); ריטב"א מו"ק (כב:) ועוד ועוד.

27 עיין מו"נ (ח"ג פמ"א): כי לבעלי האבל מנוחה בבכיה ועוררם אבלם עד שיחלשו כחות
הגופנים מסבול המקרה ההוא הנפשי.

28 יומא (פג.).

זכינו לראות שיש בסיס ליסוד של המהרש"ל בהרבה מגדולי הראשונים: רש"י, ר"ת,
הרמב"ם, הרמב"ן, רבינו יחיאל מפריש, המהר"ם מרוטנברג, ר"י מלוניל, והר"ן.

ד. היסוד של הלכות אבילות

נראה שיש כאן נקודה נפלאה: הלכות אלו מצביעות על מהותו של עניין האבילות בכלל.
חז"ל (במועד קטן כז:) למדו אותנו יסוד גדול באבילות:

> אל תבכו למת ואל תנדו לו אל תבכו למת מדאי ואל תנדו לו יותר מכשיעור
> הא כיצד שלשה ימים לבכי ושבעה להספד ושלשים לגיהוץ ולתספורת מכאן ואילך
> אמר הקדוש ברוך הוא אי אתם רחמנים בו יותר ממני.

לפי מה שראינו, יש לפרש שביסודה אבילות באה למעט ולצמצם, לא לאסור
ולהרחיב.[21] כמו שהזכרנו, הצער של אבילות היא, בדרך כלל, תגובה טבעית. המטרה של
הלכות אבילות היא לתת גדרים וגבולות לצער ולביטויו, לומר לנו "תבטא את הצער כך
ולא אחרת, עד כאן ולא יותר". מצד אחד לתת ביטוי לאבל בדרך ובמידה נכונה ומצד שני
למנוע ביטוי שלילי או מוגזם.

ומצאתי תנא דמסייעא לן בדברי הגאון רב צוריאל שליט"א באוצרות התורה (פרשת
נשא) ע"ש. ובין היתר כותב שם:

> כללית, יש לנו לשים לב שמצוות האבילות היא מדרבנן בלבד, ויש לתקנה זו הסבר
> מעניין מאד ברמב"ם, הסבר שהאבילות היא למען צמצום וריסון, שלא נבוא להגזים
> באקסטזה שלילית (מו"נ ג/מא).

ואם כן, מובן היטב למה אין בכלל מקום להלכות אבילות כשאין צער. אם הלכות אלו
באות לרסן ולצמצם את הרגש הטבעי של צער על מתו, מסתבר שאין להן מקום כשאין
שום צער מלכתחילה, וכמו שראינו מדברי הראשונים.

ה. היוצא להלכה בעניין אבילות במקום שאין צער

לפי מה שביררנו, נראה פשוט שבת שהוריה התעללו בה, ואין לה שום קשר חיובי עמיהם,
אינה מוגדרת כאבל ולכן אין לה שום חיוב לנהוג עליהם אבילות.[22] והוא הדין כל אבל

---

21 ואולי יש מקום גם להבין הכלל של שמואל (מו"ק יח.) שהלכה כדברי המיקל באבל על פי
יסוד זה, אבל הרבה יש לדון בזה [ועיין בתורת האדם (מה' שעוועל עמ' ריא) ובהל' שמחות
למהר"ם מרוטנברג (סי' קכב)] ואכמ"ל.

22 כשו"ת במראה הבזק שהזכרנו למעלה בהע' 2, ולא כשו"ת משפטי עוזיאל ח"ט (סי' מה).
הנלע"ד כתבתי, והמעיין יבחר.

כל זאת שוללת הסברא שאדם מוגדר כאבל באופן מוחלט ואוביקטיבי מגזרת הכתוב,
מאחר שהוא קרוב של הנפטר. אין הדבר כן, אלא הצער של אובדן קרובו הוא המחייב,
ולא עצם העובדה שקרובו נפטר.[14]

וכן מבואר גם ברמב"ם[15] הל' אבל (פ"א ה"י):

כל הפורשין מדרכי צבור והם האנשים שפרקו עול המצות מעל צוארן ואין נכללין
בכלל ישראל בעשיית המצות ובכבוד המועדות וישיבת בתי כנסיות ובתי מדרשות
אלא הרי הן כבני חורין לעצמן [כשאר האומות] וכן האפיקורוסין [והמומרים]
והמוסרין כל אלו אין מתאבלין עליהן, אלא אחיהם ושאר קרוביהם לובשין לבנים
ומתעטפים לבנים ואוכלים ושותים ושמחים שהרי אבדו שונאיו של הקדוש ברוך
הוא, ועליהם הכתוב אומר הלא משנאיך ה' אשנא.

הרי שבמקום שאין באובדן הנפטרים צער לאבל- אין אבילות אף שהם קרוביו, ואין
אומרים שמכל מקום יש כאן איסור של אבילות.[16]

ויש מקור חזק להבנה זו בדברי רש"י המובאים בדברי כמה מהראשונים[17] (בשינוים
קלים) ובבית יוסף.[18]

כך מובא בספר הפרדס[19] וז"ל:

וכן פ' במועד קטן מי שמת לו ולא נודע לו ונודע לבני עירו מותרין היודעין
לזמנו לסעודת מצוה שהרי אבלות מן התורה אינו חל עליו עד שעת אנינות לב.
שהרי שבעה ושלשים אינו אלא ששמע.

יש לדייק כאן שרש"י אינו מפרש שמותר משום שהאבל אינו יודע שיש כאן איסור
והוא כמתעסק, אלא משום שאינו מוגדר כאבל. הסברא כאן הוא שמי שאינו מרגיש באבלו
אינו אבל ואינו מחויב, וזה בסיס חזק לדברינו.

וחשוב להדגיש שהמהר"ם מרוטנבורג[20] הביא הלכה זו בהלכותיו, והוסיף שאין לחלק
בין אבילות על או"א ועל שאר קרובים. ועיין מה שכתבתי בעניין זה בהמשך.

---

14 אין הכוונה שיש חיוב להיות מצטער (כדברי הגרי"ד"ס שהבאנו למעלה) אלא שצערו מגדירו
כאבל, וכמו שביארנו למעלה, ודו"ק.

15 על פי מסכת שמחות (ב:ח).

16 ודו"ק שאבילות ביסודה מצוה ולא איסור, עיין מו"ק (יד:), הל' אבל (פ"א ה"א) וסה"מ (מ"ע
לז). אלא שמתבטא באיסורים (ולכן במקום שאין חיוב אבילות אין איסורים).

17 כגון מחזור ויטרי (סימן רעה), סידור רש"י (סימן תקפן), רוקח הלכות אבילות (סימן שטז),
שבלי הלקט הלכות שמחות (סימן מז), אורחות חיים הלכות אבל (אות יז).

18 תמצית דבריו מובאים בב"י יו"ד (סי' תב).

19 פרדס הגדול (סוס"י רצ).

20 עיין הלכות שמחות השלם (סי' קנב) וע"ע בהע' שם.

והנה תמהו העם על ככה, ושלחתי דברי לזקני ירושלים, וכתב לי זקן אחד וחכם
מופלא שחכמי ירושלים הסכימו לקל וחומר שדנתי מדברי הרשב"ם:

אלא שמבואר ברש"י ובשאר הראשונים עוד יותר ממה שמפורש במהרש"ל.
בראשונים מבואר שאף בקרובים ממש,[11] ואף במקום שיש אהבה ביניהם- אין חיוב
אבילות במקום שאין צער ומרירות על אובדן!

בנוסף לראשונים שהזכרנו, מצינו כסברא זו גם בדברי רבינו תם בהקשר אחר.
הא"ז הל' אבילות (סי' תכח) מביא דבריו:

...אבל קטן בן שנה בן שנתים שנשתמד עם אמו ומת יש אומרים שמתאבל עליו...
אבל ר"ת זצ"ל אומר שאין מתאבלין עליו... ועוד היה ר"ת נותן טעם ששמחים על
מיתתו יותר מחייו כי אם חי סופו היה לעבוד ע"ז וללכת בדרכי העכו"ם...

הרי שלשיטת המהרש"ל יש בסיס גם בדרבי ר"ת.
וכן מצינו בדברי הרמב"ן בתורת האדם:[12]

נראה בעיני שלא מפני ספק של דבריהם הקלו בהם אלא מפני שכל ספק בן קיימא
אין לבו של אדם דוה עליו ואין בו אנינות בלבו של אדם ולא מיקיים ביה ואחריתה
כיום מר, הלכך אין מתאבלין עליו.

הרי מפורש גם בדברי הרמב"ן שאין אבילות כשאין מרירות.
וכן מבואר מהצד השני בדברי הרמב"ם[13] בהל' אבל (פ"ו ה"א), שדוקא כשיש צער
יש להגדיר את האדם כאבל (ומכלל הן אתה שומע לאו):

מדברי סופרים שיהיה האבל נוהג במקצת דברי אבילות כל שלשים יום, ומנין סמכו
חכמים לשלשים יום, שנאמר ובכתה את אביה ואת אמה ירח ימים, מכלל שהאבל
מצטער כל שלשים יום.

---

11   אמנם בשו"ת במראה הבזק (שם) באמת הוכיחו כן אף למהרש"ל עצמו. אבל הדבר יותר
מבואר בראשונים. ובאמת אפילו אם לא נודה לעניין המהרש"ל, הרי מבואר בדברי
הראשונים ולכן אין לפקפק בזה.

12   מה' שעוועל (עמ' רי- ריא). וע"ע שם (עמ' ריב).

13   על פי הירושלמי, כמו שכתב הרדב"ז על הרמב"ם שם. ודו"ק שהרמב"ם לא כתב שלומדים
שיעור ל' יום לאבילות מאשת יפת תואר, אלא שלומדים כמה אדם מצטער משם, וממילא
שאין אבילות אלא ל' יום שאין אבילות אלא במקום צער.

לא תעטה על שפם פי' וקרא בפורענותן של רשעים משתעי שלא יהו סופדין ומתאבלין זה על זה מרוב מתים שיהו בהם ולא יוכלו להתאבל עליהם ומרוב הפורענות הניתן עליהם בחייהם ישמחו כל א' וא' במיתתו של חברו ולא יקשור אבל עליו.

ובמיוחד חשוב לענייננו לציין שכן הוא בשיטה לתלמידו של רבינו יחיאל מפריש (שם):

... רמז להם לישראל שלא יוכלו להתאבל אלו על אלו מרוב הפורענות שתבא על שונאיהם בחייהן וישמח כל אחד במיתתו של חבירו ולא יקשר עליו אבל.

אם כן, מבואר בדברי הראשונים שאין חיוב להתאבל אלא במקום שיש צער על אבדון הנפטר. וזה מקור נאמן ליסודו של המהרש"ל בים של שלמה למסכת גיטין (פרק ב סימן ד):

... ומעשה בא לידי, באחד שהיה בקטט עם אשתו, והיה לו דעת ברור לגרשה, ובתוך אותו הקטט מתה, והוריתי לו שלא לישב ז' ימי אבילות, ושלא להתאבל עליה, והבאתי ראיה מדברי הרשב"ם, שפסק כך אפילו לענין ירושת הבעל שהוא דאורייתא, כגון לר' עקיבא בפ' ד' וה' (ב"ק מ"ב ע"ב) ולרשב"ג בפ' הכותב (כתובות פ"ו ע"א) וכן הלכה, רק שרב פסק (שם) שהוא דרבנן והוי הפקעת ממון שלא כדין, אפילו הכי אמרינן כיון שנתן עיניו לגרשה חשבינן כאילו כבר גירשה, ונילף מיניה קל וחומר לענין אבילות, שהוא לכולי עלמא מדרבנן, דפטור מאבילות, ואף שכתבתי שליתא לדברי רשב"ם, היינו משום דס"ל דהלכה כרבנן, דסברי אליבא דר"י שיש לבעל פירות עד שעת נתינה, והיינו טעמא, מאחר שתקנו לו חכמים לזכות בפירות לא נפקעת אותו זכות עד שעת גירושין, דמנא לן להפקיע ממונו שלא כדין, שיכול לומר כל זמן שלא גירשתי הרי היא אשתי, וכל זכות שיש לי בה לא אמחל, בפרט מאחר שירושת הבעל דאורייתא, אבל מנין לנו לחייבו באבילות דרבנן, ועוד, מאחר דלר"ש דסבר כיון שנתן עיניו לגרשה שוב אין לו פירות, אם כן קל וחומר לענין אבילות, ונהי דחכמים חולקים, והלכה כוותייהו, מכל מקום הלכה כמיקל באבל (מו"ק י"ט ע"ב), אם כך הלכה כר"ש לענין אבילות, ועוד, **איך יעלה על דעת האדם להאבילו מה שאין לבו אבל, ואין יום מר לפניו, ונהי דבאבל ממש לא חלקו רבותינו בין אוהב לשונא,[10] הכא יש יש לחלק, ועוד, התם מאחר דאית ליה קורבא בגביה, אפילו הוא שונאו מכל מקום בשרו הוא ונכמרו רחמיו, ושייך ביה אבילות ומרירות הלב, אבל כהאי גוונא כולי עלמא מודו דחשיב ליה בלביה כאלו אזלה מיניה, ואין כאן אבילות ומרירות הלב,**

---

[10] חילוק זה אינו נוגע לענייננו, וכמו שביארו היטב בשו"ת במראה הבזק (שם).

וכל היכא דטריד הכי נמי דפטור אלא מעתה טבעה ספינתו בים דטריד הכי נמי
דפטור וכי תימא הכי נמי והאמר רבי אבא בר זבדא אמר רב אבל חייב בכל המצות
האמורות בתורה חוץ מן התפילין שהרי פאר נאמר בהן פאר הכא טריד טירדא דמצוה
התם טריד טרדא דרשות.

רש"י (שם) מפרש[7]:

טירדא דרשות. שאף על פי שהוא חייב לנהוג אבילות של נעילה רחיצה וסיכה
להראות כבוד מתו אינו חייב להצטער.

נראה מבואר שאין הצער מצוה, אלא תגובה טבעית. אין בעצב של האבל שום חיוב או
קיום הלכתי. ואם כן, צריכים להבין את דברי השיטה לתלמידו של רבינו יחיאל מפריש
(ודרכה את דברי הגאונים).

ג. הגדרת אבלים ואבילות

כדי לעמוד על כוונת נימוק זה של הגאונים וראשונים, יש לעיין ביסוד חשוב בעניין
אבילות בכלל. כידוע, הגמרא לומדת הרבה דיני אבילות ממה שפירט הקב"ה ליחזקאל,
כשצוה אותו לא להתנהג כאבל. בין היתר, הגמרא (מו"ק טו.) אומרת:

אבל חייב בעטיפת הראש מדקאמר ליה רחמנא ליחזקאל ולא תעטה על שפם מכלל
דכולי עלמא מיחייבי.

רש"י[8] מפרש (שם):

... רמז לשונאיהם של ישראל שלא יהו סופדין ומתאבלין זה על זה מרוב מתים
שיפלו מהם ולא יוכלו להתאבל עליהן ומתוך פורענות שיבא עליהם **בחייהם ישמח
כל אחד ואחד במיתתו של חבירו ולא יחול אבל עליו.**

כך גם בחידושי הר"ן[9] (שם):

---

6   קושיא זו מובא כבר שם.

7   רש"י גם מפרש כן בכתובות (ו:). [וכדברי רש"י מבואר גם בשאר ראשונים.] ובאמת יסוד זה
    מובא כבר בשם רב האי גאון ברשב"א לברכות (יא.) וז"ל: אבל העוסק במצוה ולא טריד כגון
    כונס אלמנה או דטריד ולא במצוה כגון מי שטבעה ספינתו בים וכגון אבל חייב. ועיין
    בריטב"א לכתובות (שם) שכתב שאבל טריד טירדא דרשות לגמרי ואינו מחמת מצוה מצוה כלל.

8   רש"י כ"י. [כנראה שהוא פרש"י האמיתי, כמו שמוכח מההשואה לציטוטים בהרבה ראשונים
    בהרבה מקומות במו"ק, ואכמ"ל.]

9   וכן פי' גם רבינו יהונתן מלוניל.

ב. האם יש חיוב על האבל להצטער

שנינו במשנה במועד קטן (יט.):

הקובר את מתו שלשה ימים קודם לרגל בטלה הימנו גזרת שבעה שמונה בטלו
הימנו גזרת שלשים מפני שאמרו שבת עולה ואינה מפסקת רגלים ואינן
עולין.[4]

הגאונים מנמקים חילוק זה, כפי שאנו מוצאים בספר הלכות פסוקות:

והילכתא שבת עולה ואינה מפסקת מאי טעמא ענג כתיב ביה. הרגלים מפסיקין ואינן
עולין מאי טעמא שמחה כתיב בהו.

וכן בבה"ג (סימן כא - הלכות אבל):

והילכתא שבת עולה ואינה מפסקת, מאי טעמא, עונג כתיב בה. רגלים מפסיקין ואין
עולין, מאי טעמא, שמחה כתיב בהו.

וכן בשאילתות דרב אחאי [פרשת חיי שרה (שאילתא טו)]:

שבת עולה ואינה מפסקת מאי טעמא עונג הוא דכתי' ביה הרגלים מפסיקין ואינן
עולין מאי טעמא שמחה הוא דכת' בהו.

הסבר זה מבואר בהרחבה על ידי הראשונים, ביניהם השיטה לתלמידו של רבינו יחיאל
מפריש למו"ק (שם):

ויש ליתן טעם למה שבת עולה ואינה מפסקת ורגלים להיפך. כי שבת אינו נקרא יום
שמחה אלא יום עונג. שחייב אדם להתענג בעצמו, במאכל ובמשתה ובכסות... וכל
זה מותר [לאבל] אלא שיהא אונן ודואג ולא ישמח בו. וגם זה הוא יכול לעשות
בשבת. ולכן יש לה לעלות ואין לה להפסיק כיון שאין שמחה מפסיקתו. אבל רגלים
הם ימי שמחה שחייב אדם לשמח לבו ולהסיר ממנו כל אנינות לב וכל דאגה מד'
ושמחת בחגך. וכת' והיית אך שמח וכל זה הוא הפך האבל. ולכך יש לו להפסיק
ואין לו לעלות.

לכאורה, כוונתו שאבילות ביסודה היא מצוה רגשית, עקרו להתעצב- ולכן יש סתירה
בינה לבין שמחת יו"ט.[5] אמנם קשה לפרש כן, מאחר שלכאורה אין כן שיטת הגמרא
והראשונים.[6] הגמרא אומרת בסוכה לענין קריאת שמע (כה.):

---

4 בעניין שבת ויו"ט לעניין אבילות, עיין בין היתר ברמב"ם הל' אבל (פ"י ה"א וה"ג) ובטור
   וב"י יו"ד (סי' שצ"ט, ת' ות"ב).

5 כשיטה הידועה של הגרי"ד סולוביצ'ק, עיין ברשימות שיעורים לסוכה (כה.) ד"ה לפום
   ריהטא ובהע' 5, ועוד.

האם יש חיוב להתאבל במקום שאין צער?

מאת: יצחק אברהם טברסקי

א. הקדמה

למאמר זה[1] יש שתי מגמות:

א'- בירור הלכתי בשאלה האם יש חיוב לנהוג אבילות במצב שאין האבל מצטער על פטירת קרובו,[2] שאלה שכנראה נעשתה יותר נחוצה בזמנינו. האם חייבים ע"פ הלכה לנהוג דיני אבילות בעד הורים [או קרובים אחרים] אלו, אף שיגרום לו הרבה צער ונזק נפשי עמוק? ובכלל, האם יש חיוב לנהוג אבילות אם האבל מרגיש שאין כאן עצב וקשה לו נפשית לנהוג אבילות על הנפטר שפגע בו בחייו. כבר דנו בשאלה זו בשו"ת במראה הבזק[3] ופסקו שאין חיוב משום שאין חיוב אבילות במקום שאין צער כלל על הנפטר (ולא רק במקרה של רשעות כמו בדוגמא שבו דנו שם, כמו שמבואר למעיין היטב בדברי התשובה). ובאתי כאן ליסד ולחזק מסקנתם באופן עקרוני על פי דברי הגמרא והראשונים.

ב'- עיון יסודי בהגדרת חיוב אבילות והלכותיה.

נשתדל לענות על הראשונה מתוך עיסוק בשניה. ויהי רצון שדברי ימצאו חן בעיני האב הרחמן האמיתי.

---

1. תודה רבה לחתני היקר, ר' אביהו שינפלד שליט"א, שעבר על המאמר ועזר לי בענייני לשון וניסוח. הטעויות וחסרונות שנשארו הם, כמובן, אך ורק שלי.

2. לדוגמא, המקרה המובא בשו"ת במראה הבזק (עיין בהע' הבא): אשה שהורּיה התעללו בה ואין לה יחס עמהם.

3. שו"ת במראה הבזק ח"ז (סי' פג).

רב יצחק אברהם טברסקי היה רבי בכיר ויו"ר מחלקת התנ"ך בישיבת פריש במשך 14 שנה, עד שעלה ארצה לפני 16 שנה. במהלך שהותו בארה"ב, העביר שיעורים בישיבה אוניברסיטה, פרינסטון, קולומביה, מחנה מושבה ובקהילות ואוניברסיטאות רבות במשך למעלה משני עשורים לאלפי סטודנטים, רבנים ומורים. הוא חיבר "אמיתה של תורה" על חומש "ואמיתה של תורה 2" בעניין השנה התורני www.realtorah.com, ועשרות מאמרים שפורסמו בגמרא, הלכה, תנ"ך ומחשבה. כיום הוא מעביר שיעורים במכללת מבשרת ירושלים ובנווה דניאל. יש לו יורה יורה וידין ידין מישיבה אוניברסיטה.

מדרשית אחרת, לעומת ערעור "דתן ואבירם" על סמכות משה, בספרא אמור פרשה יד כאן בא: "וַיֵּצֵא בֶּן אִשָּׁה יִשְׂרְאֵלִית": מנין יצא? **מבית דינו של משה**", שמצרף מוטיב המשפט בשלושת הפרשיות ("**מִשְׁפַּט** אֶחָד יִהְיֶה לָכֶם" עם "מִי שָׂמְךָ לְאִישׁ שַׂר **וְשֹׁפֵט**" ו"וְאֵלֶּה **הַמִּשְׁפָּטִים** אֲשֶׁר תָּשִׂים").

דברי תורה בתורת משה ילמדו לא רק מן המפורש על הסתום, אלא גם מן המפורש על המפורש אם כי בצורה סתומה, בערבוב סוגתית הילכתית ונרטיבית, כש"מקרא עשיר במקומות הרבה" (מכילתא דר"י שירה,ד) וכן "עשירים במקום אחר" (ירושלמי ר"ה פ"ג ה"ה), והעיון בממשק הפרשיות והסוגות כאחת עשוי להעשיר את הבנותינו בשניהם. ೞ

פרשת משפטים	פרשת המקלל
וְכִי יִנָּצוּ אֲנָשִׁים וְנָגְפוּ אִשָּׁה הָרָה וְיָצְאוּ יְלָדֶיהָ וְלֹא יִהְיֶה אָסוֹן	וַיִּנָּצוּ בַּמַּחֲנֶה בֶּן הַיִּשְׂרְאֵלִית וְאִישׁ הַיִּשְׂרְאֵלִי
מַכֵּה אִישׁ וָמֵת מוֹת יוּמָת	וְאִישׁ כִּי יַכֶּה כָּל נֶפֶשׁ אָדָם מוֹת יוּמָת
וְאִם אָסוֹן יִהְיֶה וְנָתַתָּה נֶפֶשׁ תַּחַת נָפֶשׁ	וּמַכֵּה נֶפֶשׁ בְּהֵמָה יְשַׁלְּמֶנָּה נֶפֶשׁ תַּחַת נָפֶשׁ וְאִישׁ כִּי יִתֵּן מוּם בַּעֲמִיתוֹ כַּאֲשֶׁר עָשָׂה כֵּן יֵעָשֶׂה לּוֹ
עַיִן תַּחַת עַיִן שֵׁן תַּחַת שֵׁן יָד תַּחַת יָד רֶגֶל תַּחַת רָגֶל	שֶׁבֶר תַּחַת שֶׁבֶר עַיִן תַּחַת עַיִן שֵׁן תַּחַת שֵׁן
כְּוִיָּה תַּחַת כְּוִיָּה פֶּצַע תַּחַת פָּצַע חַבּוּרָה תַּחַת חַבּוּרָה	כַּאֲשֶׁר יִתֵּן מוּם בָּאָדָם כֵּן יִנָּתֶן בּוֹ
וְכִי יְרִיבֻן אֲנָשִׁים וְהִכָּה אִישׁ אֶת רֵעֵהוּ	וּמַכֵּה בְהֵמָה יְשַׁלְּמֶנָּה וּמַכֵּה אָדָם יוּמָת

באים דיני נזקי אדם ובהמה כאותם אחרי דיני הכאת אדם בפרשת 'אלה המשפטים'. וכן מתוך ההקבלה המכילתא לפרשת משפטים למד שדין "וּמְקַלֵּל אָבִיו וְאִמּוֹ מוֹת יוּמָת" (שמ' כא, יז) יענש רק בנוקב שמם, כמקלל שנקב שם ה' כאן.

באופן מרתק המדרש מגשר במנהרה תת-קרקעית בין תכנים ומרכיבים המשותפים לשני הפרשיות. בפרשת המקלל, בן איש המצרי נקב בשם ה', כשבמדרש משה הרג המצרי "עם שם המפורש"[13] ו"בן איש המצרי" היה אותו בן "איש מצרי" שהרג משה[14], והבן "התגייר בתוך בני ישראל"[15]. איש המצרי הכה איש העברי מפני שנתן עיניו באשת העברי[16], אשת דתן[17] (או אחותו[18]), שהיא אם בן איש המצרי "שְׁלֹמִית בַּת דִּבְרִי לְמַטֶּה דָן" שבא עליה ונתעברה ממנו[19].

ובגישור אומנותי דק ומפתיע בשמו"ר א, כ, כשכמשה ראה איש המצרי מכה את העברי: "אמר ודאי זה חייב מיתה, כמו שכתוב: "וּמַכֵּה אָדָם יוּמָת" (ויק' כד, כא)". הפסוק שפוסק עליו אינו זה שבפרשת משפטים ("מַכֵּה אִישׁ וָמֵת מוֹת יוּמָת") אלא בפרשת המקלל בפרשת אמור. הציון לפסוק זה דייקא מקשר פרשת משה ופרשת המקלל בשילוב סיפורי בהקשר הלכתי וכרומז שבן איש המצרי שקלל את השם היה כעוס כבר מזמן על שם זה שבו הרג משה את אביו המצרי. מניע זה מובא במפורש בזוהר כאן ובעוד פרשנים. בזיקה

---

13 שמו"ר א, כט-ל; ויק"ר לב, ד; תנחומא שמות ט: "הַלְהָרְגֵנִי אַתָּה אֹמֵר כַּאֲשֶׁר הָרַגְתָּ אֶת הַמִּצְרִי": "אתה אומר", מכאן אתה למד ששם המפורש הזכיר על המצרי והרגו."

14 תנחומא שם.

15 ספרא אמור פרשה יד.

16 שמו"ר א,כט; תנחומא שם; תנחומא אמור כד; ויק"ר שם.

17 שמו"ר שם.

18 גירסת רד"ל בשמו"ר שם.

19 שמו"ר א, ל; ספרא שם.

אֶל מֹשֶׁה ... : וַיַּנִּיחֻהוּ בַּמִּשְׁמָר לִפְרֹשׁ לָהֶם עַל פִּי ה': וַיְדַבֵּר ה' אֶל מֹשֶׁה ... וְאֶל בְּנֵי
יִשְׂרָאֵל תְּדַבֵּר לֵאמֹר אִישׁ אִישׁ כִּי יְקַלֵּל אֱלֹהָיו וְנָשָׂא חֶטְאוֹ: וְנֹקֵב שֵׁם ה' מוֹת יוּמָת
רָגוֹם יִרְגְּמוּ בוֹ כָּל הָעֵדָה כַּגֵּר כָּאֶזְרָח בְּנָקְבוֹ שֵׁם יוּמָת: וְאִישׁ כִּי יַכֶּה כָּל נֶפֶשׁ אָדָם
מוֹת יוּמָת: וּמַכֵּה נֶפֶשׁ בְּהֵמָה יְשַׁלְּמֶנָּה נֶפֶשׁ תַּחַת נָפֶשׁ: (וְאִישׁ כִּי יִתֵּן מוּם בַּעֲמִיתוֹ
כַּאֲשֶׁר עָשָׂה כֵּן יֵעָשֶׂה לּוֹ: שֶׁבֶר תַּחַת שֶׁבֶר עַיִן תַּחַת עַיִן שֵׁן תַּחַת שֵׁן כַּאֲשֶׁר יִתֵּן מוּם
בָּאָדָם כֵּן יִנָּתֶן בּוֹ: וּמַכֵּה בְהֵמָה יְשַׁלְּמֶנָּה וּמַכֵּה אָדָם יוּמָת: מִשְׁפַּט אֶחָד יִהְיֶה לָכֶם כַּגֵּר
כָּאֶזְרָח יִהְיֶה כִּי אֲנִי ה' אֱלֹהֵיכֶם ...

באים כאן דיני נזקים כפרשת 'משפטים' בלשונות זהות ודומות ("כִּי יַכֶּה" "מוֹת
יוּמָת"; "וּמַכֵּה אָדָם"; "שֶׁבֶר תַּחַת שֶׁבֶר, עַיִן תַּחַת עַיִן, שֵׁן תַּחַת שֵׁן"; "נֶפֶשׁ תַּחַת נָפֶשׁ"),
וכן הקבלה סיפורית על מריבה בין "בן איש מצרי" ו"איש ישראלי" לסיפור יציאת משה
עצמו לשלושת משימותיו הראשונות. לעומת "וַיִּגְדַּל מֹשֶׁה וַיֵּצֵא אֶל אֶחָיו ... וַיַּרְא אִישׁ
מִצְרִי מַכֶּה אִישׁ עִבְרִי מֵאֶחָיו (שמ' ב, יא) בא: "וַיֵּצֵא בֶּן אִשָּׁה יִשְׂרְאֵלִית וְהוּא בֶּן אִישׁ
מִצְרִי" (ויק' כד, י), כשמשה עצמו נקרא "אִישׁ מִצְרִי" בהתערבותו השלישית: "וַתֹּאמַרְןָ
אִישׁ מִצְרִי הִצִּילָנוּ מִיַּד הָרֹעִים". מלבד מרכיבים סגנוניים המשותפים, הדגשת עקרון צדק
המשווה בסיפור כאן פעמים, "כַּגֵּר כָּאֶזְרָח", "מִשְׁפַּט אֶחָד יִהְיֶה לָכֶם כַּגֵּר כָּאֶזְרָח" (טז;
כב) משקף למופת עקרון הנרטיבי-הלכתי של צדק המשווה בסיפור שלושת משימותיו
הראשונות בתחילת דרכו.

פרשת המקלל	פרשת משה
וַיֵּצֵא בֶּן אִשָּׁה יִשְׂרְאֵלִית וְהוּא בֶּן **אִישׁ מִצְרִי** בְּתוֹךְ בְּנֵי יִשְׂרָאֵל	וַיְהִי בַּיָּמִים הָהֵם וַיִּגְדַּל מֹשֶׁה וַיֵּצֵא אֶל אֶחָיו
וְאִישׁ כִּי יַכֶּה כָּל נֶפֶשׁ אָדָם **מוֹת יוּמָת\ וּמַכֵּה אָדָם** יוּמָת	וַיַּרְא בְּסִבְלֹתָם וַיַּרְא **אִישׁ מִצְרִי מַכֶּה** אִישׁ עִבְרִי מֵאֶחָיו
וַיִּנָּצוּ בַּמַּחֲנֶה בֶּן הַיִּשְׂרְאֵלִית וְאִישׁ הַיִּשְׂרְאֵלִי	וַיֵּצֵא בַּיּוֹם הַשֵּׁנִי וְהִנֵּה שְׁנֵי אֲנָשִׁים עִבְרִים **נִצִּים** וַתֹּאמַרְןָ **אִישׁ מִצְרִי** הִצִּילָנוּ מִיַּד הָרֹעִים

וציווי "מִשְׁפַּט אֶחָד יִהְיֶה לָכֶם כַּגֵּר כָּאֶזְרָח" כאן מלמד בהקשר הסיפורי ש"אִישׁ
הַיִּשְׂרְאֵלִי" (רש"י: "זה שכנגדו שמיחה בו מטע אהלו") גם היה אשם במריבת ההכאה
בנצייתו עם "רֵעֵהוּ" בן איש המצרי, ומלמד במישור ההלכתי שאלימות ההכאה הלקאה או
הריגה כזאת גם ענישה, בהקבלה לפרשת הניזקין שבפרשת משפטים:

תנן (ד, יד): "הוי גולה למקום תורה". על כן כשראה משה רבינו ע"ה **שיש בו חובת גלות** הוזהר מאוד בדברי תורה **והיה גולה למקום תורה, כי מקומו הוא מקום תורה.".**

ונוסיף: עם שמשה הבדיל ערי המקלט בהכנה לכניסה לארץ בדב' ד, מא-מג, הלכות ערי המקלט בארץ כבר הוצגו בפרשת "אלה מסעי בני ישראל" (במ' לה, י-לב) בסוף ספר במדבר. בסיפור המסעות מוזכרת פטירת אהרן הכהן הגדול, ושלא כבפרשת חוקת, "וַיָּמָת **אַהֲרֹן** שָׁם בְּרֹאשׁ הָהָר" (במ' כ, כח) כאן הוא במפורש: "וַיַּעַל **אַהֲרֹן הַכֹּהֵן** אֶל הֹר הָהָר עַל פִּי ה' וַיָּמָת שָׁם" (לג, לז-לח). בערבוב הסוגיות, אחרי סיפורי המסעות באה סדרת הלכות בהכנות לקראת הכניסה לארץ, ובינם דיני ערי המקלט שם לרבות דין שמוזכר כאן לראשונה, שחרור רוצח בשוגג במות כהן הגדול:

דַּבֵּר אֶל בְּנֵי יִשְׂרָאֵל וְאָמַרְתָּ אֲלֵהֶם כִּי אַתֶּם עֹבְרִים אֶת הַיַּרְדֵּן אַרְצָה כְּנָעַן: וְהִקְרִיתֶם לָכֶם עָרִים עָרֵי מִקְלָט תִּהְיֶינָה לָכֶם וְנָס שָׁמָּה רֹצֵחַ מַכֵּה נֶפֶשׁ בִּשְׁגָגָה ... **וְיָשַׁב בָּהּ עַד מוֹת הַכֹּהֵן הַגָּדֹל** אֲשֶׁר מָשַׁח אֹתוֹ בְּשֶׁמֶן הַקֹּדֶשׁ ... כִּי בְעִיר מִקְלָטוֹ **יֵשֵׁב עַד מוֹת הַכֹּהֵן הַגָּדֹל וְאַחֲרֵי מוֹת הַכֹּהֵן הַגָּדֹל** יָשׁוּב הָרֹצֵחַ אֶל אֶרֶץ אֲחֻזָּתוֹ ... וְלֹא תִקְחוּ כֹפֶר לָנוּס אֶל עִיר מִקְלָטוֹ לָשׁוּב לָשֶׁבֶת בָּאָרֶץ **עַד מוֹת הַכֹּהֵן.**

ור' מאיר שמחה כהן, "משך חכמה", קישר כדרכו בין הרובד הסיפורי וההלכתי בחידוש מפתיע, לבמ' כ, כט: "ויבכו את אהרן וכו' כל בית ישראל" "הכתוב מספר לנו בזה שלא היה זה כל הארבעים שנה רוצח נפש בשוגג שהיה נגלה ... שאם היה הלא חזרו במיתת אהרן, "מות הכהן הגדול" (לה, כה) והיה להם לשמוח".

ואם נשאל אם כן למי מיועדת כפרת מות אהרן כהן הגדול הארכי-טיפוסי ("מיתת כהן הוא דמכפר", בבלי מכות יא ע"ב), אפשר להציע תשובה בעמימות הכתוב עצמו: "וְיָשַׁב בָּהּ עַד מוֹת הַכֹּהֵן הַגָּדֹל **אֲשֶׁר מָשַׁח אֹתוֹ בְּשֶׁמֶן הַקֹּדֶשׁ**" (לה, כה). ברש"י: "מן המקראות הקצרים הוא שלא פירש מי משחו... (ועל פי בבלי מכות שם: "וכי הוא משחו לכהן או הכהן משח אותו?"). אולם בעירוב נרטיבי-הלכתי ניתן לקראות ישירות במי שמשח את אהרן הכהן הגדול לראשונה: משה עצמו: "וְאֶת **אַהֲרֹן** וְאֶת בָּנָיו תִּמְשָׁח", ו"אֶת **אַהֲרֹן אָחִיךָ** וְאֶת בָּנָיו אִתּוֹ וּמָשַׁחְתָּ אֹתָם" (שמ' ל, ל; כח, מא), ויתפרש "וְנָס שָׁמָּה רֹצֵחַ מַכֵּה נֶפֶשׁ ... וְיָשַׁב בָּהּ עַד מוֹת הַכֹּהֵן הַגָּדֹל **אֲשֶׁר מָשַׁח אֹתוֹ בְּשֶׁמֶן הַקֹּדֶשׁ**"—במשה, שהכה נפש המצרי.

בבואה לפרשת משפטים: עוד סיפור נרטיבי\הלכתי

בספר ויקרא שרובו הלכה בא סיפור המקלל (כד, י-כג) שתואמת לתוכן פרשת משפטים, עם הקבלות לסיפור משה:

וַיֵּצֵא בֶּן אִשָּׁה יִשְׂרְאֵלִית וְהוּא בֶּן אִישׁ מִצְרִי בְּתוֹךְ בְּנֵי יִשְׂרָאֵל וַיִּנָּצוּ בַּמַּחֲנֶה בֶּן הַיִּשְׂרְאֵלִית וְאִישׁ הַיִּשְׂרְאֵלִי: וַיִּקֹּב בֶּן הָאִשָּׁה הַיִּשְׂרְאֵלִית אֶת הַשֵּׁם וַיְקַלֵּל וַיָּבִיאוּ אֹתוֹ

על כך כתב המלבי"ם: "ושמתי לך מקום": ובהכרח שגם במדבר היה מקום קליטה ...
וכן אמר ב[מסכתות] מכות וזבחים ... **וגם רמז לו שהוא יפריש בחייו**". כוונתו לסיפור
ההלכתי בהבדלת משה את ערי המקלט לפני הכניסה לארץ: "אָז יַבְדִּיל מֹשֶׁה שָׁלֹשׁ עָרִים
בְּעֵבֶר הַיַּרְדֵּן מִזְרְחָה שָׁמֶשׁ. לָנֻס שָׁמָּה רוֹצֵחַ אֲשֶׁר יִרְצַח אֶת רֵעֵהוּ בִּבְלִי דַעַת ... וְנָס אֶל אַחַת
מִן הֶעָרִים הָאֵל וָחָי" (דב' ד, מא-מג). ועל פי זה, באה הטרמה אינטרטקסטואלית בפרשת
משפטים ההלכתית לסיפור נרטיבי של יסוד משה את ערי המקלט לפני מותו. המדרשים
הרגישו בכסגירת מעגל סיפורי במימד ההלכתי בסמטריות הסיפורית של הריגת המצרי,
"פעילותו הציבורית" הראשונה, עם הבדלת ערי המקלט כפעילותו בסוף ימיו:

דברים רבה ואתחנן: "אז יבדיל משה" ... זה שירה, שנא': "אז ישיר משה" (שמ'
טו, א) ... וכיון שאמ' ליה הקב"ה רפואתו [של רוצח בשוגג] התחיל משה אומר
שירה ... שהרג את המצרי וברח ... מי שאכל את התבשיל הוא יודע טעמו ... מה
ישראל אמרו שירה על הבאר אף משה אמר שירה על הבאר ... לפי שאירעה פרשת
רוצח על ידו בערי מקלט.

ילקוט שמעוני, ואתחנן תתכט: אמר משה: "שירה חייב אני לומר, שאף בי אירע
הדבר הזה, שהרגתי את המצרי".

במדרש "פטירת משה רבינו" הקב"ה מנמק גזירת מותו בהריגת המצרי. הזוהר (קיד
ע"ב) אף מקשר "וְשַׂמְתִּי לְךָ מָקוֹם אֲשֶׁר יָנוּס שָׁמָּה" למשה בממד כפרה (בתרגום): "מצוה
להפריש ערי מקלט למי שהרג בגלל אותו מצרי שהרגת ... והקב"ה נתן לך ערי מקלט
והן שערי תשובה". האר"י ז"ל [12] פירשו כככפרת גלות: "ושמתי **לך** מקום אשר ינוס
שָׁמ"ה, אותיות **מֹשׁ"ה**" ... הסוד הוא כי משה תיקן ערי המקלט כדי לתקן עצמו": "אָז
יַבְדִּיל מֹשֶׁה שָׁלֹשׁ עָרִים בְּעֵבֶר הַיַּרְדֵּן מִזְרְחָה שָׁמֶשׁ לָנֻס שָׁמָּ"ה רוֹצֵח", אותיות **'מֹשׁה'**;
"הַיַּרְדֵּן מִזְרְחָה שָׁמֶשׁ", ר"ת **'מֹשׁ"ה'**. מוסיף עליו החיד"א (נחל קדומים, מסעי):
"מֹשׁ"ה גימטריא "המצרי" "שמקלטו במדבר היה דיו כיון שפעל בצדק ... רק לגודל
מעלתו היה צריך למקלט ככפרה" (צירוף פירוש התלמודי ש"וְשַׂמְתִּי לְךָ" שמגלין במדבר,
עם פירוש הקבלי).

הכפרה בתוך הטקסט

השל"ה (תורה אור, ואתחנן) הציע כפרה טקסטואלית במרחב הטקסט: "**אָז יַבְדִּיל מֹשֶׁה
שָׁלֹשׁ עָרִים** ... וְזֹאת הַתּוֹרָה אֲשֶׁר שָׂם מֹשֶׁה לִפְנֵי בְּנֵי יִשְׂרָאֵל**"] (דב' מא-מד) "קיים
בעצמו הא דתנן (אבות א, יא): "חכמים הזהרו בדבריכם שמא תחובו חובת גלות". עוד

---

[12] כוונות האר"י (מד, ב): ספר הגלגולים פרק לג; ספר הליקוטים וישב מח.

זכר **העבד והאמה** כי צריך לפרש משפט **מכה עבדו ואמתו**". תוכנם והצגתם, לרוב בניסוח קזואיסטי סיפורי ("כי ... אם ... אם"), מזכירים סיפורי משה במפגשיו הראשונים:

(יב) **מכה איש** וָמֵת מוֹת יוּמָת: (יג) וַאֲשֶׁר לֹא צָדָה וְהָאֱלֹהִים אִנָּה לְיָדוֹ **וְשַׂמְתִּי לְךָ** מָקוֹם אֲשֶׁר יָנוּס שָׁמָּה ... (טו) **וּמַכֵּה** אָבִיו וְאִמּוֹ מוֹת יוּמָת ... (יח) וְכִי יְרִיבֻן אֲנָשִׁים וְהִכָּה אִישׁ אֶת רֵעֵהוּ ... (כ) וְכִי **יַכֶּה אִישׁ אֶת עַבְדּוֹ** אוֹ אֶת אֲמָתוֹ בַּשֵּׁבֶט **וּמֵת** תַּחַת יָדוֹ **נָקֹם יִנָּקֵם** ... (כב) **וְכִי יִנָּצוּ אֲנָשִׁים** ...

הד הלשוני ב"סיפורים" ההלכתיים "וְכִי יְרִיבֻן אֲנָשִׁים **וְהִכָּה אִישׁ אֶת רֵעֵהוּ**"; "**וְכִי יִנָּצוּ אֲנָשִׁים**" (יח; כב) משחזר מריבת "שני העברים" "וַיֵּצֵא בַּיּוֹם הַשֵּׁנִי וְהִנֵּה שְׁנֵי אֲנָשִׁים עִבְרִים נִצִּים וַיֹּאמֶר לָרָשָׁע לָמָּה **תַכֶּה רֵעֶךָ**" (ב, יד). כן דין הכאת ונקמת עבד מוכה ("וְכִי **יַכֶּה אִישׁ אֶת עַבְדּוֹ** ... וּמֵת תַּחַת יָדוֹ נָקֹם יִנָּקֵם") (כא, כ) דומה לנקמת משה להכאת העבד.

ובאים כאן שני מובני "הכאה" כהלקאה או הריגה: "**מַכֵּה אִישׁ וָמֵת** מוֹת יוּמָת" ו"**וּמַכֵּה** אָבִיו וְאִמּוֹ מוֹת יוּמָת" (יב; טו). ראב"ע: "בעבור שהזכיר "**מַכֵּה אִישׁ וָמֵת**" הוצרך לפרש כי יש מכה בלא מיתת המוכה שימות כמו "**וּמַכֵּה** אָבִיו" ו'מכה' ישרת בעבור אחר". משמעות הכפולה מקבילה להתערבות משה ב"וַיַּרְא אִישׁ מִצְרִי **מַכֶּה אִישׁ עִבְרִי**... **וַיַּךְ** אֶת הַמִּצְרִי וַיִּטְמְנֵהוּ בַּחוֹל" (ב, יא-יב), כשהראשון (רש"י: "מלקהו ורודהו") גרם לשני (וַיִּטְמְנֵהוּ בַּחוֹל"), כדברי איש העברי: "**כַּאֲשֶׁר הָרַגְתָּ אֶת הַמִּצְרִי**". במרחק המובנים רמב"ן פירש הריגת משה את המצרי כגואל נוקם על הלקאה במחאה נגד העוול ולא כמציל מרצח: "נסתכל בסבלותם ועמלם ולא יכול לסבול ולכן הרג המצרי המכה הנלחץ".

משה ועיר המקלט

ובעיקר בהקשר זה ברובד ההלכתי של הכאה בא דין בריחת מכה שהורג ומקלטו: "מַכֵּה אִישׁ וָמֵת מוֹת יוּמָת: וַאֲשֶׁר לֹא צָדָה וְהָאֱלֹהִים אִנָּה לְיָדוֹ **וְשַׂמְתִּי לְךָ מָקוֹם אֲשֶׁר יָנוּס שָׁמָּה**" (כא, יב-יד), שמשקף סיפור משה ברובד הנרטיבי במפתיע: "וַיִּשְׁמַע פַּרְעֹה אֶת הַדָּבָר הַזֶּה וַיְבַקֵּשׁ לַהֲרֹג אֶת מֹשֶׁה **וַיִּבְרַח מֹשֶׁה מִפְּנֵי פַרְעֹה וַיֵּשֶׁב בְּאֶרֶץ מִדְיָן** וַיֵּשֶׁב עַל הַבְּאֵר". ואכן קיימת פרשנות רווחת שמקשרת התכנים במפורש.

הקשר בטקסט מתמקד ב"וַאֲשֶׁר לֹא צָדָה וְהָאֱלֹקִים אִנָּה לְיָדוֹ **וְשַׂמְתִּי לְךָ** מָקוֹם אֲשֶׁר יָנוּס שָׁמָּה" בגוף שני לנוכח כאילו למשה, נמען "וְאֵלֶּה הַמִּשְׁפָּטִים אֲשֶׁר תָּשִׂים", לעומת "אֲשֶׁר לֹא צָדָה וְהָאֱלֹקִים אִנָּה לְיָדוֹ" בגוף שלישי נסתר. לכן פירש רש"י: "ושמתי לך מקום": "אף במדבר שינוס שמה ואיזה מקום קולטו? זה מחנה לויה" [ע"פ בבלי זבחים קיז ע"א ומכות יב ע"ב: "ושמתי לך"—בחייך; "מקום"—ממקומך; "אשר ינוס שמה"— מלמד שמגלין במדבר ... למחנה לויה"]. (ר' בחיי העיר: "ויראה לי כי על כן הזכיר מלת "לך" בדין הזה מה שאין כן בשאר הדינין כנגד משה שהיה משבט לוי".

סיפורי של אירוע ("כי ... אם ...") ולא בסגנון אפודיקטי של חק מוחלט של "עשה כך" או "לא תעשה כך". אף באות תופעות לשון נופל על לשון, כרצף ההומונימי (שוה-שם) שציין ראב"ע (כב, ד-ה): "וזאת הדרך צחות בלשון הקדש לאמר מלה שוה והיא משני טעמים":

ד. כִּי יַבְעֶר אִישׁ שָׂדֶה אוֹ כֶרֶם וְשִׁלַּח אֶת בְּעִירוֹ [=בהמתו] וּבִעֵר בִּשְׂדֵה אַחֵר מֵיטַב שָׂדֵהוּ וּמֵיטַב כַּרְמוֹ יְשַׁלֵּם. ה. כִּי תֵצֵא אֵשׁ וּמָצְאָה קֹצִים וְנֶאֱכַל גָּדִישׁ אוֹ הַקָּמָה אוֹ הַשָּׂדֶה שַׁלֵּם יְשַׁלֵּם הַמַּבְעִר אֶת הַבְּעֵרָה [=אש]

ועוד באים מצלולים בשילוב צלילים ומשמעויות, כבמערכת העניים במבנה כיאסטי של צלילים במובנים שונים: "וְכִי יְרִיבֻן אֲנָשִׁים וְהִכָּה אִישׁ אֶת רֵעֵהוּ ... אִם יָקוּם וְהִתְהַלֵּךְ בַּחוּץ עַל מִשְׁעַנְתּוֹ וְנִקָּה הַמַּכֶּה \\ וְכִי יַכֶּה אִישׁ אֶת עַבְדּוֹ ... וּמֵת תַּחַת יָדוֹ נָקֹם יִנָּקֵם: אַךְ אִם יוֹם אוֹ יוֹמַיִם יַעֲמֹד [אונקלוס: "יִתְקַיִּים"] לֹא יֻקַּם כִּי כַסְפּוֹ הוּא" (כא, יח-כא).

א. אִם יָקוּם   ב. וְנִקָּה הַמַּכֶּה...

ב'. וּמֵת תַּחַת יָדוֹ נָקֹם יִנָּקֵם   א'. אַךְ אִם ... יַעֲמֹד לֹא יֻקַּם

רובד סיפורי בפרשת 'משפטים'

הזיקה לקורות משה מורגשת בחטיבה פותחת בדיני עבדים עברים (מדרש הגדול: "והלא לא היה לו לסמוך ל"אלה המשפטים" אלא "כי יריבון", "כי ינצו", "כי יכה איש", שהן דיני?"). רמב"ן העיר (כא, ב): "התחיל המשפט הראשון בעבד עברי מפני שיש בשילוח העבד בשנה השביעית זכר ליציאת מצרים הנזכר בדבור הראשון [של עשרת הדברות] כמו שאמר בו [בשילוח העבדים בדב' טו, טו] "וזכרת כי עבד היית בארץ מצרים ... על כן אנכי מצוך את הדבר הזה". הקשר ל"אָנֹכִי ה' אֱלֹהֶיךָ אֲשֶׁר **הוֹצֵאתִיךָ** מֵאֶרֶץ מִצְרַיִם מִבֵּית **עֲבָדִים**" מתאשר בתיאור העקבי לשחרור עבדים: "וּבַשְּׁבִעֵת יֵצֵא לַחָפְשִׁי... בְּגַפּוֹ יָצֵא ... וְיָצְאָה אִשְׁתּוֹ עִמּוֹ... וְהוּא **יֵצֵא** בְגַפּוֹ... לֹא **יֵצֵא** חָפְשִׁי... לֹא **תֵצֵא כְּצֵאת הָעֲבָדִים**... **וְיָצְאָה** חִנָּם" (כא, ב-יא), וכציון רס"ג בהקדמה לפרשה. בהקבלה רעיונית, דין עבד המסרב לצאת מעבדות, "וְהִגִּישׁוֹ אֶל הַדֶּלֶת אוֹ אֶל הַמְּזוּזָה וְרָצַע אֲדֹנָיו אֶת אָזְנוֹ" (כא, ו) נדרש בבבלי קידושין כב ע"ב: "דלת ומזוזה שהיו עדים במצרים בשעה שפסחתי על המשקוף ועל שתי המזוזות ... **וְהוֹצֵאתִים** מעבדות לחירות, והלך זה וקנה אדון לעצמו, ירצע בפניהם."

סיפורי ודיני הכאות

אחר נושא עבדים עברים באים דיני הכאה והרמת יד בין אנשים ועד למות ודין הכאת עבד. אבן עזרא העיר בעירוב הפרשיות: "**מַכֵּה אִישׁ**" (כא, יב): "טעם להזכיר זה אחר

הערעור והאישור

תוך התהליך, המערערים על תפקידו הם קהלו העיקרי, העברים: "וַיֵּצֵא בַּיּוֹם הַשֵּׁנִי וְהִנֵּה שְׁנֵי אֲנָשִׁים עִבְרִים נִצִּים וַיֹּאמֶר לָרָשָׁע לָמָּה תַכֶּה רֵעֶךָ", בטענת: "וַיֹּאמֶר **מִי שָׂמְךָ** לְאִישׁ שַׂר **וְשֹׁפֵט** עָלֵינוּ? הַלְהָרְגֵנִי אַתָּה אֹמֵר כַּאֲשֶׁר הָרַגְתָּ אֶת הַמִּצְרִי" (ב, יג-יד)[10]. תשובה לשאלתם הנוקבת אינה מופיעה. היה סביר שתשובה לשאלת ה' בבואם להר האלקים: "**מִי שָׂם** פֶּה לָאָדָם אוֹ **מִי יָשׂוּם** אִלֵּם אוֹ חֵרֵשׁ ... **הֲלֹא אָנֹכִי ה'**" (ד, י-יא) היתה מספקת גם לערוערם, אך אינו מוכרע עדיין באופן מבורר.

אולם המדרש (שמות רבה, ל, י) חש בקשר מילולי ורעיוני כמענה בתוך הכתוב עצמו:

"**וְאֵלֶּה הַמִשְׁפָּטִים**": "מהו '**וְאֵלֶּה**'? בא וראה כמה חיבב הקב"ה למשה. שבשעה שחיסדו [=ביזו] אותו דתן ואבירם במצרים, שאמרו לו "מי שמך לאיש שר **ושפט** עלינו", אמר להם הקב"ה: "בזה שחיסדתם אותו אני נותן לו גדולה שנאמר: "**וְאֵלֶּה המשפטים.**"

ברור שמלבד דרשת "**וְאֵלֶּה הַמִשְׁפָּטִים**" כהנגדה, גם "אֲשֶׁר **תָּשִׂים** לִפְנֵיהֶם" נדרש בקשר ל"**שָׂמְךָ**?" וכמפורש ב'מדרש הגדול': "אֲשֶׁר **תָּשִׂים** לִפְנֵיהֶם": "שמסר נפשו עליהן ... כשהוא אומר "וַיֹּאמֶר מִי **שָׂמְךָ** לְאִישׁ שַׂר וְשֹׁפֵט עָלֵינוּ?". המדרש מבליט ברמה לשונית מה שפשוט ונכון ברובד הסיפורי, שבפרשת 'המשפטים אשר תשים לפניהם' באה מענה בתורה לערעור הנרטיבי. וברובד שמיעתי, "**וְאֵלֶּה הַמִשְׁפָּטִים אֲשֶׁר תָּשִׂים לִפְנֵיהֶם**" היא תגובה צלילית רעיונית הולמת בעיצורים ותנועות ל"**מִי שָׂמְךָ** לְאִישׁ שַׂר וְשֹׁפֵט עָלֵינוּ?" שרצף השׁ'יׁ-שׁי'ׁ ן[11] שבו צוּיֵּן כמשדר כעס ואיבה בשילוב מצלול ומשמעות.

מרכיבים ספרותיים בפרשת משפטים

גם בפרשיות הלכתיות וסיפוריות ברורות קיימת חפיפה ניכרת וקשה לחלק ביניהן באופן חד. הלכות נלמדות מסיפורים בתורה ולעתים גם הלכות מוצגות במרכיבים ספרותיים. בפרשת משפטים עצמה הלכות מנוסחות במושאל "כמין משל" (מכילתא) כ"אִם יָקוּם וְהִתְהַלֵּךְ בַּחוּץ עַל מִשְׁעַנְתּוֹ" (כא, יט), כ"עַל בֻּרְיוֹ"; "אִם זָרְחָה הַשֶּׁמֶשׁ עָלָיו דָּמִים לוֹ" (כב, ב): "פשוט לך שאינו בא להרוג". ובעיקר, דיני נזיקין באים לרוב בניסוח קזואיסטי

10   המדרשים מזהים האנשים העברים עם "דתן ואבירם", מורדיו האבטיפוסיים: שמו"ר א,כט; בבלי נדרים סד ע"ב; פרקי דרבי אליעזר מ"ח (היותם **נצים** נדרש על שם "הוא דָתָן וַאֲבִירָם קְרִיאֵי הָעֵדָה אֲשֶׁר הִצּוּ עַל מֹשֶׁה וְעַל אַהֲרֹן בַּעֲדַת קֹרַח **בְּהַצֹּתָם** עַל ה'" (במ' כו, ט) .

11   יונתן גרוסמן, גלוי ונסתר: על כמה מדרכי העיצוב של הסיפור המקראי, ירושלים 2015, ע' 99.

נראה שעל משה רבינו כמנחיל התורה, לישראל ולגרים ואף לאומות העולם, לפעול
כגואל פעיל ובפועל עם כל אוכלוסיות אלו באכיפת הצדק טרם בואו להר האלוקים. יש
לקרוא את שלושת המפגשים כרצף נחון ומגדיר בשלוש משימות הכרחיות וכתנאי מוקדם.
עליו למלא ייעוד כגואל ומנחיל תורה לכל פלג בפני עצמו, לא רק כמשה "ספרא רבה
דישראל"[8] אלא כ"משה רבינו" של כל אותן אכלוסיות. לתפיסה זו של משימות מחויבות
כתב הרמב"ם במורה נבוכים (ח"ב, מה):

> תחלת מדרגות הנבואה שילוה לאיש אלהי עזר אלהי שיניעהו ויזרזהו למעשה טוב גדול,
> כהצלת קהל חשוב ... או השפיע טוב על אנשים רבים ... **זה הכח לא נבדל ממשה
> רבינו** מעת השיגו לגדר האנשים ולזה **התעורר להרוג את המצרי, ולמנוע הרשע
> משני הנצים**, ומחוזק זה הכח בו עד שאחרי פחדו וברחו **והגיע למדין** והוא גר
> ירא, **כאשר ראה ראה מאומה מן העול לא משל בעצמו מהסירו ולא יכול לסובלו,
> כמו שאמר, "ויקם משה ויושיען."**

כעין מקור לכך יש לראות אולי במכילתא[9] בציון (במשחק לשון נופל על לשון) על
התמסרותו העקבית על ה"דינין" אף ב"הגיער למדין": "ומנין שנתן נפשו עליהם, שנאמר
'ויצא ביום השני וגו' ויאמר מי שמך לאיש שר ושופט עלינו ... [ויברח משה ... וישב
בארץ **מדין**]" וכתיב: "ויבאו הרועים ויגרשום [ויקם משה ויושיען]": "**מדינין** ברח
ולדינין חזר".

ברצף שלושת המפגשים ואכיפת הצדק בכל אחד קיימת זיקה הלכתית בלתי-נפרדת
ברובד הסיפורי שמקשרת אוכלוסיות היעד ביעודו כגואלם ומנחיל תורתם. מבחינה
נרטיבית שום דבר אחר אינו מסופר עליו מלבד שלשה אירועים אלו עד לקריאתו בהר
האלוקים (נחמה ליבוביץ', שם: "פסוקים יא-כב הם היחידים המספרים משהו על משה
רבנו לפני התגלות ה' אליו בסנה; לא מסופרים לנו אלא שלושה מקרים בלבד"). הסיפור
הנאה במדרש (שמו"ר ב, ב) על גדי הצמא שברח שמשה הרכיב על כתיפו ודאי מורה על
אצילות נפשו להיות רועה צאנו של הקב"ה, אבל אינו בא בפשטו של מקרא מפני שאינו
מגדיר תפקידו הכפול של גואל מנחיל תורה שלא ניתן לחלק. אכן ראוי בחילוף בבואת
גומלין שמרכיב ההלכתי האינטגרלי בסיפורו ישתקף כממד נרטיבי בפרשיות ההלכה
בתורתו שינחיל.

---

8   בבלי סוטה יג ע"ב; מדרש תנאים, דבר' לד, ה. תרגום יונתן דב' לג, כא: "משה ספריהון
     דישראל".

9   בשלח מסכתא דשירה א; ומדרש תנאים לדברים טז, יח.

וּלְכֹהֵן מִדְיָן שֶׁבַע בָּנוֹת וַתָּבֹאנָה וַתִּדְלֶנָה ... וַיָּבֹאוּ הָרֹעִים וַיְגָרְשׁוּם וַיָּקָם מֹשֶׁה וַיּוֹשִׁעָן
...

על כך העירו: ר' יצחק קארו, תולדות יצחק:

"ויפן כה וכה" (ב, יא): סיפרה התורה שלשה מעשיות ... להודיע שמשה היה דיין
בטבע ובעל משפט, שלא די המצרי שהכה לישראל שהרגו, אלא גם ישראל עם
ישראל שהיו מריבין שלא הכריח לו יהירות שהאחד ישראל והאחד מצרי, אבל עם
היות ששניהם ישראלים אמר לרשע למה תכה, ולא די אלו שהם בני ישראל, אבל
עם היות ששתי כתות גוים היה בעינו העול שעושה זה לזה רע, "ויקם משה
ויושיען".

ר' עובדיה ספורנו: (ב, יא)

"וירא איש מצרי מכה איש עברי מאחיו": ומצד האחוה התעורר להנקם. (ב, יג)
"ויאמר לרשע": מפני היות כל אחד מהם אחיו לא התעורר להנקם, אבל הוכיח
במישור. (ב, יז) "ויקם משה ויושיען": בהיות שני בעלי הריב נכרים לא התעורר
להנקם גם לא הקפיד ליישר ארחותם בתוכחות מוסר, רק קם להושיע את העשוקים
מיד עושקיהם.

נחמה ליבוביץ:

שלוש פעמים הוא מתערב בסכסוכים, שלוש פעמים הוא מציל עשוק מיד עושק ...
כל אחד מהם מיצג ארכיטיפוס. הראשון: סכסוך בן עברי לבן נכר, השני: סכסוך בין
עברי לעברי, השלישי: סכסוך בין בן נכר לבן נכר. ובשלשתם מתייצב משה לימין
הצדק.[7]

ממד ההלכתי

אך נראה בחילוף הסוגות שבשלשת הסיפורים מצוי ממד הלכתי מובהק והכרחי. מעבר
לתיאור נפשו ואופיו הנעלה, אציל וישר ככל שיהיה, כרוך ממד הלכתי ביעודו כגואל
שלושת האכלוסיות, במובן שניסח הרמב"ם בהלכות מלכים, ח , י-יא:

משה רבינו לא הנחיל התורה והמצות אלא **לישראל** ... **ולכל הרוצה להתגייר**
משאר האומות ... וכן צוה משה רבינו מפי הגבורה לכוף את **כל באי העולם לקבל
מצות שנצטוו בני נח** ... והוא שיקבל אותן ויעשה אותן מפני שצוה בהן הקדוש
ברוך הוא **בתורה והודיענו על ידי משה רבינו** שבני נח מקודם נצטוו בהן.

7 'עיונים בספר שמות', ע' 35. ה'צריכותא' שבשלשה התערבויות, שם ע' 37.

מִמִּצְרַיִם תַּעַבְדוּן אֶת הָאֱלֹהִים עַל הָהָר הַזֶּה" (ג, יב)[3]. כשם שאין לחלק בתפקידו האחיד בסיפור, במובן מסוים אין להפריד בין סוגה סיפורית והלכתית בסיפור תורתו "תורת משה."[4] רמב"ן ציין (הקדמה לפירוש על התורה) שכל התורה באה בהקשר סיפורי כ"וידבר אלהים אל משה"[5] וכדומה. גופי וקבצי הלכות נלמדות על רקע וכתוצאה מסיפורים בתורה (כבסיפור עצמו): "וַיֹּאמֶר לָרָשָׁע לָמָּה תַכֶּה רֵעֶךָ" (ב, יד): "שֶׁנִּקְרָא רשע בהרמת יד" (תלמוד בבלי סנהדרין נח ע"ב; רמב"ם, חובל ומזיק ה, ב; שולחן ערוך חושן משפט תכ, א וסמ"ע שם)). בחילוף מקביל ניתן לקרוא יחידות הלכה ברובד נרטיבי מעבר לאופיין ההלכתי, ובמיוחד בסיפור משה כמנחיל התורה.

יעוד גאולה ואכלוסיות יעד

עמדו על כך שבתהליכו להר האלוקים טרם מנויו נתקל משה בשלש מפגשים סיפוריים שבכולן התערב ביוזמה עקבית נגד העוול ובצעדים מתאימים לנסיבות ואוכלוסיות: בין מצרי ועברי, בין שני עברים, ובין שני קבוצות שאינם מישראל, הרועים במדין ובנות יתרו שלמים יבוא להתגייר[6] (ב, יא-יז). (נראה שמקור הרעיון הוא ב'מורה הנבוכים' וכמו שיתבאר):

וַיְהִי בַּיָּמִים הָהֵם וַיִּגְדַּל מֹשֶׁה וַיֵּצֵא אֶל אֶחָיו וַיַּרְא בְּסִבְלֹתָם וַיַּרְא אִישׁ מִצְרִי מַכֶּה אִישׁ עִבְרִי מֵאֶחָיו: וַיִּפֶן כֹּה וָכֹה וַיַּרְא כִּי אֵין אִישׁ וַיַּךְ אֶת הַמִּצְרִי וַיִּטְמְנֵהוּ בַּחוֹל. וַיֵּצֵא בַּיּוֹם הַשֵּׁנִי וְהִנֵּה שְׁנֵי אֲנָשִׁים עִבְרִים נִצִּים וַיֹּאמֶר לָרָשָׁע לָמָּה תַכֶּה רֵעֶךָ: וַיֹּאמֶר מִי שָׂמְךָ לְאִישׁ שַׂר וְשֹׁפֵט עָלֵינוּ הַלְהָרְגֵנִי אַתָּה אֹמֵר כַּאֲשֶׁר הָרַגְתָּ אֶת הַמִּצְרִי וַיִּירָא מֹשֶׁה וַיֹּאמַר אָכֵן נוֹדַע הַדָּבָר: וַיִּבְרַח מֹשֶׁה מִפְּנֵי פַרְעֹה וַיֵּשֶׁב בְּאֶרֶץ מִדְיָן וַיֵּשֶׁב עַל הַבְּאֵר:

---

3 שמו"ר ג, ד: "הוי יודע שבזכות התורה שהן עתידים לקבל על ידך על בהר הזה הם יוצאים משם". היעודים מתגשרים בתלמוד בבלי סוטה יב ע"ב (ומגילה יד ע"א; שמו"ר א, ג) במוטיב "האור כי טוב" (בר' א, ד) בלידתו כגואל: "וַתֵּרֶא אֹתוֹ כִּי טוֹב הוּא" (שמ' ב, ב): "שהיתה [אֲחֹתוֹ] מתנבאה ... עתידה אמי שתלד בן שמושיע את ישראל וכיון שנולד משה נתמלא כל הבית כולה אור"; וכמנחיל התורה: "וַתִּצְפְּנֵהוּ שְׁלֹשָׁה יְרָחִים [לֹא יָכְלָה עוֹד הַצְּפִינוֹ]" (שם): "משבעה באדר ועד ששה בסיון תלתא ירחי ... אותו היום ששה בסיון היה, אמרו מלאכי השרת לפני הקדוש ברוך הוא: רבש"ע, מי שעתיד לקבל תורה מהר סיני ביום זה, ילקה ביום זה?"

4 יהוש' ח, לא-לב; מלאכי ג; מל"א ב, ג; מל"ב יד, ו; כג, כה; דני' ט, יא-יג; עזר' ג,ב; ז, ו; נחמי' ח,א; דהי"ב כג, יח; ל, טז.

5 "שלא כתב משה רבינו התורה כמדבר בעד עצמו ... יאמר "וידבר אלהים אל משה", "ויאמר אליו" ... מפני שקדמה לבריאת העולם אין צריך לומר ללידתו של משה רבינו". על כך כתב רבי שניאור זלמן מליאדי במובן קבלי (ספר המאמרים תקס"ח): "מה שכל התורה אינו אלא כמו סיפור מעשה כמו "וידבר ה' אל משה" ... שהתורה בחינת סיפור דבריו של עצמות המאציל ... כמו סיפור דברים על פי חכמתו העצמיות הקדומה."

6 מכילתא דרבי ישמעאל יח; מכילתא דרשב"י יח; תרגום יונתן, יח, ז; תלמוד בבלי זבחים קטז ע"ב.

משה ו'משפטים': פרשיות הלכה כנרטיבה

מאת: נחמן לוין

מבוא

כאן נסיון לקרוא עירוב פרשיות בין סוגה הלכתית וסוגה סיפורית בממשק בין-סוגתי של
גומלין[1] בראשית מינויו הכפול של משה רבינו כגואל וכמנחיל התורה. נראה שתחילת
פרשת "וְאֵלֶּה הַמִּשְׁפָּטִים" (שמו' כא) (כפרשיות הלכתיות-סיפוריות אחרות, פרשת המקלל
(ויקר' כד) ועוד) משקפת ומשחזרת להפליא קורות משה הראשונות (שמו' ב, יא-יז)
בהקשר הלכתי ורובד לשוני. כבר העיר המדרש[2] ש"וְאֵלֶּה הַמִּשְׁפָּטִים אֲשֶׁר תָּשִׂים
לִפְנֵיהֶם" (כא, א) יותפס כתגובה טקסטואלית לשאלה שהקשו עליו שני אנשים
העברים בראשית דרכו: "מִי שָׂמְךָ לְאִישׁ שַׂר וְשֹׁפֵט עָלֵינוּ?" (ב, יד). מאחר וה"משפטים"
שעליו "לשים לפניהם" (עבד עברי, יציאה מעבדות, הכאות עבדים ובין איש לרעהו,
מקלט לבורח שהכה הנפש) נשמעים מוכרים למדי מסיפור עצמו, דומה שגישׁור
האינטרטקסטואלי בפרשת המשפטים יתפקד בפשוטו של מקרא כאישור הלכתי הכרחי
ונחוץ כמענה טקסטואלי לערעור לזכאותו לתפקידו, ובהשלכות מרחיקות לכת למחויבותו
בכך.

כל המסופר על משה עד הגיעו להר האלוקים לראשונה כרוך ישירות ביעודו הכפול
כגואל ומנחיל התורה, כדברי ה' שם: "וְזֶה לְּךָ הָאוֹת כִּי אָנֹכִי שְׁלַחְתִּיךָ בְּהוֹצִיאֲךָ אֶת הָעָם

---

1   על תפקיד מערכת סוגות הספרותיות וממד הפרשני במקרא, ראה י' ליונסון, 'הסיפור שלא
סופר', הוצאת מגנס, תשס"ה. על עירוב הלכה וסיפורים בתשתית העומק: י' גרוסמן, "מדוע
דין נדרי נשים פותח את פרשת מטות?", בית המדרש הוירטואלי שליד ישיבת הר עציון,
תשס"ד; "Divine Command and Human Initiative: A Literary View On
Numbers 25-31," *Biblical Interpretation* 15 (2007).

2   שמות רבה, ל, י, י, ומדרש הגדול שם, שידונו להלן. בקריאה שכזאת מאד כדאי להיעזר
במדרשי חז"ל בשל פרשנותם הבנויה על אינטרקסטואליות בין הכתובים. ("השתייכותם יחד
של חלקי המקרא השונים בתוכן רעיוני אחד הוא מעיקרי דרכי המדרש", י' פרנקל, דרכי
המדרש והאגדה, ע' 161. "אילו רצית להגדיר מדרש מהו, הייתי אומר שהוא קריאה אינטר-
טקסטואלית של הקנון שבה עשוי כמעט כל חלק להתייחס לכל חלק אחר ולהתפרש על פיו",
D. Boyarin, *Intertextuality and the Reading of Midrash*, Bloomington, 1990
p. 16). רגישות המדרש לקשרים טקסטואליים עשויה לתרום אף לקריאה צמודה ברובד
הראשוני של פשוטו של מקרא בקשרים "תת-קרקעיים" בכתובים (כביטוי י' אליצור, "מילות
מפתח ככותרת תת-קרקעית לפרשיות במקרא", מגדים, לח (תשס"ג)).

נחמן לוין מלמד תנ"ך ומדרש בדטרויט והוא עמית מחקר במרכז ללימודי ישראל שליד
ישיבה יוניברסיטי.

חקירה

כרך ל"ב – שנת תשפ"ב

תוכן עניינים

חקירה

כרך ל"ב — שנת תשפ"ב